"Michael Norton is a one-man 'ideas factory' whose new book suggests some whacky ways in which, with a little bit of effort, people really can change the world for the better."
Guardian

"If you want to help bring about change but don't know where to start, this is the book for you...packed with ideas, information and useful websites." *Woman and Home*

"By far the most enticing and informative book... I finally stopped being a cynic." *Daily Mail*

"If you want to make a difference then I can do no better than to recommend this book...it offers thousands of ideas."
Daily Telegraph

"I can't think of another person who could dream up so many ideas. It is a great antidote to the cynicism of the chattering classes." *Susanna Cheal OBE, Who Cares? Trust*

"Life-improving...a sound manual."
Evening Standard

"This inspiring read has an idea a day...all are simple and enjoyable...what are you waiting for?" *Fresh Direction*

"You really can find something you believe in and do something to help with the aid and encouragement of this book...Big or small there is a resolution here for everyone. This is not just for laughs and it's not just for Christmas."
Latest

"Any joker can sit back and moan about life. So here's a collection of practical steps to help you make a difference."
Source

"Essential reading for every would-be activist." *Insight*

"This book has something for every day of the year and makes you think about the state of the planet; pollution, corruption, aids, starvation, disease and the lack of freedom to name but a few." *Impac News*

Myriad Editions is an independent publisher
of innovative non-fiction, original fiction and documentary comic books.
Founded in 1993, it has won international acclaim for its award-winning
State of the World atlases and remains committed to mapping
the most pressing issues facing the world today.
Visit Myriad Editions at: www.MyriadEditions.com

365 ways to change THE WORLD

Michael Norton

Myriad Editions

First published in the UK in 2005
by Myriad Editions

Reprinted 2006
This revised edition 2008

Myriad Editions
59 Lansdowne Place
Brighton
BN3 1FL
UK

www.MyriadEditions.com

1 3 5 7 9 10 8 6 4 2

A CIP catalogue record for this book is available
from the British Library.

ISBN: 978-0-9549309-6-7

Text design: Corinne Pearlman
Cover design: Colin Kennedy

Printed on paper sourced from well-managed forests
in accordance with the rules of the Forest Stewardship Council.

Contents

About the author

Michael Norton is the founder, and was until 1995 the Director, of Directory of Social Change, the UK's leading agency providing information, training and support to voluntary organisations. In 1995, he founded the Centre for Innovation in Voluntary Action (CIVA) to promote innovation and new thinking on the role of charities. See: www.civa.org.uk

CIVA's current projects (in addition to *365 Ways to Change the World*) include: encouraging low-carbon living on public housing estates so people can compensate for the impact they have on global warming; helping young people set up and run their own banks in schools and homeless foyers as a practical way of increasing financial literacy and encouraging enterprise skills; bringing the Canadian Otesha Project to the UK to promote sustainable living in a fairer world; village publishing and village libraries in India; and producing materials for young activists in the UK.

Michael Norton established Changemakers, which challenges young people to design and manage their own community projects in response to an issue or concern of importance to them. He is also the founder of YouthBank UK, which enables young people to make grants in their local communities.

He is a Founder and Trustee of unLTD – the Foundation for Social Entrepreneurs, which received an endowment of £100 million from the Millennium Commission, and makes awards to over 1,000 individuals in the UK each year who wish to create change in their communities.

He is author of numerous books on fundraising and charitable status, including *Writing Better Fundraising Applications*, *The WorldWide Fundraiser's Handbook*, *The Complete Fundraising Handbook* and *The Everyday Activist*.

To access Michael Norton's blog or receive a monthly newsletter, go to: www.365act.com

Acknowledgements

The idea for this book had been in the back of my mind for some time, but it was only after discussing it with Vicki Saunders, a Canadian social entrepreneur, and her telling me to get on and do it, that I felt able to get started. Christen Eddy got the original website going to solicit ideas, arranged brainstorm evenings and got a team of young volunteers involved. Particular thanks should go to Victoria Stanski for agreeing to contribute to, and edit, the Peace section, and to all the named contributors who submitted material for the book:

Before you get started	Christen Eddy	5 September	Victoria Stanski
What you will need	Isabel Losada	20 September	Victoria Stanski
15 May	Greg Buhrman	3 November	Victoria Stanski
22 June	Peter Sweatman	4 November	Kathryn Blume
4 July	Peter Tatchell	25 November	Margaret Murray
10 July	Victoria Stanski	7 December	Rebecca Sherman
14 July	Toby Lloyd	9 December	Bob Barclay
17 August	Jillian Frumkin	10 December	Victoria Stanski

Thanks to my agent Mary Clemmey and her assistant Niamh Walsh for their help in getting this book published around the world, and to all the team at Myriad Editions: Candida Lacey and Bob Benewick for making it happen; Jannet King for such excellent project management; Corinne Pearlman and Isabelle Lewis for the design and graphics; and Martine McDonagh, Sadie Mayne, Catherine Quinn and Helen Kingstone for additional editing. Thanks also to Colin Kennedy and Roger Harmar for additional design and graphics.

For the use of other photographs and illustrations, the publisher and author would like to thank the following:

January: 1: James Parr; 7: World Food Program / Robert Maas; 13: Derek Chung / Tactile Pictures; 14: GLINN Media Corporation Gay/ Lesbian International News Network; **February**: 5: WaterAid; 13: Jason Stitt; 15: Neve Shalom; 20: Robert Benewick; **March**: 9: Daniel Tan; 20: UNICEF India / Ami Vitale; 22: WHO / P Pirot; 25: David Lawson/WWF-UK; **April**: 3: Simon Edwin; 5: Laurie Knight; 7: Rotary International; 14: Phototag; 15: Dania Lolah; 16: Linda Bucklin; 20: World Bank / Francis Dobbs; 25: Sean Locke; **May**: 5: World Bank / Tran Thi Hoa; 26: Marc Gold; 31: Woodrow Phoenix © Comic Company; **June**: 2: Friends of Nature Burial Ground; 3: worldnakedbikeride.org; 7: Nancy Durrell McKenna; 17: Excellent Development Ltd; 24: Colin Kennedy; 27 Gemma Sisia; **July**: 5 Charlotte Krahé; 8: Anna Mockford © Bare Witness.org; 16: US State Department; 17: Augusta Riddy; 18: Lee Dowse; 19: Kenneth C. Zirkel; 24: Jonathan Ling; 27: Peter Morenus; 28: Daniel Fletcher; **August**: 1: Judi Ashlock; 4: Björn Kindler; 9: Anupam Mishra; 10: Rene Mansi; 13: Dane Wirtzfeld; 17: © Vo Cong Thong / Street Vision / PhotoVoice; 21: Rafal Zdeb; 23: Erik Millstone; 25: Kamila Kingstone; 29: Woodrow Phoenix © Comic Company; **September**: 7, 22, 23 & 24: Colin Kennedy; **October**: 13 Fran Crowe; 14: Graham Higgins © Comic Company; 16: WFP/ Tom Haskell; 18: FAO / J Holmes; 20: Room to Read; 21: angelhell / iStockphoto; 30: Jen Fariello; **November**: 27: World Bank; **December**: 9: Tina Rencelj; 10: Paiwei Wei; 11: Daniela Andreea Spyropoulos; 13: World Bank / Eric Miller; 14: World Bank; 15 Maxine Jones; 16: Theodora Children's Trust; 17: World Bank / Curt Carnemark.

Every effort was made to obtain the necessary permissions for use of copyright material, both illustrative and quoted. If there have been any omissions, we apologise and shall be pleased to make appropriate acknowledgement in any future edition.

Themes

 Community and neighbourhood

Getting to know your city or neighbourhood, ways of brightening it up, bringing fun and laughter into local life, working with socially excluded people and with prisoners.

 Culture and creativity

Connecting up with people, new ideas for getting your message across, communicating through language and stories, listening in to get inspired.

 Democracy and human rights

Fighting for freedom of information, participating in elections, lobbying your elected representatives, human rights and human wrongs around the world.

Discrimination

Fighting for disability rights, tackling racism and sexism (and all the other -isms in society), dealing with violence and abuse.

Employment and enterprise

Sharing skills and resources, open-access software, internet collaboration, social enterprise, micro-credit.

Environment

Global warming, pollution, pesticides and toxins, conservation of species and resources, trees and forests, sustainable living, waste and recycling, transport.

 Globalisation and consumerism

Multinationals and responsible business practice, fairer trade and ethical consumption, consuming less.

 Health

Battling HIV/AIDS, malaria and other global diseases, water and sanitation, better health, sport and fitness, hunger and obesity, food and diet.

 International development

Achieving the Millennium Development Goals, addressing inequality and social injustice in the world with skills, money and ideas, recycling to benefit the world's poor, paying off foreign debt, enhancing livelihoods and using appropriate technology.

 Peace

Ridding the world of weapons, waging war on war, promoting peace, preventing genocide.

 Volunteering and citizenship

Getting your message across, being nice to others, gearing up for action, having the right attitudes, donating cash and raising money, giving in kind, volunteering your time.

Young people

Improving education and schools, fighting for children's rights, supporting children in need, dealing with child abuse, providing opportunities for play and exercise, being a young activist.

Introduction

What's the big idea?

The world is full of all sorts of problems, including:

HIV/AIDS which is infecting more and more of the world's population

A widening North-South divide

War and terror (and the 'War on Terror')

All the 'isms' (racism, sexism, age-ism etc) that deny people opportunities

Environmental degradation and pollution

A scarcity of water for living and working

Hunger for far too many of the world's population

A lack of universal primary education

Corruption and bad governance in too much of the world

Abuse of human rights (including slavery and torture)

Global warming, which will have an impact on almost everything

...and many more besides.

Everyone has their own ideas about what's wrong with the world. They'll argue about which are the most important issues. But they'll all agree that things could be a lot better than they are, and that something really does need to be done. But then what? Do we just leave it to governments and international institutions? Or are there things we can do that will actually make a difference?

The issues that confront us may seem so huge, so complicated, so difficult to deal with that it's hard to believe that anything we can do will have a meaningful impact. But there are a lot of us in the world. A lot of people doing a lot of little things could have a huge impact. And by doing something, we are also demonstrating that lots of people really do care.

Together we can change the world. That is the idea underlying this book. By adjusting the way we live our lives and by taking action on the issues that really concern us, we can begin to make a difference.

This book has an idea-a-day for changing the world. Most are quite simple, can be done from home (access to the internet will be useful), and will not take up that much time. Some require a bit more time, energy and commitment.

So why not get going on changing the world? You can make a start at any time. But the best time is right now! Just open the book at today's date, read, enjoy, be inspired to action...and do something.

www.365act.com: To complement the book, we have created a website that includes some of the 365 ideas and givers you access to a blog and a monthly newsletter fro more ideas on changing the world.

This book is just a starting point for an ideas bank for changing the world. We need your help, your ideas, the feedback from what you have tried to do in order to help us make our dream of people everywhere doing all they can to change the world a reality. Use the website to provide us with ideas and feedback.

We look forward to hearing from you.

Michael Norton
January 2008

Before you get started

You watch the news every night. You turn off your television set, disturbed by what you've seen and wondering what, if anything, you can do to make a difference. The fact that you picked up this book is evidence that you want to do something positive for the planet. Are you are ready to act? Before you eradicate AIDS, end the illegal arms trade, abolish world debt, bridge the digital divide, take a brief look at your own lifestyle. There are things you should be doing on a regular basis. Some of these, even the most selfish, mean-spirited idiot knows are 'the right thing to do'. Some are saintly, others fun.

Find out if you are 'eco-sinner' or 'socially minded saint'. Tick each thing you do on a regular basis:

☐ **Turn off the lights** whenever you leave a room.

☐ **Fill up your kettle** with only as much water as you need.

☐ **Take your own bags** when shopping.

☐ **Don't leave the tap running** when you're not using the water.

☐ **Put on a sweater in the house** if you're feeling cold, instead of cranking up the heat.

☐ **Hang your clothes out** to dry in the summer, rather than use a tumble drier.

☐ **Walk or ride a bike** for short journeys, instead of using a car.

☐ **Don't drop your litter** or throw it out of the car window. This includes cigarette butts and gum.

☐ **Pick up rubbish** in the street when you see it.

☐ **Try to spread a little happiness.** You smile at everyone and chat with your neighbours.

☐ **Perform an occasional random act of kindness** to a complete stranger.

☐ **Buy local** and support local small businesses.

☐ **Recycle** everything that is recyclable.

☐ **Make a compost pile** with your food waste, and invite worms to feast on it.

☐ **Take a shower instead of a bath,** or share your bath with a friend.

☐ **Do things for others** or for the community. You volunteer at least two hours a week.

☐ **Buy fairtrade tea and coffee.**

☐ **Try to stop the barrage of junk mail** by signing off from bulk mailing lists.

☐ **Use the political process:** vote at election time; speak out on issues; lobby your local representative about anything important.

☐ **Have never smoked,** or have now quit smoking.

Check your eco-score

Now it's Judgement Day, the moment when you discover if Mother Earth will banish you to the molten core, or give you a palace in the clouds. Award yourself one point for each tick, then add up your score.

Score 0–5 You are a hopeless barbaric eco-hating hooligan.

Score 6–10 You are not a hopeless case, but you need to wise up.

Score 10–15 You are a credit to the planet.
Pat yourself on the back, but don't be too smug.

Score 16–20 You are the saviour of the planet.
You deserve a throne next to Gandhi and Mother Theresa.

What next? It's pretty obvious, isn't it? You should start living more responsibly. You should also start reading this book. Be inspired. Do one thing each day to make a better world.

What you will need

Isabel Losada is the founder of Act for Tibet, and author of *For Tibet with Love: a beginner's guide to changing the world*. Here are Isabel's top ten indispensable things that you will need in order to change the world:

1　A storage cupboard – to put your TV in.

2　A crazy, wonderful, foolish, positive, joyful, plan (like Noah).

3　Selective deafness (complete inability to hear the word 'No' or 'Can't' or 'That's a bad idea', etc).

4　A coffee addiction – it's impossible otherwise.

5　Unconditional love for others 24/7 – essential.

6　Deranged friends (*see below*).

7　An irrational desire to do mad things (jump out of planes, etc), sometimes called fundraising.

8　A website that you made yourself and can maintain yourself.

9　An unbalanced sense of humour.

10 Persistence, joy, persistence, joy, persistence, joy, persistence. . .

Act for Tibet: **www.actfortibet.com**
Isabel Losada: **www.isabellosada.com**

To find out more and to send us your ideas, go to the website: www.365act.com

Now get going. Start to change the world.
Get started today. Start at the beginning of the book. Or go to today's date.
Or browse to find those issues you are particularly interested in.
Just turn the page and you're on your way.

New Year's REVOLUTION

The best way to predict the future is to invent it.

– Alan Kay

New Year's Day is traditionally a time for looking forward, when we resolve to make a fresh start, do better, try harder, live up to expectations. But all too often these resolutions evaporate by the time we have cleared up the remains of the previous night's party and almost certainly by the time we get into work the next day. And if nothing is changing in the world around you, and the same old problems – war, famine, injustice, torture, poverty, disease – are reported in the news day after day, it sometimes feels as though there is little point in resolving to give up smoking, lose those extra pounds, walk to work. So, here's a suggestion: instead of watching, wracked by guilt, as world events unfold on your TV screen, bring about a New Year's Revolution. Change your life by resolving to change the world.

Taking the first step is important. Once you've got started, everything will get a lot easier. So, today, commit yourself to taking that first crucial step. Once you have resolved to make poverty history, to stop global warming (or whatever it is you want to do), the first thing you need is a plan of action. So make a plan. Set targets for what you want to achieve. Be ambitious. But make sure that your plan is achievable.

At the end of the year, you will want to review your progress. You will want to know whether you achieved your goals. You will want to see how much impact you have had on the issue. You will want to learn from your experience. And you will then need to plan what to do next.

www.mygoals.com/about/NewYearsTips.html

Don't be frightened of failure.
Do something, and try your best to succeed.

But even if you don't, you will have shown that you care enough to want to do something, you will probably have made some difference, and you will have learnt a lot from the experience – which you can put into practice next time.

...resolve to change the world

Make a New Year's Resolution.

Go to www.tomphillips.co.uk/portrait/sbec and download the portrait of Samuel Beckett which is ringed by the quotation:

No matter
Try again
Fail again
Fail better

Cut this picture out, frame it and put it somewhere you will see it every day. Let Samuel Beckett's words become your motto for the efforts you will be making to change the world.

MAKE *amends*

It is almost certain that there is someone you've done wrong to, harmed, had a huge argument with, insulted, let things get to a point where you are not speaking, lost contact with. You've thought about this person more times than you can count, but for some reason, you've never make an effort to wipe the slate. Make amends. Bury the past by apologising for what you've done. Admit responsibility. Heal the situation. In doing this, you will have done good – and it will be one less thing to worry about.

Whole communities can make amends. In Greensboro, North Carolina, on 3 November 1979, members of the Ku Klux Klan and the American Nazi Party killed five people and wounded ten others, as activists gathered for a rally and conference for racial and social justice. 25 years later, the City of Greensboro decided to confront the past in the style of the Truth and Reconciliation Commission that Nelson Mandela so successfully instituted for post-Apartheid South Africa. The past can never be erased, but people and communities can make amends – and move forward.

Greensboro Truth and Community Reconciliation Project: www.gtcrp.org

Pavel's story

Forced to work in a carpentry shop by day, locked in barracks at night, Pavel Kotlyarov will never forget the hunger and the hardship. Pavel, a Ukrainian, was one of millions forced into slave labour by the Nazis. 'They fed us so badly, the only thing we were thinking about was a piece of bread.'

50 years later, some German students in Gersthofen, the town where Kotlyarov was enslaved, tried to make amends for the past. They sent Kotlyarov and other former slave labourers from Kiev a letter of apology and money that they had collected as a gesture of compensation.

The German government has paid compensation of $1,000 to Ukraine's 600,000 surviving former slaves, but the students, as well as many others in Germany, feel the need to do more.

Cities have been sponsoring trips to Germany and raising money to provide aid packages for former slaves, who are mostly now in their 80s or even older.

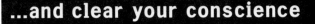

...and clear your conscience

Make amends. Today's the day to do it!

Pick up the phone, write a letter, or send an email to someone you have hurt, or someone you have lost contact with. It doesn't matter whether it is your fault or theirs that you are no longer speaking. It doesn't matter if they choose not to respond. You've taken the first step. That's what's important.

What you need: a little humility

Time invested: about 10 minutes

The pay-off: a clean conscience

2 JANUARY

climate CHANGE

What is happening to the world's climate is a cause for intense concern. Heat waves, droughts, monsoons and hurricanes are breaking all previous records. These are the most obvious signals of climate change, and are already proving costly in terms of human life, but there are others that are more surreptitious and likely to be even more deadly.

Warmer average temperatures, leading to melting ice. In the Antarctic peninsula, vast areas of ice-sheet are disintegrating. In parts of Canada, Alaska, Siberia, the melting of the permafrost is undermining roads, airports, and buildings. Most significantly, there are signs that the huge ice-sheet over Greenland is beginning to thin, releasing millions of cubic kilometres of fresh water into the north Atlantic. ♣ Mountain glaciers in temperate zones are retreating, and as they shrink, summer water flows will start to drop sharply, creating severe shortages of water for irrigation and power in areas that rely on mountain watersheds. ♣ Melting ice, and increasing temperatures that cause sea water to expand, are likely to lead to a rise in sea-level of around 92 cm over the next 100 years. Some low-lying areas will simply cease to exist; others will experience catastrophic flooding.

These climate changes are being caused by the emission of greenhouse gases. The scale of the problem means that coordinated government action will be required if climate change is to be slowed down. But it is the sum of our own individual choices and actions that is causing the problem.

Lick Global Warming: www.lickglobalwarming.org
COIN – Climate Outreach Information Network: www.coinet.org.uk

How to cut your carbon emissions by 50%

In the UK, George Marshall did everything he could to reduce his personal carbon emissions. In just one year he achieved a reduction of 50% through energy saving and changes to his lifestyle. To encourage others and even whole communities to do the same, he set up COIN – Climate Outreach Information Network. One of their ideas is Carbon Pioneers, a group of 100 people who commit to reducing their emissions, and then encourage and support each other through the process.

...needs to be stopped

Take a carbon pledge to reduce your own carbon emissions. And get all your friends to do the same. The average European emits directly and indirectly around 12 tonnes of carbon a year into the atmosphere. Pledge to save 5%–10% of your carbon emissions. For example:

- ♣ **Replace three standard light bulbs** with low-energy bulbs and save 136 kg a year.
- ♣ **Turn the thermostat down** by 2°C and save 272 kg a year.
- ♣ **Install a modern programmable thermostat** and save 453 kg a year.
- ♣ **Travel 15 miles fewer each week** by car and save 408 kg a year.

Pledge to cut your personal consumption by at least 1 tonne a year at:
www.lickglobalwarming.org/pledge.html

JANUARY 3

COFFEE *at a fair price*

Fairtrade coffee provides a higher income and greater security for small producers than is offered by the vagaries of the world market. ● The current fairtrade price for coffee is more than double the market price, which can fluctuate wildly. In 1994 coffee reached a high of $4.40 per kilo, caused by frost and drought in Brazil, but by 2001 prices had fallen to $1.10 – where it has pretty much remained since. ● The impact of low coffee prices is felt particularly by small family producers, who depend on this cash crop for their livelihood. In countries such as Ethiopia, Uganda and Honduras, coffee is a particularly important export commodity, and a slump in prices can depress the whole economy.

Some recent trends in coffee production: More coffee is being produced than is being consumed, much of it funded by agricultural development schemes. The price has dropped as a result. ● New technology is being used to remove the bitterness from the lower-priced Robusta variety, making it taste more acceptable to consumers. This means more Robusta coffee is being consumed. It is grown intensively, on large estates, which are introducing increasing mechanisation, considerably reducing the need for labour. What 1,000 people might achieve on a small estate in Guatemala, can be achieved by 12 people on a state-of-the-art mechanised farm in Brazil. ● Sales of premium coffees (single estate coffees, speciality brands, FairTrade, organic and shade grown which is sometimes called bird-friendly) are all growing rapidly. Fairtrade coffee represents 1% of the US market, and 2% in the UK.

Oxfam have just launched a chain of fair trade coffee shops called Progreso. The first two are in London's Covent Garden and Portobello Road: www.progreso.org.uk

Sharing the price of a cup of coffee

tax 15%

coffee 5%
dairy 5%
cup and lid 5%
other packaging and sugar 5%

corporate costs and profit 30%

labour 18%

rent of premises 16%

...enjoy the taste of doing good

Buy and drink fairtrade coffee. The higher price will help small farmers.

Ask whether a cup of coffee made with fairtrade coffee is a fairly traded cup of coffee. Roasted ground coffee wholesales at around £5 per kilo. 1 kilo is sufficient to make 100 cups of coffee. When you buy a coffee in a coffee shop, the coffee costs about 5p. The consumer will be paying £1 upwards. The grower will get only about 2p of this, even at fairtrade prices.

Write to the Managing Directors of Starbucks, Costa, Caffe Nero and ask them to:

● **Sell only fairtrade coffee** through their outlets

● **Include a voluntary premium** of 5p per cup to be added to your bill and paid to the Fairtrade Foundation to benefit small coffee producers.

4 JANUARY

start DRINKING

When you have a drink with your friends, there are a number of things you can do to support the local economy and help the environment.

Reduce your beer miles. This is the distance the beer has travelled from the brewery to get to you, the consumer. Support your local brewer – and your local whisky distiller and winemaker.

Choose bottles of wine that have natural cork stoppers. Oak corks bio-degrade. The oak cork woodlands in Portugal and Spain produce over 80% of natural cork. These woodlands support a huge population of wildlife and are at risk of being felled to create even more intensively farmed fields when they no longer fulfil an economic purpose.

Recycle all your bottles and cans.

Buy organic beer and wine. Organic producers don't use pesticides that can harm wildlife and contaminate water sources. Organic beer and wine will contain fewer additives so you won't have such a killer headache when you wake up.

Drink real ale, and keep traditional breweries in business. And why not brew your own?

Campaign for Real Ale: www.camra.org.uk

How to brew your own beer – all you need to know from Brew Your Own: www.byo.com

The Brew Your Own website has some adventurous recipes:

Black Pear Oyster Stout has oysters as an ingredient. There's no strong oyster flavour, but it does have a slight salty/briny character.

Wild Rice Helles Bock, a strong light-coloured beer made with wild rice.

Original Hempen Ale, a dark ale made with roasted hemp seeds, which contain a trace of THC, which is the active ingredient in marijuana. But hemp is completely legit!

Smoked Maple Amber Ale uses maple sap (you can improvise by adding water to maple syrup). For a strong smoky flavour, use hickory smoke.

Stonehenge Stein Beer uses hot stones to heat the wort and caramelise the sugars; it requires heat-resistant tongs and some ingenuity to make it.

...for the environment

Try brewing your own beer. You could start simple, or try one of the exotic varieties listed above, which were compiled to celebrate the first ten years of Brew Your Own magazine.

Or, if that is too daunting, make a point of drinking local beers. If your local doesn't offer any, ask why not.

JANUARY 5

HUMAN RIGHTS *and wrongs*

Open your newspaper – any day of the week – and you will find a report from somewhere in the world of someone being imprisoned, tortured or executed because his opinions or religion are unacceptable to his government. The newspaper reader feels a sickening sense of impotence. Yet if these feelings of disgust all over the world could be united into common action, something effective could be done.

— Peter Benenson

Amnesty International was started in 1961 by Peter Benenson, a British lawyer, after he read about the imprisonment of two Portuguese students who had drunk a toast to liberty in a Lisbon restaurant. This was during Portugal's 32-year rule by right-wing dictator, Dr Antonio Salazar. ♪ He wanted to harness the enthusiasm of people all over the world concerned about human rights abuse. ♪ Local supporters were asked to adopt three 'prisoners of conscience', one from the West, one from the Soviet bloc and one from the non-aligned world. They energetically campaigned for the release of their prisoners by writing letters, mobilising political support and showing the jailers (and the prisoner) that the prisoner had not been forgotten.

Human rights violations are as numerous today as when Amnesty was founded. Amnesty International, based in the UK, and Human Rights Watch, based in the USA, are the world's two leading human rights organisations. Amnesty campaigns on violence against women, arms control, the death penalty, torture, refugee rights, child soldiers and many other issues.

Amnesty International: www.amnesty.org
Human Rights Watch: hrw.org

Resources for human rights activists:
Human Rights Network International: www.hrni.org
International Service for Human Rights: www.ishr.ch

The Amnesty Urgent Action Network

A peasant activist 'disappears' in Mexico... in Turkey, a journalist is arrested and at risk of torture... environmentalists in Kenya are imprisoned and beaten... an elderly political prisoner in Indonesia is denied insulin for his diabetes...

Every day Amnesty receives information like this. If an immediate international response is needed to deal with a specific human rights violation, the Urgent Action Network is set in motion.

Members of the Network send a flood of letters to try to right the wrong. They may be trying to save someone from torture, death or medical neglect, from an unfair trial, a judicial death penalty or political killing, or from forcible repatriation to a country where they may be at risk of further human rights abuse.

...urgent action is needed

Here are two simple things you can do:

♪ **Download a screensaver** from the Amnesty website and remind yourself every day that human rights are the foundation of freedom, justice and peace in the world.

♪ **Join Amnesty's Urgent Action Network** and participate in campaigns on urgent issues.

6 JANUARY

visit the **HUNGER SITE**

24,000 people die every day from hunger. Three-quarters of the deaths are children under the age of five. 🌐 A website that focuses the power of the internet on the eradication of world hunger was launched in June 1999. A visitor to 'The Hunger Site' just clicks the 'Give Free Food' button and a cup of food is donated to feed a hungry person. 🌐 The food donation is paid for by a sponsor, and the cost of running the site is paid for by the advertisements of up to 10 sponsors and the sale of merchandise (such as jewellery, crafts, t-shirts and wristbands).

More than 200 million visitors gave more than 300 million cups of food in the site's first five years. In a typical month in 2005, 3.2 million people visited the site, and 3.6 million cups of food. weighing a total of 207 tonnes, were distributed as a result of this online clicking. 🌐 The food is distributed to those in need by Mercy Corps (through food donations and food for work programmes in over 70 countries in Africa, Asia, Eastern Europe, the Middle East and Latin America) and America's Second Harvest (which collects food to help feed an estimated 26 million hungry people in the USA).

The Hunger Site: www.thehungersite.com
Mercy Corps: www.mercycorps.org
America's Second Harvest: www.secondharvest.org

Hunger in the world

10% of children in developing countries die before the age of five. (CARE)

The majority of hunger deaths are caused by chronic malnutrition. Families are simply not getting enough to eat because of their extreme poverty. Famine and wars cause just 10% of hunger deaths. (The Institute for Food and Development Policy)

Chronic malnutrition also causes impaired vision, listlessness, stunted growth and greatly increased susceptibility to disease. (United Nations World Food Programme)

It is estimated that one in six people in the world suffers from hunger and malnutrition, about 100 times as many as those who actually die from it each year. (Food and Agriculture Organization of the United Nations)

It can take just a few simple resources for impoverished people to grow enough food to become self-sufficient: this includes seeds, tools, access to water and improvements in farming techniques. (Oxfam)

...and provide a square meal

🌐 **Visit the Hunger Site daily and trigger a donation.** It will cost you nothing, but you will be feeding a hungry person. There is a facility on the site for you to be sent a reminder each day.

🌐 **Develop a start-up routine for your computer** that automatically gets your computer (or all the computers in your office) to visit the Hunger Site each morning and trigger a donation.

🌐 **Tell all your friends.** There is a facility on the site to do this or you can send an e-card by asking them to click on this weblink: www.thehungersite.com/seasonoflight.swf

JANUARY 7

DEBT *write off*

During the 1970s and 1980s, the world's poorest countries were encouraged to borrow. The idea was that they would invest in projects that would produce an economic return sufficient to repay the loans. This did not happen. Instead they got saddled with a huge amount of debt and annual interest payments that they simply could not afford to repay. ● 'Jubilee Year' in the Bible is a time to wipe out outstanding debts. The Jubilee Debt Campaign focused on the year 2000 as a date to clear the debts of the world's poorest countries.

The Heavily Indebted Poor Countries initiative was set up in 1996 by the World Bank and International Monetary Fund. The original debt of the world's 52 poorest and most indebted countries totalled $375 billion. The initiative aimed to write off $100 billion of multilateral and bilateral debt. In return, countries would spend the debt relief on health, education and development. ● 42 countries were eligible. Of these, Benin, Bolivia, Burkina Faso, Ethiopia, Ghana, Guyana, Madagascar, Mali, Mauritania, Mozambique, Nicaragua, Niger, Senegal, Tanzania and Uganda completed the process. $46 billion was written off.

The Jubilee Debt Campaign continued to press for 100% cancellation of unpayable debt for every poor country. The leaders of the world's richest nations at the G8 summit in July 2005 agreed to write off all World Bank, IMF and African Development Bank debt for the 18 poorest African nations.

Jubilee Debt Campaign: www.jubileedebtcampaign.org.uk
African Forum and Network on Debt and Development: www.afrodad.org
Jubilee Research, developing a fair framework for debt relief: www.jublieeresearch.org

Third-world debt burden

The world's poorest countries, with a per capita income of less than $875, owed $412 billion at the end of 2005, and were paying $436 billion a year in debt-service charges.

Despite increasing levels of aid, poor countries are paying more than twice as much in debt service as they are receiving in grants.

Debt cancellation works

In Benin, 54% of the money saved has been spent on health.

In Tanzania, debt relief enabled primary school fees to be abolished, which led to a 66% increase in school attendance.

In Mozambique, debt relief enabled all children to be offered free immunisation.

In Uganda, debt relief enabled 2.2 million people to gain access to water.

...break the chains

Haiti was the destination for one-third of the slaves traded across the Atlantic. In 1804, a slave-led revolution resulted in its independence and the world's first free black republic. Today, half Haiti's population live on less than $1 a day – and it has a debt of $1.3 billion.

Liberia was founded in 1822 as a home for freed slaves from the USA. Today, average income is just $0.30 day, and it struggles under a total debt burden of $3.7 billion.

The debt relief proposed is still less than half the outstanding debt, and is subject to rigorous conditions.

Write to the Overseas Development Minister urging action. The Jubilee Debt campaign provides letters that you can send

8 JANUARY

contact YOUR MP

Your Member of Parliament is there to represent you. So make your views known on the Iraq war, on ethnic cleansing in Sudan, on GM foods, on local gangs and school bullying, on whatever concerns you. Tell them what you think. Ask them to support your views. Ask them to ask a Parliamentary Question. Get them to act for you and in the people's interest. That's democracy! New technology is transforming the democratic process and will make elected representatives a lot more accountable.

www.WriteToThem.com is a UK website that enables you to email your elected representative with a click of your mouse. Originally intended as a way of contacting UK Members of Parliament, you can now use this service to contact Members of the European Parliament, Members of the Scottish and Welsh Assemblies and local councillors. ♪ To write to your elected representatives you simply type in your UK postcode and choose which one you want to contact. Write your email and hit the 'submit' button. That's it! You have contacted your elected representative. You should get a reply within about two weeks.

If you are part of a campaign, then sending identical copied and pasted 'form' letters will probably not get a reply. It may be seen as junk email, and not worth replying to. They will treat your mail as spam! But rapid-response networks do use this technique to generate tens of thousands of letters in order to demonstrate the depth of public concern.

Find out how your MP has performed in Parliament and what they are interested in by going to: www.theyworkforyou.com and typing in your postcode.

Write to them: www.WriteToThem.com
They work for you: www.theyworkforyou.com
Your Constituency Mailing List: www.mysociety.org/ycml

Find out more about what your MP is doing by joining your Constituency Mailing List, organised by the MySociety.org project.

Enter your details, and you'll be added to a queue of other people in your constituency who want to hear more from their MP.

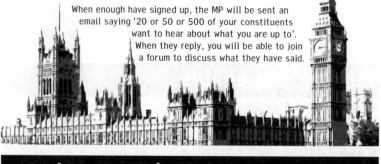

When enough have signed up, the MP will be sent an email saying '20 or 50 or 500 of your constituents want to hear about what you are up to'. When they reply, you will be able to join a forum to discuss what they have said.

...make your views known

♪ **Fax your MP today.** If their answer is unsatisfactory, then fax them again.

♪ **Telephone their office** to find out when their next 'surgery' is. Book an appointment or just turn up.

JANUARY 9

SEEING *is understanding*

There is much common ground between religions, but it is the differences that are highlighted. Religions seem to have grown from similar impulses – the desire to understand the place of human beings in the universe, the need to comprehend the mysteries of life and death, and the wish to experience meaning and happiness in the face of suffering. ❧ The troubles between Unionists and Nationalists (Protestants and Catholics) in Northern Ireland, the continuing conflict in Israel and Palestine (Jews and Arabs), the Kashmir problem between India and Pakistan (Hindus and Muslims), and the Tamil Tiger separatist movement in Sri Lanka (the Hindu minority in a largely Buddhist country) may all be based on very real grievances, but they all demonstrate how religious differences can create divisions within communities and societies, and how this can perpetuate intolerance and lead to violence. ❧ The world would be a better place if there were greater religious tolerance.

Virtual Religion Index, hyperlinks to a wealth of resources on the major religions:
www.virtualreligion.net/vri/

Faith and Food, dietary practices and beliefs of nine religions:
www.faithandfood.com

The world's major religions are:

Buddhism	Islam	Mormonism
Christianity	Jainism	Quakerism
Confucianism	Judaism	Sikhism
Hinduism		

But there are differences within religions, such as those between Catholic, Protestant, Orthodox and Evangelical Christianity, or between Sunni and Shiite Muslims.

...promote religious tolerance

Develop a better understanding of the world's religions. Here's a simple way. Get a group of friends together. Ask each to research one religion or denomination on the internet – read the main religious text (Bible, Qur'an, etc), and talk to people of that faith.

Now go to the services of as many religions and denominations as you can and observe at first hand the different practices. But a word of caution – first contact the church, temple or mosque to confirm whether outsiders are welcome at services and to find out about dress and behaviour protocol.

Here are some questions to ask yourselves:
❧ What are the basic tenets of the religion?
❧ How are concepts of peace and nonviolence highlighted by the religion?
❧ Has the getting-to-know-it process confirmed or dismissed any preconceptions you held?
❧ Does the religion promote tolerance of other religious beliefs? Does it actively seek to convert non-believers? And does it see itself as the world's only true religion?
❧ How are women treated compared with men?
❧ What does the religion say about forgiveness?
❧ Does the religion promote charity? If it does, is there an underlying motivation for undertaking selfless acts and giving to those in need?
❧ Are inter-faith services and other events held?

10 JANUARY

what's the BIG IDEA?

Are you one of those people who bores your friends, endlessly going on about the best way to deal with the burning issue of the day? Or maybe you are something of a lateral thinker, for whom simple everyday problems have elegant and imaginative solutions. 👤 Instead of keeping your good ideas to yourself (and your long-suffering nearest and dearest), you now have a chance to share them with the wired-world.

The Idea-a-Day website was launched in August 2000, and one original idea has been published on this site every day since then. 👤 You can arrange for the idea of the day to be sent to you simply by submitting your name and email address. 👤 You also can submit your own ideas, and they will be posted on the site if they are imaginative enough. 👤 All ideas posted on the site since its inception remain on the site, and it is the intention that the site will continue for ever.

500 of the best ideas have been published in The Big Idea Book, by David Owen, founder of the Idea-a-Day website – details of this book are on the website.

www.idea-a-day.com/archive.asp

Some ideas from the Idea-a-Day website:

Meeting posts in city centres. There would be 12 posts set out in a big circle in a public square in the city centre. The post at due north would be 12 o'clock. Going clockwise round the circle, the posts would be 1 o'clock, 2 o'clock, etc. You would then say to a friend: 'Hey, let's meet for a drink after work, at 6 o'clock in the city centre'. You would have agreed when *and* where.

Being able to vote against a candidate in an election. You would still have just one vote, but you could use this either to vote for or *against* a particular candidate. This would make it much easier to run a campaign against a person or a party that you don't want to see in power.

Cordoning off places of natural beauty or which have some cultural significance. The police will use 'Do not cross this line' tape not just at a crime scene, but for an ancient manhole cover or where an IRA bomb was detonated or where David Beckham proposed to Posh Spice.

The 'International Language of Love': a language school which is also a dating agency. You get paired up with someone for some 'intimate tete-a-tete conversation'. By talking together, you each learn the other's language. You would fill in a normal dating agency form to ensure that you are an ideal match with the person you are paired with.

Audio recordings of celebrities sleeping. Buy this, and when you go to bed, you can pretend that you are sleeping with your favourite pop star or A-list celebrity.

...one for each new day

👤 **Subscribe to the Idea-a-Day website and receive an idea a day.** This should set you thinking about things you could do to change the world.

👤 **Then come up with your very own brilliant idea** – and submit it.

WEAR *a wristband*

Wristbands are a way of showing that you support a particular cause.
Since Lance Armstrong's 'Livestrong' campaign for cancer survivors, which was run in association with Nike, they have replaced 'ribbons' as the must-have fashion accessory. For some wristbands, the demand has been so high, because of celebrity endorsement, that they have become virtually unobtainable. 👫 Most wristbands cost around £2. Try to buy direct from a charity rather than from a commercial supplier; then you know that all proceeds will be going to the cause:

Keep a Child Alive, AIDS drugs for children in Africa, red: www.keepachildalive.org

Make Poverty History, a campaign to end global poverty, white: www. makepovertyhistory.org

LiveStrong with Lance Armstrong, surviving cancer, yellow: www.livestrong.org

Someone you know has Lupus, lupus awareness, purple: www.lupus.org

Orange Ukraine, solidarity with Ukraine's 'orange revolution', orange: orangeukraine.squarespace.com

Victory Starts Here, the fight against women's cancers, pink: www.athenapartners.org

Support Knowledge Strength, breast cancer, pink: www.breastcancercare.org.uk

Beat bullying with a wristband

Beat Bullying was an anti-bullying campaign run by BBC Radio 1 and the Department for Education and Skills in 2004.
They produced a bright blue wristband for young people to wear in solidarity with the campaign. They got celebrities such as footballers Wayne Rooney and Rio Ferdinand and music acts such as Franz Ferdinand and Scissor Sisters to support the campaign and be seen wearing the wristband.

This created a huge demand, not all of which could be met. Eventually, 1 million were handed out before the campaign was closed. They were so popular that some were being traded for up to £30 on eBay.

...show that you care

👫 **Buy a wristband and support a cause.** Wear it with pride and tell other people why the cause is important.

👫 **Selling wristbands can be a good way of fundraising.** Try to get a celebrity to wear yours, for maximum publicity. To order a wristband for your cause, go to BAND-ITS.com at: www.mpglink.com/bands or find other suppliers on Google.

12 JANUARY

♦♦ *become a* VIRTUAL ACTIVIST

The internet is ideal for bringing thousands of people together for a common purpose. It enables you to contact lots of people extremely quickly. It allows them to make an immediate response. And you don't have to spend a lot of money on printing and postage. ♦♦ The anti-World Trade Organization demonstration in Seattle in 1999 first awoke the world to the power of internet activism. Ideas and information had spread around the world with a click of a mouse, plans had been developed and shared, and people had come to Seattle in huge numbers to fight for fairer trading arrangements for the developing world.

The starting point for internet activism is to create an email list of individuals and organisations that might be interested in hearing about what you are doing. Here are some tips for doing this:

> **Collect the email addresses** of as many friends, colleagues, helpers and supporters as possible. Research the media, potential funders, people you want to influence and anyone else you would like to communicate with regularly. Include a space for email addresses in all your promotional material, so that anyone interested can let you know.
>
> **Produce a regular e-newsletter** to let people know what you are doing in an electronic format.
>
> **Take promotional material** to any conference or workshop you attend. This could include a postcard so that those who are interested can send you their contact details.
>
> **Give people the opportunity to get involved**. Suggest some simple things for people to do to help your campaign. Ask for their views and ideas. Suggest that they pass on your details to anyone they know who might be interested.

A picture gallery of Seattle 1999: **www.globalarcade.org/wto/photo.html**
The World Trade Organization History Project: **depts.washington.edu/wtohist**

> **Tuesday 30 November 1999** – termed N30 by anti-WTO activists – dawned gray and cloudy as I made my way up Pike Street to Victor Steinbrueck Park on the Seattle waterfront. By the time I arrived at 7.00 a.m., over 1,000 demonstrators had gathered, ranging from environmentalists to union members to advocates for human rights for the people of Tibet. Soon the crowd began to march toward the Seattle Convention Center, site of the long-awaited meeting of the World Trade Organization, a group of government representatives who set the international rules regarding trade and tariffs. WTO delegates were scheduled to attend an
>
>  opening ceremony that morning at the historic Paramount Theater at 8th and Pine, but protesters were determined to ensure that WTO business did not proceed as usual. As delegates arrived, demonstrators – some dressed in sea turtle costumes and others carrying giant puppets – formed a human barrier to deny them entry...
> – Liz Highleyman, www.black-rose.com

...through the internet

Learn the skills of internet activism. Read the training materials on:
♦♦ NetAction: www.netaction.org/training
♦♦ Backspace.com: www.backspace.com/action/all.php

JANUARY 13

AIDS *Memorial Quilt*

In June 1987, a small group of people came together in San Francisco. Their aim was to create a memorial for those who had died of AIDS, and to promote a better understanding of the disease and its impact. This meeting led to the foundation of the AIDS Memorial Quilt. ☺ Since that day, more than 44,000 individual 3ft x 6ft memorial panels have been sewn – each commemorating the life of someone who has died of AIDS and contributed by friends, lovers or family members. The Quilt is exhibited from time to time, either as a whole or just a part. All the panels contributed will eventually be put on a database and form a 'virtual quilt'.

The Quilt:

Is a creative way of remembering a life cut short.

Provides a strong visual illustration of the scale of the AIDS pandemic.

Creates public awareness of HIV and AIDS.

Raises funds for the fight against AIDS.

You don't have to be an artist or a sewing expert to contribute a panel. You can use paint, needlework, iron-on transfers or appliqué – whatever technique you like. You can create a panel privately, or you might follow the tradition of 'quilting bees' by involving friends, family and colleagues. ☺ Contributing a panel is absolutely free. But donations are welcomed. The organisers (the NAMES Project) suggest a voluntary contribution of $100 a year to process and care for each panel, and $200 to add a new panel to the Quilt.

The NAMES Project Foundation and the AIDS Memorial Quilt: <u>www.aidsquilt.org</u>

How to design a panel

The finished, hemmed panel must be exactly 3 ft x 6 ft (90 cm x 180 cm). Leave an extra 3 inches (7 cm) on each side for the hem.

Use a panel to commemorate just one individual.

Include the name of the person you are commemorating, and also additional information such as date of birth and death, hometown, special talents, etc.

Use medium-weight, non-stretch fabric (such as a cotton or poplin).

Sew things on. Don't glue them – as glue will deteriorate.

If you want to include a photo or a letter, the best idea is to photocopy this on to an iron-on transfer, iron this onto a piece of cotton fabric, and then sew this on to your panel.

...sew a panel

☺ **Contribute a panel to commemorate someone you know** who has died of AIDS.

☺ **Contribute a panel to an unknown victim** of AIDS – just like the Tomb of the Unknown Soldier, which provides a remembrance to all those who might otherwise be forgotten.

14 JANUARY

uncover your hidden **BIAS**

Even though you are consciously committed to egalitarianism and strive to behave without prejudice, you might still possess strong hidden negative prejudices or stereotypes. You believe that you see and treat people as equals, but hidden biases may still influence how you think and what you do. ✖ Psychologists at Harvard, the University of Virginia and the University of Washington have created Project Implicit, and launched a series of tests on the internet – 'Implicit Association Tests' – that aim to detect any hidden bias in people's attitudes.

The test on racial bias: The first task is to sort faces identifiable racially as either black or white. The second task is to sort words associated with positive qualities (peace, pleasure, friend) or negative qualities (violent, failure, awful). Next, participants are asked to sort words into combined categories, assigning positive words and white faces to one column, and negative words and black faces into the other. As the items flash on the screen – peace, white face, awful, black face, friend – the vast majority of people continue to have little trouble doing the sorting. ✖ The signals of bias appear in the next step, when people are asked to reverse the process: to group positive words with black faces, and negative words with white faces. Theoretically, this task should have precisely the same level of difficulty as the previous step. However, most test-takers take longer and make more errors when trying to group good qualities with blacks (and in other versions of the test, with other socially excluded groups). ✖ Over 3 million tests have been completed. Consistently, the test shows bias against stigmatised groups, whether they be Aboriginals in Australia or Turks in Germany. The bias appears to cross racial lines.

In other versions of the test, people show strong preferences for young versus old. And both men and women have far more difficulty grouping women's names with words having to do with science (chemistry, biology), than with arts (drama, poetry).

Project Implicit: <u>implicit.harvard.edu</u>
Fight hate, promote tolerance: <u>www.tolerance.org</u>
A website about race, racism and life: <u>www.britkid.org</u>

www.tolerance.org is a website for people interested in countering bigotry and promoting diversity, whether at home, at school, in the workplace or in the community. It supports anti-bias activism through its online resource
 bank and downloadable public-service announcements. It tells you ten ways to fight hate and provides 101 tools for tolerance.

...test yourself and find out

Take a Demonstration Test at Project Implicit to test your bias regarding age, gender, race or nationality. Each test will take around 10 minutes to complete. At the end of the test, you will be given a summary of your results.

After taking the test on race, read the Tolerance.org tutorial to learn more about stereotypes and prejudice and the impact of these on society.

JANUARY 15

INVEST *in other people*

Directly linking a lender and a borrower is a smart and humane way of banking. The process is often referred to as 'social lending'. You choose to whom you lend or from whom you borrow – and you get better rates, because the mechanism is more efficient than traditional banking.

The world's first social lending marketplace was Zopa, which works by linking lenders with borrowers in a secure online website. Loan applicants are credit scored, and have to be A*, A, B or C-rated if they are to get a loan. The idea has now been copied around the world – for example, by Prosper (USA), Smava (Germany) and Boober (Netherlands).

To lend money, you simply have to log in with your details, and make an offer – 'I'd like to lend this much to A-rated borrowers for this long and at this rate.' Prospective borrowers size up the rates offered to them, and snap up the ones they like the look of. If they don't like the rates today, they can come back tomorrow to see if things have changed. Rates are very reasonable for borrowers as well as for lenders. At the time of writing, the average return for a lender was 6.75%, after allowing for bad debt and fees.

To reduce risk, lenders only lend small amounts to any one borrower. Someone lending £500 or more would have their money spread across at least 50 borrowers. Borrowers enter into legally binding contracts with their lenders and repay monthly by direct debit. If any repayments are missed, a collections agency is used – the same recovery process used by high-street banks. Zopa pays its way by charging borrowers a 0.5% transaction fee and lenders a 0.5% annual servicing charge.

www.zopa.co.uk

What Zopa says:

We make money human again. Instead of helping banks post record profits, your money goes to creditworthy people who'll use the cash to improve their lives. Maybe it's a couple who are building a nursery for their new baby, or maybe it's a young woman who wants to buy a car so she can start her own business. Whoever you lend to, you'll get to see where your money goes and what it's being used for.

...for enjoyable banking

Lend through Zopa, and put your savings to work to help people improve other people's lives.

The transaction is completed online. Everyone's happy. There's not a bank or a bank manager in sight!

16 JANUARY

Street papers being sold by homeless or socially excluded people are a familiar sight in many of our cities. Vendors buy bulk copies at a 50%–60% discount, and then re-sell them, keeping the profit. They will be given some training and identification, allocated a 'pitch' and be asked to comply with a code of conduct. 🏠 The organisers behind these papers aim to:

Help homeless people help themselves, by providing them with a means of earning an income and a dignified alternative to begging.

Support their re-integration into society, through a philosophy of 'a hand up, not a handout'. Any profit made by the paper is used to support homeless people.

The Big Issue in London was inspired by the first street paper, Street News in New York. There are more than 400 vendors, who between them sell 131,000 copies of each issue. There are separate Big Issues for the North, the South West, Scotland and Wales. 🏠 In the last ten years, the Big Issue Foundation has worked with 5,398 people, of whom 407 have gone into further education or attended a course, 281 have been re-housed, and 75 have been helped into permanent employment.

Street papers now exist in many big cities. The International Network of Street Newspapers has 55 members in 28 countries, with a combined annual circulation of 26 million copies. The North American Street Newspaper Association has members in 40 US and Canadian cities.

Vendor Code of Conduct

No begging
No drinking
No swearing
No harassment of the public

Big Issue website: www.bigissue.com
North American Street Newspaper Association (NASNA): www.nasna.org

John's Story: Aged 33 and after losing his job and splitting up with his partner, John found himself homeless, friendless and jobless. He started selling the Big Issue to earn money, but wanted to go back to education. The Big Issue Foundation helped him enroll on a suitable course and provided a grant towards tuition fees. 'Two years ago I was living on the streets in a cardboard box. Now I'm a mature student at the University of London.'
– from the Big Issue Foundation

...keep buying the Big Issue

🏠 **Buy a copy of your city's street paper.** Do this on a regular basis, and smile when you do it. Why not engage in small talk with the vendor? When you get to know your local vendor, why not take him or her out for a coffee at your local coffee shop.

🏠 **Download** Street Papers, a Guide to Getting Started from the NASNA or INSP website.

JANUARY 17

MONEY *talks*

Everyone uses money. Even if you are a serious credit-card addict, you will almost certainly have some banknotes in your purse or wallet. ♀ Money speaks to the masses. It promises food in your stomach, a warm home, entertainment and enjoyment and a better tomorrow. But you can also make your money serve a different purpose from just buying you a cup of coffee and a doughnut.

You can make your money speak to the world. People pay attention to money – and to red ink. So use red ink to put messages on your money, which will be passed from person to person as the money is spent. ♀ Some suggestions for hard-hitting facts to inscribe on your notes:

Over one billion people have to survive on less than a dollar a day.

842 million people across the world will go to bed hungry tonight.

1 in 5 women experience a rape or attempted rape in their lifetime.

Guns kill 34,000 Americans every year.

Wear a condom. Today 14,000 people will become infected with HIV/AIDS.

Perform a random act of kindness to someone today.

Give this money to someone who really needs it.

Make amends with someone today. Tell them you're sorry.

Make way for others. Let someone else go first.

Spread a little happiness. Smile at a stranger.

Explore the world of banknotes at: www.banknotes.com
Find out all about money at: en.wikipedia.org/wiki/Money

...give it a voice

Use your money to spread the word.

♀ **Take all the banknotes in your wallet** and write a simple, but hard-hitting, fact on each side. Don't write all over the note, or someone might not be able to use it. Write round the edges.

♀ **Your message will be spread** to everyone who gets possession of the money. Try to make it lively and interesting – so that people will want to read it. You could even direct the reader to a website.

18 JANUARY

think LONG TERM

10,000 years is about as long as the history of human technology. We have fragments of pots that old. But geographically it is a blink of an eye.

I cannot imagine the future, but I care about it. I know I am part of a story that starts long before I can remember and continues long beyond when anyone will remember me. I sense that I am alive at a time of important change, and I feel a responsibility to make sure that the change comes out well. I have hope for the future.

– Danny Hills

Progress is often measured by how quickly things happen and how cheap things become. It has been nearly 10,000 years since the end of the last ice age and the beginnings of civilisation. The Long Now Foundation was established in the year 01996 [*sic*]. It seeks to promote slower and better thinking, and to foster creativity within a framework of the next 10,000 years.

The 10,000-year clock: One of the projects of The Long Now Foundation is a clock that will tick only once a year, the century hand will advance once every 100 years, and a cuckoo will come out at each millennium. The clock will last for 10,000 years. It is being built by Danny Hills, and a prototype is exhibited at London's Science Museum.

Long Now Foundation: www.longnow.org
World Future Society: www.wfs.org

The World Future Society is a neutral clearing-house for ideas about the future, including forecasts, recommendations and alternative scenarios. These ideas will help people to anticipate what may happen in the next five, ten, or more years ahead. And when people can visualise a better future, then they can start to create it. The Society has local branches in more than 100 cities. These are some forecasts from the Society:

More emphasis will be placed on skills that cannot be automated. These 'hyper-human' skills include caring, judgment, intuition, ethics, inspiration, friendliness and imagination.

With global climate change, coral reefs will see greater changes in the next 50 years than they have faced in the last half million years.

...and predict the future

Predict the future. You can make a long-term prediction about the future on the Long Now website, and give your reasons for the prediction. To do this costs $50. You can vote on predictions that other people have made. You can also challenge a predictor with a bet of at least $200 that their prediction will not come true – whoever wins, donates their winnings to a nominated charity. Place your bet at www.longbets.org

Some predictions to bet on:

- **By 2020** bioterror or bioerror will lead to one million casualties in a single event.
- **By 2020** solar energy will be as cheap or cheaper than that produced by fossil fuels.
- **By 2060** the total population of humans will be less than what it was in 2004.

COMPUTERS *working*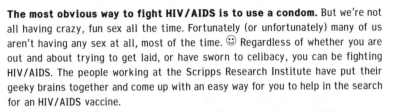

The most obvious way to fight HIV/AIDS is to use a condom. But we're not all having crazy, fun sex all the time. Fortunately (or unfortunately) many of us aren't having any sex at all, most of the time. ☺ Regardless of whether you are out and about trying to get laid, or have sworn to celibacy, you can be fighting HIV/AIDS. The people working at the Scripps Research Institute have put their geeky brains together and come up with an easy way for you to help in the search for an HIV/AIDS vaccine.

It takes an unimaginable amount of computer power to conduct the data searches necessary to create a new vaccine. Your computer sits idle with its computing power not being used, whilst it could be helping in this search. ☺ Scripps has devised a computer programme – FightAIDS@Home – you can download onto your desktop. This programme puts your computer to work when you aren't using it. ☺ When your computer has completed a computation, the results are packed up and sent back to The Scripps Research Institute, ready for its researchers to collect and analyse them. ☺ When you want to use your computer for your own purposes, the FightAIDS@Home programme instantly and automatically turns your computing power to the task you are doing.

Download the Scripps program: fightaidsathome.scripps.edu/help.html
The United Nations Programme on AIDS: www.unaids.org
Avert: a good source of information on AIDS: www.avert.org

AIDS around the world

According to UNAIDS, more than 60 million people have been infected with HIV since the epidemic began in the 1980s.

In the 45 most affected countries, it is projected that 68 million people will die prematurely as a result of AIDS between 2000 and 2020.
The projected toll is greatest in sub-Saharan Africa, where 55 million additional deaths are expected.

The average life expectancy in sub-Saharan Africa is currently 47 years. Without AIDS, it would have been 62 years. Life expectancy at birth in Botswana (which, at 38.8%, has the highest adult prevalence rate in the world) has dropped below 40 years – a level not seen in that country since before 1950.

Current HIV prevalence levels only hint at the much greater lifetime probability of becoming infected. In Lesotho, for example, it is estimated that a person who turned 15 in 2000 has a 74% chance of becoming infected with HIV by his or her 50th birthday.

...to discover an AIDS vaccine

Over 4 million people contracted HIV/AIDS in 2006.

Don't you think it's time to come up with a vaccine? Well why don't you help in the search?

Download the free Scripps programme and follow some simple instructions. There are well over 10,000 computers working on this project.

20 JANUARY

news REPORTING

The growth of the internet is changing the balance of power between journalists and readers. Dan Gillmor, in his book We the Media, writes:

> Big media ... treated the news as a lecture. We told you what the news was. You bought it, or you didn't. ... Tomorrow's news reporting and production will be more of a conversation or a seminar. The lines will blur between producers and consumers, changing the role of both in ways we're only beginning to grasp. The communication network itself will be a medium for everyone's voice, not just the few who can afford to buy multimillion-dollar printing presses, launch satellites, or win the government's permission to squat on the public airways.

Dan's book discusses some momentous changes that are taking place. Here are three examples:

OhMyNews: in Korea everyone can be a reporter. When launched in 2000, the website OhMyNews had 727 citizen reporters called 'guerrillas', who posted news based on their own informed perspectives, which was usually anti-establishment. Immediately, huge numbers of people put themselves forward, wanting to report the news, and OhMyNews changed from a weekly to a daily format. ⚑ By 2004, some 32,000 people had registered as citizen reporters. OhMyNews publishes approximately 200 articles a day, around 150 of these produced by their citizen reporters. OhMyNewsInternational, English version: english.ohmynews.com

The Memory Hole in the USA: giving the news they don't want you to know. The Memory Hole preserves and disseminates material that is in danger of being lost, or hard to find or not widely known. For example, it used the Freedom of Information Act to get photos of dead US soldiers being brought back from Iraq in flag-draped caskets into the public domain. www.thememoryhole.org

Indymedia: a global media network: Indymedia is a network of individuals, independent and alternative media activists and organisations, offering grassroots coverage of important social and political issues. It was originally set up as an information clearing-house for journalists during the WTO's meeting in Seattle in 1999. ⚑ There is now a network of Indymedia organisations spanning the globe and providing a radical, accurate, and passionate telling of the truth. 'We work out of a love and inspiration for people who continue to work for a better world.' www.indymedia.org

Download Dan Gillmor's book free on the We the Media website: wethemedia.oreilly.com

Read SchNEWS

For details of direct action events in your area – a peace festival, a demonstration, a lecture on human rights – SchNEWS' 'Party & Protest' is the activist's version of *Time Out*. Check out www.schnews.org.uk for news reports on subjects from animal rights to Zimbabwe via GATS and WTO. Order a free weekly email subscription, read back issues online, use the yellow pages directory, or buy a copy of the SchNEWS annual.

...anyone can do it

⚑ **Subscribe** to Indymedia and *SchNEWS* for a different slant on the news.

⚑ **Report the news.** When you have something important to contribute, ring up a journalist; write a letter to the editor; call a phone-in show...

JANUARY 21

QUALITY *of life*

Quality of life is not just about national and personal wealth. There are lots of other factors to take into account. But how can you compare one country with another? ♪ The Economist Intelligence Unit has devised a Quality of Life Index, which tries to measure how good a country is to live in. In 2005, 111 countries were surveyed. The survey scored each country's performance in nine different areas:

Material wellbeing gross domestic product (GDP) per person
Health life expectancy at birth
Political stability and security Economist Intelligence Unit ratings
Quality of family life divorce rate
Community life and social cohesion rate of church attendance or trade union membership

Climate and geography geographical latitude, to distinguish between warmer and colder climates
Job security unemployment rate.
Political freedom index devised by Freedom House on political and civil liberties
Gender equality ratio of male and female earnings

Ireland comes out top, because according to the report: 'it successfully combines the most desirable elements of the new (high GDP per head, low unemployment, political liberties) with the preservation of certain cosy elements of the old, such as stable family and community life.' ♪ Zimbabwe, despite its great climate, comes bottom. With widespread food shortages, one of the world's highest HIV/Aids infection rates, 200% inflation, 70% unemployment, a complete erosion of political freedom, life has become very tough for its citizens.

The World in 2005: www.economist.com

The scores out of ten for those ranked top and bottom were:

Top 6 countries	Bottom 6 countries
1 Ireland (8.333)	106 Tajikistan (4.754)
2 Switzerland (8.068)	107 Tanzania (4.753)
3 Norway (8.051)	108 Nigeria (4.505)
4 Luxembourg (8.015)	109 Botswana (4.313)
5 Sweden (7.937)	110 Haiti (4.090)
6 Australia (7.925)	111 Zimbabwe (3.892)

These are the rankings for selected other countries:
USA 13, Canada 14, UK 29, China 60, India 73, South Africa 92 and Russia 105.

...Ireland 8.3, Zimbabwe 3.8

♪ **Assess how you feel about your own quality of life.** Is there any way you can improve it?

♪ **Do something to improve the quality of life in your country.** You can't do anything about your climate (heating it up by contributing to global warming doesn't count), but there may be lots of other things you can do through campaigning or direct action.

♪ **Do something for the people of Zimbabwe or Haiti.** Go to the Human Rights Watch website to find out about some of their problems: hrw.org

22 JANUARY

lost in TRANSLATION?

Do you want send out a message in many different languages? Maybe you need to mount some text on a website, produce multi-lingual leaflets about a campaign, or publish a manifesto setting out your ideas – all in a range of languages. If you are working in the USA, you might want to translate some practical advice into Spanish for the local Hispanic community. ♀ You could find an English speaker who is fluent in other languages to do the translation for you. But there is now another way. The Altavista Babel Fish Translation programme will translate web pages or 150-word blocks of text at the click of your mouse. It will translate from English into:

Chinese	Italian
Dutch	Japanese
French	Korean
German	Portuguese
Greek	Spanish

It's a free service – although you can purchase more advanced software from Altavista. You will need to load special fonts onto your computer for translating into Chinese, Japanese, Korean and Greek. ♀ As an automatic translator, Babel Fish works best when the text you wish to translate uses proper grammar. Slang, misspelled words, poorly placed punctuation and complex or lengthy sentences can all cause a page to be translated incorrectly. If you want a polished translation, the computer-generated text will need to be properly edited.

Babel Fish: <u>world.altavista.com</u>

...here's an easy way to do it

♀ **Go to the Babel Fish website** at world.altavista.com and translate a leaflet or a page of your website into another language.

Allez au site Web de Poissons de Babel à world.altavista.com et traduisez un prospectus ou une page de votre site Web dans une autre langue.

Vaya al Web Site de los Pescados de Babel en world.altavista.com y traduzca un prospecto o las páginas de su web site a otra lengua.

Gehen Sie zur Babel Fisch Web site auf world.altavista.com und übersetzen Sie ein Faltblatt oder die Seiten ihrer Website in eine andere Sprache.

Go on. Try it!

♀ **Next time you travel abroad**, write down 20 or 25 useful phrases which you might need to use (such as 'Which restaurant sells the best pizza in town?' or 'I want to email my mother. Where is the nearest internet café?') and translate them into the languages of all the countries you will be visiting.

THE INTERNET *switch off*

We are basically trying to persuade people for just one day to do something, do anything, that involves the real world – meeting people, walking, cycling or just getting out. By all means use email to prearrange to meet up with people – but do turn it off on the day itself.

— The Global Ideas Bank

The internet is wonderful in so many different ways. It has transformed the way we live. We can contact people instantly, wherever they are. We can involve large groups of people in discussions, and capture their ideas. We can plan things together, without ever needing to meet. We have access to a world of information at the click of a mouse. We can download films and music...

But on the other hand, the internet glues us to our computer monitors, isolates us from our fellow human beings. Large offices have become eerily silent. We will now email someone a message, rather than ring them up or walk ten metres to the next office to say hello.

We need to create a balance between the world wide web and the real wide world we live in. Turn your computer off for one day a week, leave your laptop at home, get out into the real world... and get a life!

Find out about the next Internet-Free Day: www.globalideasbank.org

If you type into Google 'end of internet', you get about 118 million English pages alone. This is one of the first:

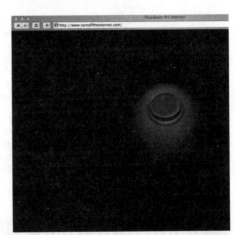

> *The End of the Internet*
>
> *Congratulations! This is the last page.*
>
> *Thank you for visiting the End of the Internet. There are no more links.*
>
> *You must now turn off your computer and go do something productive.*
>
> *Go read a book, for pete's sake.*
>
> — www.turnofftheinternet.com

...and get a life

- **Test your addiction to the internet** at: www.netaddiction.com/resources/internet_addiction_test.htm
- **Switch off your computer on Internet-Free Day** – which is the last Sunday in January. And keep it switched off for the whole day! To find out about the next Internet-Free Day, go to: www.globalideasbank.org
- **Organise your very own internet-free day** in your office, at your college, or in your community.

tackle AFRICA

Let us not equivocate. AIDS today in Africa is claiming more lives than the sum total of all wars, famines and floods, and the ravages of such deadly diseases as malaria. It is devastating families and communities.

– Nelson Mandela

TackleAfrica uses old-fashioned football to educate local African communities about HIV/AIDS. It organises football tours in Sub-Saharan Africa. Matches and mini-tournaments are set up in collaboration with local charities, and then form a focal point for wider HIV/AIDS awareness events. ☺ It was founded in 2002 by a group of young people from the UK who had either lived or worked in Africa, and felt driven to do something to stop the spread of a disease that was bringing increasing devastation to a continent that they knew and loved.

TackleAfrica provides information about HIV/AIDS and its impact on local communities. It explains how to reduce the risks of contracting the virus, and promotes acceptance of people who are living with HIV. It works with Christian Aid, one of the UK's leading international development agencies.

There were over 40 million people living with HIV/AIDS in Africa in 2005. Every nine seconds one more person becomes infected. Every 13 seconds one more person dies.

TackleAfrica: www.tackleafrica.org
Christian Aid: www.christianaid.org.uk/tackleafrica

The first TackleAfrica football tour took place in 2003–04, and visited 11 countries in west and east Africa. The team included 20 young players aged 21 to 30 – from students to bankers – four of whom were women. They travelled by truck across the continent and played 45 matches during the six-month period of the tour, making 28 school visits and playing to a combined audience of 50,000. The pitch in Burkino Faso had a tree growing in the middle until the villagers burned it down in time for kick off.

...football to fight HIV/AIDS

TackleAfrica needs any football-related goods you are willing to donate. This includes: footballs, shirts, training bibs, corner flags, goal nets, balls, boots. Most young people in Sub-Saharan Africa will never have the money to be able to buy any kind of football equipment. Yet many live for football. They will wear your donated shirts and shoes with pride.

☺ **Send your sports equipment** to The Kit Amnesty, TackleAfrica, Meadham Cottage, Hannington, Tadley, Hampshire RG26 5UA

☺ **Go to Africa for six months,** play in a football match and help spread the word about HIV/AIDS. You'll need to raise a participation fee of £2,500. Interested in participating? Write to volunteer@tackleafrica.org

JANUARY 25

OLD SPECS *new owners*

A pair of spectacles could mean a much easier life for 200 million people living in the developing world. Many of these people live in rural areas where there is no eye care available. Most are too poor to afford an eye test and a pair of spectacles. So they have to live their lives in a haze of half sight.

If they can afford to, people change their spectacles as their eyesight changes. Some people buy the latest designer brands. This means that millions of pairs of perfectly usable spectacles are discarded each year – around 10 million pairs a year in Europe and North America. ● These could help people to see in the developing world, but only if a simple way could be found of recycling them.

Vision Aid Overseas: www.vao.org.uk
Unite for Sight: www.uniteforsight.org

The story of Vision Aid Overseas

In 1985, a group of UK optometrists and dispensing opticians decided that they wanted to do something. They took a two-week holiday, ran eye clinics in a developing country and dispensed spectacles they had collected in UK. Encouraged by the success of this venture, they now send teams of volunteers each year to countries such as Ghana, India, Kenya, Malawi, Uganda and Vietnam. Each team consists of between four and eight professionals who go for two weeks and take with them thousands of pairs of carefully sorted recycled spectacles.

Rotary Clubs, schools and churches all help with collecting unwanted spectacles. Most UK opticians now act as collecting points.

Prisoners in seven prisons sort and grade the spectacles.

Vision Aid Overseas does not simply distribute spectacles; it runs 'eye camps', to check people's eyesight so that the correct lenses can be prescribed. It also acts as a centre of expertise and runs training workshops to teach optical skills to local health workers.

...transform someone's outlook

● **Donate your spectacles. Go to the Vision Aid Overseas website and locate the nearest collection point to you.** Or simply pack up your old spectacles and send them to Vision Aid Overseas, Crawley, RH10 2FZ, UK. Enclose a compliment slip so that they can thank you.

● **Start a collection in your community.** Ask all your friends and workmates to hand you their spectacles. Get publicity in the local media. You might be able to collect lots of pairs of unused, unwanted spectacles. Doing this could make an unbelievable impact on the lives of others.

Vision Aid requests all frames should be good condition, and have two unscratched lenses. Unfortunately, bifocals are of no use to them.

26 JANUARY

the HOLOCAUST

First they came for the Jews, and I did not speak out – because I was not a Jew. Then they came for the communists, and I did not speak out – because I was not a communist. Then they came for the trade unionists, and I did not speak out – because I was not a trade unionist. Then they came for me – and by then there was no one left to speak out for me.

– Pastor Martin Niemöller, resister and victim of Nazism

In 2005, the United Nations declared that International Holocaust Remembrance Day would be celebrated annually on this day. Some facts about the Holocaust:

January 1940: The first experimental gassing of Jews and other undesirables.

27 April 1940: Himmler establishes what will become the Nazi's largest and most infamous death camp at Aushwitz-Birkenau, Poland.

20 January 1942: The Wannsee Conference agrees the framework for the 'Final Solution' to the 'Jewish problem'.

1939 – 42: 6 million Jews are murdered by the Nazis, as are 7 million or more non-Jews, including communists, homosexuals, Romany people (gypsies), and physically and mentally handicapped people; 3 million non-Jewish Poles, 3 million Soviet prisoners and 700,000 Serbs.

27 January 1945: the advancing Soviet army liberates Auschwitz.

International Holocaust Memorial Day: www.un.org/holocaustremembrance
Holocaust facts: en.wikipedia.org/wiki/Holocaust and
www.holocaustforgotten.com
The Whitwell Middle School Paper Clips Project: www.marionschools.org/holocaust
Read 'Six Million Paper Clips: The Making of a Children's Holocaust Memorial',
available from: www.amazon.com
See the film: www.paperclipsmovie.com

The paper clips memorial

Eighth-grade schoolchildren in Whitwell, Tennessee created a monument to the Holocaust. They set out to collect a paper clip for each Jew who had been killed, to give them some idea of the size of 6 million, and at the same time address issues of hate and intolerance. The children had learned that Europeans had worn paper clips on their lapels to protest against the Nazis. This symbol of resistance commemorated Johann Valer, the Norwegian inventor of the paper clip, who was Jewish.

The students purchased a cattle car which had actually been used to transport holocaust victims to the death camps. Some of the 22 million paperclips they were sent were displayed in it, to provide a visible, lasting monument to the Holocaust.

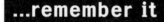

...remember it

🕊 **Wear a paper clip** on your lapel, to commemorate International Holocaust Memorial Day and to make a statement against racism and intolerance.

🕊 **Buy the book** *Six Million Paper Clips*

🕊 **Start your own** paper-clip collection.

HOUSES *for sustainability*

The Tree People Center in Los Angeles is a building with lots of green features. These include:

Extensive landscaping and a 'green roof' planted with native vegetation, which reduces heat absorption in summer.

Bicycle storage and changing facilities so as to encourage cycle use.

A 'water harvesting' storage tank and simple filtration to collect rainwater with which to irrigate the gardens.

Low-flow plumbing and waterless fixtures to reduce water use.

Renewable energy supply for at least half of the building's energy consumption.

On-site solar panels, producing 20% of the building's electricity requirements.

Insulated floors, walls and roofs, which reduce heat loss in winter and heat gain in summer.

Recycled building materials, produced locally or from sustainable sources, wherever possible.

Low-fume-emitting paints, coatings, adhesives, carpets and sealants used for decoration, which improves indoor air quality.

Daylight illumination, where possible, to avoid having to use artificial light.

In the UK, the Peabody Housing Trust built a Zero (fossil) Energy Development (ZED) of low-cost housing in Sutton in South London, and has published a handbook, From A to ZED, which sets out some basic principles for green development.

Take a green buildings tour at: **tours.virtuallygreen.com**
Find out about ZED buildings at: **www.zedfactory.com**

You can't change the design of an existing building, but there are things you can do to make it greener. Using lessons from the Tree People Centre, you might improve the way your house deals with:

Water: Store your roof-water run-off, or use it to recharge the groundwater. Use more water-efficient home appliances. What about installing a composting toilet? Plant a garden on any flat roof, and collect and use rainwater to water it.

Energy: Make sure that your roof and hot water tank are properly insulated, and use draught-excluders on windows and doors to reduce heat loss. Make sure that the curtains are not obstructing daylight through the windows, and paint the walls white or in a light colour to maximise natural illumination.

...create a greener home

🌳 **Take a Green Buildings virtual tour** and visit a green building without leaving the comfort of your home. You can find out why the building was built, what materials it's made of, some of the key design concepts that are incorporated which make it a green building. You can visit the Tree People Center, the Cleveland Environmental Center and several other green buildings. The list is growing, and there's no admission charge!

🌳 **Think about what you can do** to make your own home just that little bit greener.

28 JANUARY

fight the **SUV MENACE**

Do you live in the depths of the country and frequently have to drive off-road? If not, then you have little need to drive an SUV (Sport Utility Vehicle) or 4x4. Nevertheless, these huge cars are becoming very popular, despite being dangerous both for pedestrians and the environment. One in four vehicles sold in the USA is an SUV, and the proportion continues to rise. The same trend is now apparent in Europe.

The SUV is seen as a passport to freedom and the great outdoors. TV commercials depict them climbing snow-capped mountains, or tearing through desert sand dunes. In reality, the only off-road action most of these vehicles are likely to see is when they are accidentally driven across a grass verge!

SUVs are the most polluting form of passenger transport available. Every gallon of petrol burned emits more than 12 kg of carbon dioxide, and SUVs have gargantuan appetites. Some SUVs do as little as 13 miles per gallon in town, and not a great deal more on the open road. This makes them a major contributor to climate change. 🌳 Their enormous engines spew out twice as much carbon monoxide, hydrocarbons and nitrogen dioxide as 'greener' passenger cars. These chemicals cause ozone and other pollutants to build up around cities, leading to poor air quality, which in turn causes people to suffer from headaches, eye and throat irritation and, in the long term, lung damage.

Alliance Against Urban 4x4s: www.stopurban4x4s.org.uk
The USA Friends of the Earth website dedicated to SUVs: www.suv.org

Buy a cleaner car

When you choose your next car, do some research. There is a huge range of different models and they vary enormously in their environmental impact. Pay attention to fuel-

emission ratings, miles per gallon in the city and on the highway. Cars powered by non-carbon fuels are gaining in popularity, with rising petrol prices and fears of global warming. Consider buying an electric car or a hybrid. Use a carpool whenever possible.

www.eta.co.uk/news/car-buyers-guide. asp will help you choose the 'greenest car' for your needs.

...get the off-roads off the road

🌳 **Download fake parking tickets** for some of the London boroughs and for use elsewhere in the UK. Put these under the windscreen wipers of SUVs. They will give the owner a real shock. Download your tickets from: www.stopurban4x4s.org.uk (follow the link to Shop). You can also download posters and street signs at: www.clix.to/no4x4

🌳 **Find out what Jesus would be driving**, had he been alive today. The Evangelical Environmental network of the USA suggests that Jesus would care about his impact on global warming. www.whatwouldjesusdrive.org

JANUARY 29

SLOTHS *slowing down*

What does it mean to be a sloth? Is a sloth lazy and dirty? Is a sloth stupid and slow? Is a sloth really sloth-like? You will be surprised to find out how sloths actually live, and why we could all benefit from emulating them. An incident in the coastal jungle of Ecuador inspired the creation of the Sloth Club. A group of eco-tourists encountered a three-toed sloth, tied up in a concrete cage in a kitchen, awaiting the moment when it would be killed and eaten. Anja Light, singer and activist with the Australian Rainforest Information Centre, and several members of the Japanese Action for Mangrove Reforestation saw something in the defenselessness of the sloth that moved them to do something.

They saw all the injustice and suffering in the world reflected in the act of binding a harmless animal for three days and killing it for a tiny amount of meat: the torture of prisoners of conscience, children in poor countries starving while the rich world doesn't notice, abuse of animals, senseless warfare and degradation of the planet. The sloth is also a symbol of the forest, and the Ecuadorian forest is being destroyed at a frightening pace. It suddenly became very important for these people to find a way to release this sloth, in order to try to lessen the amount of suffering in the world, even if only for a moment. So they paid less than $5 for it, and then released it down river.

They created the Sloth Club to protect the animal's habitat and to change our way of thinking and living. The Sloth Club promotes the concept of doing less, living simply and finding joy in our life without consuming an endless chain of meaningless things. 'We want to shift from a culture of the 'more, faster and tougher' to that of 'less, slower and non-violent'. The three-toed sloth can be our greatest teacher in how to do this.'

The objectives of the Sloth Club:

Establish a sloth sanctuary in Ecuador.

Create a fund to help protect and restore the forests where sloths live.

Support communities in those forests to improve the quality of their lives.

Lead a cultural movement inspired by the sloth's low-energy, cyclical, symbiotic and non-violent lifestyle.

Promote 'Sloth Businesses' – those that are ecologically and socially conscious.

Sloth Club: www.slothclub.org

The three-toed sloth

This harmless vegetarian lives in the rainforests of Central and South America and spends most of its life upside-down about 30 metres above the ground. It has only half the muscle weight of other animals of the same size. Although this means that it can only move very slowly, it makes it light enough to climb thin branches, and therefore less likely to be attacked by predators. The sloth lives in harmony with the environment. Its fur even grows green-blue algae that support many species of insect. No wonder it has such a beatific smile.

...to protect and restore

Join the Sloth Club.

30 JANUARY

get a technological FIX

You scratch. Then it becomes like malaria, you get a high fever. If the fly has previously bitten a rabid animal, and it bites you, you could get rabies.

— Ndith

This is the worst kind of insect bite. Ndith lives in Kathekani in southern Kenya. Cattle are also affected. Her neighbour, Paul, lost all his cows to trypanosomiasis, a disease carried by the bloodsucking tsetse fly.

If the tsetse fly is allowed to spread unchecked, it will devastate the lives and livelihoods of many thousands more Kenyan farmers. Much of Kenya is dry, and crops fail three out of four years. Many families raise animals such as chickens, goats and cows. It is the one way they can meet their basic needs. ● Twenty years ago, the Tsetse fly wiped out 80% of the livestock in Kathekani. Across Africa, 55 million people and their livestock are under threat.

But there is a solution. Tsetse fly traps can eliminate 99% of flies. Farmers work together to build and maintain 'barriers' of fly traps, which are erected in key locations. In Kathekani, ten traps kill 20,000 flies every day. ● One trap costs only $40 to build. The trap is designed to look enough like a cow to trick the tsetse fly. The fly is lured to the trap by the smell of cow's urine contained in a bottle. The flies fly towards the blue cloth on either side of the trap. The black cloth in the middle invites the flies to settle. They then fall into the trap and die. ● The tsetse fly trap is one of many technological solutions developed by Practical Action. Other ideas that have been turned into action include:

Building roads in Sri Lanka.
Harnessing local river power in Zimbabwe.
Water harvesting, terracing, using donkey ploughs, damp proof grain storage in Sudan.
Solar dryers to preserve food and earthquake-proof housing in Nepal.
Solar lanterns in Kenya
Fish-breeding in Bangladesh

Practical Action: www.practicalaction.org

Intermediate Technology Development Group (now Practical Action) was set up following the 1973 publication of E F Schumacher's book, Small is Beautiful: economics as if people mattered. Small-scale water harvesting instead of big dams is a good example of his pioneering idea of small-scale solutions to problems, developed and implemented with local participation.

...find simple solutions

● **Do a global challenge.** Practical Action supporters have cycled the world, run the Andes and other incredible things to raise money for ITDG. Take a year or two off and do the same.

● **Design a machine for turning sea water into drinking water.** Of all the Earth's water, 97% is salt water found in oceans and seas. 2% is frozen. Only 1% of the Earth's water is available for drinking. Your invention could transform the world.

JANUARY 31

GIVE UP *apathy*

If the sheer weight of the world's problems induces apathy, and you don't know where to direct your energies (assuming you have any), there is a website just for you. It saves you the trouble of trawling the internet, providing 'one-stop shopping' for anyone wanting to make a difference.

The Anti-Apathy movement starts with the idea that we should all be engaged in doing *something* for a better world, and our apathy is one of the reasons why things are not changing for the better. Anti-Apathy aims to get cynical and disengaged people to connect with key issues and organisations by showing them how they can help create a more just, more democratic and more sustainable world through their awareness and action. The website provides a list of 24 key organisations. All you have to do is express an interest in five of them, and *act* on the information they send you.

Some of the organisations included on the website:

Amnesty International *human rights*
The Big Issue Foundation *homelessness*
Centre for Alternative Technology
low-energy technologies
Fair Trade Foundation *fair trade*
Friends of the Earth *environment*
Grass Roots Collective *arts and media*
Let's Kick Racism Out of Football
anti-racism

Slow Food *responsible eating and living*
Soil Association *organic agriculture*
Space Hijackers *use of public spaces*
Surfers against Sewage *marine and river pollution*
Survival International *tribal peoples around the world*
World Development Movement *tackling global poverty*

Anti-Apathy: www.antiapathy.org

WORN|AGAIN

These unique trainers, made from recycled prison blankets, towels, parachutes and suit jackets are available from the Anti-Apathy website.

...start to make a difference

This is your own personal action plan. Get moving!

The first five steps to conquering apathy

1 Admit that a life addicted to apathy is a life half lived.

2 Come to believe that the power to change things and restore society lies within each and every one of us.

3 Ponder the question, 'What can I do?' And while you're at it, list some answers to this question.

4 Make a list of all of things you do in your every day life that cause stress to the planet and to society.

5 Act on your discoveries. Find alternatives, or just stop doing the things that cause harm.
adapted from Anti-Apathy's 12 steps to personal recovery

1 FEBRUARY

the seven deadly SINS

Things used to be so cut and dried. The medieval Church laid down what constituted a sin and let people know what punishment awaited them in Hell.

Sin	Punishment in Hell
Pride or vanity: an excessive belief in your own abilities, putting yourself at the centre of the Universe.	*Torture on a large stone wheel.*
Envy: a desire for other people's status, abilities, possessions.	*Immersion in freezing water.*
Gluttony or greed: a desire to consume far more than you require.	*Enforced consumption of rats, toads and snakes.*
Lust: a craving for sexual gratification.	*Being burnt alive.*
Anger or wrath: losing your cool with aggression.	*Having arms and legs chopped off.*
Greed or avarice: a strong desire for material wealth or gain.	*Immersion in boiling oil.*
Sloth or idleness: the avoidance of work.	*Thrown into a snake pit.*

The punishments seem somewhat reminiscent of the reality TV gameshow *I'm a Celebrity: Get Me Out of Here*. Maybe there's a connection...

Mahatma Gandhi drew up a different list of deadly sins that he felt were appropriate for the modern world. These are more complex, and well worth pondering:

> Wealth without work
> Pleasure without conscience
> Science without humanity
> Knowledge without character
> Politics without principle
> Commerce without morality
> Worship without sacrifice

For more on the sins and virtues, go to: www.deadlysins.com

Biblical teaching also provides us with the seven heavenly virtues:	On a more practical level, the medieval Church stipulated *The Seven Works of Mercy*:
Faith	Feed the hungry
Hope	Give drink to the thirsty
Charity	Give shelter to strangers
Courage	Clothe the naked
Justice	Visit the sick
Temperance	Minister to prisoners
Prudence	Bury the dead

...and the seven heavenly virtues

Try to commit one less sin than you would otherwise have done. And be grateful for the punishment you won't have to suffer!

Do one work of mercy today. Visit someone you know could do with some company, cook a meal for someone who might welcome it, or take some old clothes to a charity shop. Almost certainly, you will end up getting some benefit from the action yourself – even if it is just emptier cupboards.

FEBRUARY 2

AIR PORTS *for all*

Wi-Fi (wireless internet) hot spots are springing up in public spaces all over the developed world, giving us internet access wherever we go. But the people who stand to benefit most from the Wi-Fi revolution are those in the developing world – in countries and districts where roads and telephones are basic, rare, or nonexistent.

Wi-Fi comes brightly painted. A bicycle rickshaw, decorated to resemble a Hindu temple carriage, but carrying a computer with a Wi-Fi connection, travels round villages in Uttar Pradesh, India. ♥ The driver is a computer instructor, who gives classes to young and old, providing the villagers with the skills necessary to run their own webcam, which in turn will enable them to participate in online learning. ♥ The rickshaw can also carry medical diagnostic equipment.

Wi-Fi helps isolated communities stay in contact. Yak farmers in remote regions of Nepal are using a Wi-Fi connection to stay in touch with family and friends, get help with health problems, and trade online. ♥ The project was started by teacher Mahabir Pun, who had been given some computers for his school but could not get on line. With no telephone lines, he decided to adopt a wireless solution. ♥ Signals are sent from a server about 30 miles away, to a solar-powered relay station on a tree up the mountainside. This sends the signal to another relay station (also solar- and wind-powered), from where it is distributed to five villages.

Find out more about:
The infothela bicycle rickshaw at: www.iitk.ac.in/MLAsia/infothela.htm
The Nepal Wireless Networking Project: nepalwireless.net

The MagicBike: internet connectivity on two wheels

The Magicbike was developed by Yury Gitman in New York. It is a mobile Wi-Fi hotspot that gives free internet connectivity wherever the bicycle is ridden or parked. It is ideal for art and culture events, emergency access, public demonstrations, and communities who are at the struggling end of the digital divide.

www.magicbike.net

...bring Wi-Fi to your community

Get connected to the internet by setting up your own Wi-Fi connection.

♥ **Join with your neighbours** to set up a wireless base station that all of you can use. Share the costs.

♥ **Use the money you save** to do something to bridge the digital divide.

♥ **Subscribe to www.bytesforall.org** – an online magazine on IT and development.

3 FEBRUARY

Keeping costs down and profits up is the name of the game for fashion retailers such as Gap and Diesel, and sports labels such as Adidas, Nike and Puma. One way of achieving this is to use sweatshop workers to produce their goods. ⚽ Sweatshops can range in size from hi-tech factories for 10,000 workers to individuals working from home. What they have in common is that the workers are required to work long hours for low wages, often in unhealthy and unsafe conditions.

Over 23.6 million people work in sweatshops, in 160 countries around the world. Many of them are young women and teenagers, producing cheap clothing for Western consumers. About 80% work under conditions that systematically violate local and international laws. ⚽ Some firms have pledged to clean up their act, issuing 'codes of conduct' and supporting the campaign against global poverty, but in reality the situation is getting worse as poor countries compete for low wage jobs. With complex production systems, involving thousands of suppliers, work is often subcontracted to sweatshops, which remain 'off the books', hidden from view.

Now is the time to demand that retailers eliminate the global sweatshop system. They control the industry, and they can end it. But we consumers may have to forego the pleasure of purchasing piles of dirt-cheap clothes.

No Sweat, the UK anti-sweatshop campaign: <u>www.nosweat.org.uk</u>
Behind the Label, a US union-sponsored campaign: <u>www.behindthelabel.org</u>

In 2003 David Beckham 'earned' £15.5 million by endorsing companies like Adidas. Indonesian sweatshop workers producing for Adidas earn the equivalent of £400 a year.

Workers in Tower Hamlets, London, produced jackets for Top Shop in hot and dangerous working conditions, for as little as £3.70 an hour. Philip Green, owner of Top Shop denied knowledge of this transgression of his company's code of conduct.

Women sewing $17.99 Disney shirts in Bangladesh are paid just 5 cents for each shirt they sew, while Disney boss Michael Eisner makes about $63,000 per hour.

...look behind the label

Buy a No-Sweat t-shirt or sweatshirt. Next time you shop, ask the store the following:

⚽ Do you have a list of the factories that make your products, with information on the wages and working conditions in each factory? Can you provide me with a copy of it?

⚽ Does your store guarantee that the workers who made this product were paid a living wage, enough to support their families?

⚽ Does your store have a code of conduct that protects human rights and forbids child labour and unsafe conditions in all the factories that make the products you sell? How do you enforce these rules?

FEBRUARY 4

TOILETS *you've got one*

Most of us take a flushing toilet for granted. Yet more than half the people in the world have no access to any kind of toilet at all, let alone one we would consider acceptable. 🌐 Lack of toilets is a major health issue. It is important to prevent other people, animals, and in particular insects from coming into contact with human waste for that is how many diseases are spread. Diarrhoea kills over 2 million children a year. Many of these deaths could be prevented by proper sanitation.

Lack of sanitation is also a gender issue. Boys and men find it much easier, and less embarrassing, to urinate and even defecate in public. Women dare not be caught relieving themselves. They either have to get up before dawn, or wait until nightfall, which can be bad for their health, as well as being uncomfortable.

Many schools in the developing world have no toilets at all – even large secondary schools with several thousand pupils. This is unpleasant for all concerned, but especially difficult for teenage girls. Many agencies recognise that latrines in schools are key to the education of girls. And that well-educated young women are, in turn, key to the social and economic development of some of the world's poorest nations. 🌐 So, the answer to many of the world's problems is more toilets in schools...

WaterAid: www.wateraid.org
IRC International Water and Sanitation Centre: www.irc.nl

The simplest pit latrine is a hole in the ground, with a cover to prevent insects from entering. Some also have ventilation pipes to take away odour and insects.

A more luxurious version is a pour-flush latrine, which has a u-bend kept continually full of water to create a seal. Each user takes water in with them to pour down the latrine.

These simple devices have to be properly managed, and resited when they become full.

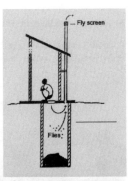

...now give one to someone else

If everybody with a toilet helped provide one for someone without, the problem would be solved. There are plenty of international development agencies working on sanitation. Find a scheme you like, and start raising money for it. According to WaterAid:

🌐 **£8** pays for enough cement to produce four latrine slabs in Malawi.

🌐 **£15** buys an ecological sanitation latrine in Mozambique.

🌐 **£350** pays for a school sanitation block for 150 boys and girls in India.

Ask people at work to help. Construct two collecting boxes. Put one in the men's and one in the women's toilet at your workplace, with a poster inviting people to drop a coin in the box every time they use the toilet.

5 FEBRUARY

minimally invasive **EDUCATION**

Mere curiosity will lead groups of children to explore, and this will result in them learning.

Dr Sugata Mitra of NIIT – a leading computer training and software company in India – came up with the idea of **Minimally Invasive Education (MIE).** The NIIT office was located next to a slum, where none of the children had access to computers, nor were particularly familiar with the English language. A hole was made in the wall of the office, and a computer was installed there with a monitor and a mouse, accessible from the street through this 'hole-in-the-wall'.

Within three months, the children had achieved a certain level of computer skills without any instruction at all. They were able to browse the internet, download songs, go to cartoon sites, work on MS Paint. They even invented their own vocabulary to define terms on the computer, for example, *sui* (needle) for the cursor, *channels* for websites and *damru* (Shiva's drum) for the hourglass (busy) symbol. By the fourth month, the children were able to accomplish tasks such as creating folders, cutting and pasting, creating shortcuts, moving/resizing windows and using MS Word to create short messages, which they were able to do without using a keyboard.

Ten more kiosks have been set up in towns and cities across India, and 100 are planned. When the idea of removing the original kiosk was discussed, parents and children strongly opposed this. The kiosk is still there, and approximately 80 children use it daily.

Read about the Hole-In-The-Wall project at: <u>www.hole-in-the-wall.com</u>

Children working intently at the Stok Learning Station in Ladakh in the Himalayas, another hole-in-the-wall project.

A Stok Learning Station.

...it's a hole-in-the-wall thing!

- **Find out** as much as you can about the **Hole-In-The-Wall** project. Write a simple manual about it.

- **Bring the idea to the attention** of organisations working in education and urban issues – in your own country as well as in the developing world.

- **And next time you travel,** try to find an organisation working in a slum and discuss with them how they might set up a **Hole-In-The-Wall** project in their community (with your support?).

FEBRUARY 6

KEEP FIT *in a green gym*

You want to keep fit, so you go along to your nearest fitness centre. All those people pedalling away at exercise bikes or jogging along on a treadmill – it seems so pointless. All that body odour. And the membership fee will cost you almost a month's salary. Well, here's a green and healthy alternative – healthy for you and good for the environment.

The idea is called a Green Gym, and this is how it works. A local group will meet usually once a week for a 4-hour session. After some basic warm-up exercises, you will be put to work doing practical gardening or conservation work. You might find yourself planting a new hedge, cutting back an overgrown footpath or helping build a community garden. When you get hot there will be cool-down activities. You don't need any experience, and you will be trained in the use of tools. You don't need the latest lycra gear or Nike trainers; you just turn up in some old clothes. And all sessions are free.

The Green Gym scheme was developed by BTCV, the UK's leading environmental volunteering agency. There are now around 70 all over the UK. If there isn't one near you, then start one yourself!

Green Gyms: www2.btcv.org.uk/display/greengym
Green Drinks: www.biothinking.com/greendrinks

Green Drinks

Green Drinks groups are a self-organising network. The first was set up in London in 1989, and there are now over 200 Green Drinks groups in North America, Europe, Mexico, Brazil, Chile, Argentina, South Africa and China.

Every month, people who are interested in green issues meet informally. There's usually a lively mixture of people from NGOs, education, government and business. New members can just turn up, say 'Are you green?', and regular Green Drinkers will look after them and introduce them to other people.

It's a great way of catching up on the issues and for making new contacts. Regular members are asked to invite someone else along, so there's always a different crowd. The latest initiative is 'Green Teens'.

You're invited to 'GREEN DRINKS'

...and then go for a Green Drink

☺ **Find your nearest Green Gym** and give it a go.

☺ **Check out if there's a Green Drinks group near you**, when and where it next meets, and join them.

7 FEBRUARY

make **A LOAN**

Invest your money in an entrepreneur, using the brilliant Kiva website.
The internet has opened up channels for giving that link people more closely with those they are supporting. For the price of a meal out, why not help someone start or expand a business, and thereby help them escape from poverty? This is not charity – it is an investment – although you don't get any interest.

Four steps to changing someone's life

Step 1: Choose a business. Go to the Kiva website and find a business that appeals to you. Each one has been put forward by a local microfinance agency.

Step 2: Make a loan. Use your credit card to transfer money to the business you select. The minimum amount is $25.

Step 3: Receive progress reports. Your loan will typically be outstanding for between six and 12 months. Over this period, you will receive progress reports about the business.

Step 4: Withdraw your money or re-lend it. When your Kiva loan is repaid, you can choose to have the money back, or you can re-lend it to another business.

www.kiva.org

Name: Rustam Gadoev
Location: Khujand, Tajikistan
Activity: Clothing sales
Loan requested: $1,200
Repayment term: 18 months – repaid monthly
Loan use: To expand his women's clothing store.
Rustam is married with two children. He has a university degree and was a geography teacher, but his teacher's salary was too low to support a family, and in 1997 he rented a shop in which to sell women's clothes. He would like to start a second shop for his wife to run, and to be able expand his range of clothing to attract new clients.

Name: Nguyen Thi Thin
Location: Do Luong, Viet Nam
Activity: Food production/sales
Loan requested: $200
Repayment term: 12 months – repaid monthly
Loan use: To get better prices from her suppliers

Nguyen is 44, and lives with her husband and two sons in a rural province in Vietnam. She sells snacks at the local market, and needs a loan to buy ingredients in greater quantities from her suppliers, thereby obtaining a discount, and enabling her to increase her profits.

...and change a life

Don't go out for a meal this weekend. Eat in and use the money you save to invest in a poor family's future, and help them to achieve economic independence. It'll be a lot more fun in the long run.

FEBRUARY 8

ORGAN DONATION *a gift of life* ☺

Transplants save lives – but there is a desperate need for more organs, and the more people discuss their wishes regarding donation, the more lives can be saved. More than 7,200 people in the UK are waiting for an organ, and around 400 people die each year while waiting for a transplant.

Transplants depend on the generosity of donors and their families. To donate your organs you need to have expressed a wish in writing during your lifetime (or orally in front of two witnesses), or the person in possession of your body at the time of your death needs to be willing to donate your organs and have no reason to believe you would not have wished this. ☺ The law differs from country to country, but there are two basic models: 'Opt-in' (the UK model), whereby individuals are asked to register their consent, or 'Opt-out', which assumes that individuals consent unless they register an objection.

Organs that can be donated include:

heart
lungs
kidneys
pancreas
liver
small bowel

Tissue that can be donated includes:

corneas
skin
bone
heart valves
tendons

Corneas can be transplanted to restore the sight of a person who has a severe eye disease or injury. ☺ Bone and tendons are used for reconstruction after an injury or during joint replacement surgery. ☺ A bone transplant can prevent limb amputation in patients suffering from bone cancer. ☺ Heart valves are used to help children born with heart defects and adults with diseased or damaged valves. ☺ Skin grafts are used as protective dressings to help save the lives of people with severe burns. ☺ Tendons can be used to restore mobility.

Register online as an organ donor at: **www.uktransplant.org.uk**

In the UK in the year to 31 March 2007:

3,086 organ transplants were carried out as a result of the generosity of **1,495** organ donors following their death.

A further **2,402** people had their sight restored through a cornea transplant.

Nearly 1 million people added their names to the National Organ Donor Register, bringing the total registered to over 14 million.

...that costs you nothing

☺ **Make known your wish to be an organ donor.** Tell your partner, your family and your friends. Tell your doctor.

☺ **Join the NHS Organ Donor Register** and carry an Organ Donor Card. This will alert those who are dealing with you in an emergency situation.

☺ **Get nine of your friends and family to register too.** This is a gift of life that costs you nothing, but will help to tackle an interntional shortage of donors.

9 FEBRUARY

♟ *collect your* **SMALL CHANGE**

Loose change in your pocket really does 'burn a hole' – or at least wears away at your pocket linings. And bulky purses full of change only add to the weight most of us end up lugging around with us. ♟ The only thing to do is *offload it*. Empty your pockets or your purse each night and bung it in a jar, a piggy bank, under your mattress, or wherever takes your fancy.

You'll be amazed at how quickly your spare change mounts up. And you probably won't even miss it! ♟ At the end of the year – or whenever the container gets full – you will then have the pleasure of deciding which project to donate the money to. You might decide to give it to a project near to home, or to respond to one of the many charitable appeals in the media. Even small sums of money can make a huge difference.

Here are some good online giving websites:

Global Giving: a marketplace for high impact social and economic development projects around the world: www.globalgiving.com

Give India: lots of different types of project, and many give you several options for giving. Surf the site, and you might end up by building a well, sponsoring a child's education, helping provide eye operations: www.giveindia.org

Just Giving: an Anglo-US website with lots of options for giving both at home and abroad: www.justgiving.com

...and donate a fortune

What a difference your small change can make! There are all sorts of interesting things you can donate to. Put your money to work changing the world.

You could give:

♟ £5 to send four carefully selected books to Africa: www.bookaid.org

♟ £17 for an adult cataract operation: www.sightsavers.org

♟ £250 for an 'elephant pump': www.pumpaid.org

Or you could be more ambitious and choose a longer-term project on the Global Giving website. Here are two examples in El Salvador:

♟ Enable one farming family to buy the land that they are working.
   Cost $7,535

♟ Save the El Impossible rainforest, helping over 50 volunteers working with SalvaNATURA to ensure that the trees don't get cut down. Cost $10,000.

These are suggestions just to illustrate the good that you could be doing with your money. Make a big change with your small change!

FEBRUARY 10

TOOLS *in the right hands*

Giving a tool enables people to make a living for themselves and their family – it is the same principle as teaching a hungry person how to fish, rather than just handing out fish. ◉ In countries such as Tanzania and Ghana, it can be incredibly difficult and far too expensive for people to buy the tools they need to make a living. This is tough for the people involved. But there's an imaginative solution.

Tools for Self-Reliance (TFSR) collects and sends over half a million pounds' worth of high-quality tools every year to six countries in Africa. The tools they send are used by skilled craftspeople to earn a living. TSFR also trains people how to use and take care of their tools. ◉ The organisation has over 100 collection points across the UK. You can join a local TFSR group, or just collect some tools, which TFSR will ship to people in some of the poorest parts of Africa.

What tools are needed?

The tools most requested are for:

woodworking

blacksmithing

building and plumbing

shoemaking and leather working

car and bicycle repairing

metal working and tin smithing

Shipping costs are the same for good tools or bad tools, so wherever possible only the best are sent.

Tools for Self Reliance: **www.tfsr.org**

My African people have great skills, initiative and energy. They work so hard to develop their communities and their continent, against such heavy odds. But you cannot work with bare hands.
– Archbishop Desmond Tutu speaking to the BBC about Tools for Self-Reliance

...foster self-reliance

Organise a tool collection drive.

◉ Contact Tools for Self Reliance. They will supply you with a list of needed tools as well as a nearby collection point.

◉ Contact your friends, family, and local businesses. Tell them what you are doing and what you need. Ask them to donate tools.

◉ Take all the tools to the drop-off location.

11 FEBRUARY

organise a FLASHMOB

FlashMobs are designed to amuse and to bemuse. A FlashMob seems to be a spontaneous gathering, but has actually been organised in secret by email or text message. It requires meticulous timing if it is to be effective. Large groups of people converge at a public (or semi-public) place for a brief period of time. The mob is formed – and then just as quickly the mob disperses again. At a pre-set time, all members depart in different directions.

The FlashMob phenomenon started in New York City in 2003. The craze quickly spread across America and migrated to Asia and Europe. Germany is now the FlashMob centre of the world. There are groups registered in 21 cities and FlashMobs are staged every night of the week.

A FlashMob is a seemingly pointless activity, but it doesn't have to be so. A FlashMob will be talked about by those who participated and also by those who hear about it. So it could be a creative way of getting across an important message – even if only subliminally.

FlashMobs in the UK and around the world: www.flashmob.co.uk

London's first FlashMob took place at precisely 6.30pm on August 7, 2003. Sofas UK in central London was besieged by 250 sweaty people speaking English without using the letter 'o'. Emails had been sent to people who had signed on to the LondonMob website. Instructions were given to meet in one of three pubs at exactly 6.17pm, when more information would be given. When the mob arrived at Sofas UK, although on time, they found that the Manager had closed up early to go for a refreshing pint – it was a really hot day! But he was persuaded to open up, and the Mobsters congratulated him on the quality of the furniture before departing.

On another occasion, 200 people with umbrellas sang in the evening sunshine to the accompaniment of their mobile phones in the courtyard fountains of Somerset House, London's former central public record office. The mob arrived at precisely 6.25pm from pubs around the West End. Participants were asked to text a mate en route to the venue with the message 'call me at 6:30' in order to provide a ringing accompaniment to the FlashMob's choral efforts. Mobsters were also asked to click their fingers every time they heard or spoke the letter 'Y' and to compliment strangers as they departed from the mob.

Flashmob.co.uk
Out of knowhere

...and make a statement

Become a FlashMobster.

Join in a local event.

Then organise your own 'spontaneous' FlashMob event and link it somehow to your cause. Be really creative in designing your event. Try to get a lot of publicity for what you have done.

FEBRUARY 12

ELECTRICITY *time to switch*

About 30% of CO$_2$ emissions are produced by the burning of fossil fuels to generate electricity. Green electricity (which is electricity produced from renewable sources such as wind or wave power) produces no CO$_2$ at all. ♣ How does this work? Electricity generators in the UK are required by law to generate 3% of their electricity (rising to 15% by 2015) from green (renewable) sources. Some other countries have similar requirements. ♣ The generating companies obtain a certificate showing that they have produced a certain quantity of green electricity. But if they produce more than their quota, they are allowed to sell certificates for the surplus to other electricity companies – which then use these rather than generating their own green electricity.

Demand and supply. The best way of encouraging the generating companies to produce more green electricity is for consumers to demand more of it.

Friends of the Earth, campaigning on green energy: www.foe.co.uk – click on 'climate', and then, through 'fossil fuels and nuclear', on 'green energy'.

Information on green electricity from Green Electricity Marketplace: www.greenelectricity.org/domestic.html

Electricity sources:

Bright green: Wind turbines, solar-electric, solar heating, hydro-electric and wave power all use natural sources of energy and produce no carbon emissions.

Pale green: Biomass takes plant material and burns it. Landfill sites and sewage produce methane, which can then be burned. Carbon taken from the atmosphere is returned to it – which is better than...

Conventional: Burning oil, coal and gas. Burning non-renewable fossil fuel is the major factor in increasing carbon in the atmosphere.

Nuclear: No carbon is produced, but disposal of the waste is a problem.

...to a responsible supplier

♣ **Switch to green electricity.** Compare prices and do this online at www.uswitch.com/green-energy. Suppliers include:
Green Energy: www.greenenergy.uk.com,
Good Energ: www.good-energy.co.uk and Ecotricity: www.ecotricity.co.uk.

♣ **Ecotricity builds its own wind generation capacity.** Visit the Swaffham turbine in Suffolk, which has a viewing platform 60 metres high, up a 300-step spiral staircase.

♣ **Try to reduce your energy consumption** as much as you can.

learn a new language # SIGN UP

Sign is the primary means of communication for many profoundly deaf people. It is in effect their first language. ✖ Sign uses hand gestures that are interpreted visually. Each word has its own gesture. There are also signs for each letter of the alphabet. ✖ There are two different versions of sign: British Sign Language (BSL) and American Sign language (ASL). And, just as with spoken language, there are colloquialisms and slang.

Social inclusion is one of the dominant ideas of our age – finding ways of including people whatever their difficulties or disabilities. For example, enabling people with learning difficulties to attend regular schools, making public buildings accessible for wheelchairs, and so on. ✖ If you meet a profoundly deaf person, find out how they prefer to communicate. Learning to sign will show your commitment to a just, tolerant and inclusive society. It isn't hard – many words are based on gestures which reflect the essence of the word. For example:

How are you?	**Hungry**	**Thank you**
Open your hands and touch your chest with them, then move them outwards, making them into fists with raised thumbs.	With a clenched fist draw a circle on your stomach. The same actions are used to sign the country, Hungary.	With straight fingers put your hand to your chin and gently bring it forward, once or twice.

For BSL contact: www.british-sign.co.uk or www.learnbsl.org
For ASL contact: www.masterstech-home.com/ASLDict.html www.signlanguage.org

I Love You (ASL)

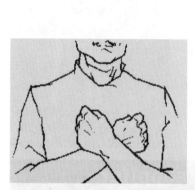

I Love You (BSL)

...and speak to deaf people

Get started in sign. Here's a simple phrase to get you going. First, find someone you want to say this to. And then say it to them. With passion!

I (Point to yourself.)

LOVE (Cross either your closed or flat hands over your heart with palms facing in.)

YOU (Point to the person you are addressing.)

KNITTING *cast off*

Peace Fleece seeks to find a common ground across political and religious divides. It was started by Peter Hagerty and Marty Tracy in 1985 when they bought wool from the Soviet Union in the hope that through trade they could help diffuse the threat of nuclear war. ❧ Since then they have created links with shepherds in Russia, Kyrgyzia, Israel and Palestine, as well as in Montana, Ohio, Texas and Maine, seeking to develop a mutual understanding and economic interdependence.

Combining wools from around the world into one yarn symbolises peace. In response to the Iraq war, Peace Fleece came up with 'Baghdad Blue', a vibrant new Peace Fleece colour as bright as the desert sky. All profits from the sale of Baghdad Blue are donated to Neve Shalom/Wahat al Salaam, an international community in Israel, founded by a Dominican monk, Father Bruno Hussar.

Knitting can itself be a political act. Knitting is about self-sufficiency and designing-it-yourself, as an alternative to responding to the whims of the fashion industry and buying garments made in developing-world sweatshops. Boys who knit challenge gender stereotypes. So believes Cast Off, a guerrilla knitting group launched in the UK in 2000 by designer Rachael Matthews and artist Amy Plant.

Peace Fleece: www.peacefleece.com
Cast Off: www.castoff.info/shop.asp

In Neve Shalom peace village
Jews, Christians and Muslims live in peace, each one faithful to his or her own faith and traditions, while respecting others. The village is the setting for a school for peace. The inspiration is the biblical quotation: 'Nation shall not lift up sword against nation, neither shall they learn war any more'.

Peace is an art. It doesn't happen spontaneously; peace-making has to be learnt. You can go to Neve Shalom/Wahat al Salaam as a volunteer. For more information about the village and the peace school, go to: www.nswas.com

...plain and purl for peace

If you've never knitted, now's the time to learn.

❧ Order some Peace Fleece wool and make a woolly jumper.

❧ Or use the yarn to try out some of the wackier ideas on the Cast Off website. They include: a dishcloth, shoe-laces, a first aid kit, a blindfold, a deluxe lipstick, an exfoliating sponge cover, a knitted willy, and even a knitted hand-grenade that doubles as a purse.

the One-Straw REVOLUTION

My method of 'do-nothing' farming is based on four major principles:

1 No cultivation (that is, no ploughing and no hoeing)
2 No fertiliser
3 No weeding
4 No pesticides

I will admit that I have had my share of failures during the forty years that I have been at it. But because I was headed basically in the right direction, I now have yields that are at least equal to or better than those of crops grown scientifically in every respect. And most importantly my method succeeds at only a tiny fraction of the labor and costs of scientific farming, and my goal is to bring this down to zero.

At no point in the process of cultivation or in my crops is there any element that generates pollution, in addition to which my soil remains eternally fertile…and I guarantee that anyone can farm this way.

– Masanobu Fukuoka, author of *The One-Straw Revolution*

Masanobu Fukuoka is a Japanese farmer who devised a revolutionary method of farming. Ploughing the land, large-scale monoculture, and chemical fertilisers and pesticides were all discarded. To everybody's surprise, year by year his yields rose, eventually exceeding those obtained using modern farming techniques. ● Disciples all over the world continue to experiment with Fukuoka's methods of natural farming. These challenge the whole basis of the world's agricultural policies. ● Fukuoka believes they can also be used to transform the arid lands of Africa.

The One-Straw Revolution is available on Amazon and from Other India Press. For details contact: oibs@bom2.vsnl.net.in   There is more information on Fukuoka and natural farming at: www.seedballs.com/2seedpa.html

Other books that have revolutionised thinking:
Gaia by James Lovelock. The earth's biosphere is seen as a self-regulating entity with its own capacity to keep the planet healthy in the long term.

Small is Beautiful: economics as if people mattered by E F Schumacher, the inspiration for appropriate technology.

Pedagogy of the Oppressed by Paolo Friere, which influenced a generation on the role of education in the fight for social justice.

Rules for Radicals by Saul Alinsky, which gives practical ideas for effective organising. His techniques have are used by community organisers around the world.

Limits to Medicine: Medical Nemesis, the Expropriation of Health and *De-schooling Society* both by Ivan Illich. Two books that show the need for radical new approaches for the two public services that have the most impact on our lives. All these books were written a generation ago. But their ideas remain relevant.

...change your thinking

Make a list of your own 'Six books to change the world'. Encourage others to read them.

FEBRUARY 16

MEETING UP *is fun*

We believe that the world will be a better place when everyone has access to a local Meetup Group. That is our goal.

Meetup.com helps people find others who share their interest or cause. This can be a starting point for creating or joining a lasting and influential local community group. ✊ Meetups are usually informal, held monthly, open to anyone – you can bring along friends if you like – and held in public places such as cafes and parks, although some take place in offices or private houses. ✊ Some Meetups are based on activities such as knitting or speaking a foreign language; others focus on a cause – such as planning a women's rights march or getting a political candidate elected; others are self-help groups at which people can swap information and stories.

There are literally thousands of local Meetup Groups for thousands of interests all over the world. There are Meetups for:

Spanish speakers...	Quit-smoking optimists...	Trigger-happy
Philosophy freaks...	Poker-playing nuts...	photographers
Elvis fans...	Quilting sororities...	Stiff-upper-lipped Expat
Atkins dieters...	Marathon trainers...	Brits...
Red Sox supporters...	Pekinese dog walkers...	Linux lovers...
Alternative-energy bores...	Harry Potter aficionados...	Bloggers with attitude...
Wine lovers...	Pregnant women...	Environment savers...

Over 1 million people all over the world have joined local Meetup Groups, which have brought communities together, shaken up politics, given people a voice...and provided a lot of fun. *United we Meetup!*

Meetup: www.meetup.com
Green Drinks: www.greendrinks.org

The Meetup Bill of Rights for members:

The right to meet: free, local monthly Meetups should be open to all.

The right to privacy: your email address will not be shared without permission.

The right not to get annoying ads: No pop-up ads, no spam.

The right to meet about almost anything: Meetup. com is non-partisan and non-denominational. Everyone should have access to a Meetup Group about almost anything (except hate and obscenity).

The right to choose where to meet: Meetups can take place anywhere. If it is a place of business, buy a drink to thank your host location!

...a chance to learn, do, change

✊ Join a Meetup near you that brings a group together around a topic that interests you. If there isn't one, start your own group.

✊ Or if you care about the environment and like drinking, why not join a Green Drinks group to meet, talk and do things together?

17 FEBRUARY

stop eating **SHRIMPS**

Huge quantities of shrimp are produced in developing countries. More than 4 million tonnes are shipped annually for consumption by the rich world. And this is causing major environmental problems in the poor world.

Shrimp fishing is a major threat to marine life and ecosystems. 75% of shrimp are fished, mostly by boats dragging huge conical trawling nets over estuaries, bays and continental shelves. ●This destroys the seabed and scoops up whatever lies in the path of the trawler. About 10kg of dead fish, turtles and other marine species are discarded for every kilogramme of shrimp caught. Shrimping accounts for 33% of the world's discarded catch, while producing less than 2% of seafood.

Nor is shrimp farming the answer. It destroys fields and rural livelihoods in coastal areas. When fishponds are built, chemicals, fertiliser and salt water inevitably leach out into the soil, degrading the land and making it unusable for agriculture. The average shrimp farm provides 15 jobs on the farm and 50 for security around the farm, while displacing up to 50,000 people through loss of traditional fishing and agriculture. ● It destroys natural coastal environments. Nearly 25% of the world's remaining tropical mangrove forests have been destroyed over the past 20 years, most of them to make way for shrimp farms. ● Each kilogramme of farmed shrimp requires 2 kg to 4 kg of fish protein, which is mainly derived from captured wild fish.

Find out more from the WorldWatch Institute:
www.worldwatch.org/pubs/goodstuff/shrimp

Ecuador's shrimp industry has expanded rapidly over the past 30 years. It now takes up some 500,000 acres of former mangrove forests, salt flats and agriculture land along the coast.

Corrupt government officials and land-hungry illegal shrimp producers collude to rob coastal people of their traditional fishing and food-gathering lands, and traditional mangrove forestry activities such as charcoal-making and wood production can no longer be carried out.

Coastal village people wanted to evict illegal shrimp producers and reforest the devastated mangrove areas around Muisne. Supported by Greenpeace and Fundecol, and using only shovels, pieces of wood and their bare hands, they cut out a breach in an illegal shrimp pond, drained the water and planted mangrove seedlings to try to restore what had been destroyed.

...and help the environment

Pledge to stop eating shrimp. For every 1,000 people who stop eating shrimp, this will save more than 5.4 tonnes of marine life per year.

Grassroots environmental groups are working with international activists to develop more ecologically sound shrimp farming. In Sri Lanka for example, the Small Fishers Federation (www.shrimpaction.com/SFFL.html) and the Mangrove Action Project (www.earthisland.org/map/) work with shrimp farmers to curb mangrove destruction and protect fish habitat. Visit their websites and lend your support.

FEBRUARY 18

EMAIL *Bill Gates*

Bill Gates receives about 4 million emails a day. Much of this is spam – unwanted, unsolicited mail. This is being sent to him because of his wealth, or because some people believe he exercises too much control on the virtual world, or just because he is Bill Gates III.

All this unwanted email should focus his mind on the fact that spam is a major internet problem – as well as a time-consuming nuisance. Up to 80% of all email traffic is spam, much of it trying to sell pornography or aids to increase your sexual performance, or some sort of scam that aims to part greedy fools from their money.

As the biggest software company in the world, Microsoft is in a position to take action – to protect all of us from receiving spam and to stop it being sent. ♥ Bill Gates has a department that sifts through the mountain of email he gets each day. So he won't actually read what you send him. But if his mail mountain continues to rise, perhaps this could spur him into action.

Email Bill at: billg@microsoft.com or askbill@microsoft.com
The unofficial Bill Gates website: www.zpub.com/un/bill
Microsoft Corporation, with the official Bill Gates web pages and contact details for the company: www.microsoft.com
The Bill and Melinda Gates Foundation: www.gatesfoundation.org

Today's problems are solvable. While the world around us fuels our sense of urgency, it also fuels our optimism. We believe that by increasing equity and opportunity, the world will become a better place for generations to come... As the years ahead bring more advances in health and learning, we share the global responsibility to ensure that they reach the people who need them most.
– Bill Gates and Melinda French Gates

Bill and Melinda are putting their money where their mouth is.
The Bill and Melinda Gates Foundation has an endowment of $27 billion and funds initiatives in global health, libraries and US schools – and community initiatives in the USA's Pacific North West, where Microsoft is located. Bill is not only the richest person on the planet, but also the most philanthropic.

...to put a stop to spam

Email Bill Gates and tell him that you are fed up with receiving pornographic emails, Nigerian fund-transfer scams and advertisements for cheap Viagra, and tell him that you expect Microsoft to find a workable solution. Ask him to do something about spam...ask him to do it now!

The Microsoft website does have tips for hiding your address from spammers, avoiding phishing and other email scams, blocking junk mail, and reporting spammers to the authorities: www.microsoft.com

19 FEBRUARY

non-violent DIRECT ACTION

Non-violent direct action can be a really effective way of getting things changed. It is often misunderstood and criticised as being too 'radical', too 'political', or even 'illegal'. It is certainly radical, often political and it may even challenge the law, but it has a long tradition of success: **The Boston Tea Party**, when tea was dumped into the sea, was the starting point for America's independence. **Gandhi's Salt Marches** highlighted the injustice of British rule in India and mobilised popular support for the Quit India campaign. And Gandhi successfully built non-violent direct action into a political philosophy. Peter Hain (subsequently a British cabinet minister) led the **Anti-Apartheid** campaign to stop South African sportsmen touring the UK by digging up rugby pitches. **The US Civil Rights Movement** involved sit-ins and boycotts to end segregation. **Friends of the Earth** in the UK started by returning non-returnable bottles to Schweppes' head office. Stunts such as this are now a common campaigning technique.

The environmental movement has incorporated significant components of direct action in its campaigns against nuclear power, to save ancient forests, to achieve a global ban on high-seas drift-net fishing and to end dumping on the high seas. Ditto the anti-war movement, the Campaign for Nuclear Disarmament and the efforts to stop the growing of GM crops.

Greenpeace: www.greenpeace.org
Ruckus Society: ruckus.org

The functions of direct action:

Alarm – to get attention to a burning problem or issue.

Reinforcement – to get publicity to support your campaign.

Planned escalation – to raise the stakes and show you mean business.

Morale – to raise spirits and renew energy.

Before you take action, you need to clearly define the issue, who is responsible and what you want to achieve. You need to design an action that will have impact. You also need to know the law and what your rights are.

...create change

Get skilled in organising. The *Ruckus Society* is a resource centre for organisers. It runs free training camps in the USA – you are asked to make a donation of $100, but nobody is refused for lack of funds. They also have a range of resources for direct action, including an *Action Planning Manual* and a practical guide to *Hanging yourself from a Billboard* or other outdoor structure – downloadable free from their website.

If you want to campaign for the environment, join Greenpeace. They use direct action really effectively. Visit the Greenpeace website, and play games on themes such as GM foods, toxic chemicals, oil discharges, nuclear waste, global warming, wind farms and *Spank Esso!* These will make you think. And you may then decide to get involved.

FEBRUARY 20

CAN YOU SAY *Adios in Ainu?*

Only eight elderly people spoke Ainu on Hokkaido Island, Japan by the late 1980s. But once it was decided to do something, the language was revived. Cornish died out in 1777. Using surviving written documents, descendants of Cornish speakers began to learn their former language and speak it to their children. Road signs began appearing in Cornish and English. Now, about 2,000 people speak Cornish.

Why is this important? Without words to express things, knowledge and ideas begin to disappear. The loss of any one language means a reduction in the sum total of human thought and knowledge and an impoverishment of the human race. It is predicted that at least half the world's 6,000 or so languages still in existence will be dead or near death by the year 2050. An *Atlas of Endangered Languages* reports that 50 European languages are in danger, with France having 14 near death. In Siberia, in the Russian Federation, nearly all the 40 or so local languages are disappearing. Languages are becoming extinct at twice the rate of endangered mammals and four times the rate of endangered birds. While there are huge campaigns to preserve animal and plant species, there is far less concern about preserving the world's languages.

Foundation for Endangered Languages: **www.ogmios.org**
Ethnologue, an online resource on lesser-known languages: **www.ethnologue.com**
UN website on cultural diversity: **www.un.org/works/culture**
Free Online Language Courses: **www.word2word.com/coursead.html**

First-languages speakers in the world today
Source: Ethnologue

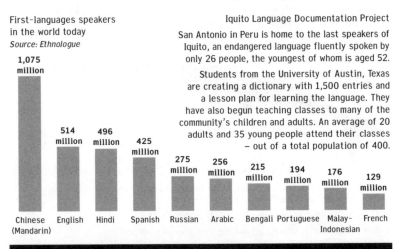

Iquito Language Documentation Project

San Antonio in Peru is home to the last speakers of Iquito, an endangered language fluently spoken by only 26 people, the youngest of whom is aged 52.

Students from the University of Austin, Texas are creating a dictionary with 1,500 entries and a lesson plan for learning the language. They have also begun teaching classes to many of the community's children and adults. An average of 20 adults and 35 young people attend their classes – out of a total population of 400.

Chinese (Mandarin)	1,075 million
English	514 million
Hindi	496 million
Spanish	425 million
Russian	275 million
Arabic	256 million
Bengali	215 million
Portuguese	194 million
Malay-Indonesian	176 million
French	129 million

...save a vanishing language

Do something to revive an endangered language.
Find out more. Investigate the languages that are indigenous to your own locality or region.

Take a course in or buy a recording of an endangered language.

Go to: www.word2word.com/coursead.html for free resources for learning 100 different languages online. Get started with Cornish or Cherokee.

say NO to PLASTIC BAGS

Bags that you use for just a few minutes may last for between 15 and 1,000 years. Every time you go shopping at the supermarket and accept a plastic bag at the check-out, you'll be doing something that harms the environment – even if you walk or cycle to get there. Even biodegradable bags take years to degrade.

Plastic bag litter creates huge problems. The bags can trap birds or kill livestock (if eaten). One farmer in Australia found eight plastic bags in the stomach of a dead calf – the loss of this calf cost him around $500. And when a dead animal decays, the plastic bags will be re-ingested by other animals – this cycle will continue for many years. ♣ That's not all. Plastic bags can block drains and foul waterways. They can accumulate along the roadside or on beaches. They can be a blot on the landscape as well as an environmental hazard.

Government action can help. In Ireland, where a law was introduced in 2002 that taxed retailers on the non-reusable bags they issued, plastic check-out bag usage was reduced by 90%. That was a saving of nearly 1 billion bags in just one year. ♣ In Australia, retailers were required to reduce their use of plastic bags by 25% during 2004 and by 50% by 2005.

Customers also need to act. Use re-usable bags when you go shopping. Recycle any plastic bags you take home with you as bin liners or freezer bags.

Planet Ark organises anti-plastic bag campaigns in Australia and the UK. Its book, Greeniology – how to live well, be green and make a difference, shows how to change your ways without sacrificing your lifestyle: www.planetark.com

Onelessplasticbag, a fabric bag that folds up to put in your pockets: www.oneless.co.uk

Did you know…

There are now over 46,000 pieces of plastic waste in every square mile of the world's oceans. Plastic-bag litter kills at least 100,000 birds, whales, seals and turtles every year.

During the manufacture of plastic bags, benzene gas, a known carcinogen, enters the atmosphere.

Plastic can take centuries to decompose. When it is burned, poisonous dioxins and hydrogen cyanide enter the soil and natural water supply.

In Australia at least 80 million bags end up as litter each year.

In China, plastic bags blowing around are called 'white pollution'.

In South Africa, there are so many bags in the countryside that they have become known as the 'national flower'.

…save the environment

Just say No! to plastic bags. Buy cloth bags, jute bags, straw bags, bags made out of recycled bottle tops. Use these instead. Take one with you whenever you go out shopping. And use it again and again and again.

FEBRUARY 22

STREETS *for people*

There was a time when streets comfortably accommodated a full range of human activity. In villages, towns and cities, they were places for trading, socialising, playing, entertaining, meeting and demonstrating in. They were also routes for travel and the movement of goods. Until the motor age, all this was kept in balance. Today the balance has been lost. Streets have become traffic corridors, cutting swathes through local communities. Traffic management is more important than the quality of local life. Streets are dirty and dangerous. Communities everywhere suffer.

Let's give the streets back to the people. Let them be living streets. This 10-point manifesto has been adapted from the Pedestrian Association's Living Streets campaign:

1 **Lots of people out and about.** Living Streets need people living on them, walking down them and overlooking them. There needs to be a mix of housing, shops, offices, pubs, schools and places of worship within reasonable walking distance.
2 **A balance between people and traffic.** Streets have become ugly and intimidating for pedestrians. Streets should be designed for people as well as for traffic.
3 **Traffic volume and speed** should not be too high. Traffic kills people. Too much traffic also kills communities.
4 **The street environment.** People are being overwhelmed by clutter on the pavements, squeezed between the buildings and the traffic, with 'street furniture' everywhere.
5 **Street upkeep.** Streets need to be properly managed to get rid of litter, dog fouling, dumped cars, petty vandalism and graffiti.
6 **Safe and well-lit streets.** If people don't feel safe, they won't use the streets.
7 **Facilities to relax.** Living streets have benches and walls where people can pause and pass the time.
8 **A nice place to be.** The street environment needs to be attractive and interesting.
9 **Accessibility.** Access in and out should be made easy.
10 **Information for pedestrians.** Maps and signs for pedestrians should be informative and helpful.

The Living Streets campaign: **www.livingstreets.org.uk**
Reclaim the Streets campaign: rts.gn.apc.org

> *On Saturday 21 August, a little bit of Cardiff's busy road network was liberated from the sound of traffic and the smell of petrol fumes for a few hours. For one afternoon only, the streets were filled with the sounds of free-spirited souls partying and the smell of... well... free-spirited souls partying!*
>
> A local Reclaim the Streets event, which described itself as a 'disorganisation for a people-centred world'

...put pedestrians first

Do a 'Liveability Survey' to see how much the street where you live or shop scores on the 10 points. Score each point out of 10, and the total out of 100. Are you satisfied with the result? If not, come up with some ideas for what to do.

become the EXPERT

When a new issue hits the headlines, experts are in great demand. The broadcast media are desperate to fill their airtime, and print journalists need help in filling their column inches. Policymakers often seek out experts for advice. The world needs information about so many different issues. There must be something on which you have more information than anyone else...or in which you are interested or about which you are concerned enough to go out and collect all the information. By doing this, you will quite soon become *the expert* on your subject.

Tell people about the importance of what you know. You could, for example:

Write and publish a report. This makes you an 'instant expert'. Make sure the report contains accurate facts and is well designed and produced.

Contact relevant journalists to tell them about it. Make them believe that you are *the expert*.

Get publicity for your ideas. You'll have to work at this. Organise a stunt to get media attention.

Collect as much information as you can, and put it on a website. Googlebomb it to make sure that your website comes up top when people are searching on a related keyword.

Get references and endorsements from as many prominent and respected people as you can.

Send out a press release whenever the issue is topical.

You might then turn from being *the expert* to being *a pundit*, and be asked for your views on a range of topics.

Read: *The Know-It-All: One Man's Humble Quest to Become the Smartest Person in the World*, **by A J Jacobs, from Amazon**

Some ideas to get you thinking:

Steven Millman wrote to every chocolate manufacturer to ask if they used slave labour in any stage of the production of the chocolate they were selling. This made him the expert on the use of slave labour in chocolate.

Documenting change over time enables you to compare what things were like then and what they are like now. You will have real evidence of change. Keep a diary, take photographs, collect published information and press cuttings.

...know your facts

Think of a topic that really interests you – preferably one that nobody else is expert on, and something that is or is likely to become important and newsworthy. Start collecting as much information as you can. Then put up a website and write a definitive article for Wikipedia, the open-source internet encyclopaedia at: en.wikipedia.org

Get a group of 100 young people to be 'The Voice of Youth' on topics as diverse as gender and democracy. If the group is 'representative', then their views will be more authoritative. Get advice from a polling agency on how to construct such a group.

FEBRUARY 24

INFLUENCE *the media*

You ask me what I came into the world to do. I came to live out loud.
— Emile Zola

The internet has provided us all with an opportunity to make our views known. Political 'blogging' is an effective way of keeping democracy alive using the latest technology. ♀ Use your freedom of expression as an individual to keep government transparent and accountable – locally or nationally. Even if you live under a tyrannical government, the internet may still provide a space for you to express your views.

'Blog' is short for 'web-log' – an internet diary reflecting the ideas, experiences and views of the blogger, often linked to other web-based information. ♀ People blog for every reason under the sun. Some just do it to keep a diary, some because they are keen to share their ideas or expertise. And some do it for a political purpose. ♀ Some people just want to share their secrets. One of the most visited websites, and a web publishing sensation, is a weblog of a call girl known as 'Belle de Jour': belledejour-uk.blogspot.com

These are some good examples of political blogs:

andrewsullivan.theatlantic.com – Andrew is a British-born gay republican with great sources and a sharp outlook on American politics.

gotze.eu – e-government from enterprise architecture to e-democracy.

www.instapundit.com – a hyperactive blogger who focuses on the intersection between technology and individual liberty.

Most blogs have the following features for easy access:

Photographs and links to text, audio and video files and to other websites.

One or more columns, with new content put prominently in the largest column. Side columns include links to other blogs, previous posts or reader comments.

Updates published in reverse chronological order, so regular readers just need to read what's at the top.

Frequent updates, sometimes daily, sometimes several times an hour.

...become a political blogger

Become a blogger. A free basic blogging service that will help you get started is: www.blogspot.com. Setting up a blog will take you less than five minutes. Then how much time and energy you put into making it really good and in finding readers is up to you.

♀ **Are there issues in your community that no one is addressing**: traffic, homelessness, gangs, police brutality? Become the voice that brings this issue to the forefront so it can no longer be ignored.

♀ **Provide the latest news**. Praise and criticise government officials. See that they live up to the promises that got them elected. Research the candidates running in the next election. Find out about their campaigning platforms and their stance on important issues.

25 FEBRUARY

give up # GROUP THINK

Do you ever find yourself listening to a group discussion, disagreeing with what is being said, or feeling that an important point is being missed, but afraid to speak up? It is quite likely that others are feeling the same way. This is Group Think.

We will all find ourselves in a Group Think situation sometime. It might be about a tiny issue, or something much more important. Whatever it is, speak up; get your point of view heard; influence the discussion *and* the decision. Your view is important and needs to be heard.

Six symptoms of group think

1 Believing there are good reasons for what you know are poor decisions, and explaining away facts that do not support the line of thought.
2 Believing what you are doing is morally correct, even when the evidence suggests otherwise.
3 Using shared negative and positive stereotypes to inform the decision.
4 Exercising direct and indirect pressure on members of the group who would like to express contrary views.
5 Self-censorship: failure to speak up means that your views remain hidden.
6 Maintaining an illusion of unanimity, where silence is taken for assent.

And six ways to avoid group think

1 Understand how Group Think affects decision making.
2 Find someone neutral to chair the group.
3 Give space for everyone to express their views.
4 Always compare the proposed decision with a less popular alternative. Ask someone to play devil's advocate.
5 After reaching what seems to be a consensus, encourage people to express their doubts.
6 Break into several smaller groups to discuss the issue and suggest a course of action. Then try to reach a consensus.

'1984' by George Orwell, a frightening parable of Stalinist Russia and a couple's attempt not to conform: www.online-literature.com/orwell/1984

'12 Angry Men', an Oscar-winning film in which the Henry Fonda character is the only juror to believe that the defendant is not guilty: www.filmsite.org/twelve.html

Here are two examples of Group Think in recent history:

The treatment of the Jews in Nazi Germany; people must have known what was happening was wrong.

The McCarthy crusade against Communism, and the witch hunts in the middle ages (which Arthur Miller used as a parable of McCarthyism in his play *The Crucible*).

...speak up if you disagree

Next time you go to a meeting, don't remain silent. Speak up. Say what you think. Don't be frightened of seeming foolish. Others in the group may also not be happy with how the discussion is going, and welcome your intervention.

If you are chairing a group, encourage everyone to say what they think, and make sure everyone's point of view is respected. Sharing ideas leads to better decisions – and better decisions are needed for a better world.

FREECYCLE *for fun*

'Think globally, recycle locally'– the Freecycling Network has been set up for those who want to recycle things, rather than throw them away. 🏠 Whether it's a chair, a fax machine, a piano or an old door, your local Freecycling group will provide you with an opportunity to advertise the things you no longer need in the hope that you can find someone who would like them. 🏠 Or if you're looking to acquire something yourself, this is a good place to start.

Freecycling helps keep good stuff out of landfills. It is a virtual response to a global problem. There is just one rule – everything that is advertised must be free. 🏠 There are now over 1,500 cities all over the world with a Freecycling group, with over 525,000 members in total. The largest group is in Portland, Oregon, with over 10,000 members. There are 120 groups in the UK. 🏠 Freecycling can be started in any city, and is open to any individual who wants to participate. Groups are run by a local volunteer, who facilitates the group. The Freecycling Network gives itself a pat on the back by saying: 'This is grassroots action at its best!'

Freecycle: freecycle.org

The Freecycling Oath of Honour

Those starting a new Freecycling group, take the following oath:

I (*your name*) pledge to be a really nice and patient person when moderating our new Freecycle webpage.

I promise to use the Freecycle name only for our non-commercial *Yahoo* group.

I will remain open to the occasional democratic discussion on our webpage, but will know when to make the tough calls and decisions in order to spare the rest the long debates.

With great honour I shall also keep spam, ads and money-makers out of my group with the 'two strikes, you're out' rule.

I'll suggest people give preference to nonprofits when giving stuff away.

And, finally, I shall come clean of my rat pack ways and clean out my own garage before asking the same of others.

...find homes for your discards

Check if there is a local Freecycling group for your city, town or neighbourhood. If there is, join it. Dispose of your old stuff and get new stuff by Freecycling. Enjoy!

If there isn't a local Freecycling group, then start one. The Freecycle website tells you what you need to do to get started. It essentially means moderating a Yahoo group whilst being a passionate advocate for recycling.

27 FEBRUARY

be a good NEIGHBOUR

In these days of high-speed communications, you can feel close to someone thousands of miles away. The sense of a 'global village' is being used by NABUUR, a Dutch Foundation, to help give urban and rural communities in developing countries (which they call 'villages') access to the resources they need to solve their problems: information, expertise, experience gained by projects that work elsewhere, ideas for funding.

This is how NABUUR.com works:

1 A community is in urgent need of help. After an assessment, the village is given a page on NABUUR.com. A representative of the local community then describes an urgent question or problem which needs to be solved.
2 People who want to help sign up as virtual neighbours of that village. They look for answers to the question, working together with other good neighbours.
3 The best solutions are then put forward to the village. A neighbourhood representative discusses these with the community.
4 The community decides what to do, and the solutions are implemented. The good neighbours are able see the results through photos and stories posted on NABUUR.com.
5 A new question may then be put forward; and the process starts all over again.

The neighbours mainly help by searching for information on the internet, contacting organisations that could be helpful, using their creativity and other skills, and providing specific expertise and advice.

NABUUR.com is the brainchild of Siegfried Woldhek, who was previously the Chief Executive of WWF Netherlands.

NABUUR Foundation: <u>www.nabuur.com</u>

Welcome to Chimaltenango, Guatemala: The Kaqchikel Maya who live in Chimaltenango are the direct descendants of the precolumbian Maya. The majority are peasant farmers, growing maize, beans and vegetables. The population has grown rapidly in recent years. This has led to widespread deforestation. To stem the tide, the community wants to develop ecotourism. The area has much to offer: beautiful forests (despite the deforestation), volcanoes, ancient temples and indigenous arts and crafts. The community needs information on what tourists find interesting, what sorts of activities could be developed and how to promote Chimaltenango as an ecotourist destination.

...help in someone else's village

Become a good neighbour. Choose from around 60 villages in Africa, Asia and Latin America with problems covering community development, income generation, education, environment, sanitation, agriculture, health and much else.

Go to NABUUR.com and select a village that interests you. Become a neighbour of that village. Get to work. Post your answers and ideas on the discussion board for that village.

FEBRUARY 28

A DAY OFF *clear your head*

Today is an extra day added to the calendar to keep it aligned with the seasons. Why not mark it by taking the day off, if you can, and doing something out of the ordinary: an extreme sport, an act of generosity – something you've been meaning to do for four years? ♟ If you're usually a very busy person, you could treat it as a day to get yourself back in alignment and just chill out. Do whatever you think you need to do most. Of course this could include thinking up some really great ideas for changing the world...

Here are some suggestions, but don't feel pressured to do any of them!

Soak in a hot tub. Relax. And start thinking about how to change the world.

Ask your friends to come round and celebrate Leap Day with you. Ask them to bring a bottle and one good idea.

Take your local Big Issue seller for a cup of coffee and a chat. Ask him or her to give you one idea for doing something about homelessness.

Surf the internet. Type in two or three words that best describe the issue you are interested in, and see what appears. Follow up any interesting links that are suggested.

Write to your head of government (or any other famous person), and ask him or her to give you one good idea for what you and other people can do to make the world a better place.

Check out these ideas websites:
Why not? www.whynot.net
Global Ideas Bank: www.globalideasbank.org
Idea Explore: www.ideaexplore.net
Idea a Day: www.idea-a-day.com
Brainflower: www.brainflower.com
Creativity Poo:l www.creativitypool.com
Premises Premises: www.premisespremises.com
Half Bakery: www.halfbakery.com

... and these ideas blogs:
World Changing:
www.worldchanging.com
Global Ideas Bank blog:
www.globalideasblog.com
The Demos Greenhouse:
www.demosgreenhouse.co.uk
Café Utne: www.newcafe.org

The Innovation Tools website catalogues the best resources for innovation, creativity and brainstorming: www.innovationtools.com

...make room for new ideas

Organise an impromptu 'Ideas Party' for changing the world.

♟ **Decide on an issue you really care about.** Identify some of the problems around that issue. For each problem, ask everyone to come up with one practical idea that they – either by themselves or as a small group – could do that would have some impact (however small) on the problem.

♟ **List all the ideas** and then select those that are relatively simple to do and likely to have some impact. At the end of the evening, review all the good ideas, and ask each person to do at least one thing from the list.

♟ **Eat, drink, be merry** – and get your creative juices flowing.

29 FEBRUARY

keep up with **THE NEWS**

There's so much information on the web, and so little time to sift through the billions of web pages. Keeping up to date with the news can be extremely time-consuming.

How about getting the latest news and features delivered to your desktop? Now news updates can be sent straight to your computer using a service called RSS. No more hopping from site to site looking for new information updates – RSS sends it to you direct.

RSS stands for Really Simple Syndication. It enables you to choose websites you're interested in, and get their news delivered to your computer or Blackberry. RSS makes it easy for people to access multiple blogs and news websites simultaneously. Instead of surfing 20 web pages, RSS shows new content on your favourite sites at the click of a button. To use RSS, simply install an RSS reader and log your favourite websites. Then click the update button, and your RSS reader lists all new items on your preferred websites by headline, brief description, date and time.

RSS News Reader Downloads: for Windows: www.newzcrawler.com
for Mac: ranchero.com/netnewswire
See also the How Stuff Works website for interesting facts about almost everything: www.howstuffworks.com/rss-feeds.htm

Websites offering Really Simple Syndication:

A growing number of websites offer RSS, including news providers such as *The Guardian*, *Reuters*, the BBC and CNN. As Really Simple Syndication becomes more widely used, more information providers will offer the service.

Here are a few websites already offering RSS:

National Public Radio: www.npr.org/rss/index.html
BBC: news.bbc.co.uk/1/hi/help/rss/default.stm
CNN: www.cnn.com/services/rss/
Reuters: today.reuters.com/rss/newsrss.aspx
The Guardian: guardian.co.uk/webfeeds
Wired: feeds://wired.com/rss//index.xml

...with Really Simple Syndication

Get started with RSS.

♟ **Get a News Reader.** One may be included in your browser software, or you can download one from the internet. There are lots of programmes available, although free versions have fewer features.

♟ **Check your favourite website for an RSS link.** If it has one, click on the link and choose the categories of information you want to be updated on. Then follow the instructions on how to hook up, and get news updates from this site to your computer.

MARCH 1

JUNK MAIL *cancel it*

Everyone gets junk mail – the endless stream of unsolicited letters and leaflets arriving through the mailbox each day: loan invitations, credit card applications, mail order catalogues, offers of fabulous prizes, etc. The generic envelope instantly shatters dreams of a premium bond win or letter from a loved one. As soon as we recognise junk letters we throw them away unopened.

Junk mail is a complete waste of paper, extra weight for the postman to carry and extra rubbish for the refuse collector to cart away, not to mention personal aggravation for us.

Mail Preference Service. UK: www.mpsonline.org.uk
USA: www.dmaconsumers.org/cgi/offmailing

Do-it-yourself: stop junk mail, e-mail and phone calls:
www.obviously.com/junkmail

New American Dream: www.newdream.org
Forest Ethics: www.forestethics.org/

How to make junk mail more environmentally friendly

New American Dream and Forest Ethics are calling on five of the USA's biggest catalogue companies (all of whom currently use little or no recycled paper) to start greening the 600 million catalogues they produce each year.

Help persuade mail order catalogues to be more environmentally friendly. Write a letter urging companies sending you mail to reduce the frequency of their mailings, and start printing on at least 10% recycled content immediately. Ask them to commit to improving this to 50%–60% over the next five years. Tell your friends to do the same.

...stop junk mail

If you're fed up with junk mail, you'll be glad to know you can do something about it:

🍄 **Get in touch with the Mail Preference Service** and tell them you don't want to receive unsolicited mail. Mailing list organisations servicing the direct marketing industry will delete your name from the addresses sold to marketers. Your name will be removed for five years and you should start to notice a reduction in junk mail after three months. It's much better to stop junk mail at the source rather than recycle, and this organisation will show you how to do it.

🍄 **Tick the box on any reply form** you fill in stating you do not want information about future special offers.

🍄 **Do not fill in the warranty applications for consumer goods** as these are often used as a way of collecting names and addresses. Your rights are protected under law.

2 MARCH

go on a CARBON DIET

The USA is responsible for 25% of the world's energy consumption – most of which is generated by burning fossil fuels. ♣ Each person in the USA is directly or indirectly responsible for the release of 20 tonnes of CO_2 each year. ♣ In the UK, it's about 12 tonnes. The world annual total of carbon emissions is 6.5 billion tonnes, which is four times the 1950 level. ♣ The Earth's capacity to absorb CO_2 is fairly constant, and the excess adds to the concentration of greenhouse gases in the atmosphere.

Cut your CO_2 emissions. When it comes to CO_2, most of us in the rich world are over-indulging. To prevent the climate from changing even more, we all need to go on a CO_2 diet.

Work out your carbon footprint with the National Energy Foundation's carbon calculator: www.nef.org.uk

Identify the best ways of saving energy in your home with The Home Energy Saver: hes.lbl.gov

Some tips for living lite

Buy locally grown fresh produce wherever possible. This cuts down on the air miles of getting the food to you.

Don't leave the TV and other appliances on 'standby': 8% of electricity consumed at home is from items you aren't using.

Ensure that your home and your hot water tank are properly insulated.

Use more energy efficient household appliances. Switch to low-energy bulbs for all or most of your lighting.

Switch to a renewable electricity tariff – it needn't cost anything extra, but it shows your commitment to a renewable future.

Purchase goods from suppliers who have teamed up with a Carbon Reduction company to offset some or all of the carbon cost of what you are purchasing. The 'Market Place' at Climate Care shows some of the options available in the UK: www.climatecare.org

Drive more slowly. If you do 60mph rather than 80mph on the motorway, you will use 25% less fuel. But better still, cut out some journeys, and travel wherever possible by bicycle or on foot – or rollerblade if you really want some fun.

...get a taste for living lite

♣ **Play the Carbon Game** to get some ideas for saving energy and money, and reducing your impact on global warming: www.pbs.org/wgbh/warming/carbon

♣ **Plant one tree.** This will consume more than enough CO_2 to offset the CO_2 you are breathing out. It's nice to know that a tree is working to reduce your body's carbon emissions!

♣ **Live lite.** Go on a carbon diet. Change your lifestyle to cut down on your own CO_2 emissions.

MARCH 3

TOXINS *in your TV*

Many electronic products contain toxic chemicals. Small amounts of these chemicals can cause widespread pollution once the product has reached the end of its useful life and is discarded.

What is being done? One solution is to put pressure on the manufacturers to remove toxic chemicals from their products. Samsung, Nokia, Sony and Philips have all promised to do this as soon as they realistically can.

> **If your cellphone is made by:** Motorola, Panasonic, Sharp, Siemens, Sony Ericsson...
>
> **Or if your TV is made by:** Akai, Bang & Olufsen, Daewoo, Grundig, JVC, Panasonic, Sharp...
>
> **Or if your computer is an:** Acer, Apple, Dell, Fujitsu-Siemens, HP/Compaq, IBM, Panasonic, Toshiba, Tulip...

...then your pressure could push these companies to follow the good example of those that have already made a decision to phase out toxic chemicals.

Do the Toxic Tech Test at the GreenpeaceWeb.org website:
www.greenpeaceweb.org/consumingchemicals/ddtest.asp

Form letter you could send to a manufacturer

Dear Sir/Madam,

I have a product from your company *(insert name of company)*. As a customer of your company, I am asking if the computer/electronic equipment *(insert item and model)* I have bought from you contains toxic chemicals.

Toxic chemicals, if used by your company in the production of these products, would cause damage to the environment and to people. I am particularly concerned about brominated flame retardants and phthalates.

More and more companies are choosing to phase out all these toxic chemicals in all their products and production. If your products contain toxic chemicals, are you planning to phase all these chemicals out of your products or not?

If you do *not* plan to phase out all these toxic chemicals, then I will consider buying from a different company next time.

Yours sincerely,

Your Name, Your email

...take the Toxic Tech Test

Go to the Greenpeace website:

🌳 **Do the Toxic Tech Test.**

🌳 **Send a letter to a manufacturer** of the electronic product you have just bought. The site provides a form letter, with space for you to fill in your details.

4 MARCH

join the **GREAT ESCAPE**

Stuck in a job you don't like? Dissatisfied with the work you are doing? Feeling that your values are at odds with those of your employer? Want to fulfil your potential, do something more meaningful and exploit your talents and creativity?

You are not alone. Many people settle for a job that gives them a certain status and brings in a reasonable income, but this may not be what they really want to be doing. You only have one life, so try to use it to do what you really want to do – something you feel passionate about: where you can make a positive contribution and get real satisfaction.

The Escape Club was set up for people like you, by Alok Singh and Satu Kreula. These two Pioneers of Change saw many of their friends unhappy at work, and wanted to help them find a way of addressing this. The Escape Club provides people making a career change with what they need: specific tools, courses, connections with people who can help, real-life stories, etc. The club also includes lots of feedback and ideas from members.

The Escape Club: www.escape-club.org
Career Shifters: www.careershifters.org
Downshifting Down Under (for Australians): downshifting.naturalinnovation.org

Advice from an Escapee

Never let your perceived limitations hold you back. Chance your arm. Take a risk and go for it.

Get passionate about something and turn it into your work.

Remember to do the groundwork – plan it and fuel it with passion.

Be flexible enough to pull your ideas apart every so often, look at what works and what doesn't, and take it forward from there.

Be humble enough to ask for help and guidance.

– Helena Dennison, June 2004

...change your career

Make your own Great Escape.

Read the archive of the Escape Club's monthly newsletter, *Escape Stories*. Each issue has real-life stories of people who said 'Okay isn't good enough', and went on to pursue what inspired them in their lives.

You'll read about the changes they made, but you'll also find out what their journeys were like, what obstacles they faced, how they overcame these and the advice they'd give to others contemplating a career change.

There is a resource section with inspirational books and other resources. And there is information on workshops, courses and networking events that you can attend to support you on your escape journey.

MARCH 5

MAKE A CHOICE

'Be the change you wish to see in the world.' These words, spoken by Gandhi, mean that we should live according to our values. From the moment we get up we know that we can either be contributing to the exploitation of people and natural resources, to pollution and climate change, or we can be contributing to fair trade, sustainable agriculture and an emissions-free bicycle culture. The change we make in the world is up to us.

A dream born in Kenya has become a charitable organisation of hopeful young people, uniting as the Otesha Project. Otesha means 'reason to dream' in Swahili, and the project was founded in 2002, after 21-year-olds Jocelyn Land-Murphy and Jessica Lax met in Kenya and took back to Canada with them the message of sustainable living. In 2003, they organised a 5,500-mile cycle ride across Canada which reached over 12,000 people with their presentations and performances as they went from town to town.

They have continued to spread the word by organising cycling tours throughout Canada, inspiring young people to change how they think and live, and creating the smallest possible eco-footprint whilst doing this.

The Otesha Project: www.otesha.org.uk

Morning Choices

The Otesha Project's *Morning Choices* comedy show demonstrates how people can choose to make a positive or a negative impact on the world through what they do when they get up. It features the Careless Consumer, the Hopeful Hooligan, Mother  Earth and a variety of live props to connect everyday actions in a typical morning between 8am and 9am with global problems – including what you do in the bathroom, getting dressed, drinking coffee, packing lunch and getting to school.

...and be the change

See what you can do in the first hour of your day – today and every day – that will help create a better world through your choice of:
- How much water to use.
- What clothes to wear.
- The newspaper or TV that informs you.
- The breakfast you have.
- Your packed lunch.
- How you get to college or work.

If you are stuck for ideas on what to do, then get the funky, inspiring *Otesha Book*. Download it free, or order a copy. It comes in two versions: a traditional paperback, or bound in recycled cardboard packaging.

6 MARCH

save the RAINFOREST

Originally there were 6 million square miles of tropical rainforest worldwide. Today, as a result of deforestation, just over 2 million square miles remain. The rainforest continues to shrink rapidly: almost two acres disappear every second. This leads to soil erosion, loss of biodiversity and an increase in carbon dioxide in the atmosphere.

But you can do something to help. You can help save the rainforest by visiting one of the many 'click to donate' sites. The Rainforest Site has so far preserved more than 17,000 acres in Paraguay, Mexico, Peru and Brazil.

And you can even buy your own area of rainforest, and help to preserve it.

The Rainforest Site: www.therainforestsite.com
Race for the Rainforest: rainforest.care2.com
World Land Trust: www.worldlandtrust.org
Cool Earth: www.coolearth.org

Cool Earth

The destruction of the rainforest releases carbon dioxide into the atmosphere. At current rates, over just 24 hours, deforestation is releasing the equivalent amount of CO_2 as that created if 8 million people were to fly from London to New York.

The forests are critical to the global climate, acting as a huge thermostat, and providing a fifth of the world's water and oxygen, but they are cut down for their

wood, and to create land for farming, even though their poor-quality soil is exhausted in just five years.

Cool Earth asks you to help them buy areas of rainforest, and put it in local trust to protect it against the loggers. They also help fund community health and education services, making sure that the rainforest really is valuable to the local people. You can keep and eye on 'your' patch of forest via Google Earth.

...with a click of your mouse

🌳 **Visit the Rainforest Site daily at: www.therainforestsite.com.** Click on the 'Save Our Rainforests' button, and trigger a donation from the sponsors of the site. Each click saves one square metre of rainforest – that's about as much space as you take up sitting at your computer.

🌳 **Visit the World Land Trust or Cool Earth sites** and consider purchasing some rainforest. At as little as £25 for half an acre, it's a bargain!

MARCH 7

WOMEN'S *day*

The history of International Women's Day:

In 1909, after a declaration by the Socialist Party of America, the first US National Woman's Day was held on 28 February.

In 1910, the Socialist International meeting in Copenhagen established an International Women's Day to honour the movement for women's rights and to assist in achieving universal suffrage for women. The first International Women's Day was held on 19 March 1911.

In 1913, as part of the peace movement on the eve of World War I, Russian women observed their first International Women's Day on the last Sunday of February 1913.

In 1917, with 2 million Russian soldiers dead in the war, Russian women again chose the last Sunday in February to strike for 'bread and peace'. Four days later the Czar was forced to abdicate and the new Provisional Government granted women the right to vote. That Sunday fell on 23 February on the Julian calendar then used in Russia, which was 8 March on the Gregorian calendar used elsewhere.

International Women's Day has become a global opportunity to celebrate acts of courage and determination by ordinary women in the advancement of women's rights.

International Women's Day: www.un.org/events/women/iwd

The Nobel Peace Prize has been awarded to 12 women since it was founded in 1901:

1905 **Bertha von Suttner** (Austria), who helped set up the Nobel Peace Prize.
1931 **Jane Addams** (USA), leader of the women's suffrage movement.
1946 **Emily Balch**, co-founder of the Women's International League for Peace and Freedom.
1976 **Mairead Corrigan and Betty Williams** (Northern Ireland), peace activists.
1979 **Mother Teresa** (Calcutta, India), working with the most marginalised.
1982 **Alva Myrdal** (Sweden), campaigner for nuclear disarmament.
1991 **Aung San Suu Kyi** (Burma), opposition leader and prisoner of conscience.
1992 **Rigoberta Menchú** (Guatemala), protecting the rights of indigenous peoples.
1997 **Jody Williams** (USA), banning and clearing landmines.
2003 **Shirin Ebadi** (Iran), improving the status of women and children in Iran *(see right)*.
2004 **Wangari Maathai** (Kenya), tree planting.

...to celebrate achievements

Do two things to promote the achievements of women in creating social change:

⊗ **Spend 15 minutes researching a current woman leader** whose achievements and ideas have impressed you.

⊗ **Interview a woman in your community** who is doing fantastic things. This could be a person of power or a cleaning lady. What's important is what they are doing to change the world.

⊗ **Tell at least five people about this amazing woman** and what she has achieved.

making MUSIC

In 1992, a small community music school in Soweto, South Africa, was struggling to keep going. The British viola player Rosemary Nalden heard about it on the BBC. She enlisted the support of her professional colleagues, who agreed to take part in a simultaneous 'busk' on various railway stations. They raised £6,000, and Rosemary was able to buy musical instruments and equipment for the school.

Five years later Rosemary moved to South Africa to teach the children, and the Buskaid Soweto String Project was established. Many children were keen to learn. So Rosemary taught in large groups, sometimes for hours at a time.

BuskAid Soweto String Project now has around 70 students aged between 6 and 26, with the younger ones attending music classes after school and at weekends. They have a string ensemble which has developed a considerable reputation, and performed in France, London, New Zealand and the USA. They have recorded five CDs.

Rosemary started a teacher-training programme to provide her with teaching assistance. She wants to give all township children the opportunity to channel their creative energies into learning and playing classical music to the highest international standards.

BuskAid: www.buskaid.org.za and www.buskaidusa.com

Instrument repair

String instruments are made of wood and therefore react badly to changing weather conditions – especially in Johannesburg's cold dry winters. And then there are the occasional accidents that inevitably befall such relatively delicate instruments.

Buskaid started its own repair workshop. A longer-term aim is to train and employ local young people to make string instruments for the school.

...the BuskAid way

Why not use your musical talents – or those of your friends – to raise money for Buskaid. You could:

🎗 Busk on a street corner.

🎗 Organise a small concert.

Failing that, why not buy one of their CDs, listen, enjoy.

WEBSITE *build your own*

Do you really exist? French philosopher René Descartes declared: 'Cogito ergo sum', which is Latin for, 'I think, therefore I am'. He was looking for certainties in life. One thing he was absolutely certain about was that he was thinking. And this led him to another certainty – that in order to think, he must exist.

'I don't have a website, therefore I don't exist.' If someone wants to find out more about you, your ideas, your organisation and the cause you are involved with, the first thing they will do is type your name into Google. If the search comes up with nothing, then as far as the searcher is concerned you just don't exist. In the internet age, you need a virtual web identity.

Four steps to setting up a website: www.havingmyownwebsite.net

Virtually Ignorant, an online web design course for beginners: www.virtuallyignorant.com

WebSpawner.com, a free and easy way to create your own webpage: www.webspawner.com

Charity Focus was founded in 1999 by 23-year-old Nipun Mehta, and four of his friends from the San Francisco Bay Area. They decided that most non-profitable organisations at that time couldn't afford to create good websites, so they offered to build websites free for charities. Quite soon demand began to grow exponentially. Charity Focus now receives around 40 requests a week. It can't help everybody, so it concentrates on smaller organisations without a current web presence. The service is volunteer-run and completely free, apart from domain and web hosting charges (which have to be paid to third parties).

Charity Focus has developed a pledging system, a charity shop facility for selling things from websites, enlightening banners of inspiring quotations instead of advertisements and a quote-for-the-day email service.

– charityfocus.org

...tell the world you exist

Design a website:

- For yourself, or
- For your community, or
- For the organisation or ideas you are putting your energies into.

If you don't know how to do this, you can:

- Find a professional website designer.
- Visit WebSpawner.com and teach yourself.
- Find a virtual volunteer.

10 MARCH

sell BOOKS ONLINE

GreenMetropolis.com is an online bookstore for recycling books. If you are a buyer, you can find the book you've been looking for at a great price. All paperbacks sell for £3.75. There is no minimum order and no postage to pay. Browse the bookstore to see if they've got what you want to read.

If you are a seller, you can turn the books you've read and no longer want into cash. Just log on to GreenMetropolis.com, and enter the book's ISBN number (usually printed on the back of the book) and its condition. Once the book is sold, you are notified by email of where to send the book and your account is credited with £3.00. You have to pay postage and packing costs.

GreenMetropolis.com also donates 5p for every book sold to the Woodland Trust's Plant a Tree scheme, so you are helping grow wood to make more paper. Another alternative is to sell on Amazon, where you pay a fixed fee (75p in the UK) and 15% of the selling price. When you are notified of a sale, you send the book to the purchaser. You are given a credit towards the postage costs, and the proceeds are credited to your account.

Green Metropolis: www.greenmetropolis.com
Amazon: www.amazon.co.uk
Oxfam: www.oxfam.org.uk
World Environmental Organization: www.world.org/reuse/Books

Donating books to charity

If none of the above appeals to you, you can always donate your books to a charity shop. Oxfam is the largest retailer of second-hand books in Europe, selling around 11 million books per year. Most of the 750 or more Oxfam shops in the UK sell books, and over 70 are specialist bookstores. Take your unwanted books into an Oxfam shop, or use one of the 1,000 plus Oxfam 'Book Banks' around the country, usually found next to glass and newspaper recycling bins.

...and buy them second hand

What to do with your old books and magazines

Recycle all the books you no longer need. Get your books into the hands of new readers (this will save trees), and use any cash you raise to support a good cause.

Advice from the World Environmental Organization:

🌳 Donate books to a library.

🌳 Sell study books directly to other students – let *them* save a ton of money.

🌳 Set up a table at your community centre where people can drop off old magazines for others to buy. Then donate the money to charity.

ABOLISH *capital punishment*

The death penalty is no more effective a deterrent than life imprisonment. It is also evident that the burden of capital punishment falls upon the poor, the ignorant and the underprivileged members of society.

– US Supreme Court Justice Thurgood Marshall

Governments all over the world are ending capital punishment. Each year since 1976, three more countries have abolished the death penalty. But judicial killing continues to be used in some parts of the world. The USA, China, Iran and Saudi Arabia today account for over 80% of recorded executions. ᛁ The USA has executed over 800 people since 1976, and over 3,700 men and women are held on death row. Despite popular support for the death penalty, it does not stop violence. Other reasons for pressing for its abolition are that it affects poor and black people disproportionately, and that it is irreversible (and evidence can turn up when it is too late, demonstrating the innocence of an executed prisoner).

Befriending a person on death row by writing to them regularly allows an element of humanity to enter an inhumane system. Organisations exist to advise you about what is involved, and tell you whether they feel you are suitable as a pen friend. All being well, they put you in contact with a prisoner who is under sentence of death. Here is a quote from a death row prisoner with a Human Rights pen friend from the UK:

> *As a condemned man I have felt alone and isolated and completely cut off from everybody and the world. Human Writes gave me hope by connecting me to compassionate people … I love watching the world through your eyes.*

Human Writes: www.humanwrites.org
Cyberspace Inmates: www.cyberspace-inmates.com/death.htm
National Coalition to Abolish the Death Penalty: www.ncadp.org/lifelines.html

Ernest Willis was the 117th death row prisoner to be freed in the USA since 1973. He had been sentenced to death 17 years previously, for allegedly setting a house on fire that killed two people. The District Judge held that the State had administered medically inappropriate anti-psychotic drugs without Willis' consent, had suppressed evidence favourable to Willis, and had provided ineffective legal representation at his trial. The District Attorney hired a fire expert to examine the evidence, and his conclusion was that there was not a single item of physical evidence supporting a finding of arson. He concluded Willis 'simply did not do the crime… I'm sorry this man was on death row for so long.'

...champion human rights

ᛁ **Become a pen friend of a prisoner on death row:**

ᛁ **Help Reprieve,** which is based in the UK, fight for the lives of people facing the death penalty. They offer internships for people wishing to spend three months to two years in a law office in the USA or Caribbean helping out on cases. www.reprieve.org.uk

12 MARCH

Starbucks FREE COFFEE

Starbucks and other coffee house chains use a lot of coffee. And they have a problem about what to do with all the coffee grounds. Rather than seeing them as waste and throwing them away, they can be used as a fertiliser to help your garden grow.

Coffee grounds have a high nitrogen content, but are also slightly acidic. Dry leaves and grass, mixed with the grounds, balance the acidity though, and can be used to:

- Enrich your garden soil so you can grow prize-winning marrows.
- Turn on the heat to speed up your composting.
- Give a caffeine-high to the worms in your vermi-composter.

Starbucks and composting: www.starbucks.com/aboutus/compost.asp

Companies are coming under increasing pressure to adopt environmentally sustainable business practices. Here are some of the things that Starbucks is doing from bean to cup and beyond to try to reduce the environmental footprint of the cup of coffee you are drinking:

Promoting ecologically sound practices for growing beans, advised by Conservation International.

Paying farmers according to CAFÉ guidelines (Coffee and Farmer Equity Practices), rewarding farmers who meet strict environmental, social, economic and quality standards.

Recycling the burlap bags in which beans are transported, for use in agriculture, furniture-making and carpets.

Controlling emissions at its coffee-roasting plants.

Reducing waste by offering a discount to customers who bring their own mugs.

Donating used coffee grounds to customers, parks, schools and nurseries.

...grounds for your garden

🌳 **Go into your local Starbucks** and ask for a bag of used coffee grounds. Starbucks is giving these away free. Apply these to your garden according to instructions.

🌳 **Get several bags.** They come in shiny silver with a cheerful label, and would make nice presents.

🌳 **Ask other coffee chains**, hotels, fast-food outlets and other mega-users of coffee. Fairtrade coffee grounds work even better!

MARCH 13

TOXIC TOURS *organise your own*

Our society spews out unbelievable quantities of effluent and waste, all of which has to be disposed of. But mostly this process is kept hidden from us. What we see are rows of attractively designed products on the shelf, not the factories manufacturing either the packaging or the contents, nor the solid waste they produce and the chemicals they discharge.

We don't see the mountains of garbage collected from our houses and piled up in landfills. Nor do we see human waste and how that's disposed of. This is the hidden backside of our society. If we knew the mess we were causing, we might choose to live differently and be a lot more environmentally conscious.

Friends of the Earth, campaigning against incineration, landfill and toxic waste:
www.foe.co.uk/resource/briefings/toxic_tips.html
Play a Toxic Waste Team-building exercise:
www.wilderdom.com/games/descriptions/ToxicWaste.html

International dumping of toxic waste

In November 1998, the cargo ship *Chang Shun* slipped into Cambodia's southern port of Sihanoukville. The cargo was unloaded and dumped 15 km away. Soon, villagers nearby started to complain of diarrhoea, headaches and vomiting.

Dumping toxic waste is a serious problem for poor countries, who may need the money but do not have the resources for proper waste treatment or public safety. The Basel Convention controlling shipments of toxic waste was adopted in 1989. The Basel Action Network (BAN) campaigns on toxic waste issues, including ship breaking, electronic waste, mercury pollution and ratification of the Basel ban on exporting hazardous waste from rich to poor countries.

...go on a waste watch

Organise a Toxic Tour to raise community awareness and to stimulate action on pollutants and those who are generating them.

- **Take members of the public and local decision-makers** to see how waste is disposed of in and around your town or city. Visit any or all of the following: a local sewage treatment facility, a landfill site, a waste incinerator (if one is nearby), a municipal recycling centre, a hospital to look at medical waste disposal, a local manufacturer using chemicals to see how they dispose of effluent, and a battery chicken farm or a pig production unit.

- **You will all be intrigued and horrified** at how much we waste and how our waste is disposed of. Discuss the problem, and develop a plan of action to do something about it.

14 MARCH

green BABIES

Seven million trees are felled to manufacture the nearly 3 billion disposable nappies that are needed to supply the UK market each year. And all those nappies, each of which takes between 200 and 500 years to decompose, have to be disposed of. Because of the huge environmental impact of disposable nappies, there is now active encouragement for parents to try reusable nappies instead.

In the USA, the story is much the same – only on an even grander scale. Each year, parents and babysitters dispose of about 18 billion disposable nappies, which consume nearly 100,000 tons of plastic and 800,000 tons of tree pulp in the process. The estimated cost of disposal is $350 million a year.

The Women's Environment Network encourages the use of washable cotton nappies and co-ordinates Real Nappy Week, which is held in the UK at the end of March each year and acts as a focus for its campaigning: www.wen.org.uk/rnw

For general advice you can also contact NappyLine: www.uknappyline.co.uk

Give reusable nappies a go

Things have moved on. A modern, fitted, reusable nappy is far better than anything available just a few years ago. You will find that you can pamper your baby without buying Pampers, and you will save money at the same time. The cost of kitting out a baby with reusable nappies can be as little as £50. Even if you add the cost of washing them, you'll save around £500 for each baby.

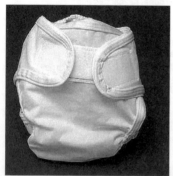

For suppliers of reusable nappies, go on the internet. Babygroe produces a catalogue of green, recycled, organic and ethical products: www.babygroe.co.uk.

Also, contact Real Nappy Networks run by mums experienced in using cloth nappies and valuable sources of impartial information and advice.

...in reusable nappies

🏆 **Find out the facts.** Search the web to find out the environmental impact of disposable diapers. Go to: www.wen.org.uk/nappies/cost_comparison.htm for a cost comparison.

🏆 **Tell every expectant parent you know** about the environmental and cost-saving benefits of reusable nappies. Produce and hand out a leaflet to every parent with a baby you come across in the street.

🏆 **Participate in Real Nappy Week.** Help the organisers with their annual stunt. In 2004, the Mountains of Nappy Waste stunt involved building mountains of waste all around the country to draw attention to the amount of waste created when a baby uses disposable nappies for a year.

MARCH 15

ESSO *stopped*

Exxon/Mobil, trading in the UK as Esso, is the world's largest non-state-owned oil company. It played a significant role lobbying the US government against Kyoto, and promoting the idea there is no provable link between carbon emissions and global warming. *The Economist* has described Exxon/Mobil as 'the world's most powerful climate change sceptic'. Exxon/Mobil has also done much less than it could in investing in renewable energy technologies. ⚽ The Esso UK website says: 'As a citizen, sometimes direct action is necessary to make a positive contribution to something you care about.' The Stop Esso Campaign replies: 'Esso chooses to wreck the climate. We can choose not to buy Esso's products. Don't buy Esso!'

Consumer power can change corporate attitudes. According to the Stop Esso Campaign, one million people are now boycotting Esso in the UK (MORI poll). Since its launch in May 2001, the Campaign has spread to the USA, Germany, Canada, Austria, Australia, France, Norway, Luxembourg and Slovakia. ⚽ The second Stop Esso Day saw 400 Esso stations with protests outside. A leading oil analyst has said that the Campaign 'has to be considered a brand risk'.

The Corporate Watch website lists Exxon/Mobil's 'corporate crimes and dirty tricks': www.corporatewatch.org.uk/profiles/oil_gas/exxon_mobil

The Stop Esso Campaign is organised by Greenpeace, Friends of the Earth and People and Planet: www.stopesso.com/about.php and www.greenpeace.org.uk/climate

Quietly taking on ESSO – best done at full moon!

See if you can find yourself an ESSO (or EXXON) station on a long stretch of road.
Make yourself posters saying:

ESSO Garage 100m ahead, PLEASE DO NOT USE!

ESSO Garage 50m ahead, DEFINITELY DO NOT USE!!

ESSO Garage 25m ahead, AVOID AT ALL COSTS – DRIVE ON!!!

Once you have prepared these signs, go out at night (a full moon will be a help) and place the signs at the required distances.

– as seen in northwest London; the originator of this idea is unknown

...fight Big Oil

The Stop Esso Campaign also suggests lobbying customers and staff.

⚽ **Download the Alternative Staff Magazine** from the Stop Esso website, and give it out to Esso staff at service stations.

⚽ **Organise peaceful legal actions** to get the message out to Esso customers, from picketing Esso stations and handing out leaflets, to promoting the Stop Esso Campaign in the area where you live. The Campaign can provide you with a full how-to briefing.

16 MARCH

check out the IDEAS BANK

The Global Ideas Bank contains a mixture of weird and wonderful ideas for changing the world. Some have been tested in practice, some are work in progress, others are just good ideas. You can vote on the ideas and add your own comments.

Here are some of the ideas:

Mayor on a park bench. The mayor turns up each week to discuss the city and its problems with local residents.

A web page for every prescription drug, for information and patient discussions. The best advice comes from users rather than experts.

A pig in every neighbourhood. People in inner cities have virtually no exposure to animals other than domestic pets. This cuts them off from nature.

Free wireless internet access. Canada is currently installing wireless access throughout its library network – this idea is a must!

Print statistics on toilet paper. This will grab people's attention, and inform them about an interesting problem they did not know about.

The Global Ideas Bank: www.globalideasbank.org

An idea submitted to the Global Ideas Bank by Dr G Caldwell

Committees, decision-making groups and governments may think they know what they are talking about, but they hide it in fancy language. I suggest that at every meeting of any decision-making group (e.g. at 10 Downing Street, The White House, the local pub darts team, etc), there is a cardboard cut-out of an 11-year old. My boy is called Jack.

Then as the meeting continues, everyone has to check that Jack understands what they are talking about, and if he is getting bored and fidgety. If Jack can understand and is interested, then the meeting is going well, and it is likely that more sensible decisions will be made.

...and contribute a great idea

❦ **Send** in your ideas to the Global Ideas Bank. There's a prize for the best idea of the year.

❦ **Read** *The Problem Solving Pocketbook: An introduction to creativity techniques for the budding social inventor*, from the Global Ideas Bank, £3.50.

❦ **Visit** the Enterprise Insight website, which has a manual for turning your ideas into action. This is aimed at business enterprises, but is equally applicable to social enterprises. You can find it on the web at: www.starttalkingideas.org

❦ **Enter** The World Challenge, which is run by Newsweek and BBC World, and aims to find individuals and groups from around the world who have shown enterprise and made a difference to their communities. See: www.theworldchallenge.co.uk

MARCH 17

WIND-UP RADIOS *a lifeline*

How can you listen to the radio if you have no source of power? As well as bringing people pleasure, the radio is a vital source of information and education – but one that is unavailable to the millions of people who have no electricity, and cannot easily afford batteries. ◉ British inventor Trevor Baylis struggled with this problem, and came up with the Clockwork Radio. He proposed that the radios be used for spreading the word about safe sex, as a way of combatting the spread of AIDS in Africa.

Clockwork technology can be used for other electronic gadgets, as Chris Staines and Rory Stear realised when they set up the Freeplay Energy Group. As well as radios, the Freeplay product range now includes torches, mobile phone chargers and stand-by power units.

The Freeplay Foundation was created by Freeplay Energy in 1998, to ensure that the technology reached those who needed it most. Over 300,000 Freeplay radios have been brought into communities in more than 40 developing countries. This has benefited over 6 million people directly (and many more indirectly) by enabling them to listen to radio for pleasure and information.

The Foundation created the Lifeline radio in 2003, based on feedback from children orphaned by AIDS and conflict in Kenya, Rwanda and South Africa. The rugged self-powered Lifeline radio is the first created specifically for humanitarian projects, especially for children living on their own.

Radio can help children learn. The Zambia Education Project donates radio to community schools, enabling children not having formal schooling to receive primary-level education. ◉ Radios also bring hours of listening pleasure.

Freeplay Energy Group: www.freeplayenergy.com
Freeplay Foundation: www.freeplayfoundation.org

In Malawi, the Ministry of Agriculture distributed 9,100 Freeplay radios to farmers' clubs in remote areas throughout the country. Each of the clubs, or listening groups, elected a chairperson who was responsible for the use and care of the radio and for notifying club members of the broadcasts.

In Madagascar, a radio drama series for women's listening clubs has been developed, aimed at improving health education, family planning and AIDS prevention. Wind-up radios, funded by the Rotary Club, have been distributed to clubs, who provide regular feedback on the programmes.

...around the world

Give the gift of a radio

A gift of just one radio can make a positive difference to a family, a classroom or a whole community for years to come. Through the Freeplay Foundation it costs just £35 to bring a radio to a family of a community. Save up the money, and donate it. It'll make a wonderful gift.

18 MARCH

global SISTERHOOD

If you want to know how women's lives are changing around the world, then visit the Global Sisterhood Network. This organisation monitors electronic and print media for developments likely to have a direct impact on women's lives. These include developments in agriculture, economics, employment, environment, health, law, militarism, politics, technology, trade and science.

Subscribe to Global Sisterhood Network List for daily online feminist comment and information: www.global-sisterhood-network.org

How does the Global Sisterhood Network describe itself?

GSN provides regularly updated information including critical comment and displays of newspaper and journal articles that reinforce patriarchy/misogyny, but have attracted sparse attention and/or comment as the world moves closer to un-democracy.

– The Global Sisterhood Network

...for a feminist perspective

❌ **Visit the GSN website** and click on Links and GSN Network to find a list of women's groups worldwide who are doing their share towards making a better world:

Afghan Women's Mission, (USA) supporting Afghan women refugee projects: afghanwomensmission.org

Friends of the River Narmada, supporting Narmada Bachao Andolan, India, which is protesting the construction of a big dam: www.narmada.org

Gramya, female infanticide prevention in Andhra Pradesh: home.vicnet.net.au/~gramya

Revolutionary Association of the Women of Afghanistan, Afghan women for human rights and social justice: www.rawa.org

❌ **Link to the following groups** associated with the Global Sisterhood Network:

Feminism on Line, feminist links: home.wanadoo.nl/~vidabo/FeminismOn-Line.html

Feminist Peace Network, ending violence towards women and children: www.feministpeacenetwork.org

International Women's Tribune Centre, connecting women globally for social change: www.iwtc.org

Saidit Online: feminist news, culture and politics: saidit.org

WINGS, women's voices on radio worldwide: www.wings.org

Women's International League for Peace and Freedom, which is the oldest women's peace organisation in the world: www.wilpf.int.ch

MARCH 19

EARTH DAY *needs your pledge*

The one thing we all have in common is our planet. So let's pledge our lives and fortunes to aid the great task of the earth's rejuvenation, and each do our part as a trustee of the earth to take charge and take care of the planet.

— John McConnell, founder of Earth Day.

Earth Day is an annual event dedicated to celebrating the wonder of life on the planet, and making a pledge to ensure a sustainable future for all its inhabitants. It is held each year at the Spring Equinox, which falls on 20 or 21 March. Earth Day is celebrated around the globe by people of all backgrounds, faiths and nationalities.

The Earth Day Network was founded by the organisers of Earth Day and promotes environmental citizenship and year-round worldwide action. Earth Day Network links up action campaigns in the USA and across the world. 🌳 At the network website you can find ideas for action on: animals and plants; clean air and water; food and agriculture; forests and wilderness; global warming and clean energy; nuclear and toxic waste; oceans, planes, trains and automobiles; politics and people; recycling and solid waste; urban growth and more. If you're stuck for ideas on how to save the world, this would be a good place to start!

Earth Day Network: www.earthday.net
Earth Day site: www.earthsite.org

I Will Not
A poem by a student of class 5 of Karachi High School for Earth Day 1991

Today on Earth Day we are celebrating by making promises,
but I will not:
    I will not stop throwing paper on the ground
    I will not stop using plastic bags
    I will not go to clean the beaches
    I will not stop polluting
I will not do all these things because I am not polluting
the world
    It is the grown-ups who are dropping bombs
    It is the grown-ups who have to stop
One bomb destroys more than all the paper & plastic
that I can throw in all my life
    It is the grown-ups who should get together and talk
    to each other
    They should solve problems and stop fighting and
    stop wars
    They are making acid rain and a hole in the ozone layer
I will not listen to the grown-ups!

...promise to help the planet

Sign the pledge at the Earth Day website:

I will act as a Trustee of the Earth by:
    Promoting actions to preserve peace and planet;
    Conserving nature and its resources;
    Encouraging environmental stewardship; and
    Asking others to do the same.

eliminate **RACISM**

21 March is International Day for the Elimination of Racial Discrimination
– a time to think of the millions of people all over the world being persecuted as a result of extreme prejudice. They are denied rights and opportunities because of their race, their gender, their religion or some physical disability. Don't just sit there and do nothing!

How can we stop racism? Consider the case of Mal Hussein, an Asian, and his partner Linda Livingstone, who bought the Ryelands Mini-Market corner shop on the Ryelands Estate near Lancaster in June 1991. They were subjected to a 24/7 campaign of intense racial harassment, including death threats, stoning, firebombing, physical attack, graffiti and verbal abuse. Their shop was routinely attacked and customers threatened. They have now sold their shop and moved away. ⊗ Such behaviour in a civilised society should be completely unacceptable. Citizens need to take a stand against racial violence, and bring pressure to bear on the police and the judicial system to intervene more fairly and more effectively.

Friends of Mal Hussein Campaign: www.naar.org.uk/family/mal.asp
Justice for Jay: www.naar.org.uk/family/jay.asp
National Assembly Against Racism: www.naar.org.uk

Commission for Racial Equality, the official body working for a society free from prejudice, discrimination and racism: www.cehr.org.uk

Jay Abatan, a 42-year-old black man, was attacked by a gang in Brighton on 24 January 1999. He died in hospital five days later from severe head injuries. His brother Michael and a friend, who were out celebrating with Jay, were also attacked. Two men were arrested and charged with manslaughter, but by the time of the trial were only charged with affray and Actual Bodily Harm to Michael because of a lack of witnesses. The jury was not allowed to hear of Jay's death as the judge ruled that this would prejudice the trial. No one has yet been tried for Jay's murder.

This investigation was the subject of an inquiry by Essex police. The original investigating team was replaced by another team as a result of this inquiry. It was announced that the murder was being treated as a racist killing – two years after it took place. However, the family have not been shown the findings of this second report. NAAR supports the family in its campaign to get the police to release the report.

:...unite for justice

How can you help stop racism?
You can help NAAR and the Abatan family by joining their campaign. And you can join the campaigns of others who have experienced extreme racial violence.

When you come face to face with racism or discrimination, you can:

⊗ **Intervene personally** – but do so with caution – telling the racists that their behaviour is completely unacceptable, and showing solidarity with the victim.

⊗ **Report the matter to the police,** the local Council for Racial Equality, your MP and anyone else who might be interested, and ask them to act.

⊗ **Get publicity for the incident** in your local newspaper.

MARCH 21 *International Day for the Elimination of Racial Discrimination*

HARVEST *the rain*

Rainwater comes direct to you whenever it rains. If your house sits on a 400-square-metre plot and a storm dumps 2 centimetres of rain, you've just received 8,000 litres (1,750 gallons) of water on your house and garden. This water is largely clean and chemical-free. ♣ Most people don't utilise this rainwater – they just let it run away. But in countries where rain comes seasonally or where there is simply not enough of it, communities will set up elaborate water-catching systems to collect rainwater and stop it running off into the sea.

This is called rainwater harvesting. It can include storing and utilising the water that falls on roofs, building dams, ponds and other systems for stopping the water running away, and using the rainfall to recharge the ground water. Harvesting rainwater and using water sensibly are crucial in a world running short of water.

A great site entirely dedicating to rainwater harvesting: www.rainharvesting.com

A 'how to' guide, complete with simple drawings and a photo-gallery of rainwater harvesting projects: www.dot.co.pima.az.us/flood/wh/index.html

The Barefoot College in India has a good resource list: www.barefootcollege.org

Think of others on World Day for Water

Any time we need water in the rich world, we just turn on a tap. You probably give little thought to the amount of water you use, or to how all this clean and drinkable water is brought to your home. But for billions of people around the world, getting enough clean water to meet their daily needs is a major struggle. Women and children may have to walk hours every day to get to their local water source – which might be a lake or a pond. They may have to make several trips just to meet their family's daily water needs, and this water is not always clean.

...catch that water

♣ **Design a rainwater-catching system** to harvest all the water that falls on to the roof of your house. Spend as little as possible. What materials will you need? What will it look like? How much will it cost? If you had to purchase a domestic rainwater-harvesting system, it would cost around £2,000.

♣ **Build your rainwater-catching system.** Use the rainwater to water your garden and your pot plants, and to wash your dog and your car. You would need to filter it, if it is to be drinkable.

♣ **Produce a simple design manual** and circulate it to your friends. Your ideas might even help solve the water crisis around the world!

Give someone a **HUG TODAY**

Scientific studies have shown the benefits of a good hug. Human touch reduces levels of cortisol, a stress hormone, and increases serotonin, a feel-good hormone. People who live in cities are often isolated. They have too few social connections, nobody to smile at them. The Free Hugs campaign provides a simple way to show someone that you care.

Juan Mann started hugging in 2004. This is how it all happened.

> *I'd been living in London when my world turned upside down and I had to come home to Sydney. By the time I landed all I had left was a carry-on bag full of clothes and a world of troubles. No one to welcome me back, no place to call home.*
>
> *Standing there in the terminal, I watched other passengers meeting their waiting friends and family with open arms and smiling faces, hugging and laughing together. I wanted someone out there to be happy to see me, to hug me. So I got some cardboard and a marker and made a sign. I found the busiest pedestrian intersection in the city and held that sign aloft, with the words 'Free Hugs' on both sides.*
>
> *The first person who stopped, tapped me on the shoulder and told me how her dog had just died that morning on the anniversary of her only daughter dying in a car accident, how what she needed now, when she felt most alone in the world, was a hug. We put our arms around each other and when we parted, she was smiling. To see someone who was once frowning, smile even for a moment is worth it every time.*

The free hugs movement really took off when Juan Mann's Free Hug video was posted on YouTube in September 2006, and was viewed over 10 million times in the following three months. There are now Free Hugs groups all over the world.

Free Hugs: www.freehugscampaign.org
Juan Mann on YouTube: www.youtube.com/watch?v=nJC28OCYBwY
Hugz4U: www.wellbeingproject.co.uk/hugz4u.htm

Hugz4U!

The Hugz4U! campaign, organised by the Wellbeing Project, encourages everyone to seek out five hugs a day to promote positive mental health and wellbeing.

> *A hug is one of those innate human behaviours that can promote a warm, fuzzy feeling that we like to call wellbeing. Hugs help to promote a sense of feeling connected and supported by people around us. If you think about it, we hug when we're happy, to celebrate and share good news; and we hug when we're sad, to show others that we care and want to help.*

...for that warm fuzzy feeling

🚶 **Download a sticker** from the Hugz4U website.
🚶 **Join a free hugs group** and participate in an event in your area. You could even start your own group.
🚶 **Spread the word** and convert others to the idea of Free Hugs.
🚶 **If hugging is just not your thing**, or if you are too embarrassed to do it, then just smile at the next stranger you pass in the street.

MARCH 23

DUBBLE *(chocolate) agents*

Cocoa production in Ghana is suffering. In the 75 years up to 1976, Ghana was the world's leading cocoa producer, contributing nearly 40% of world output. There are still around 1.6 million people in Ghana involved in growing cocoa, and many more work in associated industries. In the late 1970s the world market price for cocoa plummeted by two-thirds. Ghanaian cocoa farmers were receiving less than 40% of the world market price from the State Purchasing Board, so many stopped producing cocoa altogether. The situation got even worse after the droughts and bush fires of the early 1980s: cocoa production in Ghana fell from one-third of the world's total in 1972 to just 12% by 2005.

The Kuapa Kokoo co-operative are trying to change things in Ghana. They are a group of farmers, who formed a co-operative in 1993 to sell cocoa for the benefit of its members. The Kuapa Kokoo co-operative now has a membership of 35,000 and sells about 1,000 tonnes of cocoa annually to the European fairtrade market. They currently receive $1,600 a tonne, plus a $150 fairtrade premium for their cocoa, whilst the world price has been around $1,000. This additional income makes a huge difference to the lives of the farmers and their families.

The Dubble website: www.dubble.co.uk
Divine Chocolate: www.divinechocolate.com

The Dubble chocolate bar

Kuapa Kokoo decided that another way to increase farmer's income was to produce their own brand of chocolate to sell in Western markets. In 1998 they founded the Day Chocolate Company in partnership with Twin Trading and several international development agencies, and launched Divine fairtrade milk chocolate. Divine chocolate is now available in UK supermarkets nationwide. The Dubble Bar is part of the Divine range, and is a fun bar aimed primarily at children.

...on a mission for fairtrade

Become a Dubble Agent

- **Sign up to become a fully-fledged Dubble Agent** and receive your free choc-secret Mission Pack, complete with everything you need to start changing the world chunk by chunk!

- **Become a Stock the Choc Sleuth.** Your mission is to help get fairtrade chocolate more widely distributed and properly displayed in stores. To do this, you are asked to visit local Dubble stockists as often as possible and check Dubble chocolate bars are on the shelf and displayed in a prominent position. If your local shop, school or work canteen doesn't stock Dubble, try to persuade them to do so.

- **Throw a Dubble Agent party.** Invite friends to dress up as Dubble Agents or Dubble lookalikes, sample some chocolate and plan tactics for promoting fairtrade chocolate.

24 MARCH

become a ZOO CHECKER

An adult lion's roar can be heard up to five miles away. One of the few places you can still hear the sound is at your local zoo. There are approximately 1,500 zoos around the world, providing an amazing opportunity for people (and especially children) to experience the diversity of animal life existing on our planet. But if you think the lions and tigers and bears living in zoos are happy campers, you are wrong.

Some zoo animals are kept in quite appalling conditions. It's a tragedy when creatures are treated badly, and animal abuse may also be occurring in circuses, magic shows, dolphinaria and other tourist attractions where performing animals are used. Many establishments do not provide their animals with adequate living conditions. A lion's roar of distress may not bother some zookeepers, but if you care enough you should try to do something.

Sign up to be a Zoo Checker: **www.bornfree.org.uk/campaigns**

Did you know?

An albatross can sleep while it flies. It apparently dozes while cruising at 25 miles per hour.

Clams can change sex. All start out as males, but some decide to become females later in life.

Elephants have a gestation period of over 20 months.

Mockingbirds can imitate any sound from a squeaking door to a cat meowing.

Sharks are the only animals that never get sick. Current research suggests they are immune to every known disease, including cancer.

The Kiwi can't fly, lives in a hole in the ground, is almost blind and lays only one egg each year. Yet is has survived for 70 million years.

The poison-arrow frog has enough poison to kill about 2,200 people.

You can see all these animals and many more in a zoo.

...grass on animal-abusers

The Born Free organisation has set up the Zoo Check and Travellers' Alert systems for reporting maltreatment of animals.

🐾 **If you see animals being badly treated** or kept in appalling conditions at your local zoo or at a tourist attraction (at home, or on holiday abroad), take photographs or make video evidence of the conditions in which the animals are being kept.

🐾 **Send your evidence to Zoo Checker,** and a campaign will be started to improve the treatment of these animals.

MARCH 25

DESIGNER *ambitions*

Architecture for Humanity is a non-profit organisation founded by Cameron Sinclair, a London-trained architect. It promotes architectural and design solutions to global, social and humanitarian problems, and brings design services to communities in need.

Architecture for Humanity runs design competitions, open to everyone. These competitions don't focus on designing the next Trump hotel. The aim is to obtain designs of low-cost structures for international communities in crisis. ● Entrants are provided with a list of materials and costs local to the area where the winning project will be built. They are then asked to formulate a design, taking into consideration factors such as how to get water, what resources are available locally, whether there is electricity, and the budget. If your design is selected, they build it.

Architecture for Humanity: www.architectureforhumanity.org

Some Architecture for Humanity projects:

2004: A competition to design a football pitch in Somkhele, an area in South Africa with one of the highest rates of HIV in the world. The pitch had to offer a place for young people to play football, and to host the first-ever girls' football league in the area. It also had to offer a place to learn about HIV/AIDS, and a mobile healthcare facility. The design by 2nd-placed finalists David Mathias and Tim Denis is shown here.

2004 and ongoing: Rebuilding Bam in Iran. Architecture for Humanity is collaborating with Relief International to provide permanent housing for the many thousands of residents left homeless by an earthquake that killed over 41,000 people.

2002: A design competition for mobile health clinics to provide basic healthcare, health education and AIDS/HIV testing in Sub-Saharan Africa.

Architecture for Humanity is also working on mine clearance, building playgrounds in the Balkans and refugee housing on the borders of Afghanistan.

...architecture for humanity

● **See if there is an Architecture for Humanity group near you.** There are 132 groups in cities around the world, some with memberships of over 300 (and some with just one member looking to find some architectural soul mates). Meetings are held on the first Tuesday of each month at 7pm to discuss design and development issues. Everyone is welcome. If there *is* a local group that meets near you, why not go along?

● **Check out the latest competition.** Your design could be featured in a top architectural magazine and exhibited in international design shows, not to mention help to solve a humanitarian crisis and save thousands of lives.

● **Go to the People We Like section** of the Architecture for Humanity website – it offers information on interesting people and organisations promoting socially responsible design.

26 MARCH

protest through SONG

Songs are enormously important for peace or protest. They create a sense of unity and purpose. They bring people together. They make you feel good. Here are some songs for peace and for protest selected by Toby Blume, who lives in London:

Songs of peace

Bob Marley & The Wailers 'War' (from the album *Rastaman Vibration*, 1976)

Faithless 'Mass Destruction' (from the album *No Roots*, 2004)

Boogie Down Productions 'Stop the Violence' (from the album, *By All Means Necessary*, 1988)

Curtis Mayfield 'We've got to have Peace' (from the album, *Roots*, 1972)

Spearhead 'Piece O'Peace' (from the album *Home*, 1994)

Basement Jaxx (featuring Yellowman) 'Love is the Answer' (from the album *Peace Songs*, 2004)

Songs of protest

Public Enemy 'Fight the Power' (from the album *Fear Of A Black Planet*, 1994)

Levellers 'Liberty Song' (from the album *Levelling The Land*, 1992)

Johnny Cash 'I Shall not be Moved' (from the album *My Mother's Hymn Book*, 2004)

Chumbawumba 'Enough is Enough' (from the album *Anarchy*, 1998)

The Pogues 'Streets of Sorrow/Birmingham Six' (from the album *If I Should Fall From Grace With God*, 1987)

Jimmy Cliff 'Viet Nam' (from the album *Wonderful World, Beautiful People*, 1970)

Anti-war songs at: www.lacarte.org/songs/anti-war/index.html
Peace songs at: www.newsongsforpeace.org and www.songs4peace.com

Producers of songs for peace and protest

The Smithsonian Museum publishes a wide range of folk songs, some of which are classics of peace and protest, including Pete Seeger's 'Songs of Protest and Struggle', Woody Guthrie's 'Struggle', 'Good Morning Vietnam' and 'Poems for Peace'. www.folkways.si.edu

Amaze Me: Songs in the Key of Peace is a peace CD featuring female musicians from across the USA who care about their country and want to see it become a leader for peace. All of the album proceeds are being donated to organisations working for peace, such as Women Against Military Madness, DemocracyNow and CodePINK. For more information, go to: www.peacecd.com

...call for a better world

Be inspired.

● Download the above songs on to your iPod, listen and be inspired.

● And if you'd like to, write your own song or poem for peace and post it on the *365 Ways to Change the World* website: www.365act.com

MARCH 27

HUMAN MANURE *what to do*

If Britain were planning sewage disposal from scratch today, we wouldn't flush it away, we would collect the solids and compost them.

— Michael Rouse, former chief drinking-water inspector.

We take the disposal of human waste for granted. We just flush the toilet and watch it disappear. Most human waste is disposed of through the sewerage system. But there are a number of problems with this. ♣ Raw sewage starts to break down, using oxygen dissolved in the water. But once the oxygen is used up, micro-organisms continue the process anaerobically (without oxygen). This produces a nutrient-rich effluent (which could be used as fertiliser) and methane gas (which could be used as a fuel). But the untreated effluent is often left to run into rivers and ends up in the sea. The nutrients cause algae to bloom; and when they die they decompose, which uses up dissolved oxygen in the water. The reduction of oxygen in the water kills marine animals.

To ensure sustainability, everything taken from the land needs to be put back. If this doesn't happen, the natural fertilisers contained in the soil diminish, and have to be replaced with chemical fertiliser. These chemicals run off into rivers and lakes, and pollute the water table. ♣ Clean water is piped to us, often over hundreds of miles, and around 40% of it is flushed straight down the toilet. There has to be a better way. Composting toilets are the answer.

Composting Toilet World, which describes itself as 'the official website of composting toilets': www.compostingtoilet.org

Composting toilets

Composting toilets use little or no water; they are not connected to an expensive sewage system; they cause no environmental damage; and they produce compost as a by-product, which you can use in your garden _ or sell.

There are two ways of composting. The batch system uses a container, which is filled, then replaced with an empty container. The composting process is completed inside the filled container. In a continual process system, the waste moves downwards and is harvested as compost after about six months.

If your carpentry skills aren't good enough, then think about buying a composting toilet. There are lots of models to choose from. Go to the Composting Toilet World website for advice and information.

Diagram labels: Fan → | Vent pipe extends through roof → | Floor | This chute variable in length | Access Doors | Air inlet | Air flow | COMPOST | Drain

...with all that poo

- ♣ **Read** *The Humanure Handbook*. This is a guide to composting human manure. The authors claim that 'after reading this book, you will never flush a toilet with indifference again'.

- ♣ **Build your own composting toilet** using wood and sawdust. A simple design will cost you only £15 to build. Get the plans from: www.jenkinspublishing.com/sawdustoilet.html

28 MARCH

people with DISABILITIES

We are not the source of the problems; we are the resources needed to solve them. We are not expenses; we are investments. We are citizens of this world.

– Andrew Biyinzika, Ugandan Disability Rights Activist

This is Andrew's Story: I am Andrew Biyinzika. I move with the help of a wheelchair. During my education I faced a lot of challenges in the schools I attended. The classrooms, toilets and labs were totally unfriendly environments for persons with disabilities. It was not easy, but I had no alternative. I encountered many difficult situations, which had a big psychological influence on my life. But I wouldn't give up. ❌ I started an organisation called RENYAD (Reach the Needs of Youth and Young People with Disabilities) with the aim of fighting for the fundamental rights of people with disabilities. It is vital for disabled people to be given equal opportunities in all aspects of life. Until the world accepts its responsibility to us, I will continue to fight for our rights. I have the will, knowledge, sensitivity and dedication to do this.

RADAR, the UK's disability network: www.radar.org.uk
Disability rights in the UK: www.disability.gov.uk
Action on Disability and Development: www.add.org.uk

Andrew's suggestions for making a difference to those with disabilities

Join a campaign to support the right to human dignity of people with disabilities. Force governments to implement appropriate measures to ensure that people with disabilities are able to realise their full mental and physical potential. This is a human rights issue.

Counter negative attitudes towards disabled people and stop judging people by their appearance.

Stop governments going to war. War increases the number of disabled people in the world.

...fight to end inequality

❌ **Identify a problem that a person with a mental or a physical disability in your community might encounter.** Maybe the local bank has no disabled access, or the traffic lights in town do not emit a sound to let a visually-impaired person know when it is safe to cross, or a theatre does not have space for a wheelchair user. Discuss the problem with people you know who have disabilities. Then commit yourself to solving it.

❌ **Start a letter writing campaign** to the local bank. Set up a meeting with your local government official to tell him/her the traffic light system needs to be changed. There are a hundred and one things in every community that could improve to the lives of people with disabilities; and there are thousands of ways of making these things happen.

MARCH 29

HITCH-HIKE *to Morocco*

Imagine a classroom, but take away the books, desks, chairs, and windows. Remove the roof as well for good measure. Next put an under-trained teacher in charge of too many children – some of whom have walked 5 km to school, or had no proper breakfast, or both. ♠ These are the conditions in which many children in the world today are trying to get an education. It is not their fault that they were born in a country without the resources for a decent education system.

Without education, it is hard for any community to escape from poverty. But things can be done. ♠ Link Community Development is based in South Africa, and also works in Ghana and Uganda. It supports head teachers implementing development plans for their schools. It trains teachers, helps schools raise money for improvements, twins schools in Africa with schools in the UK, and provides educational electives for UK teachers to share their expertise with an African school.

Link has helped improve education for over 500,000 children. Only 700 organisations like Link would be able to improve education for all Africa's children.

Link Community Development: www.lcd.org.uk
Morocco Hitch: www.lcd.org.uk/events/hitch
Camfed, extending girls' access to education in Africa: www.camfed.org
Information on girls' education: www.educategirls.org

Dance classes in Morocco

While working as a Peace Corps Volunteer in Morocco, I noticed that instead of going to school, young girls were required to stay at home to take care of the household chores while their mothers wove carpets to sell at the weekly market. I wanted to give young girls an opportunity to be themselves, express their creativity, and most importantly have fun! I started a series of dance classes. Wrapped in headscarves and long skirts, we twisted, turned and let loose. This increased the girls' self-esteem and gave them something to look forward to.

– Kari Detwiler, New York

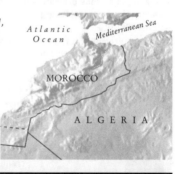

...give children a chance

Hitch-hike to Morocco

♠ **Join the Morocco Hitch during the spring holiday period.**
The registration fee is only £25, and gets you a t-shirt and a *Rough Guide*. Your minimum fundraising target is only £300, and each £250 raised provides a development grant for one school. For every £500 you raise you can claim back £75 towards the cost of your trip.

♠ **Travel in a group of two or three people,** and get to Morocco however you can. The average journey time starting from London is four to five days.

♠ **When you get to Morocco,** you might even visit a school or two.

become a FOOTBALL FAN

Street League uses the power of sport to transform people's lives – people from underprivileged, poorly educated, socially excluded and conflicting communities. This includes the homeless, rough sleepers, people participating in drug and alcohol rehabilitation projects, refugees and asylum seekers, long-term unemployed and others. Founder, Damian Hatton says, 'As well as the structure given to their lives through practice and match timetables, players might be motivated to make positive changes in their lifestyles through a desire to improve their sporting performance.' Anyone can participate, regardless of footballing ability. There are weekly training sessions with qualified coaches, monthly match days and a cup competition.

Street League was founded in 2001, by Dr Damian Hatton (whilst doing a stint on an infectious disease ward in a London hospital). The idea grew. There are now more than 850 players in Street League teams across the UK, in cities as far apart as London and Glasgow. A year ago there were just 260 players. Graz 2003, Gothenburg 2004, New York 2005: The Homeless World Cup brings together teams from national Street Leagues and homeless football projects in 26 countries. It is organised though the International Network of Street Newspapers. The World Cup provides a shared international goal, and also great publicity for the homeless football movement.

Homeless World Cup: www.streetsoccer.org
Street League: www.streetleague.co.uk

These organisations promote anti-racism football tournaments:
www.mondialiantirazzisti.org
www.farenet.org

And these promote football amongst young people in developing countries:
globall.streetfootballworld.org
www.playsoccer-nonprofit.org

Jose's story

Drug dependency lost 42-year old Jose everything – his job, his family, his home. After seven years of sleeping rough and watching friends die from AIDS or go to prison, he started rehab. Now he's got an apartment, attends college and is reconnected with his children. The credit 'goes to God – and to soccer'. Jose was a member of the US team that competed in the first Homeless World Cup in 2003. He didn't actually get to Austria, as he had to complete his rehab. But the months of exercise and practice helped him clean out his body and open his mind.

...the action's on the street

 Become a football fan. Adopt a side and turn up to see them play. This will provide real encouragement.

 You can even sponsor a side, just as Vodafone sponsors Manchester United. You won't have to pay so much, but £300 gets your name on their t-shirts and £30 pays for a Cup: www.goodgifts.org

MARCH 31

MASTURBATE *for peace*

Today is All Fools Day, otherwise known as April Fool's Day – a day to play practical jokes on your friends and colleagues. Tradition has it that the practical joke should be performed before noon.

Is this website a joke? Or is it for real? Go to www.masturbateforpeace.com and decide for yourself.

This is their mission statement:

> *There's no greater antidote for war than love. Feelings of hatred and distrust form the necessary basis of armed confrontation. Replace those negative feelings with love and you're halfway towards resolution of any conflict.*

> *However, any real love must start from within. You can't love others without loving yourself first. And, of course, masturbation is the greatest expression of self-love. So it's natural that we, the citizens of the world, are joining together to masturbate for peace.-*

> *As we begin with this act of self-love, we encourage others to do the same, to take pleasure in life and to share masturbation's positive energy with a world in need.*

> *Joining this movement is simple. Just masturbate in your own way, focusing your thoughts and energy towards love and peace. Encourage others to do the same. Also, please fill out our petition and tell us how you intend to masturbate for peace.*

From the Unrepentant Liberal: liberal.home.comcast.net/slogans.htm
Top April Fool's Day hoaxes of all time: www.museumofhoaxes.com/hoax/aprilfool

Slogans for Peace:

Anything war can do, peace can do better

Collateral damage is HUMAN LIFE!

Drop Bush, not Bombs

Go solar, not ballistic

How many lives per gallon?

If you can't pronounce it, don't bomb it!

War is expensive; peace is priceless

War is so 20th century!

⊕ *PEACE* ⊕
IS PATRIOTIC

...self-love to end conflict

Make and distribute bumper stickers on the theme Make Love, Not War.

Masturbate for Peace is an international movement for peace, with over 17,000 petitions from 91 countries and all 50 states of the USA. You can sign their petition, and in your own words and say why making love (even if it's with yourself), is better than making war.

Remember, testosterone is potentially the world's most dangerous chemical. We should all try to do something for peace.

guerrilla GARDENING

Armed with trowels, seeds and vision, you can garden everywhere. Anywhere.

– Guerilla Gardeners

Our cities are a sad concrete mess. More parking lots than parks. More traffic signs than trees. Whilst you're looking at the cityscape, ask yourself: Does it have to be like this? Guerrilla Gardeners are people who anonymously plant herbs, flowers and vegetables on vacant land, in cracks in the pavements and by the sides of roads and footpaths.

Planting-as-protest began in the 1970s with a New York group called the Green Guerrillas. These urban horticulturalists lobbed seed grenades (Christmas tree ornaments filled with soil and wildflower seeds) into hundreds of abandoned, debris-filled building sites, which eventually became hundreds of beautiful flower and vegetable-filled community gardens. Their slogan was: 'Resistance Is Fertile'.

Why not become a guerrilla gardener? Start to sow the seeds of change. Start to reclaim the urban environment for nature. All you need is:

Some seeds and a small bag of soil.

A trowel and a watering can.

Used packaging – recycled of course.

Some friends (doing it with others is always more fun).

As much creativity as you can muster.

Primal Seeds, a network protecting biodiversity: www.primalseeds.org
Guerrilla gardening and reclaiming public space: www.publicspace.ca

Plant for peace, Toronto Peace Gardeners Mission Statement, May 2003

The most revolutionary action is to plant in a spirit of peace. Join us as we reclaim Ecology Park beside the subway as a place for community and peace. Community includes all the birds, the sky, trees, people, little animals, stones, plants, and insects. Peace means a place to sit, smile, breathe and enjoy all the treasures of the present moment. Guerrilla Gardening is a revolutionary idea - the way to peace.

...sow the seeds of revolution

🏠 **Walk around and look for good places to start planting.** Derelict front gardens, buildings awaiting redevelopment, car parks, roundabouts and central reservations, beneath trees – these are just a few places where you might find a crack in the concrete where you can start planting.

🏠 **You can plant seeds and cuttings in spring and summer,** and bulbs in the autumn. You can plant flowers, vegetables, shrubs, trees. If you're planting seeds, sprout them at home and allow them to grow for four to eight weeks, before transplanting them at your chosen site.

🏠 **Protect your new plants for the first few days;** cut the tops and bottoms off plastic water bottles and put these over the plants.

🏠 **Design a wonderful garden.** Label the plants. Take photos as they grow.

APRIL 2

LOCKS *of love*

Alopecia Aresta has no known cause or cure, and many children suffer from it. Locks of Love provides hairpieces to children in North America aged 18 or younger who are suffering any form of medical hair loss and who are in financial need. Other recipients are cancer patients undergoing chemotherapy. This restores self-esteem, and helps them have better relationships with their peers.

Wigs made from human hair are not always an option for cancer patients. There are two main reasons. The wigs are made to order, and this can take two months – but most people don't know two months beforehand that they are going to have chemotherapy. They want their wig a bit sooner. Human hair wigs are expensive; if your hair is going to grow again, it may seem a bit of a luxury.

Anyone can donate their hair to Locks of Love from anywhere, provided these conditions are met:

10-inch (25-cm) minimum hair length (tip to tip). Pull curly hair straight to measure its length.

Hair supplied bundled as a ponytail or braid. Layered hair may be divided into multiple ponytails for donation.

Hair to be clean, dry, placed in a plastic bag, and then in a padded envelope.

Hair can be from men as well as women, young and old, all colours.

Hair may be coloured or permed, but must not be bleached or chemically damaged (if unsure, ask your stylist).

Hair swept off the floor is not usable.

Hair cut years ago is usable if it has been kept in a ponytail or braid.

Hair that is short, grey, or unsuitable for children will be separated out and sold at market value, which will offset the cost of manufacturing.

Most hair donated to Locks of Love comes from children wishing to help other children.

Locks of Love: www.locksoflove.org
Wig Bank: wigbank.com

Agnes Lennox was diagnosed with breast cancer in January 2003. The worst part of her treatment was losing her hair during chemotherapy.
A National Health Service prescription wig is expensive – £53 for a synthetic wig and £204 for one made of human hair. So Agnes decided to set up a Wig Bank to help others.

Donated wigs are washed and reconditioned, then sold for £10–£20, with £5 from each transaction going to Maggie's Cancer Caring Centre. Agnes has set up a network of Wig Banks throughout the UK.

...donate your hair

𝕟𝕩 Grow your hair to more than 10 inches, then get it cut off. Send it to Locks of Love.

𝕟𝕩 If you have a wig you no longer use, donate it to Wig Bank.

3 APRIL

emulate **GANDHI**

Apply the following test: recall the face of the poorest and the weakest man [or woman] whom you may have seen, and ask yourself if the step you contemplate is going to be of any use to him. Will he gain anything by it? Will it restore him to a control over his own life and destiny?

– Mahatma Gandhi

Reading this book makes you a very fortunate person. Seriously. You have the resources to buy it. You can take the time to read it, even if you are just flicking through it. You are literate, so you can understand what the words mean. And you can see with your eyes, helped perhaps by contact lenses or spectacles. All this makes you one of the world's more fortunate.

Every single day you probably walk past people down on their luck. Your natural instinct, most likely, is to ignore the people who are sitting in the street begging for a few pennies. For you, this is a moment of discomfort that you shrug off when you get round the next corner.

There are many reasons why people are living rough. But it is always hard and often lonely. A small act could transform their whole day – an act of kindness, a smile, a little conversation, a coin or two from your pocket that you can well afford. For you this could be insignificant; for them it could mean everything.

Find out about Gandhi, his life and his ideas from:

Mahatma Gandhi Foundation: web.mahatma.org.in
Gandhian Institute: www.mkgandhi.org
Kamat's Mahatma Gandhi album: www.kamat.com/mmgandhi/iink.htm

Who was Mahatma Gandhi?

Mahatma means 'Great Soul', a title given to Gandhi as a mark of respect. Mohandas Gandhi was born in 1869 in Western India. He went to London to study law, and qualified as a barrister in 1891. He then went to South Africa, where he was appalled by the conditions and lack of human rights of immigrant Indians, and he set out to change their lives, developing the idea of non-violent resistance as a protest tool.

He remained committed throughout his life to religious tolerance and to improving the lives of the very poorest.

...do something today

ᚸ **Practise the Gandhi principle.** Gandhi believed that no day was worth living unless by the end of the day you could say that you had done something to improve the plight of someone less fortunate than you.

ᚸ **Today, when you are out doing whatever you do,** stop when you pass someone begging. Take them out for a pizza. Ask them how their day is going. Listen to their dreams for the future. Share ideas about the state of the world.

APRIL 4

SPEED DATING *for change*

Use social occasions with your friends not just to gossip about who is dating whom; or how much so-and-so is earning. Not just to discuss the problems of the world and moan about politicians, but to focus on a particular problem that you are interested in and to discuss solutions and practical ideas for actually doing something.

Adapt the speed dating dynamic to discuss ideas for changing the world:
Fill a room with people who are eager to change the world.
Get people into pairs with five minutes to share their ideas.
Each fills in a score out of ten, based on how interesting the other person's idea is, whether they think it feasible and whether they would like to join with that person in taking the idea forward.
A whistle is blown after five minutes, and everyone moves to another pairing.
The process continues until the end of the evening.

Or have a dinner party discussion. Ask seven people to dinner. Every guest is invited to think of a practical idea to change the world that they could do with a group of people. Over dinner or after eating, each person is invited to talk about their idea for 2–3 minutes, followed by discussion. At the end of the evening, the best idea is chosen – by consensus if possible – and everyone is then invited to work on it.

Speed dating for crickets

To determine whether male crickets were attractive or unattractive, Australian researcher Megan Head organised 'dating tournaments' where pairs of male and female crickets were timed to see how long it took them to have sex. Males that got the females interested quickly were labelled 'attractive'. Megan then looked at what happened afterwards.

Females who mated with attractive males died earlier and had slightly fewer children. But they had a greater number of attractive sons and their grandchildren were born much sooner. This means that their genes are more likely to be passed down into future generations.

Megan's work has implications for the long-term consequences of human mating choice. It's the quality of the offspring that's important, not just the quantity.

...a transforming event

Revive your love life and make new friends.

- **Organise a** 'Change the World Dinner Party' or 'Speed Dating to Save the World'.
- **Do this by candlelight** for a romantic atmosphere and to save electricity. Then see what happens!

5 APRIL

Genocide occurs, and we say 'Never again'. But we always seem to allow it to recur. So, with Rwanda, Kosovo, and Darfur fresh in our minds, with communal violence between Hindus and Muslims on the rise in India, it's a good time to act. The Rwandan Genocide started on 7 April 1994. One million people were massacred in 100 days. We must do our best to stop anything like this ever happening ever again.

The first step in preventing genocide is awareness. Educate yourself about what is happening on the planet. Often major media sources do not cover the atrocities which are happening. Know where injustice is occurring. Mary Kayitesi Blewitt, originally from Rwanda, founded SURF (the Survivors Fund) after losing 50 family members herself during the Rwandan genocide. SURF helps survivors deal with and recover from the tragedies of 1994. ❧ Remember Rwanda preserves the memory of the Rwandan genocide by remembering its victims and those who tried to aid its victims, and through public education on the Rwandan and other genocides.

The Elie Wiesel Foundation for Humanity creates forums for the discussion and resolution of urgent ethical issues. It is particularly concerned with hate, intolerance, injustice and indifference. It organises an annual essay contest for undergraduates in US colleges (read what they have to say).

Prevent Genocide International: www.preventgenocide.org
SURF: www.survivors-fund.org.uk
Elie Wiesel Foundation: www.eliewieselfoundation.org

Assumpta's story.

I was 18 at the time of genocide. I lost my mother, father, brothers and sisters and 30 other relatives, and suffered rape and beatings. My surviving sister went back to my home village after the genocide and was attacked again with machete by the killers of my family, who feared that she would denounce them to authorities. She was in a coma for months and slowly gained consciousness. She lost her hearing ability and she lives with constant headache and mental problems. I have tried to commit suicide twice but failed to die. I live in the shadow of genocide. Sometimes I imagine meeting my mother on the street. Sometimes I see people wearing similar clothes like my dead relatives, and I follow them and tap on their shoulders...

...stop genocide

Learn about the tragedies of Rwanda.

❧ **Download** the personal testaments of Rwandan genocide survivors, adults and children, being collected by the Memory and Remembrance Project of the Survivors Fund (SURF) at www.survivors-fund.org.uk/remember/index.htm.

❧ **Print out** and frame the photos at the Remember Rwanda website collected as a 10th-anniversary memorial:
www.visiontv.ca/RememberRwanda/main_pf.htm.

❧ **Create** your own mini-exhibition to 'Remember Rwanda'.

APRIL 6

POLIO *let's make it history*

Polio is one of a very few diseases that can be totally eradicated. As the disease only affects humans, an effective and inexpensive vaccine exists, and immunity is life-long. Polio will die out through mass immunisation. ☺ In 1988, the Global Polio Eradication Initiative was launched, spearheaded by the World Health Organization, Rotary International (who have provided volunteers and fundraised all over the world), Centre for Disease Control and Prevention (CDC) and UNICEF. The effort has so far galvanised more than 200 countries, 20 million volunteers, and an international investment of $3 billion. The number of polio cases worldwide has decreased from 350,000 in 1988, to 1,998 in 2006.

An estimated 5 million people are able to walk due to this initiative. These people would otherwise have been paralysed. The campaign has also helped strengthen health delivery in many countries. Hundreds of thousands of health workers have been trained, and millions of volunteers have been mobilised to support immunisation campaigns.

Polio is endemic in only four countries: Afghanistan, India, Nigeria and Pakistan. And they have all publicly pledged an all-out effort to end the disease. The ultimate success of the world's largest public health campaign is now within reach. ☺ If the world seizes the chance to end polio, no child will ever again experience the crippling effects of this devastating disease. And drug companies could play a stronger role in helping combat malaria and the spread of HIV, and in extending the lives of those living with AIDS.

World Health Organization: www.polioeradication.org
Rotary International: www.rotary.org/foundation/polioplus/

Bob's bike ride

After working for the US Centre for Disease Control for 33 years, Bob Keegan retired in 2007. His next challenge was a 4,165-mile cycle ride across the USA to raise money for polio eradication and inspire others to take action.

At the end of the day, polio eradication is merely a simple question about whether or not the most wealthy and enfranchised people of the world are willing to provide the political will, technical assistance, and funds to stop polio from affecting the poorest children in the world. Although polio eradication will be a humanitarian benefit for these children, it will be an even greater balm for the soul of humankind.

www.bobsbikeride.org

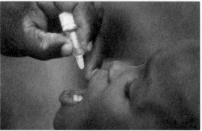

...through global eradication

Donate to Polio Eradication. Since 1988, some two billion children around the world have been immunised against polio, thanks to the Global Polio Eradication Initiative. One last push and with your help polio could be history. £20 pays the cost of 6 immunisations.

consider TITHING

Tithing means giving away 10% of your annual income to charity. The idea of giving a proportion of your income to charity, and the idea of this specific amount – 10% – comes from the Old Testament. But many religions encourage tithing.

There are lots of good reasons for giving to charity:
If you have more than enough money, you can help others who don't.
If you have more than enough things, buying more is a waste.
Using your money creatively to help others or to change the world can be a lot of fun.

You might not be willing to give 10% just now. In which case give a smaller proportion of your income. And increase your level of giving as your income rises and as you start to enjoy what you are achieving with your money. And you don't have to be limited to 10%. You can give more!

If you feel already over-committed financially, you might consider donating your time or talents to a charitable cause instead.

To calculate how much a tithe is per annum, per month, per week or per day, put in the figure for your annual income and use the tithe calculator at:
www.nacba.net/tithe.htm

To donate tax-effectively in the UK, contact the Charities Aid Foundation:
www.cafonline.org

If you want to give your money away, there are a number of decisions to make.

How much of your income to give away. Decide whether this is to be a certain proportion of your income, or a fixed annual sum, or some other amount.

Whether to plan your giving, by setting aside a monthly or annual sum into a separate bank account.

How to give tax-effectively, so that you benefit from the tax reliefs that are on offer.

...give 10% to charity

Start giving a portion of your income or of your time to charity.

Calculate how much money you actually need to live at the standard you want. Then donate everything in excess of this.

Tithe your time instead of your money. Cash might be tight, so you may be able to give your time instead. 10% of your work time equals four hours a week. Donate that by volunteering.

Tithe your talent instead of your money. Do you have a skill or an expertise or a talent which you can donate?

Donate a valuable item which you don't really want, or which you no longer need. Whatever the item, it will have value. Donate this as your contribution. Or sell it on eBay and donate the proceeds.

Get a part-time job specifically to donate your earnings from this. You could baby-sit, work as a bartender, or mow someone's lawn through the summer.

APRIL 8

ELECTIONS *make a difference*

You can stand for election. You need to be aged at least 21 and be a citizen of the UK, the Republic of Ireland or a Commonwealth country. Peers, bishops, members of the police and armed forces, prisoners serving sentences of more than one year and bankrupts cannot stand.

You need ten people to nominate you for Parliament, and you must put up a deposit of £500 (which is returnable if you get at least 5% of the vote). You can send out one letter (not more than 60 grammes) free of charge to everyone on the Electoral Roll – this could save you to £10,000 in stamps alone, but you have to pay for the leaflet.

Screaming Lord Sutch founded the Monster Raving Loony Party in 1983. He contested over 40 elections, often getting a respectable number of votes. Lord Sutch (who was not a proper Lord, but a UK pop singer), was easily recognised by his flamboyant clothes and top hat. Shortly after he polled several hundred votes in Magaret Thatcher's Finchley constituency in 1983, the deposit paid by candidates was raised from £150 to £500. This did little to deter the legendarily deposit-losing Lord Sutch, who increased the number of rock concerts he performed at to pay for his mock political campaigns.

For how to stand, see: www.electoralcommission.org.uk

William Pitt the Younger became Prime Minister of Britain in 1783 at the age of 24, whilst still technically a 'young person'. He had gone to university at age 14, entered parliament at age 22 and was made Chancellor of the Exchequer at age 23.

Pitt is remembered for his fight against corruption, taxation reform, and for shifting power towards the House of Commons. He was also responsible for the Act of Union 1800, which brought Ireland into the United Kingdom. This Act included Catholic emancipation, which was rejected by the King. Pitt resigned in protest in 1801.

Pitt was Prime Minister again in 1804 up to his death in 1806. He ran the country for a total of 20 years.

...take part in running things

At the next election if you meet the criteria, decide to run for office. Your friends will vote for you. If you campaign vigorously, other people might too. You may not get elected, but you could get a great deal of publicity for an important cause.

9 APRIL

Choose where to put your savings, and who you choose to borrow from. This can have an impact not just on the banks, but also on the companies they choose to invest and not to invest in. Financial companies such as banks rely on your money to keep them in profit. Many people bank with a regular commercial bank, such as Barclays or HSBC (which advertises itself as 'The World's Local Bank').

An alternative is to use a bank which is a co-operative. This means the bank doesn't have to pay out dividends to its shareholders, and so has more commitment to invest locally and uphold socially responsible values.

Co-operative banking has a huge appeal to people who want to bank ethically. In the UK, the Co-operative Bank is part of the Co-operative movement, together with its Smile online banking operation. Other UK ethical banks are Triodos and the Ecology Building Society.

Websites for socially responsible investors:
Social Investment Forum: www.uksif.org
Ethical Investment Research and Information Service (with free online magazine): www.eiris.org

Affinity cards

Your credit card provides another opportunity to do good with your money. There are hundreds of different credit cards on offer. Some are issued by a financial institution in partnership with a charity, which gets an upfront fee for every new customer plus a small percentage of the amount spent on the card. These are known as 'Affinity Cards'.

If you are interested in an Affinity Card, think about these four things:
Are you prepared to forgo other benefits, such as Air Miles, that are available on other credit cards?

Are the interest charges fair?

Does the card give enough to the charity? Some give more than others.

Do you believe enough in the cause to want to support it through an Affinity Card?

Still keen? Then this is a painless way of supporting a charity.

...invest to make it work

Swap your credit card for an affinity card, and bank with an ethical bank.

If you have stocks and shares (or a pension fund), think about investing ethically – putting your money in companies which do not degrade the planet or exploit their workers or make dangerous products.

There is a good deal of advice available on ethical investing. There are specialist unit trusts for the ethical investor. Some ethical shares are traded on Ethex: www.triodos.co.uk

NEEM *the village pharmacy*

The neem tree is known as the 'Village Pharmacy' in India because of its many healing properties. It is the source of a large number of natural medicines. It helps protect crops against insect pests and people against disease-carrying mosquitoes. Its twigs are used as a toothbrush and toothpaste all in one.

The neem tree was largely unknown to the rest of the world until 1959, when a German scientist witnessed a locust swarm in Sudan. After the swarm had passed by, the only tree left untouched by the locusts was a neem tree. On closer investigation it was concluded that the locusts did indeed land on neem trees, but they always left without feeding.

There has been worldwide scientific interest in neem since this discovery, and intense research into its many properties. We now know that the neem tree contains many natural active ingredients which make it resistant not only to locusts but also to more than 300 different types of insects, as well as to fungi, bacteria, and even viruses. These chemical defences are not only useful in protecting neem trees, but can also be used as the basis for natural medicines.

Neem Foundation, promotes the growing and use of neem: www.neemfoundation.org
Where to get neem products: www.theneemteam.co.uk

Properties of the neem tree

Healing and soothing
Leaves from the neem tree can be used to ease a variety of skin conditions, complaints and wounds. In India, Neem leaf poultices and infusions and Neem oil are widely used in the treatment of skin and nail complaints.

Insect repellant
Neem is also a powerful insect repellent. The oil was extensively tested in Scotland on the Highland midge by a team of leading experts. Neem seed extract, the highly concentrated extract from neem seeds, is an extremely powerful way of eliminating insects, particularly head lice.

Economic fuel
Neem has a huge potential for solving global agricultural, public health, population and environmental pollution problems. The demand for neem products, especially the seed as the basic raw material, is set to increase by leaps and bounds, and with it income generation and job opportunities.

...a tree for global problems

Go neem! Buy neem soap, neem shampoo, neem mosquito and insect repellant, and neem treatment for headlice.

Big drug companies have become interested in identifying the active ingredients of neem and patenting them. But the neem tree is part of India's indigenous knowledge base. For bio-piracy issues around the attempts to patent neem, go to: www.american.edu/TED/neemtree.htm

11 APRIL

visit the world's HERITAGE

Heritage is our legacy from the past, and what we pass on to future generations. Our cultural and natural heritage are both irreplaceable sources of life and inspiration. Places as unique and diverse as the wilds of East Africa's Serengeti, the Pyramids of Egypt, the Great Barrier Reef in Australia and the Baroque cathedrals of Latin America make up our world's heritage.

What makes the concept of World Heritage exceptional is its universal application. World Heritage Sites belong to all the peoples of the world, irrespective of the territory on which they are located.

World Heritage Sites encourage the preservation of cultural and natural heritage around the world. This is embodied in an international treaty called the Convention concerning the Protection of the World Cultural and Natural Heritage, adopted by UNESCO in 1972.

The UNESCO World Heritage Centre: <u>whc.unesco.org</u>

Some World Heritage Sites in the United Kingdom

Giant's Causeway and Causeway Coast
Durham Castle and Cathedral
Ironbridge Gorge
Stonehenge and Avebury
St. Kilda
Blenheim Palace
Westminster Palace
City of Bath
Hadrian's Wall
Tower of London
Canterbury Cathedral
Old and New Towns of Edinburgh
Maritime Greenwich
Heart of Neolithic Orkney
Blaenavon Industrial Landscape
Dorset and East Devon Coast
Derwent Valley Mills
Royal Botanic Gardens, Kew
Liverpool - Maritime Mercantile City

...contribute to conservation

Plan a visit to a World Heritage Site.

🌳 **Prepare a picnic.** No pre-prepared foods; no packaging; no plastic bags; no cans, no plastic water bottles. Just good friends, real food, proper plates and cutlery. Make sure that everything but the food is re-usable. Have a great day out.

🌳 **Visit every World Heritage Site** in your country.

🌳 **Go on a conservation holiday** with Earthwatch to help save World Heritage Sites. No experience is necessary – only a thirst for adventure and a passion to make a real contribution to heritage conservation.

APRIL 12

PLANT *a sunflower*

The sunflower's head follows the sun from sunrise until sunset. Its scientific name is *Helianthus*, derived from *Helios* meaning sun and Anthos meaning flower. The sunflower is making a silent, simple and spontaneous statement about the importance of sunlight.

'Sunflowers instead of missiles in the soil would ensure peace for future generations.' These are the words of US Secretary of Defense, William Perry, spoken on 4 June 1996. This was when the defence ministers of the USA, Russia and Ukraine met at the Pervomaisk missile base to celebrate Ukraine's transfer of its nuclear warheads to Russia for dismantling. The ministers planted sunflowers where missiles were once buried.

The Sunflower Project is dedicated to taking the 1996 Ukrainian missile gesture and fostering a worldwide campaign to encourage people everywhere to plant sunflowers throughout their cities, towns, communities, and countryside as living symbols of peace and to celebrate our connection to nature.

The Sunflower Project: www.sunflowerproject.com

The Sunflower Petition

The Sunflower Project is a global appeal to all people on planet earth concerned about nuclear war, pollution, violence, injustice, and threats to the balance of nature, to plant at least one sunflower seed in a sunny place where it will be noticed.

This simple act of planting a seed will demonstrate the energy, simplicity, and practicality of nature. The incredible sunflower is a symbol of our hope for Nature and for Peace.

We make a collective, conscious, and powerful statement by planting sunflowers where they will be noticed. We encourage all to plant a sunflower seed and watch it grow to become a majestic symbol – to summon harmony between humans, and with nature – toward peace on earth.

...for peace and prosperity

Click and sign the Sunflower Petition on the Sunflower Site.
Plant a sunflower:
- in your garden
- on waste land
- beside a road
- around a car park – wherever you think it will make a statement.

The larger varieties grow up to 3.5 metres tall.

13 APRIL

plant a TREE

Trees renew our air supply by absorbing carbon dioxide and producing oxygen. Just two mature trees can provide enough oxygen for a family of four.

> **One tree produces nearly 118kg of oxygen** each year.
>
> **One acre of trees removes up to 2.6 tonnes of carbon dioxide** each year.
>
> **Shade trees can protect against fierce sunlight** and make buildings up to 10C cooler in the summer.
>
> **Trees cool the air** by evaporating water in their leaves.
>
> **Tree roots stabilise the soil** and prevent erosion.
>
> **Trees improve water quality** by slowing and filtering rain water, as well as protecting aquifers and watersheds.

– Adapted from 'Fun Facts' on the
Trees Are Good website of the International Society of Arboriculture

Trees are Good has information on trees and caring for them:
www.treesaregood.com

Trees for Cities: www.treesforcities.org

Tree Aid: www.treeaid.org.uk

Tree charities plant trees for you

Charities such as Trees for Cities plant trees in cities in return for donations of around £15 a year. They also have a partnership with Ben & Jerry's, whereby they supply free tree-planting kits (in a Ben & Jerry's ice cream tub of course).

Trees for Cities also works overseas. You can plant banana, lemon or avocado trees somewhere exciting such as Addis Ababa.

Trees for Cities runs a number of interesting training courses, including: 'How to operate a chain saw', and 'How to hang from a tree'.

Tree Aid runs tree nurseries, plants trees and manages woodlands in Ethiopia, Mali, Burkina Faso, Niger and Northern Ghana, all in the arid zone of central Africa. Help regenerate the desert by getting Tree Aid to plant a tree.

...improve air quality

Grow your own trees

🌳 **Go to your local ice cream shop** and ask them for some large empty cartons. Find some seeds (acorns if you want to plant oak trees), and plant the seeds in the cartons. Put the tubs in sunny window, water from time to time, and add some plant food if you feel that your trees are getting hungry. Transplant into a bigger pot as your trees grow.

🌳 **Find a suitable spot** to plant out your trees: on a bit of waste land, the canal towpath, the edge of an existing grove of trees.

🌳 **Visit your trees.** Look after them. Take pride in what you have done.

PEACE *imagining*

Imagine peace. Think about what peace means to you.

Here are some ideas to reflect on:

If soldiers fought for peace instead of going to war, what would they be doing?

If all guns were replaced with flowers, what would the world look like?

How can we get rid of hate and violence in the world? In your neighbourhood?

Listen to the song 'Imagine' by John Lennon. Make a drawing of what you imagined.

What animal represents peace? What animal represents violence? Why are they different? How are they similar?

If peace grew from a tree, what would it look like?

What ingredients would you use to make a 'peace meal'? Write a recipe for this.

If peace could be embodied in a person, who would that person be?

Read the full text of 'Imagine' at:
www.john-lennon.com/songlyrics/songs/Imagine.htm

Art for peace

Young people can teach us a lot. As future adults and even future leaders of the world, their visions of the future and their ideas for dealing with the world's problems are important.

Enabling young people to express their ideas for peace through art is a step closer towards making peace a reality. It can inspire young people to share their dreams, and even to take action for a better world.

Focusing on peace creates optimism. Focusing on the terrorist threat only makes us more afraid.

...a world without war

Organise a local art show on the theme of peace. Why not do it to commemorate those who died in a conflict or a violent event that has touched your community.

❧ **Contact** schoolteachers and after-school programme organisers.

❧ **Find a venue** to exhibit the work. Ideally, a centrally located space such as a library, grocery store, shopping mall, town hall, etc.

❧ **Have an official opening.** Ask the young artists to bring their family and friends to admire the show.

❧ **Get a sponsor** and offer prizes for everyone.

The young people can express their views in a variety of media (drawing, painting, sculpture, an installation, a happening). Ask the young artists to use their imagination. It is important to remove the idea of competitiveness from the event, as the purpose is to promote peace and co-operation, which means respecting everyone's views and ideas.

15 APRIL

ChessBrain was the first distributed network to play a game against a single human opponent. On 30 January 2004 this earned an official World Record for the largest networked chess computer in history. One chess Grand Master competed against 2,070 PCs from over 50 countries. The game ended in a draw.

Some projects require too much computing power to solve. So much that it is impossible for any one computer or any one person to solve them in a reasonable amount of time. Using a large number of small computers via the Internet in a 'distributed network' is a way of overcoming this problem.

Small parts of the problem are given to lots of different computers to solve. And the solution is combined from the component parts. Distributed computing projects use the computers of hundreds of thousands of volunteers all over the world. Besides playing chess, projects include:

Prime numbers: Finding larger ones – now with more than 10 million digits.
Extraterrestrial radio signals: The search continues.
Exploring protein folding: To try to find treatments for diseases such as Alzheimers and Huntingtons Chorea.
Finding new and more effective drugs to fight cancer and AIDS.
Mapping the World Wide Web at grub.org

Choose the project that interests you the most. Go to: distributedcomputing.info

Search for Extraterrestrial Intelligence

SETI is a scientific experiment that uses radio telescopes to listen for narrow-bandwidth radio signals from space. Such signals are not known to occur naturally, so detecting them would provide evidence of extraterrestrial technology.

Radio SETI has an insatiable appetite for computing power. More computing power enables searches to cover greater frequency ranges with better sensitivity. You can help in the search for intelligent life outside Earth by running a free program that downloads and analyses radio telescope data.
setiathome.berkeley.edu/index.php

...join a distributed network

Join a distributed network. This will involve your visiting a website and downloading some software whilst keeping your computer connected to the internet. After that you won't notice a thing. Your computer will be using its unused storage and processing capacity to solve some of the world's big problems, which are either to large or too expensive for a supercomputer to manage on its own.

APRIL 16

AIR MILES *donate them*

Today, more than 120 million people worldwide belong to airline loyalty schemes. The Air Miles scheme awards air miles as a customer loyalty bonus in other retail sectors. According to *The Guardian*, air miles have become 'a new global currency'.

Frequent flyer schemes started in 1981. Almost 14 trillion frequent-flyer miles have been accumulated. ⚥ Each mile is worth between two and ten cents. The total stock of air miles issued is worth more than $700 billion, which is more than the value of all dollar bills in circulation, and far more than the UK's £42 billion issued notes and coins. ⚥ You can spend air miles on travel and other benefits. Some schemes allow you to donate them for use by a charity.

The Make-A-Wish Foundation grants wishes to children who have a life-threatening medical condition. Children over the age of two-and-a-half, and under the age of 18 at the time of referral, are potentially eligible to have their wish granted. The Foundation contacts the doctor treating the child to determine if the child is medically eligible for a wish (based on the Foundation's medical criteria), and that the child has not received a wish from another wish-granting organisation.

Most wishes fall into one of these categories:

I wish to go somewhere...
To a favorite theme park, an exotic beach, go on a cruise, see snow for the first time, or attend a major sporting event or concert.
I wish to be somebody...
To be someone for a day – a fireman, a police officer, a model.
I wish to meet someone famous...
To meet their favorite athlete, recording artist, television personality, movie star, public figure.
I wish to have something...
A computer, a shopping spree, something special they've wanted for ages.

To donate air miles, go to: <u>donate.wish.org/donate/miles</u>

Beat Cancer with a video game

Ben Duskin was diagnosed with cancer aged five. His mother used a video-game analogy to explain what was going on inside his body. Ben asked Make-A-Wish to create a video game to help other people battle cancer. In the game, Ben whizzes around on his skateboard killing bad cancer cells. The game is based on the idea that attitude is what gets you through cancer.
Play the game at www.makewish.org/ben

...make a wish come true

⚥ **Help make a child's wish come true.** Put a smile on their face. Help their recovery. Go to Make-A-Wish Foundation: www.worldwish.org

⚥ **Donate your airmiles to the Foundation.** Participating airlines include: America West, American, British Airways, Continental, Delta, Northwest, Southwest, United, US Airways.

17 APRIL

use recycled TOILET PAPER

Reducing the amount of paper you use and increasing the amount that is recycled, can help reduce the pressure on the world's timber resources. This saves energy as well as trees, as recycled paper manufacture only uses half the energy and water required for new paper.

Everyone in the UK uses about six trees worth of paper every year. This is six times more than 50 years ago. Most paper in the UK has been imported, which adds to transport pollution. Making paper uses a huge amount of energy. To produce a tonne of paper requires the same energy as is used in producing a tonne of steel. New paper is often white, not because this is paper's natural colour, but because it is bleached. This bleach is a major cause of water pollution.

Toxic wastes, including dioxins and other waste, are discharged from pulp mills. Yet until recently there was little control of these discharges. Even though paper can be recycled and the amount being recycled has been increasing, more than half of all paper used is still thrown away. 🌳 One in five of the world's trees is used to make paper. Check out your own dustbin. On average 30% of your waste is paper and card. That's two trees' worth each year just caused by you!

Paper facts and lots of other information from Wildlife Watch:
www.wildlifewatch.org.uk/helpingwildlife

ShitBeGone toilet paper

ShitBegone is 100% recycled, because who wants to flush trees down the toilet? Only an asshole would sell people something made of trees when they don't need it.

ShitBegone toilet paper is non-embossed. Instead of being puffed up with air, ShitBegone is wound tightly on the roll. This makes ShitBegone rolls smaller and harder than the rolls that other companies sell. But ShitBegone is just as soft, just as long-lasting, and cheaper too!

ShitBegone expresses hope and belief that a better world is possible!

From the ShitBegone website:
www.shitbegone.com

...and roll back waste

🌳**Use recycled toilet paper.** This is available from many supermarkets, and also from eco-shopping services.

🌳**Buy some now.** And just for a challenge, see if you can cut down on the number of squares you use.

🌳**Start to use other recycled paper products** – tissues, and kitchen rolls.

CYBERSPACE *connecting up*

The internet creates all sorts of opportunities for connecting people. Some intriguing projects have been developed to do this.

The 1,000 Journals project consists of 1,000 journals, which travel at random through the world. Each person completes a page, and then sends it to another person. The first 700 journals were sent to people who asked for them, who then passed their journal to a friend. People add whatever they like to the journal that is in their possession before passing it on – writing, painting, bits and pieces. Sightings of all 1,000 journals are logged on the website. The first journal to return had travelled to 13 US states and also to Brazil and Ireland. The completed journal was exhibited on the 1,000 Journals website.

The Degree Confluence Project's aim is to visit each point on the surface of the earth where a degree of latitude and a degree of longitude intersect, and for the person visiting each location to take a photo. The pictures and stories from that location are then posted on the website. So far 3,430 points have been photographed in 155 countries. There is an intersection point within 49 miles (79 km) of everyone, and a total of 12,737 intersection points on dry land. Anyone can participate in this project.

1000 Journals: 1000journals.com
Degree Conference Project: www.confluence.org
PhotoTag: www.phototag.org

PhotoTag – releasing cameras into the wild

This fun, not-for-profit venture captures the chance wanderings of disposable cameras, which are labelled and sent out with instructions for those who find them to take one picture and then pass the camera on. A pre-paid and addressed envelope is included with the camera so that it can be mailed back to PhotoTag when all the film has been used up.

People who stumble upon a camera can log on to the PhotoTag website to update the progress of their particular camera. And when the camera is returned (if it ever is) then the photo-images are posted on the website. 40 cameras have been released since 2000, of which only 6 have so far been returned.

...see what can happen

- 🏵 **Visit these websites** and find out as much as you can about these projects.
- 🏵 **Let this be a spur to your imagination.** Think up a project that will connect people in your community or across the world.
- 🏵 **Take the first crucial step** in developing your idea.
- 🏵 **Keep going** until your project is out there.

19 APRIL

link up with # SLUMS

There are 923 million people around the world living in slums: 554 million people in Asia, 187 million in Africa, 128 million in Latin America and the Caribbean and 54 million in the rich world. This represents nearly one-third of the world's urban population, and 43% of people in developing countries. 🌍 In the next 30 years, the number will increase to 2 billion if no action is taken.

The UN defines a slum as a household lacking:

Access to sufficient and affordable water.

Access to a private or shared toilet.

Secure tenure without threat of eviction.

A permanent and adequate structure in a non-hazardous location.

Sufficient space – with not more than two people sharing a room.

Most slum dwellers live in homes of less than 150 square foot with no amenities or services. When people begin to feel more secure, they will often build brick walls, put a better roof on their house and consider themselves the owner. Instead of rent, they will be paying money to a 'local boss', who will protect them from being evicted by the authorities or the landowner. 🌍 Sometimes a slum community will be resettled, with the city authorities providing a site and services, and the people building their own homes. More often, they will be evicted with nowhere to go, and have to find somewhere to live all over again.

Slum/Shack Dwellers International: www.sdinet.org
UN Habitat: www.unhabitat.org

Shack/Slum Dwellers International provides a forum for slum dwellers all over the world to report on what they are doing to improve their housing. The success stories include accounts of how they are:

Advocating their needs, and obtaining basic rights.

Obtaining land, designing and building their own housing.

Developing income-generating activities.

You can read the good news about how the government in Thailand has approved a $470-million plan to upgrade and develop housing in 2,000 communities in 2005–08. The people living in the communities will be the key actors and owners of the project, and will develop it collectively.

Or you can keep up to date with darker developments in the slum-clearing in Zimbabwe.

...help upgrade homes

Contact one of the slum-dwellers associations listed on the SDI website and set up a link between them and your own community. Organise fundraising on the theme of housing. Here are some ideas:

🌍 **Hold a mass sponsored sleep-out** on your street or in someone's garden, under home-made shelters.

🌍 **Raise sponsorship** to spend 24 hours with no mains water supply, collecting all your water from a neighbour at least 100 metres away.

🌍 **Try making some 'Shack Chic' objects** (see Craig Fraser's photographs on: www.quivertree.co.za) and selling them on a stall.

APRIL 20

SLOW *down*

Most people agree that modern life is lacking something. Life in the fast lane means stress, worries about status and money, and a feeling that you are somehow missing out. Here are two interesting reactions to an ever-faster world:

Downshifting: swapping a high-octane, high-earning, stressed-out career for a more relaxed existence. In other words, going slow and enjoying it. One source estimates that 16 million people in Europe will have downshifted by 2007. ⚑ Broadcaster and journalist Tracey Smith organises an annual National Downshifting Week in the UK and the USA in the last week of April to highlight ways in which people can live simpler and happier lives, while being kinder to the environment. Among her suggested activities are:

Book half a day off work to spend entirely with someone you love.

Cut up a credit card.

Eliminate three non-essential purchases a week.

Slowing down: The Society for the Deceleration of Time campaigns for slowness. Its 1,000 members undertake to contribute to a general process of deceleration and to pause for reflection wherever appropriate. The society was founded in 1990 and is based in Klagenfurt, Austria. It organises talks and workshops, and an annual symposium. It also organises stunts to get publicity for the idea of deceleration. For example:

Gold medals for the slowest competitor in Olympic events – an idea they put to the International Olympic Committee.

Pedestrian 'speed traps', which time people over 50 metres. If the pedestrian takes under 37 seconds, they are pulled over and asked to explain their haste. As a punishment they are then asked to walk a tortoise puppet along the same 50-metre stretch.

Society for the Deceleration of Time: **www.zeitverein.com** (an English language version of this website is being created at a snail's pace!)

Tracey Smith's downshifting website: **www.frenchentree.com/fe-downshifting**

The National Downshifting Week website has lots of good links: **www.downshiftingweek.com**

In Praise of Slow by Carl Honore has chapters on: slow food, slow cities, slow mind and body, slow medicine, slow sex, slow work, slow leisure and slow childrearing. The author writes:

I am a speedaholic, and so this book is also a personal journey. I want to be free of the constant itch to go faster. I want to be able to read to my son without watching the clock. I want to find a way to live better by striking a balance between fast and slow.
www.inpraiseofslow.com

...enjoy being relaxed

Sign up to the idea of slowing down. Think of ten ways in which you could slow down your own lifestyle. Make a pledge today to do all of these.

be a backyard BEEKEEPER

Bees are essential to life on earth. They transfer pollen from the male parts to the female parts of flowers. Without this process, many garden plants would not be pollinated and so would fail to produce the fruits, vegetables and flowers that we need and enjoy. Around 80% of the food we eat comes from crops that have been pollinated by bees.

Beekeeping can be a lot of fun. The bees will do most of the work. To collect 454 grammes of honey, bees will need to visit over 2 million flowers. This means a journey of around 55,000 miles – the equivalent of more than twice round the world. A worker bee will visit up to 100 flowers each trip and make up to 15 trips each day.

To get started you will need:

a hive

some basic equipment

protective clothing

and, of course, some bees.

A typical hive will produce around 12 kg to 15 kg and possibly as much as 30 kg of honey each year.

Backyard Beekeeping – notes on keeping bees in urban and suburban neighbourhoods: outdoorplace.org/beekeeping/citybees.htm

Somerset Beekeepers has lots of practical information: www.somersetbeekeepers.org.uk

British Bee Keepers Association: www.bbka.org.uk

Where to put your bees

You don't even need your own garden. You can do it on your rooftop. Or you can arrange with a park or a landowner or ask a local allotment gardener to put your hive on their

land. Your bees will be doing a useful job for them, so they may welcome you.

You will need to put in around half an hour per week per hive from mid-April to August to look after your bees. You can buy a complete hive of bees, or you can obtain a swarm, when a bee colony divides into two, with half leaving to form a new colony elsewhere; or you can buy a nucleus and grow this into a colony.

According to the British Beekeeping Association you might need to invest £150–£230 for equipment and £80 for a second-hand hive with bees.

...pollinate the world

Become a beekeeper!

Even if you live in a concrete jungle, you can do it. You'll be a friend of the earth, a pollinator and a food producer.

There are around 40,000 beekeepers in the UK. Most are hobbyists rather than commercial producers.

You can sell the honey you produce to earn an income. Or you can distribute it amongst your friends.

COPYRIGHT *and copyleft*

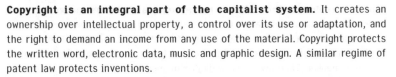

Copyright is an integral part of the capitalist system. It creates an ownership over intellectual property, a control over its use or adaptation, and the right to demand an income from any use of the material. Copyright protects the written word, electronic data, music and graphic design. A similar regime of patent law protects inventions.

Copyright has a value. It may be owned by the original author, or it can be assigned or sold on to another person. For example, Michael Jackson purchased the copyright to a large number of Beatles' songs, and the copyright to *Peter Pan* was donated by J M Barrie to the Great Ormond Street Hospital for Sick Children, for which it has produced a steady stream of income over the years.

Copyright exists for 70 years from the original publication date or the author's death, whichever is the later, according to international conventions. After this, the work goes out of copyright and can be used freely by anyone without payment.

The GNU General Public License project: www.gnu.org/copyleft/gpl.html
Free Software Foundation Copyleft site: www.gnu.org/copyleft/copyleft.html

There is an alternative to copyright: 'Copyleft'. This has been developed by the Free Software Foundation. It asserts the author's ownership over the work, but allows it to be distributed free, whilst at the same time preventing anyone else claiming copyright over it.

Copyleft should be used by anyone wanting to promote free and wide dissemination of any work, both to set out the terms for doing this and as a statement of commitment to the idea of sharing. In a world where genetic sequences and traditional medicines and foods (such as Basmati rice) are being patented, the idea of Copyleft shows that there is an alternative.

...property is theft

Add the following to anything and everything you write:

This work is 'Copyleft' as part of the author's commitment to a fair and sharing society. This means you are free to publish any part or all of it under the following licence:

Copyright © year of publication, author name.

Permission is granted to anyone to make or distribute verbatim copies of this work, in any medium, provided that this copyright notice and permission notice are preserved, and that the distributor and any subsequent distributor grants the recipient permission for further redistribution as permitted by this notice.

Modified versions may not be made except with the permission of the author.

Failure to comply with this may result in legal action to obtain financial compensation for the illegal use of the intellectual property.

effective **FUNDRAISING**

Fundraisers donate their time to raise money and change the world. There are many causes worth donating to, and a number of routes to raise the cash.

1 **Prepare a short talk**, perhaps with a PowerPoint presentation. Contact local groups (such as a Round Table) or the local school. Ask if they would like a speaker. Then invite the audience to support you or to raise money for you.

2 **Ask your friends, family and colleagues at work.** You only need 50 people to give you £2 a week for a year, and you will have raised over £5,000. This is little more than the price of a cup of coffee. Prepare a leaflet explaining your project. Ask everyone you can think of – in person, by telephone, by email or by letter.

3 **Organise a fundraising event** – party, a disco, a quiz evening, a picnic or an outing. There are lots of ways of raising money!

4 **Organise an Auction of Promises.** Get people to promise to do something for you, such as baby-sit once a month, mow your lawn every week through the summer, or serenade a loved one's apartment. Then auction these promises at a fundraising event.

5 **Run in a marathon or cycle from one end of your country to the other.** Do something that seems very difficult, and then ask people to sponsor you.

6 **Make a wish-list of all the things that you need**, which people or companies can donate or lend to you. Think about who might have these, and then ask them.

How to be a Fundraising Champion is a simple, practical, lively workbook for improving your fundraising skills. Download it from: www.millenniumcampaign.org

Effective fundraising

To change the world you need a great idea, lots of time and energy, tenacity and friends to help you. You will almost certainly also need money to pay the costs of your project.

First draw up a budget. Write down all the things you need. Estimate how much each will cost. Once you know how much you need to raise you can start fundraising.

Remember to say thank you to all your supporters. Report back on progress. If your project is going well, then people might be happy to give you more support next time you ask.

...how to do it

Raise some money today.

👫 **Set yourself a target.** This could be £10 or £50 or £500.

👫 **Think of who might be interested in giving.** Then find a way of asking them.

👫 **Make people so excited by your project** that they want to help you.

BOYCOTT *bad companies*

As a consumer you are in a powerful position. You can support companies that behave ethically, but you can also exercise your buying power to boycott companies who are behaving in unethical ways. 'Taking action' then involves doing nothing other than *not* buying products from suppliers you disapprove of.

Boycotts work. Canadian forests, Mexican salt marshes, whales and the seabed have all benefited from boycott activity in the past. Animal rights campaigners have also been sophisticated users of the boycott technique, with successes in the fields of live animal transport, hunting, pet shops and animal testing. Last but not least, human rights boycotts have also made a string of gains, most notably perhaps over corporate activity in Burma.

See the boycott list and contact details at Ethical Consumer:
www.ethicalconsumer.org

Find out about company practice at: www.responsibleshopper.org

Co-op America's boycott and action site includes a downloadable guide to organising a consumer boycott: www.boycotts.org

Some ongoingcampaigns:

Boycott Bush has been called by Ethical Consumer because of President Bush's rejection of the Kyoto Agreement on global warming. The top five brands to boycott are: Esso, Maxwell House, Microsoft, MBNA and Asda. Log on to www.boycottbush.net to find out the biggest corporate funders of Bush's re-election campaign and ethical alternatives.

Boycott Coca-Cola is supported by the Colombia Solidarity Campaign and India Resource Centre following environmental and human rights abuses in both countries. In Colombia, Coca-Cola stands accused of complicity in the assassination of eight trade union leaders since 1990. Many other leaders have been imprisoned, tortured, forcibly displaced and exiled. In India, the company has depleted and polluted groundwater in Kerala. Show your solidarity by checking out www.colombiasolidarity.org.uk and www.indiaresource.org

Boycott De Beers has been called by Survival International in support of the Bushmen of the Kalahari in Botswana, who claim they have been forcibly evicted from their ancestral land to make way for future diamond mining, and continue to be persecuted. Seven claimed to be tortured by wildlife officials for hunting to feed their families. Support the Bushmen at www.survival-international.org

Boycott Nestlé is another long-running campaign, called by Baby Milk Action, originally in response to the irresponsible marketing of breast-milk substitutes for babies. It's estimated that 1.5 million babies die each year because they are not breast fed. Recently, the group has broadened its remit to include information about Nestlé's water extraction exploits at historic Sao Lourenco, Brazil.
Find out more on www.babymilkaction.org

...the power of not buying

Boycott those companies and products you strongly disapprove of.

Your actions can make a difference. Make an effort to withdraw your financial support from immoral organisations, and stop buying their products.

25 APRIL

high street DIVERSITY

Starbucks is one of just a few big corporations that are taking over our high streets. It may serve good coffee, support fairtrade and donate some of its profits to good causes, but it also drives local shops out of business and creates a uniform look to shopping centres in whichever city or country they are in.

Space Hijackers opposes the way that public space is being eroded and being replaced by corporate profit-making space. They want to reclaim public ownership for these spaces.

A particular target of Space Hijackers is Starbucks, which is massive in the USA and expanding fast in the UK – its second biggest market. 🏠 In 1997, a 25-year-old Houston-based computer programmer called Winter started a quest to visit every Starbucks in the world and drink an espresso or a black coffee at each. By 2005, he had visited 4,765 Starbucks in North America, and 213 elsewhere. The problem is that Starbucks is opening, on average, 25 new outlets each week.

Starbucks Musical Chairs: www2.spacehijackers.org/starbucks/index.html
Space Hijackers: www.spacehijackers.org
Starbucks: www.starbucks.com

'Starbucks Musical Chairs'

You're sitting down in your local Starbucks. The people who sit next to you keep moving away to other seats. So you sniff yourself to check you don't smell. Suddenly, a girl stands up at the far end of the cafe and screams at the top of her voice 'I've been Starbucked!'.

Everyone else in the store simultaneously sighs with depression. The next thing you know, everyone in the store starts laughing, they all get up and leave the cafe at once. You and the staff are the only ones left, and they look as stunned as you...

Everyone has been playing Starbucks Musical Chairs!

...give cities a human face

Get together with a group of friends to play Starbucks Musical Chairs. The rules are:

🏠 Players separately make their way to a Starbucks and sit down.
🏠 Each player smuggles in a drink of their choice disguised as a Starbucks beverage. (If players purchase anything from Starbucks, they are disqualified.)
🏠 Players move chairs each time two songs have been played on the in-store stereo.
🏠 Points are awarded, based on where the person is sitting (on the floor 5 points; sole occupant of an armchair 20 points).
🏠 The first player to reach 100 points stands up and says 'I've been Starbucked'. They are the winner.
🏠 Other players curse themselves for losing and leave the store.

APRIL 26

PETITION *the world*

Words without actions are the assassins of idealism.

– Herbert Hoover

An effective way of getting attention and gathering support for an issue is a petition. The days of knocking on the doors in residential neighbourhoods begging for signatures have passed. Not only is this hard work, it's only really appropriate for a neighbourhood campaign, when everyone has a vested interest in the subject. Nowadays, the advent of the internet has given us a fast and easy mechanism for collecting thousands of signatures.

What makes for a good petition? Explain exactly what the issue is, and what you are asking people to sign up to. Do your research. Present the reader with concrete facts. Be brief. Don't write more than half a page.

How to collect more signatures than you ever dreamed possible:

Send emails to your friends asking them to sign.

Post links on relevant discussion boards.

Contact relevant writers and journalists and tell them about your petition.

Send out a press release announcing your petition.

Talk about your petition in online chat rooms.

Add a link to your petition in your email signature and your website.

Ask special interest groups to add a link on their website or in their newsletters.

Submit your petition page to search engines (it usually takes between three and four weeks to be indexed). Type into Google 'submit search engines' to find a way of reaching a lot of search engines for free.

The Petition Site: www.thepetitionsite.com/create.html
PetitionOnline: www.petitiononline.com/petition.html
Petition the Prime Minister: petitions.pm.gov.uk

Some petitions on the PetitionOnline website:

Al-Sistani For 2005 Nobel Peace Prize
To: the Committee for Nobel Prize for Peace

Get softball back into the 2012 Olympics
To: the International Olympic Committee

Property rights in animals
To: the US Congress

Please Lindsay, eat!
To Lindsay Lohan, teen actress

1934 Total Signatures

...a mouse click and it's done

Create your petition online. It's free!

After you have collected signatures, don't just let your petition sit and rot. Send it to politicians, companies, and leaders – whoever can help you work toward getting the change you want.

27 APRIL

try experimental TRAVEL

Feeling like a day out? A long weekend away? A holiday of a lifetime? Why not do something really different, and at the same time, save energy, reduce your carbon emissions and see the world in a completely new perspective.

In 1990, Joel Henry started experimenting with travel as a form of conceptual art. He invited people in Strasbourg to travel to Zurich, view the city as a serious tourist and then bring back some memento of their visit. Each person paid his or her own costs and travelled independently. They met up on their return to discuss their visit. ♀ This was the start of Latourex, the laboratory of experimental travel.

Latourex: www.latourex.org
The Lonely Planet Guide to Experimental Travel:
www.lonelyplanet.com/experimentaltravel

Guide to Experimental Travel

Joel Henry teamed up with Rachel Antony to compile the *Lonely Planet Guide to Experimental Travel*. Here are some of the 40 ideas in the book:

A-to-Z travel: Find the first street in a town that starts with the letter A and the last that starts with the letter Z, draw a line between the two. Walk as close to your line as the roads will allow you. That's your route for exploring the city.

Backpacking at home: Go to the airport dressed as a backpacker. Take public transport back to the centre of the city, check into a hostel, and spend a few days doing backpacker things.

Chance travel: Every time you come to a crossroads, flip a coin. If it's heads, you turn left; if tails, you turn right. See where chance will take you.

Eros-tourism: Discover a city whilst looking for love. Arrange to take a holiday with your partner, but travel to the city independently with no plans for meeting up. Your task is to find your loved one.

...for a very different holiday

♀ **Become an experimental traveller.** You can use Rachel and Joel's book to give you ideas for what to do. But come up with your own ideas too. Do it by yourself, or make it a group thing. Why not set up your own Experimental Travel Group, and plan one experimental tour each month?

♀ **Spend a day at the airport:** enjoy the shopping, pray in the chapel, have a meal, wash and brush up, meet up with others waiting for their flight. And remember Merhan Karimi Nasseri, a stateless refugee from Iraq who has been living at Paris Charles de Gaulle airport since 1988, whose story formed the basis of the Hollywood film *Terminal*, starring Tom Hanks.

APRIL 28

PLANT *a community garden*

This is the story of Graham and Bob, who live in Cavendish Gardens, a low-rise housing estate built in the early 1970s by Walsall Council – near the M6 motorway just North of Birmingham.

In 1998, Graham and Bob planted a small tree in the communal area outside their apartment. They added herbaceous borders the next year and began to maintain the lawn. Soon other residents began to join in to extend the garden and create new gardens around the estate. ⌂ In January 2002, a Gardening Co-operative was set up to take full responsibility for the environmental maintenance of the estate. The landlord provided all the equipment, including a lawn tractor, mowers, tools and secure storage. Most of the new plants and garden furniture were provided by the residents. The Garden Co-operative was entirely voluntary. Everything was done through the efforts, the generosity and the community spirit of its members.

The whole estate is now filled with gardens that the residents can sit in and enjoy. A wonderful neighbourhood has been created from what was once a run-down estate. Cavendish Gardens is a stunning example of how two individuals with energy and enthusiasm transformed their community, and turned what were once hard to let flats into really desirable residences.

Cavendish Gardens: www.cgc.vze.com
Federation of City Farms and Community Gardens, for information and advice on community gardens, community orchards or city farms: www.farmgarden.org.uk

City Farms and Community Gardens are community-managed projects ranging from tiny wildlife gardens to fruit and vegetable plots on housing estates, from community polytunnels to large city farms. They exist mainly in urban areas and are created in response to a lack of access to green space, combined with a desire to encourage strong community relationships and an awareness of gardening and farming. City farms and community gardens are often developed by local people in a voluntary capacity, and usually rely on volunteer involvement. If you volunteer on a community farm or garden you might become involved in:

Looking after trees, plants, livestock and crops.
Pre-school and after-school clubs and special needs groups.
Running a cafe or a shop.
General maintenance and construction work.
Administration, marketing and fundraising.

...for a more rural life

⌂ Turn the area in front of your home into a wonderful floral garden for everyone who passes by to enjoy.

⌂ If you don't have a front garden, put hanging baskets on the walls and window boxes on all the windowsills facing the street.

⌂ If there's a piece of vacant land, get together with others in your community to turn it into a community garden.

29 APRIL

adopt NON-VOTERS

All of us know people who don't vote at election time. Are they the kind of people who give long-winded speeches about how little difference their one vote will make? Are they completely fed up with politics and politicians of all parties, seeing them as corrupt windbags who promise a lot and then deliver nothing? Or are they just so lazy that they can't be bothered to get off the sofa?

Voting is the most direct route we have to our politicians. When someone doesn't vote, one less voice is heard and the democratic process is weakened. It is our opportunity to back someone we trust and whose ideas we like, someone whom we believe will do their best for the community they represent.

We have the chance at election time to engage with politicians. After they have been elected, hold them accountable to all the promises they made and ensure that they make their best efforts as our representatives. If they are performing poorly, then we can vote next time for someone better. ♨ You accomplish all of these things and more when you vote. The actual voting process only takes a few minutes.

The Orange revolution in Ukraine: <u>orangeukraine.squarespace.com</u>
Find out about elections around the world: <u>www.electionworld.org</u>

Democracy

Democracy is the recurrent suspicion that more than half the people are right more than half the time.

– E B White

Many societies do not have true democracy. Fair elections are something that people fought hard and even died to get – for example in Ukraine in 2004 when the protests of millions on the streets achieved a re-run of the first rigged election.

...drag them to the polls

Your vote can make a difference.

♨ **If you are over 18,** make sure you are registered to vote and that you vote on Election Day.

♨ **Drag all your non-voting friends to the polling station**, no matter how much they protest.

♨ **Pledge here and now that you will vote** at the next election. Also pledge that you will take five people to the polls who wouldn't otherwise vote.

♨ **After they have voted, do something that's fun.** Take them out to lunch, have a voting party on election night just for people who have voted. Do whatever it takes!

APRIL 30

JOIN *the sex workers union*

Sex work is big business all over the world. People become sex workers because they can see no other available way of earning a living, to feed a drug habit, because they are forced into it and kept there as slaves, or out of choice.

Sex work has many dangers, whatever the reasons: the ever-present risk of violence, AIDS, prosecution, extortion and much else besides.

Sex workers conventions take place all over the world. Sex workers have now banded together to fight for a safer and more secure work environment. And there is a union that lobbies on their behalf. This is the International Union of Sex Workers.

International Union of Sex Workers. www.iusw.org

Network of Sex Work Projects, promoting health and human rights. www.nswp.org

Kids with Cameras gave cameras to the children of sex workers working in Calcutta's brothels so that they could photograph their lives. An Oscar-nominated documentary was made about this project called 'Born into Brothels'.

Find out about how the children of sex workers see their lives: www.kids-with-cameras.org

The International Union of Sex Workers demands include:

Decriminalisation of all aspects of sex work which involves consenting adults.

The right to form and join professional associations or unions.

The right to work on the same basis as other independent contractors and employers and to receive the same benefits as other self-employed or contracted workers.

No taxation without such rights and without representation.

Zero-tolerance of coercion, violence, sexual abuse, child labour, rape and racism.

Legal support for sex workers who want to sue those who exploit their labour.

The right to travel across national boundaries and obtain work permits wherever the person is living.

Clean and safe places to work.

The right to choose whether to work alone or co-operatively with other sex workers.

The absolute right to say 'No'.

Access to training – sex workers' jobs require very special skills and professional standards.

Access to health clinics where sex workers will not feel stigmatised.

Re-training programmes for sex workers who want to leave the industry.

An end to social attitudes which stigmatise those who are or who have been sex workers.

...as an act of solidarity

Join the International Union of Sex Workers. Membership is free. No, you don't need to be a sex worker to join.

Do this as an act of solidarity. Find out what's going on. Help out if you can.

wood-burning STOVES

Wood-burning stoves can change lives dramatically. The Escorts Foundation works with the people of the Changa Manga forest area in Punjab, Pakistan. They noticed that families spent many hours illegally pillaging the forest for the firewood they needed for cooking. This was damaging the forest; out of 760 trees grown per acre, 600 were being stripped for firewood. ● The cooking process also meant that the women were spending hours every day near a smoky stove (known as a 'chulla'), and this was causing serious respiratory and eye problems.

A new type of stove which used less wood and was less smoky had not caught on. This was partly due to the high cost of paying a local blacksmith to make the stove's steel chimney. ● The Escorts Foundation first modified the design by introducing a simple mud chimney, and then adapted the design of the stove itself so that it could be made out of locally available raw materials (measured in units of tins and bottles) and using a cooking-oil drum as a mould.

This stove could be built by anyone anywhere. The materials needed were mud, straw and clay. The challenge was to demonstrate to village women that the stove would actually work, and that it would save them time. The stove uses up to 75% less firewood, and it can use smaller branches and twigs. ● Escorts then trained women to become 'chulla mechanics'. The women would go back to their villages and help other women make stoves. ● One stove takes a day to make, and costs virtually nothing. So far, 12,000 stoves have been installed, with an average 70% take-up in most of the villages.

The Escorts Foundation won a 2004 Ashden Award for projects bringing renewable energy to local communities in the developing world: www.ashdenawards.org

An evaluation has shown the following benefits from wood-burning stoves:
Children attend school more regularly.
Children are cleaner.
There is a 70% saving in time collecting firewood and a 50% reduction in the use of firewood, thereby reducing carbon dioxide emissions.

...life-changing solutions

Support the Escorts Foundation in this work.

It costs just £2 to build a stove (including all the training and support). Raise a small sum and make a huge impact on people's lives.

STAND UP *for press freedom*

Today is World Press Freedom Day. This may not seem important if you have a free press. But more than a third of the world's people live in countries where there is no press freedom, where journalists are persecuted for telling the truth, and where politicians would rather their people did not know the truth.

Reporting can be a dangerous job: 42 media professionals lost their lives in 2003 for just doing their job. Around the world, 184 journalists, media assistants and cyber-dissidents are in prison. Some simply because they used the 'wrong' word or photograph.

Reporters Without Borders is an international network of journalists working to uphold press freedom by:

> **Monitoring press freedom** around the world via a network of over 100 correspondents.
>
> **Publishing regular reports** on press freedom. This includes an annual World Press Freedom Ranking. In 2003 at the bottom of the list were Burma, Cuba and North Korea.
>
> **Defending journalists** who have been imprisoned or persecuted for doing their work, and providing legal aid to get torturers and murderers of journalists brought to trial.
>
> **Campaigning to reduce censorship** and oppose laws that restrict press freedom.
>
> **Working to improve the safety** of journalists around the world, particularly in war zones.

Reporters Without Borders: www.rsf.org

Persecuting journalists in Eritrea: In September 2001, the Eritrean government ordered all the country's privately owned publications to close down. In the following days, police arrested more than 15 journalists. They were accused of having published interviews with political leaders who had been publicly calling for 'democratic reforms' in the country. Those leaders were also arrested. Today, ten journalists remain behind bars in Eritrea.

Shutting down a website in China: When state security police came to arrest Huang Qi at his home on 3 June 2000, he just had time to send this email: 'Goodbye everyone, the police want to take me away. We've got a long road ahead of us. Thanks to all those helping to further democracy in China.' Huang, founder of the website www. tianwang.com, waited nearly three years before finding out he had been sentenced to five years for 'subversion' and 'incitement to overthrow the government.' Huang has been tortured in prison. His website was closed down, and the domain name is for sale. Why not buy it and create a memorial to Huang's bravery?

...support its defenders

🕯 **Visit the Reporters Without Borders website.**

🕯 **Find out about abuses** of press freedom around the world.

🕯 **Sign and send petitions** to try to free some of the world's imprisoned journalists. Just click and send. It will remind the oppressors that their victims have not been forgotten.

More of us are living to a ripe old age. And fewer children are being born than 50 years ago. This means that the proportion of older people in the population is increasing. Living to be 100 years old used to be very unusual, but today there are around 10,000 centenarians in the UK alone. An estimated 1 million of us in our thirties today could live to be a centenarian.

In some societies, old people are seen as a nuisance – to be put in old people's homes and forgotten about. Elder abuse is commonplace. But in other societies, old people are revered. They are seen as a source of wisdom. They are people to be consulted and listened to.

Old people have a wealth of experience to share. They carry traditional knowledge from one generation to the next. They can provide important information from the past for the benefit of future generations. And many of them have been through experiences that most of us can only guess at.

Find out about the oldest centenarian at: www.supercentenarian.com
See if you are likely to live to 100: www.livingto100.com
The Honeybee Network : www.sristi.org/honeybee.html

Honeybee Network

The Honeybee Network, based in India, creates links between people in the same way as a bee links flowers through the process of pollination. The network collects information from people, but ensures that they are none the poorer for sharing that information.

They organise an annual walk through villages to speak to farmers and village elders. Their project has interviewed several hundred people aged over a hundred. Honeybee

 uses the most promising innovations to improve the lives of the poor.

Ismailbhai Gajan, a local veterinary healer, bemoaned the extinction of many herbal plants, as this had affected his ability to provide effective treatment. Deviben Lakum spoke about first aid and treatments for animal disorders and diseases.

The world would be worse off without the wisdom of Ismailbhai and Deviben and others like them!

...and find out about the past

Find a centenarian and interview them. Ask them about:

- What life was like when they were young.
- What problems they had, and how they overcame them.
- What they cooked and ate.
- Whether they led more healthy lives than we do today.
- Whether things are better or worse today than in their youth.

MAY 4

KNIT *blankets*

Every year, nearly 600,000 women die from complications during pregnancy and childbirth. That's the equivalent of a ship the size of the *Titanic* sinking every single day with no survivors. Maternal deaths account for 25% to 30% of all deaths among women of reproductive age. There are huge differences across the world: for example, a woman in Somalia is 700 times more likely to die as a result of pregnancy or childbirth than a woman in the UK.

The Partnership for Maternal, Newborn and Child Health protects women throughout pregnancy and childbirth. It means ensuring that all women everywhere receive the care they need to be safe and healthy. This can be achieved by providing high-quality maternal health services to all women during pregnancy, childbirth, and the postpartum period. This includes:

Care by skilled health personnel before, during, and after childbirth.
Emergency care for life-threatening obstetric complications.
Services to prevent and manage the complications of unsafe abortion.
Family planning and health education.

Millennium Goal 5 is to improve maternal health. The target for 2015 is to reduce by three-quarters the chance of women dying in childbirth (currently one in 48).

The Partnership is a global network to promote safe motherhood:
www.who.int/pmnch/en

Marie Stopes International, promoting safe motherhood across the world:
www.mariestopes.org.uk

Royal College of Midwives safe motherhood initiative:
www.rcm.org.uk/data/international/data/safe.htm

Maternity Worldwide: www.maternityworldwide.org

According to Marie Stopes International, every minute of every hour of every day:

380 women become pregnant; half of these are unplanned or unwanted.
110 women experience pregnancy-related complications.
40 women have an unsafe abortion.
One woman dies from complications during pregnancy. More than 99% of these deaths occur in developing countries and most could be avoided with improved obstetric care.

...to save mothers

☺ **Knit for Maternity Worldwide.** You can knit blankets which will be used for hospital beds as well as wraps for mums in Ethiopia. You can knit smaller blankets or vests to keep the babies warm. The vest may be the only piece of new clothing that the newborn baby receives. If you are interested, contact: babyvests@maternityworldwide.org

☺ **Find sponsors to support your efforts.** Get your friends to sponsor you to knit a square. Every £15 you raise will pay for a safe birth.

plant your BIRTH TREE

Each day of the year has a particular tree associated with it. The tree for the day you were born is known as your 'birth tree'. Don't just plant any tree. Plant your birth tree. Or commemorate someone else's birthday by planting their birth tree.

Your birth tree confers a set of characteristics on you. For example, if you are born on 10 July your birth tree would be a Fir. You would then be likely to have all of the following characteristics: taste, dignity, cultivated airs, a love of anything beautiful, modesty, ambition, and many friends.

To find out about your birth tree:
www.geocities.com/Athens/5341/tree.html

Jan 02 to Jan 11	**Fir**	May 01 to May 14	**Poplar**
Jan 12 to Jan 24	**Elm**	May 15 to May 24	**Chestnut**
Jan 25 to Feb 03	**Cypress**	May 25 to Jun 03	**Ash**
Feb 04 to Feb 08	**Poplar**	Jun 04 to Jun 13	**Hornbeam**
Feb 09 to Feb 18	**Cedar**	Jun 14 to Jun 23	**Fig**
Feb 19 to Feb 28	**Pine**	Jun 24	**Birch**
		Jun 25 to Jul 04	**Apple**
Mar 01 to Mar 10	**Weeping Willow**		
Mar 11 to Mar 20	**Lime**	Jul 05 to Jul 14	**Fir**
Mar 21	**Oak**	Jul 15 to Jul 25	**Elm**
Mar 22 to Mar 31	**Hazelnut**	Jul 26 to Aug 04	**Cypress**
Apr 01 to Apr 10	**Rowan**	Aug 05 to Aug 13	**Poplar**
Apr 11 to Apr 20	**Maple**	Aug 14 to Aug 23	**Cedar**
Apr 21 to Apr 30	**Walnut**	Aug 24 to Sep 02	**Pine**
		Sep 03 to Sep 12	**Weeping Willow**
		Sep 13 to Sep 22	**Lime**
		Sep 23	**Olive**
		Sep 24 to Oct 03	**Hazelnut**
		Oct 04 to Oct 13	**Rowan**
		Oct 14 to Oct 23	**Maple**
		Oct 24 to Nov 11	**Walnut**
		Nov 12 to Nov 21	**Chestnut**
		Nov 22 to Dec 01	**Ash**
		Dec 02 to Dec 11	**Hornbeam**
		Dec 12 to Dec 21	**Fig**
		Dec 22	**Beech**
		Dec 23 to Jan 01	**Apple**

...for a greener world

🌳 **Use the table to identify your birth tree.**

🌳 **Plant your birth tree** to commemorate your next birthday. Do it yourself in your own garden, or on a plot of vacant land, or in a clearing in a wood or forest. Find somewhere that desperately needs a tree. Then plant one.

MAY 6

WATER *fetching*

Millions of people worldwide lack piped water. Many also live far away from a safe water source. Women and girls have to walk long distances every day to collect their family's water needs from a nearby dam, lake or river. ● The traditional way of collecting water is using a bucket or pot carried as a head load. Most women can manage to carry around 20 litres, girls less. Collecting water is time-consuming and more than one trip may need to be made each day. Some women spend two to three hours every day of their life just collecting water. It is hard work and can cause serious health problems. But there is a simple answer.

Instead of carrying water on your head, why not roll it along the ground? The Hippo Water Roller carries 90 litres of water. It has a clip-on steel handle for pushing it along the ground. Water purification tablets can be added; the rolling motion ensures these fully dissolve in the water. ● The drum is manufactured from polyethylene and can easily withstand typical rural conditions such as uneven footpaths, rocks and even broken bottles. If it happens to meet a landmine, the water will absorb most of the blast.

Children and older people can easily push a full roller over most terrains, because the low centre of gravity, makes the effective weight around 10 kg. But the really good news is that approximately five times as much water can be collected in less time and with far less effort. If someone is spending two hours a day fetching water, they would save more than ten hours a week. ● Think what they could do with this extra free time – grow vegetables, milk a cow, do handicrafts. Think of how much extra money they will be able to earn. The Hippo Water Roller costs just £30.

The Hippo Water Roller is a Operation Hunger project: www.operationhunger.co.za

Did you know?

The average person in the UK uses 135 litres of water every day.

The average person in a developing country uses 10 litres of water every day for their drinking, washing and cooking. This is the same as an average flush of a toilet.

Around 40 billion working hours are spent carrying water each year in Africa. Maybe half of these could be saved by using the Hippo Water Roller.

...made slightly easier

Spread the word about the Hippo Water Roller.

Hundreds of millions of women all over the world would benefit if there was an easier way of fetching water. Tell NGOs in Africa and Asia to go to the Water Hippo website to find out more: www.hipporoller.org

send FLOWERS

I, Woodrow Wilson, President of the United States of America do hereby direct the government officials to display the United States flag on all government buildings and do invite the people of the United States to display the flag at their homes or other suitable places on the second Sunday in May as a public expression of our love and reverence for the mothers of our country.

– President Woodrow Wilson, 1914

Mother's Day started with the Greeks. Their spring festival honoured Rhea, who was mother of many gods. The Romans had a similar festival honouring Cybele. ⚽ Christians honoured Mary, mother of Christ, on the fourth Sunday of Lent, which also occurred at around the same time of year. In the UK this became Mothering Sunday, a day to honour all mothers.

In the USA, the idea of Mother's Day was started by Anna Jarvis. Anna was an Appalachian housewife, who decided to campaign about the poor health of her community. To focus on this, she organised a 'Mother's Work Day'. After Anna's death, her daughter continued to campaign for a day dedicated to mothers. ⚽ In 1913, the US House of Representatives adopted a resolution calling for officials of the federal government to wear white carnations on the second Sunday in May, which began to be called 'Mother's Day'. Then in 1914, Woodrow Wilson formally created Mother's Day as we now know it.

Organic Bouquet: www.organicbouquet.com
Charity Flowers: www.charityflowers.co.uk
Order Charity Flowers through Practical Action:
www.practicalaction.org/?id=flowers_by_post

Flowers for Charity

If you live in the UK, order flowers from Charity Flowers, which will be sent direct from the growers in the Channel Island of Guernsey. But if you place the order via the Practical Action website, 15% of what you pay is donated towards creating practical solutions to many of the poor world's problems using appropriate technology. Charity Flowers is owned by Age Concern and the profits generated support services for the elderly in the UK.

If you live in the USA, then order via Organic Bouquet. Their growers are small businesses, and each has a page about their family and farm. A proportion of the proceeds is donated to non-profits working for the environment and human and animal rights. If you have your own website, create a link to Organic Bouquet. They will give you a 15% commission on any sales you generate.

...with a difference

On Mother's Day, send your mum some flowers. But send flowers with a difference – flowers which will also contribute to a better world.

TRADE *fair*

Many farmers now have to work harder and longer for less money. Prices paid for agricultural commodities produced in the south have not risen in real terms over the last 40 years. At the same time, the cost of fertilisers, pesticides and machinery (imported from the rich countries) have all increased substantially. ⚽ If the market price of commodities falls below the actual cost of production, as it can do, this can force millions of small farmers into crippling debt, some losing their land and homes.

What farmers need is a fair price for their products that covers the cost of production, and an assurance that they will be able to sell what they produce. This is the basis of the fairtrade movement. ⚽ Fairtrade certification was launched in the 1980s in the Netherlands. A consumer label, the FAIRTRADE Mark, was awarded to products that met fairtrade standards. Today in the UK you can buy over 1,000 FAIRTRADE Mark products from coffee, chocolate and tea to fresh fruits. Products are available in supermarkets, independent shops and cafés, and sales are growing by 40% each year.

Make Trade Fair, a global campaign led by Oxfam: www.maketradefair.com
Fairtrade Labelling Organisations International: www.fairtrade.net
The Fairtrade Foundation: www.fairtrade.org.uk
International Fair Trade Association: www.ifat.org
World Fair Trade Day: www.wftday.org

Fairtrade Towns
In 2000, Garstang in Lancashire declared itself 'The world's first Fairtrade Town'. The idea has spread. To be a Fairtrade Town, five goals must be met:
1   The local council must pass a resolution supporting fairtrade, and serve fairtrade coffee and tea at its meetings and in its offices and canteens.
2   A range of fairtrade products must be readily available in the town's shops, local cafés and catering establishments.
3   Fairtrade products must be used by some local workplaces and community organisations.
4   The campaign should have popular support.
5   A committee must be formed.
Campaign to get your town declared a Fairtrade Town.
www.garstangfairtrade.org.uk
www.fairtrade.org.uk/towns.htm

Four facts about Fairtrade
1   Out of every $100 generated by world exports, only $3 goes to low-income countries.
2   For every dollar given to poor countries in aid, $2 are lost because of unfair trade. This costs the poor world $100 billion a year.
3   If Africa, East Asia, South Asia and Latin America increased their share of world exports by just 1%, it would lift 128 million people out of poverty.
4   Rich countries spend $1 billion a day on agricultural subsidies.

...make yours a Fairtrade Town

⚽ **Look for the FAIRTRADE Mark** on products. Go out now and buy fairtrade chocolate and a packet of fairtrade tea or coffee.

⚽ **Make a commitment to buy fairtrade** whenever you can.

be a virtual **VOLUNTEER**

Virtual volunteering means that you can give practical help without leaving your home. Anyone who has the time available and wants to change the world, who has regular, reliable access to a computer and the internet, and has skills and experience that others might need is a great candidate for online volunteering. Your skill could be computer programming, writing, fundraising, project management, fluency in another language, or simply the time you can offer to help get a task done.

You can even help an organisation halfway round the world. More than 15,000 people have registered on the United Nations online volunteering website as being interested in doing something. They work on anything from translating documents, editing press releases, and research, to creating web pages, designing brochures and newsletters, giving professional expertise and advice, and much more.

What it takes to be a good online volunteer:
Attention to detail.
Commitment to answer emails quickly.
Commitment to stay with a project through to its completion.
Enjoying working independently.
A desire to learn, and a willingness to be flexible.
Having a clear definition of what you want out of it.
Being enthusiastic about the goals of the organisation you are helping.

Online volunteering: **www.onlinevolunteering.org**

Raising the visibility of volunteer organisations in Egypt

Carlos Jimenez from Spain has been the driving online volunteer force behind the website of the Volunteer Network Egypt, a portal aimed at increasing the awareness of volunteerism in Egypt.

 The portal was launched on International Volunteer Day (5 December) in 2004. Its successful launch can be attributed to a considerable degree to Carlos's skillful and committed coordination of a team of 11 online volunteers from seven countries, spread over the Arab region, Asia, Europe, and North America.

Online Volunteering gives us the opportunity to contribute – from our homes, from our workplaces – much more than a donation. We can actively participate, as protagonists, in sustainable development.

...with a click of your mouse

Become an online volunteer today.

 Go to www.onlinevolunteering.org and register (the website used to be called NetAid).

 Or if you could use an online volunteer to help you change the world, then post your volunteering assignment on the website.

LESS *is more*

Imagine having enough money to meet all your needs. Now think about a society and economy operating without any of the problems caused by money and its unfair distribution: poverty, exploitation, homelessness, unemployment, fear, and stress. A world where everyone can afford what they need, where they can all work and have the time and facilities to play.

This is the dream of an 'Open Money Economy' where people within a community can freely exchange goods and services. LETS (Local Exchange Trading System) is a working example of an open money system. With LETS, members exchange goods and services with each other. A person receives credits for all the goods and services they provide. These can then be used to purchase other goods and services from within the LETS community. A credit cannot be exchanged for cash. A bookkeeper records all the transactions and keeps accounts for members, showing whether they are in credit or debit.

LETS relies on trust and co-operation amongst the community. If someone builds up a substantial credit and there is nothing they wish to purchase, then they will probably lose interest. If they go into debt because they have been on a 'spending spree' or because they can't provide things that other people want, then the LETS community has to sort the matter out with the person concerned. LETS really works. Around 40,000 people are involved in 450 LETS groups in the UK. LETS has a particular relevance for people who are out of work either through lack of employment opportunities, disability or retirement. LETS enables them to participate in economic life when they don't have a means of doing this within the formal economy.

All you need to know about LETS: www.gmlets.u-net.com
International LETS groups network: www.lets-linkup.com
LETS in the UK: www.letslinkuk.org

Travel without money

James Taris travelled the world without money for 400 days. This is the website he created with free tips for living on LETS: www.travelwithoutmoney.com

...let's stop using money

 Play LETSplay at www.letslinkuk.org This game enables you to understand the key concepts of LETS. It shows you:

> The difference between conventional and community money.
> The significance of that difference.
> The value of using both forms of money.
> How to use a community money system without risk.

 If you get hooked on the idea, then set up a LETS group. Start by organising a street party. Ask everyone to write all the things they think they might need on one set of cards, and all their skills and other things they could offer on another set of cards. Put these up on a noticeboard. Then see what happens.

11 MAY

say no to BILLBOARDS

Mobile billboards drive around the city, but don't actually go anywhere. They are those trucks you see being driven through the streets where you live and work, with an advertising hoarding on the back. They fill up road space and contribute to gridlock. They spew out pollution and greenhouse gases, but ignore the fact that that they're inconveniencing everybody else.

Mobile billboards are a good indication of a selfish and wasteful society. They are completely unnecessary. If people really want to advertise in the streets, they could use the sides and backs of buses as an alternative.

Here are two Canadian websites which should spur you on in your own battles with mobile billboards in your own country:

Stop Mobile Billboards: www3.sympatico.ca/alwaysweb/mobile_billboards.html

Überculture's Montreal campaign: www.uberculture.org

Say NO to mobile billboards!

Ad Trucks are Bad Trucks. They're bad for the environment, bad for driving and pretty much illegal.

– überculture, Montreal, which is campaigning to reclaim public space.

Downtown Montreal has over 30 billboard trucks each day, travelling 2.34 million kilometers a year, burning over 400,000 litres of gas and emitting 940,000 kg of carbon dioxide.

...and save our air

Campaign against mobile billboards:

🌳 **Make a note of any mobile billboard you see.** Write down where you saw it, its registration number, the company advertising and the date and time. If you have a camera, photograph it.

🌳 **Write to the company to complain.** Tell them to be more environmentally sensitive. Tell them that you will stop buying their products if they don't change their policy. And tell them that you will tell all your friends to do the same. Make sure the company knows that thanks to its advertising policy, it has lost a customer, not gained one.

🌳 **Try to get some really bad PR for the advertiser.** Think of a creative and powerful way of getting media coverage for a 'Say NO to mobile billboards!' campaign.

🌳 **Don't buy from any company that advertises on mobile billboards.** Don't vote for any politician or political party that uses a mobile billboard for campaigning.

GUTENBERG *project*

Michael Hart set up Project Gutenberg in 1971 when he was a student. His goal was to make available free electronic copies of out-of-copyright books, and books whose copyright had been donated. Project Gutenberg became the world's first digital library. Michael himself typed in the first hundred books. With the emergence of the internet in the mid-1990s, the project took off. It is now truly international.

A book is scanned into an electronic copy. This is then proofread and any corrections made. If the original is in poor condition, as with very old books, the book has to be typed in manually word by word. There are now a thousand volunteers all over the world who help with these processes. The books are produced in 'text' format, so as to minimise the size of the file. ✋ Any title can be downloaded for free from the Project Gutenberg website and then sent on to people who might be interested in reading it. ✋ Software on the website (which is still being tested) will allow users to convert books into other formats and eventually into Braille and voice.

The number of books available reached 11,000 by the start of 2004. And 350 new titles are added every month. Most titles are in English, but there are now books available in 25 languages, and the target is to extend the library to at least 100 languages. Michael's dream is to have one million titles available by 2015.

Project Gutenberg: www.gutenberg.net

Become a Distributed Proofreader

Go to the Project Gutenberg website, to the book you want to work on. Pages of the book appear side by side in two forms: one the scanned image and the other the text produced by OCR (optical character recognition). You compare the two and make corrections. OCR is around 99% accurate, which makes for about ten corrections a page. Save each page. You can then either stop work or do another page.

All the books are proofread twice (the second time by an experienced proofreader) before the final version is ready for distribution. If any further errors are noted by readers after the book has been distributed, they can then be corrected. Proofreaders aren't given a quota to fulfil, but it's suggested that you do at least one page a day. This is a small contribution towards creating a library of a million books.

...bringing people books

✋ **Read a Gutenberg book tonight.**

✋ **Send people books** they might be interested in as a virtual birthday present.

13 MAY

commemorate a CELEBRITY

The Blue Plaque Scheme was started in 1867 by the Royal Society of Arts. It was set up at the instigation of William Ewart MP as a way of honouring noteworthy or famous people who had contributed in some way to society, history or to the local area. Initially the Scheme placed more emphasis on the buildings, but more recently it has been adapted to become a way of developing an interest in local history.

Blue Plaques have also boosted tourism. Visitors to London like to see where the artists, physicists, statesmen and great literary figures of the past have been born, lived (for some period of their lives) and died. The Blue Plaque scheme has spread from London to other cities in the UK, and the idea is now beginning to be exported to other countries.

To get a plaque in London, a person has to be nominated. For this they need to have died more than 20 years ago or to have been born more than 100 years ago (whichever is earlier). 🏠 The criteria for deserving a plaque include: eminence; having made an important positive contribution; exceptional and outstanding personalities; and those judged as deserving of national recognition. If a person meets these criteria, a plaque may be placed on a building linked to them. There can only be one plaque for any individual.

How to get started in local history, advice from Local History magazine: www.local-history.co.uk/gettingstarted.html
Information on plaques in London: www.blueplaque.com

Commemorate a physicist: The Director of the Institute of Physics has set up a scheme to erect blue plaques commemorating famous scientists. groups.iop.org/HP/Bluepq/index.htm

Commemorate a Muslim: There are not many plaques that commemorate Muslims in London, although there are many for people who have an Islamic or Muslim connection. These three Muslims do have a Blue Plaque:

Mohammed Ali Jinnah (1876-1948) – Founder of Pakistan
Syed Ahmed Khan (1817-1898) – Muslim Reformer
Mustapha Pasha Reschid (1800-1858) – Turkish Statesman

At a time of negative perceptions of Islam and Muslims, join the campaign to get more Blue Plaques erected for Muslims in London:
www.masud.co.uk/ISLAM/bmh/BMH-IRO-blue_plaque.htm

...put up a plaque

Someone famous was born or lived in your street or neighbourhood.

🏠 **Find out who,** and as much as you can about them, their life and their connection with your area.

🏠 **Start a campaign** to commemorate this person through the Blue Plaque scheme, with the collaboration of your Local Council or completely unofficially.

MAY 14

AIDS ORPHANS *in South Africa*

The struggle against global AIDS is one of the great challenges of our time. And the suffering of children affected by AIDS is one of the issues that most demands our attention. ◀ Nowhere is the problem more evident than in South Africa, where it is estimated that there are nearly 1 million AIDS orphans. This is close to the number of children aged under five in the entire state of New York. Soon there will be 2 million AIDS orphans.

Africa's AIDS orphans have been described as 'an army in search of a leader'. Brought up without the protection of adults, basic material needs being met and moral guidance, these children are the most dispossessed.

Heartbeat works with 5,000 children in more than a dozen areas of South Africa. Home-based care workers serve as surrogate parents for AIDS orphans and other children who head a household. ◀ Heartbeat provides food, clothes, school fees and basic medicines to these children, and, just as importantly, supplies nurturing, attention and counselling. The care workers provide protection from sexual and physical abuse.

Find out about Heartbeat at: www.austincommunityfoundation.org
Find out about Nkosi's Haven at: nkosi.iafrica.com

Nkosi Johnson died from AIDS in 2001 aged only 12. During his short life, Nkosi saw that not enough was being done to protect children from being born with HIV or to care for those who were born with HIV and to provide for orphans. He also saw AIDS-discrimination at work when he was refused entry to school. Nkosi, with his foster mother, set about doing something. Nkosi himself became the 'human face' of AIDS orphans in South Africa, gaining a huge amount of media attention for the cause.

Nkosi and his foster mother, Gail, set up Nkosi's Haven, which is a hostel accommodating 11 mothers who are HIV positive or with full-blown AIDS, and 27 children (of whom ten are HIV positive). The next-door property has also been purchased, which will double the capacity of the hostel, and plans are being made to purchase a 12-acre farm and a property with 13 self-contained cottages and flats to set up residential communities for mothers and children living with AIDS.

...one million and rising

◀ **Organise a Dinner of Hope.** Host a dinner at your home. Book a restaurant. Have a picnic. Throw a party. Invite as many people as you can.

◀ **Ask your guests to make a contribution.** Every pound raised will help AIDS-orphaned children in South Africa. Find out more from www.starfishcharity.org which supports Heartbeat.

unite as NETIZENS

A 'Netizen' is a 'Citizen of the Internet', a member of a worldwide community. All Netizens should have rights, freedom and equality. But in order for the cyber-world to be a place for good, we need 'Responsible Netizenship'.

Citizens Coalition for Economic Justice in Korea has drawn up the following charter for good Netizenship. Netizens should:

Voluntarily develop the cyber-world as an open and sound space for everyone.

Respect and protect the human rights and privacy of others, valuing them as their own.

Try to respect the work of others whilst having access to unlimited information.

Protect the private information of others as if it were their own.

Refrain from using vulgar or foul language.

Use their real names, and take responsibility for their actions and comments.

Not produce or disseminate incorrect information.

Not engage in illegal actions, such as spreading a virus or cracking passwords.

Participate positively in the cyber-world by watching out for and commenting on irresponsible actions.

Contribute towards creating a positive internet culture by keeping and practising these principles.

One in five children are sexually solicited online every year. Online sexual solicitation is an unprovoked, uninvited, unwanted request to engage in sexual activity, engage in a sexually explicit conversation, or give personal sexual information with someone first met online. The internet allows people to masquerade behind a false identity, name, age and even gender.

Cybertipline: www.cybertipline.com

Citizens Coalition for Economic Justice: www.ccej.or.kr/English

A Worm exploits the Tsunami to spread a virus

A mass email sent out in January 2005 posing as a plea for aid to help the victims of the 26 December 2004 Asian tsunami disaster was in fact a vehicle for spreading a computer virus. The worm appeared with the subject line: 'Tsunami donation! Please help!' and invited recipients to open an attachment 'tsunami.exe'. If opened, this would then forward the virus to other Internet users. Another worm said the tsunami was God's revenge on 'people who did bad on earth'.

...ensure internet safety

Be a responsible Netizen.

Sign the charter. Do what you can to promote its principles.

Encourage others to do the same.

MAY 16

HELPLINE *volunteers*

Helplines provide comfort and sometimes direct assistance to those in real need. Samaritans was started in 1953 by Chad Varah, a young London vicar. Chad had buried a 14-year-old girl who had taken her own life, having mistaken her periods for a sexually transmitted disease. He recognised the distress caused by having nobody to talk to about confidential issues, and decided to take action. 👫 Chad organised a network of people who would be at the other end of a telephone and could be asked anything. Around 4.6 million calls are now received each year in the UK by Samaritans.

ChildLine was started in 1986 by TV presenter Esther Rantzen for children experiencing problems such as sexual and physical abuse, bullying, serious family tensions, worries about friends' welfare and teenage pregnancy. Around 650,000 calls are answered each year.

The idea of telephone helplines has now spread around the world. The Befrienders International network, now run by Samaritans, is a network for suicide lines, and Child Helpline International for children's helplines. The use of the internet, cellphones and broadcast television are all being explored as additional mechanisms of providing advice.

Telephone Helplines Association, supporting helplines in the UK:
www.helplines.org.uk

Child Helpline International, promoting children's helplines internationally:
www.childhelplineinternational.org

Samaritans: www.samaritans.org
and around the world: www.befrienders.org

Email received by the Muslim Youth Helpline:

hi my name is youssef and i am a heroin addict and i need some help, i chase about 0.5 of a gram a day. if u can help me phone me on this number. A.S.A.P. cos am suffering every min of every hour of every day. salamo alaikum.

Muslim Youth Helpline was set up by 17-year-old Mohammed Mamdani in 2001. Young Muslims contact the Helpline by phone or email.
www.myh.org.uk

...it's good to talk

👫 **Volunteer on a telephone helpline.** Whether it is physical abuse or mental distress, the fear of dying or the problems of living, dealing with a crisis or just giving advice, there is a helpline that needs you to talk to people in distress.

👫 **Volunteer at a festival or an event.** The Festival Branch of Samaritans provides a 24-hour Samaritan service at outdoor music festivals like Glastonbury or Reading, and also at various biker, dance, surf, multicultural, lesbian/gay, homeless events, and other gatherings.
Contact: www.samaritans.org/~festival/volunteer.html

unwanted **STYROFOAM**

In May 1971, 1,500 non-returnable bottles were returned to the Schweppes' Headquarters. Schweppes was then the UK's leading fizzy drinks manufacturer. This was done to protest against the switch from returnable bottles (with the customer paying a refundable deposit on purchase of the drink) to non-returnable bottles (which would just have one single use before being disposed of).

This stunt was used to launch the Friends of the Earth reuse and recycle campaign. Friends of the Earth now has 72,000 members and over 240 local groups in the UK alone. Since 1971, non-returnable bottles have become standard. But there are now easily accessible recycling points so that the glass can be collected, melted down and reused.

Most Styrofoam (polystyrene) packaging will end up in a landfill site. Until manufacturers are made aware by the purchasing public that Styrofoam packaging is not good for the environment, then goods will continue to be supplied in this way. But if manufacturers begin to get the point, then they might switch to more environmentally sensible packaging, or even come up with a way of collecting and reusing the Styrofoam.

International Foam Solutions offers a recycling scheme for schools in the USA, and produces equipment for the D-I-Y enthusiast:
www.internationalfoamsolutions.com

Styrofoam is recyclable

You could reuse it for its original purpose. Cups and plates could be washed and used for another meal or drink. Packaging could be collected by the manufacturer to be reused.

You can separate out the Styrofoam products from other trash, and shred it. It can then be dissolved in a solvent and moulded to make another product. This is not very cost-effective for mass production, so is not widely done.

...send it packing

🌳 **Send Styrofoam packaging back to the manufacturer.** Address your parcel to the Chairman at Head Office – find out the name and address from the company's website. Styrofoam may be bulky, but it's very light, so it won't cost that much in postage.

🌳 **Include a polite and positive letter** asking the company to think more carefully about the environmental impact of their packaging. Ask them to try to find a safe recycling solution or look for sensible alternative ways of packing their products.

MAY 18

GOOGLE *bombing*

A 'Google Bomb' is an attempt to get a site ranked top when people search for it on Google. This is quite easy if you understand the way the Google Search Engine works. The key factors are the number of links and the use of particular words or phrases on many linked webpages.

The first Google Bomb to get publicity was in 1999. Typing in the words 'More evil than Satan' led to the Microsoft Home Page. Such was the interest in this, that now, typing in this phrase gets you to several articles on the discovery of Google Bombing.

Google Bombs come and go. Many get too well known, and mentions in popular web journals gets these journals to the top spot. Google Bombing can be used to get your organisation or issue to the top, which should be an important goal for your PR.

Try google bombing at: www.google.com

These Weapons of Mass Destruction cannot be displayed

In 2004, by typing in 'Weapons of Mass Destruction' and clicking 'I'm feeling lucky' you got to: www.coxar.pwp.blueyonder.co.uk. This came up on your screen:

Address: @ http://www.coxar.pwp.blueyonder.co.uk/

> These Weapons of Mass Destruction cannot be displayed
>
> The weapons you are looking for are currently unavailable. The country might be experiencing technical difficulties, or you may need to adjust your weapons inspectors mandate.

Favorites / History / Search / Scrapbook

Please try the following:
* Click the Regime change button, or try again later.
* If you are George Bush and typed the country's name in the address bar, make sure that it is spelled correctly. (IRAQ).
* To check your weapons inspector settings, click the **UN** menu, and then click **Weapons Inspector Options**. On the **Security Council** tab, click **Consensus**. The settings should match those provided by your government or NATO.
* If the Security Council has enabled it, The United States of America can examine your country and automatically discover Weapons of Mass Destruction.
* If you would like to use the CIA to try and discover them, click **Detect weapons**.
* Some countries require 128 thousand troops to liberate them. Click the Panic menu and then click **About US foreign policy** to determine what regime they will install.
* Click the Bomb button if you are Donald Rumsfeld.

...issues on the net

Google Bombing will get your message out.

Try typing in a slogan, and see what comes up. For example:

End Third World Debt gets you to an article on third world debt on the Socialist Workers Party website.

Education, Education, Education gets you to the UNESCO website

Make Love Not War gets you to political posters from the Sixties Project.

19 MAY

low impact T-SHIRTS

Next time you buy a t-shirt with an environmental message, remember to think about the impact your purchase is having on the world's water problems, and the conditions experienced by the people who grew the cotton.

Cotton grows best in a hot dry climate, but requires a lot of water. The cotton needed to make just one t-shirt requires 1,170 litres of water – that's more than a tonne. In countries where cotton is a major export, such as Egypt, Pakistan and the central Asian republics of Uzbekistan, Tajikistan and Turkmenistan, it is leading to serious water and environmental problems. The Aral Sea has shrunk, the mighty Indus has become a trickle, and the intensively irrigated fields are becoming salty, which will lead to desertification of the land.

Cotton growers use huge amounts of chemical fertilisers and pesticides. Chemicals worth $2 billion are sprayed on the world's cotton crop every year, with almost half of them classified as hazardous by the World Health Organization. Cotton is responsible for the release of 16% of global insecticides – more than any other single crop. Cotton workers, many of whom are children, and people living close to the fields, are at high risk of suffering the side-effects of these dangerous chemicals.

Why not switch to hemp? It smothers weeds, grows well in cooler climates, needs little or no irrigation, and grows easily and quickly (in just 100 days).

Environmental Justice Foundation (EJF): www.ejfoundation.org
Pesticides Action Network (PAN): www.pan-uk.org
The Hemp Store: www.thehempstore.co.uk
Hemp Union: www.hemp-union.karoo.net
Planet Earth and No-Sweat labels at The Urban Shop: www.theurbanshop.co.uk

The qualities of hemp

The seeds of the hemp plant (*Cannabis Sativa*) are used as a drug (both recreational and medicinal), and are also a common ingredient of seed mixes sold in health food shops, and as bird food.

The plant's fibres can be turned into a coarse linen-like cloth, traditionally used for sacks and floor coverings because of its strength and durability, and also for rope and paper. In fact, early bank notes were made from recycled rope, hence the phrase 'Money from/for old rope'.

Its toughness makes it ideal for bags and shoes, and for clothing, but it has to be mixed with cotton to make it sufficiently pliable.

...hemp is the answer

🌳 Buy clothes, shoes and bags made from a hemp–cotton mix.

🌳 Buy organic cotton clothes.

🌳 Download and read *The Deadly Chemicals in Cotton* from the websites of the Environmental Justice Foundation and Pesticides Action Network.

MAY 20

SPEAK *to a Thai farmer*

The theory of six degrees of separation states that any person is linked to any other person on Earth by only six ties. So, if you are a Hollywood mogul you will find that you are linked to a Mongolian shepherd through six people or fewer. You know someone, who knows someone, who knows someone, who knows someone, who knows someone, who knows the Mongolian shepherd. ♥ There are over 6 billion people covering our planet. Over 600 million have some form of internet access – and the number is rising day by day. So take advantage of the absurd simplicity of email as a mechanism for disseminating information to the growing number of people who can receive it.

If you can reach hundreds of people... and they can reach hundreds of people... and they can reach hundreds of people... and they can reach hundreds of people... and they can reach hundreds of people... and they can reach hundreds of people (that's six degrees of separation)... then your message can speak to a Mongolian shepherd, or a Thai chicken farmer... or the President of a country.

Change can start with a simple message. This is like planting a seed. Put forward an idea and give one or two key facts and figures, and this could get people thinking about the world in a slightly different way. Changing people's attitudes is a first step in creating change.

End Hate has a message to get your neurons moving: www.endhate.org

Ending Hate with Email

What if we all decided, starting right now, that the colour of our skins' didn't matter?

  – or religion?
  – or nationality?
  – or ideology?

What if we stopped being afraid? Think about it for a minute... maybe it wouldn't be that hard to live in peace? Maybe it's just that simple.

It's estimated that there are 605,000,000 people on earth with internet access. If 100,000,000 see this message can they make a difference? Forward this. Maybe it's just that simple. Maybe–its–that–simple@endhate.org

...spread the word by email

♥ **Compose a clear, simple message that promotes positive change.** It can be about racism, sexism, war, peace, sex, inclusion – whatever inspires or infuriates you.

♥ **Create a simple weblink for people to access the message.** Or just put it in an email.

♥ **Forward this to everyone you know,** everyone in your address book. And ask them to forward it to everyone they know. Your message could reach the four corners of the globe in a single day. Who knows what its impact will be?

save endangered SPECIES

Some animals and plants are so sought-after that they are at risk of extinction. WWF compiles an annual Top Ten most wanted list of species threatened by unsustainable trade and consumer demand. For 2004, these were:

Humphead Wrasse: a bulbous-headed, coral-reef fish caught and displayed live in tanks for diners in East Asian restaurants.

Ramin: a tropical hardwood grown largely in peat swamp forests in Indonesia and Malaysia, used for mass-produced mouldings, doors and picture frames.

Tigers: over the last 100 years, tiger numbers have been reduced by 95% – with perhaps fewer than 5,000 tigers left in the wild. They are poached for their skins, and for bone used in traditional Chinese medicines.

Great White Sharks: the largest of the predatory sharks, they are poached for their jaws, teeth, and fins, which are in demand worldwide.

Irrawaddy Dolphins: these are entangled in fishing nets and injured by explosives used for dynamite fishing. They are also in demand for display in zoos and aquaria.

Asian Elephants: they are poached for ivory and meat in many Asian countries. There are now only 35,000-50,000 Asian elephants in the wild, with an additional 15,000 in captivity.

Pig-Nosed Turtles: a giant freshwater turtle with a protruding snout, found in Papua New Guinea, northern Australia, and Indonesia, in demand by the international pet trade. Nests are robbed of eggs, which are either eaten or sold.

Yellow-Crested Cockatoos: fewer than 10,000 of these exotic-looking birds remain. They are in high demand by the international pet trade.

Leaf-tailed Geckos: these lizards found in Madagascar, with their bark-like appearance, are also in high demand by the international pet trade.

Trade in these species needs to be regulated and well-managed. Don't even think of getting a pig-nosed turtle or a yellow-crested cockatoo as a pet.

International office of WWF: www.panda.org
UK office of WWF: www.wwf.org.uk

Save our trees: Over 8,000 tree species, 10% of the world's total, are threatened with extinction. These include the Monkey Puzzle Tree, the Nubian Dragon Tree and the Clanwilliam Cedar. Find out about these and other threatened trees at Global Trees Campaign: www.globaltrees.org

...greed leads to extinction

Campaign for wildlife conservation from your desktop.

🌳 **Get a Panda Passport from www.panda.org.** You will be asked to post letters or send emails, petitions or faxes to decision-makers.

🌳 **You may be asked to make a personal commitment,** such as buying wood products only made from FSC-certified wood or switching to renewable energy.

SEE RED

AIDS, tuberculosis and malaria are three killer diseases that are ravaging the world, and having the greatest impact on the poorest countries. These three diseases need to be eradicated or an effective treatment needs to be found. The Global Fund was established in 2002 to substantially increase resources to do this.

By December 2006, the Global Fund had committed US$5.3 billion to projects in 132 countries. It could report:

9.4 million people reached with HIV counselling and testing.

770,000 people treated for HIV/AIDS.

2 million people being treated for tuberculosis.

23 million malaria treatments delivered.

18 million insecticide-treated mosquito nets distributed.

(PRODUCT) RED was created by Bono, lead singer of U2, and Bobby Shriver, Chairman of DATA (the Debt AIDS Trade in Africa organisation that Bono set up in 2002) in order to raise awareness and money for the Global Fund by organising joint promotions with some of the world's leading brands.

The money raised goes to AIDS projects with an emphasis on helping women and children. It will help prevent mother-to-child-transmission of HIV, provide nutritional support to AIDS-affected families and anti-retroviral therapy.

(PRODUCT) RED: www.joinred.com
The Global Fund: www.theglobalfund.org

Bono Vox

Paul Hewson was born in Dublin on 10 May 1960. He was originally nicknamed 'Bono Vox' (good voice) by a friend, supposedly after a hearing-aid advertisement they passed by regularly, and because he sang so loudly that he seemed to be singing for the deaf. He later shortened this to Bono, which he is now known by. His other nicknames have included The Antichrist, The Mother Theresa of Abandoned Songs, The Sonic Leprechaun and Mirrorball Man. He joined U2 in 1976 in response to an advertisement asking for people to form a band, later becoming lead singer. Bono, along with his fellow Irishman Bob Geldof, has played a leading role in campaigning for third-world debt relief and a better deal for Africa.

...to fight AIDS

☺ **Buy a phone**, an iPod Nano, or a pair of Converse sneakers, through the (PRODUCT) RED website. A proportion of the money you spend goes to the Global Fund.

☺ **Apply for the American Express RED card.** There is no annual fee, and if you use the card in the first month £5 goes to the Global Fund, and 1% of your spend thereafter are given to the Global Fund (1.25% if you spend more than £5,000 in a year).

☺ **Check out Armani's range of (PRODUCT) RED products**, including t-shirts, vests, underwear, shirts, belts and bags. On average 40% goes to the Global Fund.

23 MAY

try VEGETARIANISM

Producing meat requires a huge amount of resources compared to growing fruit, vegetables and grains. This is a fact that nobody can refute. Whether you give a damn about animal cruelty or not, you cannot deny the enormous drain that meat eating has on the world's limited supply of fertile land and water.

Here are a few facts:

20 vegetarians can live off the same amount of land that one meat eater would require.

If Americans reduced their meat consumption by 10%, it would free 12 million tonnes of grain – enough to feed 60 million people (the population of the UK).

An average hectare field will yield 187 kg of beef or 22,680 kg of potatoes.

250 litres of water are needed to produce one kilo of wheat, and 25,000 litres to produce 1 kg of meat.

The water used to produce 5 kg of steak is equivalent to the average consumption of water for an entire household for an entire year.

Cows breaking wind and belching are estimated account for 35% of Ireland's greenhouse gas emissions, thereby being a major cause of global warming.

Here are some good websites for vegetarian recipes. There are lots of others.
VegWeb: www.vegweb.com
Nava Atlas's Vegetarian Kitchen: www.vegkitchen.com
The Vegetarian Resource Group: www.vrg.org

An incredible double green hummus

For this recipe, you need:
1 bunch fresh coriander
1 bunch fresh dill
Juice from half a lemon
4 garlic cloves (more or less to your taste)
Half cup of tahini
2 cans chick peas

Quarter teaspoon chili powder
1 teaspoon salt

Using a blender, blend everything together except the chick peas. Add the chick peas and blend until smooth. Adjust the amounts to taste. This hummus is great on sandwiches with tomato or cucumber or onion slices.

– contributed to the VegWeb site by Elizabeth Rosegunn

...to save resources

Commit to eating a vegetables-only dinner once a week. This is a start. It will be even more effective and much more fun if you do it with all your family.

Not only will you be doing your bit for the environment, you will be opening up your taste buds to a whole new range of foods and flavours. If you still hanker after meat, there are excellent meat substitutes available.

MAY 24

GOAT *revolving*

Giving poor families an animal is a good starting point for helping them out of poverty. It used to be cows, but now it's other animals as well. Very poor people, with little land and few resources, sometimes find it difficult to manage a dairy cow.

Send a Cow has launched a new programme called StockAid. This scheme provides the poorest of the poor with smaller stock, such as goats, pigs or poultry. They are thus able to begin rearing livestock even where they are unable to provide the shelter or fodder needed for a cow. This is particularly helpful to families suffering the impact of drought, AIDS and conflict.

Send a Cow: www.sendacow.org.uk
Christian Aid: www.christianaid.org.uk/learn/goats
Goats for Peace: www.goodgifts.org

Christian Aid runs a revolving goat scheme. Here's how the scheme works:

Step 1. Goats are given to a goat bank.
Step 2. The goat bank lends a female goat to a family, possibly a widow and her children.
Step 3. The goat grazes on scrub land or eats up waste, and produces milk.
Step 4. The children have nutritious milk to drink, and any surplus is sold.
Step 5. The goat produces manure. If the widow has a plot of land, this fertilises the soil and the crop yield goes up. This represents more to eat or more money for the family.
Step 6. The goat gets pregnant, and produces more goats.
Step 7. One female is returned to the goat bank to pay off the loan, and the widow keeps the others.
Step 8. A goat is lent to another widow.... and so the process of getting families out of poverty will go on.

It takes £60 for Christian Aid to provide four goats for a goat bank in Bolivia or Burundi. And £25 for Send-A-Cow to send a goat.

Goats for Peace is a scheme run by the Good Gifts Catalogue, which gives goats to widows and families in several countries, including to genocide survivors in Rwanda. £15 pays for one goat.

...help a family out of poverty

Buy a goat for a family, and help the family take a first step towards self-sufficiency.

You won't have to go to the pet shop to buy it. You won't have to gift-wrap it; you won't need to feed it. You won't have to clean up its mess. You just provide the money; and someone else does the necessary. Your bright new goat will be delivered to its proud new owner.

Provide a hand up to someone who needs it. You won't even notice the £15-£25 it costs.

25 MAY

start your own **AID AGENCY**

Many people go it alone and choose to run their own aid agencies. Often they are just ordinary people, motivated by what they see abroad. This may not be a perfect way of getting aid to the neediest, but it is direct, it involves no highly paid professionals with Landcruisers and professional jargon, and it is done with a good heart.

The first step is to find out about local problems and needs. As an outsider it isn't always easy to know who or what to support. Ask around. Talk to a teacher or the village head. Work through existing community institutions.

> **Support** obvious immediate need: medicines for eye and ear infections can save sight or hearing.
>
> **Set up** a hardship fund for distributing small grants to those in need after you've gone.
>
> **Support** people with no source of income such as widows.
>
> **Help** build facilities of obvious community benefit, such as a classroom, toilets, or village well.
>
> **Use** your support to add to the energies and efforts of local people.

100 Friends Project: **www.100friends.com**

I am Marc Gold. I started the 100 Friends project in 1989. The idea is simple. Every year about 100 people contribute to the project, and I take the money to Third World Countries and look for the neediest people I can find. I then put the money to work in the most compassionate, appropriate, culturally compatible, constructive and practical manner possible. I pay for my own travel expenses.

The project began when I visited India for the first time. I met a Tibetan woman in the Himalayas who had a terrible ear infection. I was able save her life with antibiotics that cost about a dollar. For another $30 I purchased a hearing aid

that restored her hearing. I was shocked to see that something so important could be accomplished with so little.

In 2004, Marc raised $18,300, in 2005, $40,465, and in 2006 $73,518. He is building a school in Afghanistan and creating a drop-in centre for homeless children in Iraq. He is planning to build schools, drill wells, develop livelihood projects, and provide medicines and malaria nets in Malawi, Niger and Rwanda, three of Africa's poorest countries. He is also supporting projects in Cambodia, Vietnam and Mongolia.

...and travel helpfully

Resolve to make a difference by:

🌐 **Becoming one of Marc Gold's 100 Friends.**

🌐 **Doing it yourself.** Change the world whilst travelling.

MAY 26

CANCER *survivors*

The 'Big C' can strike anyone anywhere. One in three people will be diagnosed with cancer during their lifetime. Cancer is the second most likely cause of death, coming a close second after heart failure. The main types of cancer are: bladder, breast, cervical, colonic and rectal, endometrial (womb) oesophageal (throat), kidney, leukaemia, lung, lymphatic (Hodgkins disease and other lymphomas), melanoma (skin), multiple myeloma (bone marrow), oral (mouth cavity), ovarian, prostate, testicular, and uterine.

Over the last 50 years, deaths from cancer have not reduced. But death from heart disease has halved. ☺ For men the most common cancers are lung, prostate and colo-rectal; and for women, lung, breast and colo-rectal. Together these account for more than half the incidence of cancer. ☺ The overall survival rate for all cancers is 63%. The highest levels of survival are prostate (98%), melanoma (90%), breast (87%) and urinary tract (82%).

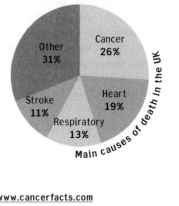

Main causes of death in the UK

- Other 31%
- Cancer 26%
- Heart 19%
- Respiratory 13%
- Stroke 11%

The Live Strong website: www.livestrong.org
Find out more about cancer from CancerFacts: www.cancerfacts.com
and from CancerHelp UK: www.cancerhelp.org.uk

Lance Armstrong's story

Lance was 25 when diagnosed with testicular cancer. This is treatable if detected early. But Lance ignored the warning signs, and the cancer spread to his abdomen, lungs and brain. Once diagnosed, Lance immediately declared himself a cancer survivor rather than a victim, and was determined to live, not die. He underwent two surgeries (one to remove a cancerous testicle and the other to remove two cancerous lesions on the brain) plus four chemotherapies.

Lance survived the treatment, and went on to become the most successful cyclist ever, winning the Tour de France a record seven times in a row from 1999 to 2005.

...live strong with Lance

- ☺ **Wear yellow and live strong** to salute a cycling legend and support his efforts to promote cancer survival. Nike launched the Wear Yellow campaign to support the Lance Armstrong Foundation. Nike donated $1 million and is helping raise an additional $5 million through the sale of yellow wristbands with the words 'Live Strong'.

- ☺ **Buy a wristband.** They can be purchased for $1 each in quantities of 10, 100 or 1,200 from the Foundation's website. These wristbands created a trend for wristbands for other causes in other colours.

- ☺ **Keep healthy.** Stop smoking, eat five portions of fruit and vegetables daily, live healthy and go for cancer screening as recommended by your doctor.

27 MAY

fight BIO-PIRACY

Bio-pirates exploit patent and trademark laws for profit. Patents and trademarks exist to protect tangible property, such as inventions or brands. But in some cases they are used to make amoral proprietary claims. Examples include ripping off indigenous knowledge, monopolising genes, patenting plants, or even trademarking a patron saint.

Examples of bio-piracy include the following Captain Hook Awards:

🌐 **The greediest:** Genetic Technologies (Australia) patented non-coded DNA (known as 'junk DNA') of all living creatures, including humans. This DNA was believed to be unimportant biologically, but scientists have now realised that junk-DNA plays a crucial role in switching particular genes on and off.

🌐 **The worst corporate offender:** Monsanto holds a European patent on soft-milling, low-gluten wheat that is derived from a traditional Indian wheat variety. Monsanto's patent covers not only the low-gluten wheat, but also the flour, dough and edible products (biscuits, cakes) produced from it!

🌐 **The worst nano-pirate:** Mr Yang Mengjun (China), secured 466 patents on nanoscale versions of traditional Chinese medicinal herbs by turning the plants into fine powders and claiming a new invention with increased solubility and bio-availability. Mr Yang has patents on barks, roots, fruit, and leaves that have been used in Chinese medicine since ancient times. Nano-piracy is a new way to monopolise traditional knowledge.

Nominate someone for a Captain Hook Award for bio-piracy:
www.captainhookawards.org

RiceTec

By patenting similar or superior Basmati grains outside India, RiceTec has ended India's ownership of the Basmati brand. Basmati rice is no longer a product unique to the specific climate and soil conditions of the Himalayan foothills (unlike sherry, which can only be made in Spain, or scotch whisky, which can only come from Scotland).

Today, the world is on the brink of a biological diversity crisis. We here in India are working towards increasing awareness of the importance of conserving our valuable genetic heritage, while challenging and opposing the forces responsible for its rapid erosion and usurpation. Join us in the struggle and research for sustainability and justice in these turbulent and uncertain times.

– Vandava Shiva

Vandana Shiva has been fighting the theft of indigenous knowledge by multinational companies, and has run a vocal campaign against RiceTec for securing US patents on Basmati rice, which is a major contributor to the Indian economy. www.navdanya.org

...for the real owners

Bring the bio-pirates to justice. Shower RiceTec with rice.

Buy Basmati rice from India. Write to John Nelsen CEO, RiceTec Inc, 1925 FM Road, 2917 Alvin, TX 77511, enclose some rice and ask him to hand back the Basmati brand to its indigenous owners.

MAY 28

PEACEMAKERS *are stars*

The Nobel Peace Prize has been running since 1901, when Henry Dunant, the founder of the Red Cross, shared the prize with Frédéric Passy, a leading international pacifist. The prize honours individuals and organisations for the exceptional contributions they have made to peace and justice.

There is now an 'alternative Nobel Peace Prize', known as the Right Livelihood Award. This award was established in 1980. The idea of 'right livelihood' is an ancient one. It embodies the principle that each person should follow an honest occupation which fully respects other people and the natural world. It means being responsible for the consequences of our actions and taking only a fair share of the earth's resources. The prize honours individuals and organisations who uphold these.

These people should be the stars in our human cosmos. But their work often entails huge personal sacrifice and being opposed or persecuted by powerful forces around them. The Right Livelihood Award now has over 100 laureates from 48 countries.

For Nobel Peace Prize Winners: nobelprize.org/nobel_prizes/peace
The Nobel Peace Prize has developed an online museum:
www.nobelpeacecenter.org/default.aspx
For Right Livelihood Winners: www.rightlivelihood.org

Nobel Winners in recent years have included:

2003: **Shirin Ebadi**, an Iranian human rights activist.

2002: **Jimmy Carte**r, who since relinquishing the US presidency has devoted himself to peace and conflict resolution through the Carter Institute.

1999: **Médecins sans Frontières**, for their medical work in areas of conflict.

1998: **John Hume** (with David Trimble), who was the architect of the peace process in Northern Ireland.

1997: **The International Campaign to Ban Landmines.**

1996: **Carlos Belo** and **Jose Ramos-Horta,** for their efforts to bring a peaceful conclusion to East Timor.

1995: **Joseph Rotblat** and the **Pugwash Conference** for their efforts to ban nuclear weapons.

Right Livelihood Award Winners in 2003 and 2004 included:

Walden Bello and **Nicanor Perlas** (Philippines), for their outstanding efforts in educating civil society about the effects of corporate globalisation, and how alternatives can be implemented.

The Citizens' Coalition for Economic Justice (South Korea), for its efforts to bring social justice and accountability to South Korea, and for promoting reconciliation with North Korea.

Bianca Jagger (Nicaragua), for her human rights campaigning.

Memorial (Russia), for prompting civil society and revealing the truth about the past.

...know their work

Find out about these and other award winners.

Be inspired by them. Learn from what they have done.

visit a PRISONER

Some prisoners are held a long way from home – so far away that their friends and family may not be able to spare the time for, or afford the cost of, a visit. Others may have been cut off by their families after getting into trouble. And some may simply lack any long-term relationships and have nobody who cares about them.

A Prison Visitor is anyone who has time to care, to share, and to listen. They are independent volunteers, recruited by prisons, who offer friendship to prisoners who have requested such a visitor. They may visit a prisoner on a regular basis, listening in confidence to their prisoner, giving them a sense of self-respect and being cared for – perhaps even changing their life.

To become an Official Prison Visitor, you apply to the prison you wish to visit. You must be of good character, most likely aged between 21 and 70, and not hold a job which might involve any conflict of interest. There should not be a faith dimension to your role.

National Association of Official Prison Visitors: www.naopv.com
The aim of the Prison Reform Trust is to create a 'just, humane and effective penal system': www.prisonreformtrust.org.uk

You never know what might happen:

The Ayrshire Post, July 20, 1984. 63

MAYBOLE

CITIZEN OF THE YEAR

JIMMY Boyle is the 1984 Maybole Citizen of the Year. At a special ceremony in the Carrick Speakers Social Club on Saturday, the trophy was presented to Mr Boyle by Mrs Kathleen Murray, chairman of Maybole Community Association.

Nominations for the honour were accepted up to the beginning of June and a committee selected Mr Boyle.

For the past 15 years Mr Boyle has been hallkeeper at the Town Hall and many organisations have spoken highly of him and how he went beyond his duty to help them.

Jimmy is a very popular man in the town and his selection was very well received by those present in the club. Community Council Chairman, David Kiltie also presented Mr Boyle with a medallion with the town's coat-of-arms embossed on it.

Jimmy Boyle, a renowned hard man and convicted gangland murderer from Glasgow serving a life sentence, was visited by Sarah Trevelyan, a young doctor training to be a psychiatrist. Sarah had been urged to do this by her father, a former film censor and penal reformer. Sarah and Jimmy fell in love and a few years after were married. Jimmy become an acclaimed author and sculptor, and on his release he founded the gateway Exchange to help young people at risk of offending.

...enjoy going to jail

Become a prison visitor. Contact the prison you wish to visit and ask for an application form. You will need patience, understanding and an ability to relate to people.

MAY 30

TOBACCO *sucks*

Tobacco is the cause of 1 in 10 adult deaths worldwide (around 5 million people a year), and this is projected to double by 2020 if current smoking trends continue. Half those who smoke today (around 650 million people) will be killed by tobacco.

Public attitudes have changed rapidly over the last few years. The complete ban on smoking in enclosed public places, which took effect in the UK in 2006–7, was broadly welcomed, even by a significant proportion of smokers, many of whom felt that it would help them kick the habit. The restriction of smoking to designated areas in the workplace is becoming much more common. ☺ Tobacco advertising has now been banned throughout the European Union, including motor racing sponsorship.

Nearly 170 countries so far have signed the UN Framework Convention on Tobacco Control, and are committed to protecting non-smokers and banning tobacco advertising. The States of New York, Delaware and California were the first in the USA to ban smoking. In New York, the ban covers bars, certain restaurants, betting parlours, bowling alleys, pool halls and even company cars. In California, smoking is now banned in prisons.

Bhutan aims to become the first country in the world to become completely tobacco-free. The sale of tobacco products, and smoking in public places in this tiny Himalayan kingdom have already been banned in 19 of the country's 20 Districts, and the Ministry of Health provides support for anyone wanting to give up.

Action on Smoking and Health: www.ash.org.uk
No Smoking Day in the UK: www.nosmokingday.org.uk

Tobacco: the killer facts

5,600 billion cigarettes are smoked every year. That's 875 for every person in the world.

There are 1.1 billion smokers, but only 15% live in rich countries. Despite warnings, 30% of adults still smoke in North America, Europe and Japan.

There are 4.8 million premature deaths a year from smoking-related illnesses. WorldWatch predicts that smoking will become the world's biggest killer by 2030, causing over 10 million deaths a year.

...reclaim clean air

☺ **If you're a smoker, give up.**

☺ **Be a pain in the bum.** Tell everyone you know who smokes, and any smoker whose smoke is curling into your face how harmful smoking is to them, and how unpleasant and dangerous to those around them.

☺ **Download information on smoking and pregnancy.** Hand this out to friends and colleagues who are or intend to become pregnant. You'll be giving a baby a better chance of good health.

go UNSHOPPING

In a throwaway convenience world, we buy so many things we don't need: things that are often over-packaged and stuffed with poisons. The principle of unshopping involves unlearning all the bad habits of our consumer society, shopping more responsibly and thinking about the future of the planet.

Coop America has come up with a list of ten things you should never buy.

Styrofoam cups: Polystyrene is forever – it's not biodegradable. Americans use enough styrofoam cups each year to circle the earth 436 times. *Don't be a mug. Use a mug.*

Paper towels: They waste forest resources and your money. *Use a dishcloth.*

Bleached coffee filters: The dioxins used in the bleaching contaminate groundwater and are linked to cancer. Find a better way of making coffee. *Use a cafetière.*

Overpackaged food: One-third of what we put in the rubbish bin is packaging. This is a complete waste of resources. *Buy in bulk; buy things with less packaging; take your own shopping bag with you.*

Hardwood products: Every year 27 million acres of tropical rainforests are being destroyed. Use products *made from sustainably harvested timber or salvaged wood.*

Chemical pesticides: They poison the soil and contaminate the groundwater. *Grow native plants and use organic pest-control techniques.*

Household cleaning fluids: Many of these release volatile organic compounds. Buy biodegradable non-*toxic cleaners and washing powders, or make your own with simple ingredients such as vinegar and soap.*

Higher octane petrol than you need: The higher the octane, the more hazardous the pollutants. *Drive less, drive a smaller car, and use lower-octane fuel.*

Toys made with PVC: Chemicals used to make PVC are known carcinogens; dangerous additives are often used; and PVC is the least recycled plastic. *Use toys made from natural materials; tell manufacturers to stop using PVC.*

Plastic forks and spoons: They are not biodegradable. *Carry your own utensils and food containers.*

Coop America: www.coopamerica.org
The Ecologist: www.theecologist.org

...10 things never to buy again

🏆 **Make a commitment not to buy any of these items.** It's a start towards creating a better world. You'll find that once you get into the swing of things you won't even notice the difference.

🏆 **For more ideas, read the following books:**

50 Simple Things You Can Do to Save the Earth and *The Next Step: 50 More Things You Can Do to Save the Earth* by Earthworks Group.

Save Cash AND Save the Planet published by Harper Collins in association with Friends of the Earth UK.

Go M-A-D: 365 Daily Ways to Save the Planet published by *The Ecologist*.

JUNE 1

GREEN *funerals*

Funerals are environmentally unfriendly. Think of the wood used for the coffins, the land taken up for burial, the access roads needed for the site and the embalming chemicals that can leach into the soil. 🌳 Funerals are also hugely expensive. The average UK funeral in 2000 cost £2,048, while the average cremation cost only £1,215, according to the Oddfellows friendly society.

There is an alternative to using the funeral industry – a green burial in a field or woodland. Natural burial grounds decompose very quickly; you're then left with an area of regenerated flora without the clutter of marble or granite memorial stones. 🌳 To avoid legal complications and bureaucracy, green burial grounds are often not consecrated, but priests can bless individual plots. The legal requirement of marking each separate grave for the burial register can be fulfilled by planting a shrub, tree or even an electronic chip. 🌳 Cardboard coffins with strap-down lids cost as little as £50, and these allow both them and their contents to decompose rapidly.

Along with a green burial, why not have an alternative funeral? Celebrate the life of the deceased as well as mourn their passing. 🌳 Find out what to do by reading the Natural Death Handbook, which is a mine of ideas and practical advice.

The Natural Death Handbook is available from the Natural Death Centre:
www.naturaldeath.org.uk

What about a bamboo coffin?

The SAWD partnership is a UK company producing bamboo eco-coffins in Hunan Province, China. The bamboo is grown and cut under licence from the government – pandas do not live in the surrounding area. The coffins are hand-woven and then transported by sea Russian-doll-style (one inside another) to minimise transport costs. This type of coffin received a best-coffin award from the Natural Death Centre.
www.bamboocoffins.co.uk

...dying to save the world

Consider expressing a wish to have a Green Funeral. The Natural Death Centre will give you all the information you need.

naked BIKE RIDERS

When I see a person on a bicycle, it gives me hope for the human race.

– H.G. Wells

There are so many reasons to cycle rather than drive: You save a lot of petrol. You aren't giving your hard-earned cash to an evil oil company. Biking produces no harmful emissions. You will get a healthy heart and body, not to mention great legs. You can't get done for Driving Under the Influence. You can laugh and make faces at all the poor fools stuck in traffic as you sail past them. Your maintenance costs are close to zero. The bottom line is that cycling benefits both you and the earth.

See how many more calories you burn when you cycle:

Activities	Number of minutes	Calories burned
Cycling (15 mph)	30	360
Walking	30	144
Sleeping	30	32
Driving	30	71
Sex (vigorous)	30	53
Kissing	30	36
Watching TV	30	27

World Naked Bike Ride: www.worldnakedbikeride.org

The World Naked Bike Ride is an annual global event. People ride as naked as they dare around town to protest against oil dependency and celebrate the power of the human body.

Every group has its own approach to cycling naked. Some focus on body painting. Some participate within the context of ancient cultural celebrations. Some use the day to promote cycling and a cleaner environment. Some use their body to call attention to political issues. Some ride at night. Some during the day. Some skip the bicycles altogether and rollerskate or rollerblade.

...go as bare as you dare

Take part in your nearest World Naked Bike Ride.

- **Date:** Early June – check the website for the exact date.
- **Dress code:** As bare as you dare.
- **What to do:** Sign up at the World Naked Bike Ride website, then tell your friends to tell their friends that it's time to take off their kit and hop on their bikes!

CHILD *prostitution must end*

In every continent, and in developed and developing countries alike, poverty, lack of education and parental pressure is forcing children into the sex industry. Some are sent by their families into what they believe is domestic service, but the children are then kidnapped, trafficked across borders and forced to work as sex slaves.

Commercial sexual exploitation of girls and boys exists in three main forms:
> **Prostitution** (which includes child sex tourism)
> **Pornography**
> **Trafficking** for sexual purposes

Commercial sexual exploitation of children is a multi-billion dollar industry. Over 1 million children worldwide are involved. Most children are aged between 13 and 18, although some are as young as five. In Vietnam, 30% of the 185,000 prostitutes are under 16. ◀ A large proportion of child prostitutes catch sexually transmitted diseases. 70% of child prostitutes in Thailand are HIV positive, and many girls have abortions. Most children suffer serious psychological problems.

Article 34 of the Convention on the Rights of the Child requires countries to act to prevent the inducement or coercion of a child to engage in unlawful sexual activity, and to prevent the exploitative use of children in prostitution, pornography or other unlawful sexual activities. Article 35 requires countries to act to prevent the abduction, sale of or traffic in children for any purpose or in any form. Despite this, child prostitution persists.

Child prostitution, like child slavery, should simply not be tolerated. It is a gross abuse of the human rights of those who are least able to do anything. Whoever you are and whatever you do, you must do something about it.

End Child Prostitution, Child Pornography and Trafficking of Children for Sexual Purposes (ECPAT): www.ecpat.org.uk
Anti-Slavery Society: www.antislavery.org

The Hearth
Many Albanian girls are being trafficked across the Adriatic to Italy, where they are forced into prostitution. In 1997, Vera Lesko founded The Hearth of Vlora Women to try to put an end to this, and to deal with related problems of drug abuse and child abuse in the family. The Hearth raises awareness of the problem, and it provides counselling and medical and legal assistance. The Hearth opened the first shelter in Albania in 2001 for trafficked women and girls. This provides secure accommodation and an opportunity for the young women to find a way out of trafficking and rebuild their lives.

...imagine it were your child

Raise public awareness. Use the internet to do some research. Then write, design and print a simple leaflet, which could include facts and figures, case studies if you can find them, and a call to action. Print off 100 copies of this leaflet, and hand them out in the street or put them through people's letterboxes.

help the ENVIRONMENT

When it comes to saving the environment, every bit helps. Turning the tap off when you brush your teeth or putting a bird box in your garden are all worthwhile contributions. To mark World Environment Day 2004, the Environment Agency came up with 60 ideas. Some of them are listed below.

UK Environment Agency: www.environment-agency.gov.uk/wed

World Environment Day: www.unep.org/wed

Visit the New Dream Foundation to see the impact of your actions: www.newdream.org/tttoffline

A few of the Environment Agency's 60 ideas:

Clean air

Drive intelligently – accelerate gradually, obey speed limits, combine several errands in one trip.

Limit how long your car engine runs when you stop.

Use a car with a three-way catalytic converter.

Wildlife

Put out a bird feeder or nesting box.

Build a pond in your garden.

Take part in a local tree planting.

Buy products made from sustainably produced wood.

Water

Take showers instead of baths.

Limit use of garden sprinklers or hoses.

Collect rain water to water your plants with.

Put a bag of water in your lavatory cistern to reduce the water flushed.

Turn the tap off when brushing your teeth.

Use full loads in your dishwasher and washing machine.

Repair dripping taps and turn taps off properly.

Use environmentally friendly cleaning products.

Energy use

Buy local produce or grow your own.

Fly less frequently.

Use thermostats that switch off the heating when you're out.

Insulate your home.

Use a fan instead of air conditioning.

Turn off appliances and lights when not needed.

Fit energy-efficient light bulbs.

Heat small meals in a microwave.

Insulate your hot water tank properly.

Dry your clothes on a clothesline.

Waste

Use a doorstep recycling scheme.

Choose products with recyclable packaging.

Make compost.

Re-use plastic shopping bags or use cloth bags.

Use rechargeable batteries.

Print and photocopy on both sides of paper.

Re-use envelopes.

Find people to use the things you no longer want.

Use a cloth hankie.

Use the front of greeting cards to create postcards or gift tags.

Cook fresh food, which has less packaging.

Drink tap or filtered water, not bottled.

...60 ways to save the world

Pledge to do at least 10 of these – 20 if you want to be a superhero – and tick them off as you go.

GUM *on the streets*

People in the UK spend an estimated £258 million on chewing gum, with half the population chewing the stuff (28 million according to Wrigley's). But gum seems to end up everywhere else but where it belongs – in the bin. An estimated £150 million a year is spent trying to clean up discarded gum, which is found on up to 91% of busy high streets in England, according to an EnCams survey. The Government has decided to clarify the litter laws and is advising on-the-spot fines for gum throwers.

Gum chewing began in ancient Greece, where they chewed mastiche made from tree resin. Thousands of years and billions of gum chewers later, it appears that we still haven't figured out how to throw gum into a bin. Gum littering became such a problem in Singapore (which has the tightest litter laws in the world) that they banned chewing gum altogether. This has just been relaxed. Sugarless gum is now available on prescription from pharmacists. The penalty for smuggling gum into the country is one year in jail and a fine equivalent to £3,000.

www.parliament.uk/post/pn201.pdf
news.bbc.co.uk/1/hi/uk/4515413.stm

Gum cleaners seem to be fighting a losing battle. So another approach is being adopted. Gum boards are being fixed to lampposts and signposts where gum-chewers can stick their used gum. The idea is to make it fun to stick your gum. In Huddersfield in the North of England, the boards had issues of public concern where people were invited to stick their gum in a 'Yes' or a 'No' box. In Poole, they used pictures of celebrities whose popularity was in decline, such as Jeffrey Archer and Jeremy Beadle.

...solving a sticky problem

- **Don't be a litter lout.** If you must chew gum, throw it in the bin when you've finished with it.

- **Make your own 'target board'** for gum disposal. Use a large sheet of cardboard, metal or plywood, and devise a funny phrase or amusing picture to attract people's attention. Put it up at a local school or on the street. In doing this, you will hopefully make your streets a little cleaner and decrease your chances of finding a big wadge of double-mint stuck to the bottom of your fancy new shoes next time you look. If you've got the time, arrange to meet a headteacher and suggest this as a 'citizenship' project.

- **Buy a Wrigley share** and own a piece of the action. They own 50% of the chewing gum market. You could attend Annual General Meetings and share your ideas on gum disposal with the Chair. The company mails a gift box of chewing gum to all its shareholders each year as a Christmas present. Buy your share at: www.oneshare.com or www.frameastock.com

6 JUNE

fight FISTULA

My name is Talana Shabera. I'm an Ethiopian. I'm 14 years old. I was promised in marriage when I was three years old, betrothed at ten years old, and pregnant at 12. After three days of labour I was carried on a stretcher to a hospital where my baby died two hours later. The obstructed labour left me incontinent. I smell and I feel so ashamed.

Talana is suffering more than any women in the world should have to suffer. Her problem is fistula – a tearing of the soft tissue between the vagina and the bladder – which occurs during a lengthy and complicated childbirth. Over 9,000 women and girls in Ethiopia suffer this painful and undignified condition. But exact numbers are impossible to obtain, as women with fistula are often hidden away or abandoned.

As long as poverty continues, so will fistula. Many expectant mothers in Ethiopia, perhaps as many as 70%, live over two-days walk from the nearest hospital. They need access to obstetric care and a skilled attendant to be with them during the birth. ● While women in the West are having liposuctions, implants and cosmetic surgery to hide the signs of ageing, perhaps as many as 2 million women in the developing world are having their bodies destroyed, simply as a result of the lottery of where they happen to have been born.

The UNFPA's campaign to end fistula: www.endfistula.org
Safehands for Mothers: www.safehands.org
The Fistula Foundation, supporting the fistula hospital in Addis Ababa: www.fistulafoundation.org

Two feisty women

Dr Catherine Hamlin decided to do something about fistula. Forty years ago, she set up the Fistula Hospital in Addis Ababa. This has become a world centre of excellence. As well as trying to repair the damage of women with fistula, the hospital provides training for obstetricians and gynaecologists from all over the world.

Nancy Durrell McKenna is a photographer who has taken some wonderful photographs of pregnancy. She has founded Safehands for Mothers to do something for mothers who don't have access to proper obstetric care. Safehands will produce and distribute training materials for health professionals.

...a hidden problem

Participate in the Fistula Hospital's Love-a-Sister programme. Help one woman obtain free, safe surgery to repair her devastating injuries of fistula and re-build her life. A £250 contribution will pay for surgery and postoperative care. This is not much to repair a life. If you don't have the money, go out and raise it.

● **Celebrate your fundraising success by** downloading some of Nancy's wonderful photos from the Safehands website. Frame them and hang them on your wall.

JUNE 7

OCEAN DAY

Today is World Ocean Day, a chance to celebrate the rich diversity of life in the seas, to highlight their problems, and to focus on what is being done to promote a healthy and productive ocean and to conserve marine resources for future generations.

But ocean environments are under severe stress due to rising sea temperatures, over-fishing, destruction of coral reefs, the impact of cruise ships, entangled animals, marine debris, pollution, mercury-contamination, offshore drilling, unsustainable coastal development and many other factors. The basic problem is humankind's greed and lack of concern for what is a common resource.

Demand for seafood products has doubled over the last 30 years and the diets of 2.6 billion people now depend on fish as a source of animal protein. A quarter of the world's fish stocks are being over-fished, and half are being fished at their maximum biological capacity.

Fish is good for our brains, but we need to use our brains when it comes to choosing which fish to eat.

World Ocean Day: www.theoceanproject.org
Marine Conservation Society: www.mcsuk.org
Marine Stewardship Council: eng.msc.org

Choose your fish with care

The Marine Stewardship Council has developed an environmental standard for sustainable and well-managed fisheries, put together in consultation with scientists, fisheries experts, environmental organisations and other people with a strong interest in preserving fish stocks worldwide.

Fish caught using sustainable fishing practices and management are entitled to carry the MSC's distinctive blue eco-label, which reassures concerned consumers that what they are purchasing has been fished sustainably, and has not contributed to the environmental problem of overfishing.

...eat fish thoughtfully

🍄 **Buy a copy of the MCS Good Fish Guide**, available from their website, and find out which fish to eat, and which to avoid.

🍄 **Buy fish with the MSC blue label.**

🍄 **Help MCS campaign** for the setting up of Highly Protected Marine Reserves – sanctuaries for marine life from which no natural resources can be taken.

words without BORDERS

The smuggler passed the slope and walked on toward the minefield, measuring each of his steps with increasing care. Bluebells bloomed and blades of grass, flattened by the wind, spread across the ground, trying to hide themselves in the stone-filled meadow that ran up to the hilltop in a gentle slant, beyond which lay the cliffs and the pass. No minesweeper had come to this place; there were no barriers, no warning signs...

– the opening paragraph of *At the Borderline* by Sherko Fatah

Storytelling is as old as the human race. Cavemen illustrated their stories with rudimentary paintings on cave walls. Today we communicate our stories through newspapers, magazines, the internet, television, radio and CDs. Even aeroplanes sometimes write messages in the sky. ❦ Storytelling gives pleasure, stimulates thinking, connects us to real and imagined worlds, enlarges our vision and generates understanding. In a world full of ignorance about other peoples and cultures, writing produced by other cultures has an especially important role to play.

If a book is written in your own language, it is increasingly easy to access it via the internet. But if it is written in another language, it must first be translated. Today, 50% of all books translated are translated from English, but only 6% are translated into English. This disproportionate flow of information is a great loss to English readers.

Words without Borders: www.wordswithoutborders.org
The International Storytelling Centre: www.storytellingcenter.com

Words Without Borders is trying to address this problem. They are translating some of the world's best writing – selected and translated by a distinguished group of writers, translators and publishing professionals – and publishing these translations on the internet.

Our ultimate aim is to introduce exciting international writing to the general public – travellers, teachers, students, publishers, and a new generation of eclectic readers – by presenting international literature not as a static, elite phenomenon, but as a portal through which to explore the world.

The International Storytelling Centre sees storytelling as a vehicle for social change. They have a resource pack to show how to use stories and storytelling in preventing conflict, reconciling differences and building peace.

...read books in translation

Sign up to Words Without Borders to get their free e-newsletter.

Find a story from their library. Read it by yourself, or read it to somebody else. Hear about life in Africa, the Americas, Asia, Europe, the Middle East and the Pacific Rim.

Soon Words Without Borders will be setting up online reading group discussions – something to look forward to.

JUNE 9

OBESITY *a growing problem* ☺

The growing waistlines of Americans are eating into the profits of the airline industry. A study by the US Centre for Disease Control calculated that $275 million has to be spent each year on 1.3 billion more litres of fuel needed to carry the extra 10lbs weight that the average American gained during the 1990s. This adds an extra 3.8 million tons of carbon dioxide to annual greenhouse gas emissions.

Obesity is a major cause of disease, primarily heart disease and diabetes. And it is becoming a global problem. ☺ In the rich world, obesity is largely caused by lifestyle (increasing calorie intake and lack of exercise). The increasing quantity of processed foods means that fat and sugar now account for more than half the caloric intake, and consumption of refined grains has largely replaced that of whole grains. Snacking between meals is also becoming routine. ☺ In the developing world, the trend towards urban living and a Westernised diet is a significant factor. ☺ There are also cultural factors at work. For example, being overweight may be seen as a sign of power and success in countries where many people go short of food. In China, the one-child policy has created a generation of 'little emperors', spoiled rotten by their parents.

Check the shape you're in by using the calculator at: www.nhlbisupport.com/bmi

In the USA 28% of men and 33% of women are obese, and 64% of the adult population is overweight. Obesity levels are rising sharply, and are also increasing in Australia, Canada and Europe, although they are still lower than in the USA.

In South Africa (urban areas) 10% of men and 33% of women are obese.

In Brazil (urban areas) 8% of men and 33% of women are obese, more than double that of 22 years ago.

In Mexico, people now drink more Coca Cola than milk.

In China: 70 million people are overweight. In Beijing, 20% of children are obese.

...that needs reducing

If you are overweight or obese, here are some ways to get into better shape:

At work:

Get off the bus or train a few stops earlier and walk the rest of the way.
Go for a walk at lunchtime.
Use the stairs instead of the lift.
Go and speak to colleagues instead of using the phone or email.
Stand while on the phone.
Schedule exercise time into your day.

In your leisure time:

Plan outings and holidays that include exercise – walk, run, swim or fly a kite.
Dance for fun.
See the sights in a city by walking, jogging or cycling.

10 JUNE

search THE INTERNET

The internet has become a huge marketplace, where companies pay to have customers visit their websites. The companies pay a few pennies when visitors to their website click on text and image links. The total revenue generated from this adds up to around $14 billion per year. A number of services have been designed to direct some of this revenue to charity. Some benefit a pre-selected list of charities. Others generate money for any charity – which can include yours if you register. The amount you receive will depend on the amount of clicking by you and your supporters.

Magic Taxi is based on the search engine Yahoo. It supports 18 national charities in the UK, with 50% of its net revenue. Each day, a different charity is featured as beneficiary, or you can choose your favourite from amongst the 18.

Everyclick is based on the search engine Ask. Half the revenue is given to charity. If a site user does not select a specific charity, the income is used to benefit all charities registered with Everyclick.

CharityClick is also based on Ask. Any charity can register and get its supporters to raise money for it.

Magic Taxi: www.magictaxi.co.uk
Everyclick: www.everyclick.com
CharityClick: www.charityclicknow.com

With the click of a mouse

Each internet search you make through the website generates around 0.5p for charity. So this is how much your charity could earn if each supporter makes an average of two clicks per day:

Small charity with 100 supporters will get an estimated £375 per annum.

Medium charity with 1,000 supporters will get an estimated £3,750 per annum.

Large charity with 10,000 supporters will get an estimated £37,500 per annum.

It is a painless way to raise money for charity. The more people who search, the more money you raise.

...generate money for charity

👫 **Select a Search Engine** that offers this service, sign up and then start searching. Choose the service on the basis of how well the search engine will work for you, and whether you want to support your own charity or just pick one from a list or support the 'charity of the month'.

👫 **Send out an email** to all your supporters, and ask them to forward it on to their friends. Over the course of a year, and with lots of your supporters doing it, the amount you raise can really add up.

PUBLISH *yourself*

You can publish your own book for as little as £4! Lulu.com has combined the technology of print-on-demand, where printing presses are set up to print individual copies, with an internet-based system for turning your typescript into a final design, to create a really cheap and simple way to publish a book.

Lulu is a website that provides you with the tools to publish and sell books, music, comics, photographs and movies. It was founded in 2002 by Bob Young, co-founder of the Red Hat open-source software company. You, the author, retain complete control over content and design.

There is no set-up fee and no minimum order, but there are simple instructions for turning your manuscript into a book. Lulu manages the printing, delivery and customer service. You can take delivery of the books and sell them yourself. Or you can set your own royalty and use the Lulu website for marketing. At the end of each quarter, you will receive the royalties generated. Lulu will take a percentage from each transaction to cover its costs.

And Lulu is cheap. Here's an idea of the cost for a 128-page paperback book, 6 x 9 inches: a single printed copy costs £4.16; 50 copies cost £4.06 per copy; 500 copies cost £3.51 per copy.

Lulu: www.lulu.com

What's in the name?

Ever hear the phrase 'Boy, that's a real lulu?' Even if you haven't, think of the word Lulu as an old-fashioned term for a remarkable person, object or idea. Well, that's exactly what Lulu, the company, is. Think of us as an open marketplace for digital content – an on-demand publishing tool for books, e-books, music, images, movies and calendars.

– How Lulu describes itself

...do it on Lulu

- **Read** *the Publish-it-Yourself Handbook* by Bill Henderson, and be inspired by some of the extraordinary people who have done just that: www.amazon.com
- **Get your manuscript out of the drawer** where it has been gathering dust for years – or find it on your computer's hard drive. Give it an editorial once-over yourself, or get someone else to do so. (You need to be sure that it makes sense and is typo-free. Remember that *rubbish in = rubbish out.*)
- **Or write your soon-to-be a bestseller today** on a subject that you're passionate about. Then upload your manuscript onto Lulu and follow the instructions.

buy local EAT LOCAL

Food is travelling further and further, often hundreds or even thousands of miles from where it was produced to where it is consumed. This pollutes the atmosphere with greenhouse gases and other harmful emissions, and clogs up the highways with articulated lorries. But there are other problems too:

> **The local food chain** is fast disappearing. Family farms, local abattoirs, small processing plants, local food distribution systems and small shops are all finding that they are unable to compete in today's global market.

> **Centralisation of food distribution** has meant the loss of local distinctiveness — traditional varieties, and a sense of belonging to the community.

> **Money leaks out** from the local economy — and into the bank accounts of distant multinational food businesses.

Much of this is our fault. As consumers we always have a choice. If we use our choice positively to buy local, then shops will put more effort into stocking local produce.

Local Food Works: www.localfoodworks.org

Farmers' markets are markets where farmers, growers and producers from the local area sell their own produce directly to the public. All products sold will have been grown, reared, caught, brewed, pickled, baked, smoked or processed by the stallholder. They offer freshly-picked fruit and vegetables, though not necessarily organic produce. They usually offer meat, fish, cakes, pies, jams, chutneys, cheeses, flour, soups, drinks and other fare. Plus a chance to talk to the stallholder.

...reduce food miles

Some simple things to do which will reduce food miles and help regenerate the local food chain:

- Buy local whenever you can.
- For food that cannot be grown in your region, such as tea, coffee, bananas or chocolate, buy fairtrade products where these are available.
- Buy seasonal fresh produce as it becomes available.
- Wherever possible, buy from small, local shops and markets.
- Avoid products that have been air-freighted in.
- Write to your supermarket's head office — to the Managing Director — asking them to stock more locally grown and made produce. Ask smaller retailers to do the same. Ask local restaurants to feature local produce on their menus.
- Consult a local food directory to see who's growing or producing what in your locality. If there isn't one, why not produce one yourself.
- Grow your own food — organically if possible — in your back garden, on an allotment or community garden, or even in window boxes and gro-bags on the roof.
- Write to your MP asking for a clearer labelling system that shows the distance the food has travelled and the country or countries of origin.
- Ask publicly funded canteens (such as schools, hospitals, local authorities and prisons) to make a point of buying more local, seasonal and organic food.

JUNE 13

CAR *sharing*

The average car commuter in the UK drives 19 miles a day. Cutting that by half through car sharing would save 648 kg of carbon dioxide over one year, the same as that absorbed by 216 trees.

– Liftshare

Commuting to work? Driving your children to school? Going shopping? Going to town? Going to a football match? Driving abroad for business or pleasure? The chances are that there will be empty seats in your car. But other people might want to travel to roughly the same place at roughly the same time and could share the journey with you. Can you find them?

It makes financial sense to share the costs of a journey. It also makes good environmental sense, as it results in one less car trip, though it'll always be better for the environment if you walk, cycle or use public transport. ♣ If you're travelling by car, think about lift sharing. The internet is a great mechanism for linking people to share a journey. ♣ You could also consider car sharing, whereby people club together to jointly own and run a car.

The benefits of sharing a journey:

Saves money – you can save up to £1,000 a year.
Reduces the number of cars on the roads – less congestion, less pollution and fewer parking problems.
Is especially beneficial for people in rural areas.
Makes an enjoyable journey out of that boring slog to work in the morning.
Provides an alternative to owning your own car.

Liftshare, for sharing a ride in the UK: www.liftshare.org
National Liftshare Day: www.liftshare.co.uk/nlsd.asp
World CarShare Consortium: www.ecoplan.org/carshare
Carplus: www.carclubs.org.uk

Here are some simple rules for internet lift sharing:
Decide if you are prepared to travel with a member of the opposite sex.
Exchange telephone numbers and make arrangements over the phone, even if the first contact is by email.
Meet in a well-lit public place.
Give someone else your journey details plus contact details of who you are travelling with.
Take basic safety precautions, ask for car details – make, model, colour and registration number. Ask the driver to bring along a driving licence plus insurance and roadworthiness certificates.

...halve the impact

♣ **Just for the fun of it, go travelling** to celebrate National Liftshare Day. Log in to a liftshare website, and find somebody who is going somewhere interesting. Share a ride with them.

♣ **Start liftsharing.** Next time you have a spare seat in your car or want to go somewhere, share the ride.

donate **SMART CLOTHES**

Imagine you are down and out, or simply very poor. All the clothes you own are shabby. But you've managed to get a job interview, and you want to look your best. You've got a problem. You've got nothing nice to wear for your interview. This makes it less likely that you'll get the job. This is the Catch 22: no smart clothes, no job; no job, no money to buy smart clothes.

Dress for Success is an organisation that addresses this very problem. Women are referred to it by government agencies and other organisations, including homeless shelters, domestic violence shelters, immigration services and job training programmes. Each client receives one suit for a job interview and a second suit when she gets the job. The Dress for Success Professional Women's Group then provides ongoing support to help clients build a successful career.

Dress for Success: www.dressforsuccess.org

A story of success
Nancy Lublin used a $5,000 inheritance from her great-grandfather to start Dress for Success, and put a great idea into practice.

Dress for Success now provides interview suits, confidence boosts and career development to more than 45,000 women in over 73 cities each year.

Most of its branches are in the USA, but there are UK branches in London and Cardiff, as well as in New Zealand and Canada.

...help to dress for success

Dress for Success needs a supply of clothes. Donate new or nearly new (and clean) office clothes. They are particularly in need of clothes in larger sizes:
Coordinated, contemporary, interview-appropriate skirt and trouser suits
Beautiful, crisp blouses
Gorgeous blazers and jackets
Professional shoes

If you've got the time and energy, why not start a Dress for Success branch in your town or city. Their website tells you how.

Charity shops would love the things that Dress for Success can't use. Donate your old clothes, jewellery you no longer wear, decorative items you are fed up with and unwanted presents. They will convert these into cash for a good cause.

Buy as many of your clothes as possible at charity shops and become the new home for someone else's perfectly good clothes. You'll be saving money and supporting a charity. And you'll also be dressing distinctively rather than being a boring old follower of fashion!

JUNE 15

POVERTY *can be conquered*

One day our grandchildren will go to museums to see what poverty was like.

– Muhammad Yunus

Muhammad Yunus, a banker from Bangladesh, had an idea for eradicating poverty. He would lend money to really poor people using a simple formula. People would save regularly for a period of time, and then they would be able to get a loan. Each borrower would join a group of borrowers who would be jointly responsible for the loan. This would create peer pressure on the borrower to repay the loan, and would make defaults less likely. No collateral would be needed from the borrower.

Grameen, the organisation that he set up, now works in 43,000 villages across Bangladesh and gives loans to 2.8 million borrowers, 96% of whom are women. Over the years, it has lent more than US$4 billion to these borrowers, of which $3.6 billion has been repaid. The recovery rate is 99%. ♛ Borrowers own 93% of the bank; the remaining 7% is owned by the government. ♛ The idea of the Grameen Bank led to the development of a 'micro-credit industry' around the world, which lends to poor people to help them escape poverty.

International Year of Microcredit 2005: www.yearofmicrocredit.org
Grameen Bank: www.grameen-info.org
Make Your Mark: www.makeyourmark.org.uk

Good Gifts, supporting small businesses in the developing world: www.goodgifts.org

Aruma is a widow in Ethiopia who was struggling to feed her family. She was offered a loan to buy a goat, which then provided milk for her family plus some to sell. The goat produced some kids, and these were sold. Soon Aruma had saved enough money to buy a cow, which produced even more milk and money for her. She was a proud mother when her eldest son got a place at college – without the original loan, he would almost certainly have had to drop out of school to start earning money.

Didier is a young tailor in Benin. He could not get hold of the funds he needed to set up a tailoring workshop. He managed to get a micro-loan of $850, which took his equipment as security. Only a week after getting the loan, he was offered a contract to make ready-to-wear shirts. He has recruited two employees, and is well on the way to becoming a successful local entrepreneur.

...a small loan is first step

♛ **Support someone in the developing world** to start a micro-business. It might be taxi-driving, brewing, tailoring, vegetable growing, livestock. You choose – just go to the Good Gifts website.

♛ **Go to the Start Talking Ideas website** and find all the information and ideas you need to become an entrepreneur.

♛ **Start your own business with a £100 loan.** You come up with the business idea. You lend yourself the money. Find four friends who will all do exactly the same. You have 365 days to see who can make the most profit from their enterprise.

transform ARID LANDS

Semi-arid land in Africa is turning to desert, in part because of poor land and water management. 🌍 In areas where electricity is simply not available, the only fuel for cooking is wood. The daily search for wood is taking people further and further afield, and is resulting in whole areas being stripped of what meagre vegetation they had. Once the trees and scrub has gone, there is nothing to hold the topsoil in place. Any rain that falls quickly evaporates, the soil dries off and the wind simply blows it away.

Water needs to be carefully managed. In much of Africa rainfall is highly erratic. It is always possible that seasonal rain will just not arrive at all. And when it does arrive, much of it simply drains off into rivers, and flows out to sea. 🌍 If only that rainwater could be retained, it could be used during the dry season to increase food production. It would also have a positive impact on people's daily lives, as they would no longer have to walk long distances to fetch water, and the water itself would be cleaner.

One answer lies in small-scale 'sand dams', which an organisation called Excellent Development has been helping to build for over 20 years. Started in 1984 by 18-year-old Simon Maddrell, it has worked with communities in East Africa to construct 50 dams, and aims to make that 300 by 2010.

Excellent Development: www.excellentdevelopment.com

SOS Sahel working with the Africa Drylands alliance in Mali, Niger, Ethiopia, Kenya and Sudan to reclaim the desert: www.sahel.org.uk

A sand dam is a reinforced concrete wall, 2 to 4 metres high, built across a seasonal river bed. A pipe is laid through the dam, and extended 20 metres back upstream. When the seasonal rains occur, sand is washed downstream and collects behind the dam. It traps water within it, which seeps out and runs through the pipe long after the soil in neighbouring valleys has dried up.

As well as helping to construct the dam, local people work to improve the land behind it, terracing the hillsides to improve water and soil conservation. The extra water enables them to grow vegetables, which improve their diets. They also grow trees in nurseries, eventually planting them out to further rehabilitate the semi-arid land.

...help build a sand dam

Excellent Development has teamed up with Virgin Wines to offer you £20 off your first order of a case of wine, with Virgin Wines kindly contributing £5 to Excellent Development's work.

Visit: www.excellentdevelopment.com/wine.php to find out how to take advantage of this special offer and turn wine into water!

And if you don't live in the UK, just go out and buy a bottle of wine and drink a toast to Simon Maddrell and his vision.

RECHARGE *batteries*

Batteries are so much part of our daily lives that we rarely think about them until they need replacing. And that's precisely the time that we do need to think about them, because we have to address the problem of what to *do* with them, and what to replace them with. 🌳 Most of us just chuck them in the bin without thinking about it, but we need to get into the habit of recycling them.

Around 22,000 tonnes of batteries are sold annually in the UK and almost all of them end up in a landfill site. Many batteries contain some very nasty chemicals, such as cadmium, which can poison the environment. They also include zinc, which could be re-used if the battery were recycled. 🌳 Battery use is increasing, which means that battery waste is becoming an ever-bigger problem. The situation is similar in many other countries around the world.

Many children's toys and games are battery powered, which is why it is great to hear of schoolchildren in West Somerset campaigning to have collection points for used batteries in all the schools in their area. If they can do it, so can you.

Find out everything you need to know about batteries at:
www.batteryuniversity.com

The different types of rechargeable battery:
   Lead-acid: heavy but cheap; used for car batteries and for equipment where weight is not an issue, such as wheelchairs.
   Nickel-cadmium: long-life, used for power tools; contain toxic matter. Avoid if possible.
   Nickel-metal-hydride: used in mobile phones and laptops; contain no toxic matter.
   Lithium-ion and Lithium-ion-polymer: high energy and low weight; used in lightweight laptop and notebook computers and for mobile phones.
   Reusable alkaline: cheap rechargeable batteries used for torches and other consumer devices.

...don't let energy go to waste

🌳 **Reduce the environmental impact of battery use:**
   Use rechargeable batteries wherever possible. Some batteries can be recharged up to 1,000 times. But you will need a battery charger.
   Purchase Nickel Metal Hydride (NiMH) batteries in preference to Nickel Cadmium (NiCd) batteries, as these are much less toxic.
   Never throw used batteries away with your household rubbish, as some of their ingredients, especially cadmium, are highly toxic.
   Recycle used batteries instead.

🌳 **Ask your employer or your school or college to provide a battery bin** for collecting and recycling used batteries. If they won't, then build one yourself. Make it bright and colourful; produce a leaflet alongside it, explaining why it is important to recycle batteries. The battery bin should be situated in a prominent place.

🌳 **Find out if your local council does anything about battery recycling.** Some do. But if yours doesn't yet, then use your lobbying skills to persuade them that they really should.

18 JUNE

put yourself in PRISON

Please, use your liberty to promote ours.

– Aung San Suu Kyi, opposition leader in Burma and Nobel prizewinner

Burma is ruled by a brutal dictatorship, which uses murder, torture and rape to keep 50 million citizens under its thumb. Hence its nickname: 'The Prison without Bars'. ♪ The Burmese government has incarcerated over 1,000 political prisoners, 38 of whom are elected Members of Parliament. Millions of people have been forced into slave labour. Living conditions are horrendous. Yet the borders are sealed, and no citizen can leave.

Aung San Suu Kyi is the face of hope for the Burmese people. She is a renowned advocate for democracy. She is also the world's only Nobel Peace Prize recipient to be kept under house arrest. ♪ For decades she has been campaigning for liberation for the Burmese people from the Burmese government. She is the leader of the National League for Democracy, the legitimately elected leader of Burma, and she is being held prisoner. ♪ Today is Aung San Suu Kyi's birthday, and has been designated 'Arrest Yourself Day'. People all over the world are invited to throw a 24-hour house party, to draw attention to her struggle.

Aung San Suu Kyi's website: www.dassk.com
US Campaign for Burma: www.uscampaignforburma.org

Aung San Suu Kyi's father, General Aung San, led his country's fight for independence from the UK in the 1940s and was killed in 1947. She studied at Oxford, married and had two sons, but returned to Burma in 1988 to tend her critically-ill mother. She became involved in the pro-democracy movement, which was gaining momentum, despite the murder of thousands of demonstrators by the 'State Law and Order Restoration Council' (SLORC). In the 1990 general election the party she headed, the National League for Democracy, won 80% of the vote, but the SLORC refused to recognise the result, and arrested her. Since then, she has been under almost constant house arrest, speaking in public on only a few occasions. She was awarded the Nobel Peace Price in 1991.

...campaign for Burma

♪ **Arrest yourself and your friends in your own house for 24 hours** to draw attention to the situation in Burma. Why not ask everybody to give £10 and use the party to raise money for the international struggle for freedom for the people of Burma. Have a great time, but make sure that you also tell the local media what you are planning.

♪ **Send a birthday card to Aung San Suu Kyi.** Send your card to the Campaign at 612 K St., NW Suite #401, Washington, DC 20006, USA to arrive by 1 June; the cards will be delivered in person on 19 June.

REFUGEES *seeking asylum*

Everyone has the right to escape persecution in their own country and to seek asylum in another. That principle is enshrined in the Universal Declaration of Human Rights (1948), reinforced by the 1951 Geneva Convention. More than 21 million people are living in another part of their country, or in a different country, because life became unsustainable at home. Many fled from conflict, suffering rape, torture, and the deaths of family members. But instead of finding the personal and economic safety they sought, they are destitute and relying on the support of international agencies.

Some people migrate because they are unable to find work, and therefore food, in their own country. Often they become illegal immigrants – hidden from sight and open to exploitation. Some have paid large sums of money for travel arrangements and work permits, and have been shipped illegally to a country where they are being kept as 'debt slaves' and forced to work for low wages. Girls and women may have arrived thinking they would be domestic servants, but end up working as prostitutes. ⅋ As parts of the world become uninhabitable through climate change and pressure on natural resources, the number of environmental migrants is bound to increase.

STAR: www.star-network.org.uk
Forced Migration Online, information on human displacement: www.forcedmigration.org
UN High Commission for Refugees (UNHCR): www.unhcr.ch
Refugee Action: www.refugee-action.org.uk

Facts and figures

Refugees are people outside their country who cannot return owing to a well-founded fear of persecution. Asylum seekers are those seeking recognition as bona fide refugees to obtain legal protection and material assistance. The UNHCR estimated that there were 8.4 million refugees and 773,500 asylum seekers in the world at the end of 2006.

The richer nations stress the need to curb the inflow of refugees, but it is the poorer countries, least able to afford it, who are receiving the greatest number of refugees.

Origin of major refugee populations and where they are living:

Afghanistan	1,908,100	Pakistan, Iran, Germany, Netherlands, UK
Sudan	693,300	Chad, Uganda, Kenya, Ethiopia,
Burundi	438,700	Tanzania, DR Congo, Rwanda, S Africa, Zambia
DR Congo	430,600	Tanzania, Zambia, Congo, Rwanda, Uganda
Somalia	394,800	Kenya, Yemen, UK, USA, Ethiopia
Vietnam	358,200	China, Germany, France, USA, Switzerland
Palestine	349,700	Saudi, Egypt, Iraq, Libya, Algeria
Iraq	262,100	Iran, Germany, Netherlands, Syria, UK

...support them

Do something positive to help people who have fled to your country. The very least you can do is to challenge the negative attitudes sometimes expressed towards refugees, asylum seekers and immigrants.

STAR is a student-run campaign for refugees in the UK. They suggest you look through your local/national newspaper to find articles about refugees or asylum seekers. Take a look at the tenor of the article and the language used. Is it fair and non-prejudiced? If it's not, write a letter to the Editor making your views known.

build a SOLAR COOKER

A few years ago, I woke up to the fact that half of the world's people must burn wood or dried dung in order to cook their food. It came as quite a shock to me, especially as I learned of the illnesses caused by breathing smoke day in and day out, and the environmental impacts of deforestation – not to mention the time spent by people (mostly women) gathering sticks and dung to cook their food.

And yet, many of these billions of people live near the equator, where sunshine is abundant and free. As a University Professor of Physics with a background in energy usage, I set out to develop a means of cooking food and sterilising water using the free energy of the sun.

– Steven E Jones, Brigham Young University

Using a solar-powered cooker in a land where the sun shines nearly every day has to be a win-win situation.

Here are some of the reasons why a solar cooker is a good thing:

It helps prevent deforestation and desertification. In developing countries, the majority of rural people cook over wood fires or stoves. The year-round removal of so much vegetation contributes to soil erosion.

It saves the time of the women whose job it is to collect the firewood, and might even free up young girls so that they can attend school.

There is no smoke pollution, reducing the risk of the respiratory disease that affects women and their children who spend so much of their time breathing in the smoke from open fires.

It reduces injuries especially.

It reduces carbon dioxide emissions and makes a small contribution to the reduction in greenhouse gases.

It can be used to produce safe drinking water as well as to prepare food, thus reducing the risk of disease.

The sun's energy is free.

Plans for building a solar cooker can be got from: solarcooking.org

There are three types of solar cooker:

Box style, which works like a mini-greenhouse.

Panel style, which directs sunlight into the cooking area using reflecting panels.

Parabolic, which focuses an intense beam of sunlight on the bottom of the cooking pot.

All can be made using simple materials: aluminium foil, cardboard, polythene, or, in the case of the one shown here, an inflated car inner tube, a sheet of wood, an aluminium saucepan and lid painted black on the outside, and a sheet of glass.

...cook your dinner for free

- 🌐 **Build a solar cooker yourself.**
- 🌐 **Organise a solar-cooked lunch party** for your friends on a sunny day.
- 🌐 **Become a passionate advocate for solar cooking** and do what you can to spread the word.

GLOBAL *warming*

It's taken the world just a few years to wake up to the threat of global warming, but it may already be too late. Many of the effects of a warming world are creating positive feedback loops. For example, as the surface-ice melts in polar regions' warmer summers, sunlight is absorbed by the pools of water and exposed rock, whereas the ice that existed before reflected it.

Water Cooler: worldcoolers.org
20 actions to Stop Global Warming: www.stopglobalwarming.org

Mark Lynas's book, *Six Degrees*, provides scenarios of what might happen with each further degree of temperature rise. Mark believes we can halt the warming process at around 2 degrees.

One degree:
- Deserts invade the high plains of the US causing severe agricultural loss.
- The Gulf Stream switches off, plunging Britain and Europe into icy winter cold.
- Coral reefs are wiped out.
- Island nations submerge under rising seas.

Two degrees
- Greenland tips into irreversible melt, accelerating sea-level rise.
- Polar bears and other ice-dependent marine animals in the Arctic become extinct.
- Declining snowfields threaten water supplies in California.
- A third of species face extinction.

Three degrees
- A permanent El Nino grips the Pacific, causing weather chaos around the world.
- Heat and drought cause the world to tip into net food deficit (people will starve).
- The whole Amazonian ecosystem collapses in a conflagration of fire and destruction.

Four degrees
- West Antarctic ice sheet potentially collapses; sea levels rise by 5 metres as a result.
- Southern Europe desertifies and all glaciers disappear in the Alps.
- Permafrost melt in Siberia releases billions of tons of CO_2 and methane, spiralling global warming upwards.

Five degrees
- The Earth is hotter than at any time in 55 million years.
- Methane hydrate is released from beneath the oceans, sparking tsunamis in coastal regions and pushing global warming into an unstoppable spiral.
- Much of the world becomes uninhabitable.

Six degrees
- Mass extinction.
- Huge fireballs sweep the planet as methane hydrate fireballs ignite.
- Seas turn anoxic (without oxygen) and release poisonous hydrogen sulphide.
- Humanity's survival is in question.

...must be reversed

🌳 **Read Six Degrees by Mark Lynas.**

🌳 **Become a Water Cooler!** Join an online community to share and receive information about global warming.

22 JUNE

recycle your BIKE

Merlin Matthews was such a genius at fixing everyone's bikes when he was at university that he earned the nickname 'Dr Bike'. He would fix bikes in exchange for beers on Friday evenings. He was even approached for advice about starting up a bike factory in Haiti. This made him realise that there are lots of bikes being thrown away that could be fixed. ● He decided to find a way of collecting old bikes in the UK and sending them to Haiti, thinking that he would be able spend most of his time in Haiti's sunshine running a bicycle repair workshop. Sadly, he realised that his time would be better spent in the UK doing the fundraising, sorting out the bikes and shipping them. ● He linked up with Institute for Transportation & Development Policy, International Bicycle Fund and Bikes Not Bombs in the USA, which had similar ideas, and as a result decided that, since US organisations are better able to help in Latin America, he should to focus on supplying bicycles to Africa.

The charity he started, Re~Cycle, has so far donated over 14,000 bikes to Africa. Many people there have to trek four hours every day just to get drinking water, or walk 11 miles to get to school – and another 11 to get back home. A bicycle can make the difference between life and death, or between a child gaining an education, or not. The charity also works with local African groups, teaching people how to repair and maintain their bicycles.

Check out these bike recycling groups:
Re~Cycle: www.re-cycle.org

Bike Recycling, a network of UK bike recycling groups: www.bikerecycling.org.uk

Bikes for the World and Bikes not Bombs both donate bikes from the USA to the developing world: www.bikesfortheworld.org and www.bikesnotbombs.org

And these organisations promoting sustainable transport solutions globally:
International Bicycle Fund: www.ibike.org

Institute for Transportation & Development Policy: www.itdp.org

Can you provide any of the help needed to recycle bikes internationally?
Storage space for collected bikes – needs to be 100% secure, but infrequent access required.
Contacts in the haulage industry and the shipping world – to get good discounts.
Containers (40 ft or 20 ft) at the end of their seaworthy life – donated to be used for secure storage or turned into a cycle repair workshop in Africa.
Second-hand bikes, parts and tools (all donated, of course).

...send it to Africa

● **Allow your old bicycle to improve someone's life in Africa.** Go and dig it out from behind the broken fridge and donate it. Someone in Africa will be very grateful.

JUNE 23

SLOW FOOD *now*

The Slow Food movement was founded in 1988 by Carlo Petrini, an Italian journalist and activist. He was protesting against the opening of a McDonald's next to the Spanish Steps in Rome, seeing it as part of a rapidly spreading global fast-food culture. He believed that the world was forgetting the joys of good food and leisurely dining.

Eating something delicious will help sustain biodiversity by preserving food plants now under threat from a food industry demanding mass production of foods that look good (rather than taste good) and which have long shelf lives. The pleasure we take in eating good food is itself a small but meaningful political act.

Eco-gastronomy isn't going to save the world, but if you can bring food politics and the pleasure of eating together, the Vesuvian apricot and Delaware Bay oyster won't be the only species to benefit.

Slow Food: www.slowfood.com

The Slow Food Manifesto:

Our century, which began and has developed under the insignia of industrial civilisation, first invented the machine and then took this as its life model. We are enslaved by speed and have all succumbed to the same insidious virus – Fast Life – which disrupts our habits, pervades the privacy of our homes and forces us to eat Fast Foods. To be worthy of the name, Homo sapiens (Latin for 'thinking man') should rid himself of speed before it reduces all of us to a species in danger of extinction.

A firm defence of quiet material pleasure is the only way to oppose the universal folly of Fast Life. Suitable doses of guaranteed sensual pleasure and slow, long-lasting enjoyment should hopefully preserve us from the contagion of the multitudes who mistake frenzy for efficiency.

Our defence should begin at the table with Slow Food. Let us rediscover the flavours and savours of regional cooking and banish the degrading effects of Fast Food. In the name of productivity, Fast Life has changed our way of being and threatens our environment and our landscapes. So Slow Food is now the only truly progressive answer. It guarantees a better future. But it is an idea that needs plenty of supporters in order to turn this (slow) motion into an international movement, with the little snail as its symbol.

...make it last

Organise a dinner party for your seven best friends.

☺ **Ask them all to prepare and bring something delicious** using only the best ingredients plus a bottle of something special. Plan the menu together or leave things to chance.

☺ **Linger over your dinner**, the longer the better. Have a really great time. Repeat as often as desired.

24 JUNE

put theories to **THE TEST**

If you saw someone pouring $1.4bn into encouraging people to eat apples, which is the amount McDonald's spends in a single year on radio, television and print advertising, you'd see apple sales go through the roof. Suddenly, you'd have Justin Timberlake on TV going: 'Man, I love apples! You should eat some apples too! Look at me − I'm running, and I'm eating apples.'
− Morgan Spurlock

Morgan Spurlock, a 33-year-old New York film-maker, was watching the news at his parents' home in West Virginia in November 2002, when he saw that two teenagers from New York were suing McDonald's for making them obese. He decided to test out the teenagers' claim that eating fast food could seriously damage your health, and film the process. ☺ For a whole month he would eat nothing but McDonald's food: for breakfast, lunch and dinner. There were three ground rules:

1 He had to eat every item on the McDonald's menu at least once.
2 He could only eat what was available over the counter (no special orders).
3 He had to order a SuperSize meal whenever a counter assistant offered him this option.

He would record the state of his health prior to this new diet and afterwards. The outcome was SuperSizeMe, an award winning 98-minute film.

In the first week he put on 4kgs. After a month he'd added a total of 11kg. His cholesterol level rose by 65 points and was 33% higher than when he started. His doctor also suggested that this diet of fast food was causing serious liver damage. It took Spurlock 14 months to return to his former physical condition.

Spurlock's film challenges the power of the huge food corporations to determine what we eat. It is not just their menus but their marketing clout, and the impact that this has on lifestyles and attitudes, which seems to be leading to an epidemic of obesity.

SuperSizeMe: supersizeme.com

Industry response
Since the first showing of the film SuperSizeMe, McDonald's has phased out its SuperSize meals and is testing a Go-Active Happy Meal with a salad, bottle of water and free pedometer!
But consumer demand seems insatiable. Hardees has launched its Monster Thickburger in the USA with 1,420 calories and 107 grammes of fat per portion. It consists of 2 slabs of Angus beef (664 calories) and 4 rashers of bacon (150 calories) with 3 slices of processed cheese (186 calories) and mayonnaise (160 calories) in a sesame seed bun (230 calories) spread with butter (30 calories). Throw in a portion of fries and a carbonated drink, and it's a day's calorie intake on a plate – a 'monument to decadence' and 'not a burger for tree-huggers', says Hardees.

...wise up, don't fatten up

☺ **Complain to the Advertising Standards Authority** (which oversees advertising to see that it is 'legal, decent, honest and truthful') if you see any advertising **on TV and in magazines** that is obviously untrue. For the advertising codes of practice and how to complain: www.asa.org.uk.

☺ **If there is something you feel needs testing,** test it out and see what happens.

JUNE 25

TORURE *is endemic*

If we fail to do anything about torture, we condone it.

– Michael Palin

Beatings, electrocutions, being suspended for hours, mock drownings, sleep deprivation, rape... The ingenuity of humans to think up ways of torturing their fellow humans is limitless. ✿ Room 101 was dreamt up by George Orwell for his novel *1984*, as the place where each person confronted his or her own worst nightmare. For Winston Smith, the hero of the novel, it was rats. In Room 101, Smith had a cage containing starving rats strapped to his face until he 'confessed' that he loved Big Brother. ✿ Would you have been able to hold out? Or would you, like Smith, have 'confessed'. What would be your breaking point?

Horrendous stories are published almost daily about people being tortured. Don't run away from them. Often, people have had to go through a second form of torture, just to recount and relive their story. As a tribute to the courage they have shown in standing up for what they believe in, we can at least do them the honour of listening to them.

Medical Foundation for the Care of Victims of Torture: www.torturecare.org.uk

World Organisation Against Torture, an international coalition fighting arbitrary detention and torture: www.omct.org

The Wikipedia article on torture, with lots of information on torture methods: en.wikipedia.org/wiki/Torture

Elizabeth is a 21-year-old student from Zimbabwe. Early in the morning, a group of men, some in Zanu-PF t-shirts, barged their way in to her house. A black hood, drawn tightly at the neck, was placed over her head and she was taken away, detained for two days, beaten and raped, and questioned about her political activities. All she had done was to participate in the youth section of a pro-democracy movement opposing the President.

Edwin, from an English-speaking area of Cameroon, was 15 when he was caught participating in a student demonstration protesting against plans to scrap the Anglo-Saxon system of education. He was held for three weeks, beaten, kicked and whipped with the buckled end of a belt. Undeterred, Edwin joined an opposition group and co-founded the Student Parliament. His university branded him a dissident and refused to let him do postgraduate studies. At one protest he was arrested by paramilitary gendarmes, had his skull split by a rifle butt and was dragged naked along the ground. Beatings have left him deaf in one ear.

...do something about it

The Medical Foundation for the Care of Victims of Torture helps over 3,000 people a year with practical assistance, medical treatment and psychotherapeutic support.

✿ Support the Foundation by torturing yourself. Identify your worst fear and resolve to face it head on. You might, for example, be afraid of heights. Arrange to do a charity parachute jump to raise money for the Foundation. They'll provide an Action Pack telling you how to do it.

✿ If you're not up to that, try ethical banking. Open a Medical Foundation Saver Account at Triodos Bank. They will donate 0.25% of your average account balance each year to the Foundation and you can choose to donate all or part of your interest.

start your own SCHOOL

If you are planning for one year, plant rice. If you are planning for ten years, plant trees. If you are planning for 100 years, plant education.

– Chinese proverb

Only 37 out of 155 developing countries have universal primary education and have managed to enrol all school-age children in a school, and to keep them at school until they have received a rudimentary education. This is helping to meet Millennium Development Goal No. 3: to ensure that, by 2015, children everywhere, boys and girls alike, will be able to complete a full course of primary schooling. Another 32 countries look likely to achieve this goal by 2015. But in 70 countries, more needs to be done.

Ethiopia is a country that is still trying to address the problem. Nearly two-thirds of Ethiopians cannot read or write. But with more than half the people in the country under 15 years old, there is an opportunity to rectify this. Primary school is free, and is supposedly mandatory, but fewer than half of all children ever begin school and only one in ten continue to the eighth grade. It is also normal for a class to have up to 100 children, making teaching and learning very difficult indeed.

Asfaw Yemiru believes that education is the only way for the poor to achieve a better life. When still only 14 years old, he opened a school for street children, outdoors under a big oak tree. That was in 1957. Four years later, he built the Asere Hawariat School for 2,000 children (classes 1 to 5). In 1972 he opened the Moya School for 2,000 children (classes 6 to 8), where children learn practical and vocational skills as well as the formal curriculum, and their education is still free of charge. School books are also free in Asfaw's schools, and students do not have to wear a uniform.

Asra Hawariat School: www.asrahawariat.org.uk
School of St Jude: www.schoolofstjude.co.tz

Fighting poverty through education

After finishing university, a young Australian, Gemma Sisia, travelled to Uganda to teach for three years. On her return, Gemma started taking $10 out of her pay packet each week to sponsor some Ugandan children she had met. Soon her family and friends were also sponsoring children's education.

This was the starting point for Gemma to build and run a school – St Jude's, near Arusha in Tanzania – which now has 850 pupils. Around 90 percent receive free education, thanks to local and international sponsors.

...one class at a time

Go to Africa, and help start a school – just like Asfaw and Gemma did. But if you can't do that, then think about supporting the costs of one child. Girls are especially in need as they have fewer opportunities. Why not support a child at Asfaw's or Gemma's school?

JUNE 27

RESPONSIBLE *travel*

Responsible travel conserves the environment and improves the well-being of local people. By being responsible you are likely to get a little bit more out of your travels – as well as putting something back.

Here are some suggestions from Responsible Travel on to how to approach travel to foreign countries in a way that will bring benefits to the country, without diminishing the self-respect of its people.

Read up on the countries you plan to visit. The welcome will be warmer if you take an interest and speak even a few words of the local language.

Think small when booking a holiday. For example, stay in bed and breakfasts, village houses and locally owned accommodation, benefiting local families.

Travel like Gandhi, with simple clothes, open eyes and an uncluttered mind.

Ask to see your tour operator's responsible travel policy.

Help the local economy by buying local produce rather than imported goods.

Bear in mind that a small amount saved when bargaining to buy an item, could be extremely significant to the seller.

Recognise cultural differences. The people in the country you are visiting may have different time concepts and thought patterns from your own. This does not make them inferior, only different. Respect local cultures, traditions and holy places.

Cultivate the habit of asking questions and discover the enrichment of seeing a different way of life through other people's eyes.

Use public transport, hire a bike or walk where convenient. You'll meet local people and get to know the place much better.

Use water sparingly. Local people may not have sufficient clean water for their needs.

Find out where locals go when they have time off. Visit the main tourist sites, but get off the tourist trail too.

Don't discard litter, take it home with you. Waste disposal is a major expense in poorer countries.

Ask permission before you photograph people. In some cultures it can cause offence.

Do not buy products made from endangered species, hard woods, shells from beach traders, or ancient artefacts (which have probably been stolen).

Take small gifts from home as gifts for your hosts. Ask your tour operator for suggestions.

Spend time reflecting on your experiences. Try to deepen your understanding. Enjoy the memories.

For a more detailed explanation of sustainable tourism, see:
www.uneptie.org/pc/tourism/sust-tourism/home.htm

International Ecotourism Society: www.ecotourism.org
Responsible Travel: www.responsibletravel.com

...a guide to good practice

Travel more responsibly next time. Why would you want to do otherwise?

28 JUNE

some more GREAT IDEAS

In compiling this book, we invited people to submit ideas for ways of changing the world. Here is a selection of those we received, but did not have space to give them their own page:

Campaign to get empty housing back in use. Do a survey. Think about who might need it. Homeless people? Asylum seekers and refugees? Students? Visitors and tourists? It's doing no good remaining empty.

Organise a carnival to kick racism out of the community. Celebrate the diversity of all the different peoples who live in your neighbourhood.

Do a litter walk with some friends. Pick a mile of road or beach, and pick up all the litter you find. Wear heavy-duty gardening gloves. Take great care of sharp objects (including discarded syringes). Start a 'Stop Litter' campaign.

Make a banner to promote an issue horizontally or vertically, and hang it up.

Befriend an elderly person. Have tea with them, do their shopping, tend their garden. Share experiences from the past and the present. Collect their stories of life long ago.

Hold a swap-shop party. Everyone brings ten things to swap for something they like better. Everyone leaves with ten new things.

Get people in your office to stop printing out emails. This could save up to 40% of office paper usage.

Make recycled paper. It's fun and it makes great gifts. All you need are scraps and a blender.

Organise a community-wide 'I have a dream' contest to find the best ideas in your community for addressing some of its key problems and opportunities.

Organise a Talk-to-your-Neighbours day in your neighbourhood. Or just invite your neighbours in for a cup of tea.

Create a catalogue that features locally made items, to stimulate the local economy.

Set up a coffee shop in your neighbourhood that is cheap, fairtrade and healthy. Fill it with posters, publications and music on how to change the world. This could be the best franchise idea since Starbucks!

Use pavement chalk as a protest tool – or just to brighten up the street. Create a floor mural. Unlike paint, chalk will wash away with the next rains.

Petition Mr Kipling to reduce cake packaging. Do a survey of food packaging. Start a campaign to get manufacturers to reduce the amount they use.

Do something with a pumpkin! After Halloween, pumpkins go to waste. But there are many things you could do wth them. Why not arrange a pumpkin soupfest? Or a competition for the best pumpkin jam? Or even a prize for turning one into Cinderella's coach?

Send your great ideas to us: www.365act.com

...keep them coming

🖐 **Take one of these ideas and make it happen.**

🖐 **Or think of a better idea and send it to us.**

WATER *purification*

The human right to water entitles everyone to sufficient, safe, ...
accessible and affordable water for personal and domestic uses.

– The Right to Water, 2002

About 1.1 billion people do not have access to safe drinking water – that is at least a third of people in developing countries. Two-thirds of these people live in Asia. In Sub-Saharan Africa, 42% of the population does not have access to a clean safe drinking-water supply. ☺ This lack of clean water supply together with no proper sanitation facilities, causes serious health problems. The main dangers are diarrhoea and cholera. Together these kill 1.8 million people each year, 90% of whom are children under five years old.

One of the UN's Millennium Development Goals is to halve, by 2015, the proportion of people who do not have access to safe drinking water and basic sanitation. The UN has declared 2005 – 2015 as the International Decade for Action, in order to provide a greater focus on water-related issues under the slogan 'Water for Life'.

There is a simple practical technology for purifying water in emergencies (such as the post-tsunami period) as well as for everyday use. It's called SODIS, which stands for solar disinfection, and it is being promoted by Fundación Sodis in Latin America and by the Solaqua Foundation in other parts of the world. ☺ SODIS is a simple alternative to boiling water (which consumes firewood) and chlorination (which requires the availability of chemicals and also adversely affects the water's taste).

Solaqua Foundation: www.sodis.ch/Text2002/T-Howdoesitwork.htm
UNESCO Water Portal: www.unesco.org/water

This is how SODIS works:
    Get hold of a transparent plastic bottle. Wash well before first-time use. Use PolyEthyleneTerephtalate (PET) plastic bottles rather than PolyVinylChloride (PVC). Whereas PET bottles smell sweet when burnt, PVC bottles often have a bluish tinge, and produce pungent smoke.

    Fill the bottle three-quarters full with water from a local water source such as a stream or river. The water should not be too muddy. Shake to aerate the water – the dissolved oxygen helps in the purification process. Then fill completely and screw on the cap.

Place the bottle on a corrugated metal roof in strong sunlight for one full day. The heating of the water and the Ultra-Violet (UV-A) radiation together destroy the micro-organisms which cause water-borne diseases.

Pour into a cup and enjoy!

...Do-It-Yourself

☺ **Try the SODIS process for yourself,** as an act of solidarity with those who have no alternative.

☺ **Share the technology** with anyone you think might be interested.

set up a **CO-OP**

In 1844, 28 craftsmen in Rochdale pooled their money to open a store that sold basic commodities such as flour, oatmeal, butter, sugar and candles. These 'Rochdale Pioneers' – Miles Ashworth (a flannel weaver), James Bamford (a shoemaker), John Bent (a tailor) and the others – were the founders of the co-operative movement. They wanted to achieve fair prices for the essential goods they needed, and they wanted to ensure that the products they were buying were not being adulterated, which was common practice at the time.

Co-operatives involve people working together, using the economies of scale for mutual financial benefit. Co-operatives belong to the members, who control trading practice and distribution of any profits (as a dividend), and are run democratically – one member, one vote. ✋ Today there are 'producer Co-operatives' jointly marketing members' products, 'consumer co-operatives' through which members jointly purchase what they need, 'credit unions', in which members pool their savings and obtain cheaper credit, 'giving co-operatives' through which members pool their charitable donations to give bigger amounts to the causes they wish to support, 'housing co-operatives' that build and manage housing on behalf of owner-tenants, 'school-run co-operatives' that hire a minibus for the journey to school, and even 'baby-sitting co-operatives' whereby young parents share babysitting. ✋ These co-operatives can be formally constituted, or they can be run informally.

Co-op On Line: www.cooponline.coop
International Co-operative Information Centre: www.uwcc.wisc.edu
Amul, an Indian milk-processing plant: www.amul.com
The National Dairy Development board: www.nddb.org

Milk co-operatives in India

Dr Verghese Kurien is known as the 'father of the white revolution' in India. He started a milk processing plant, so small producers could get a decent price for their milk. This has now grown into Amul, which collects, processes and sells 5 million litres of milk a day on behalf of 2.36 million producers. The National Dairy Development Board was set up under Dr Kurien's leadership to spread the principles of co-operation in the dairy industry across India. Dr Kurien has done more to transform rural livelihoods in India than almost anyone else.

...people working together

Start your own co-operative. It only needs three of you to get started. Decide what you want to do. Here are two simple ideas:
- ✋ **A dog-walking co-operative,** in which each person taking turns to walk everyone's dogs.
- ✋ **A food co-operative,** with each member going to the wholesale market once a week to purchase fresh fruit and vegetables.

Work out your rules. These set out what members are going to get out of it and what they are going to put in (time, skills, money, membership fee), as well as how it is going to operate (membership, meetings, responsibilities). This constitution should be signed by all the members.

MAD *pride*

☺

Mad Pride was formed in 1997 and is comprised of ex-psychiatric patients and enlightened others. Sick of the 'loony' tag, outraged by increasing stigma and legislative attempts to nab us and jab us, we campaign for urgent issues, risking our necks and the wrath of our shrinks.

– Mad Pride website

First there was Black Pride; then there was Gay Pride; now there's Mad Pride. All have in common the idea of people celebrating who they are and their differences, and campaigning for justice and equal human rights.

MindFreedom is at the centre of the psychiatric survivors' liberation movement. They have declared July as Mad Pride Month, when events are organised in Canada, France, the UK and the USA to promote self-determination for those deemed 'mad', and to highlight human rights abuses of people diagnosed with psychiatric disabilities.

MindFreedom is campaigning to put an end to involuntary electric shock and drug treatment. It seeks a voice for mentally ill people in shaping the treatments and services provided for them. It documents the oral histories of survivors, in order to assist others and to act as a clarion call for change.

For Mad Pride Month 2005, activists pushed a psychiatric bed on wheels from Bradford to Manchester, a distance of 33 miles. A mannequin was strapped to the bed, held down by four-point restraints in order to highlight psychiatric abuse.

Mad Pride: www.x-madpride-x.org
MindFreedom: www.mindfreedom.org
Mental Health Foundation: www.mentalhealth.org.uk

According to the Mental Health Foundation:

1 in 5 women and 1 in 7 men have some sort of mental problem (mostly anxiety, depression, some sort of phobia or panic attacks).

1 in 100 will suffer manic depression or schizophrenia.

The total cost of mental health in England is estimated at £23 billion each year (which includes lost employment).

...nutters with attitude

☺ **Keep sane.** Reduce the stress in your life. Do the ten simple things suggested by the 'Ways to look after your Mental Health' poster from the Mental Health Foundation. Download this from the publications section of their website.

☺ **Understand those who suffer mental illness.** Read their personal testimonies on the MindFreedom and MadNotBad websites.

☺ **Wear a Mad Pride t-shirt,** to show solidarity with the Mad Movement and find out what's happening for Mad Pride week this year.

☺ **Go to the Mad Market section of the MindFreedom website,** and buy a hypodermic highlighter for $3. This popular novelty stationery item also *highlights* the human rights issues in mental health. buy lots, and give them to all your friends.

bombard the GUN LOBBY

There are 639 million guns in the world. 16 billion rounds of ammunition are manufactured each year – that's two bullets for every person on the planet. Every year throughout the world roughly half a million men, women, and children are killed by armed violence – that's one person every minute of every day of every year. ❧ Weapons fuel violent conflict, state repression, crime, domestic abuse, slaughter of school children and accidental death. If arms continue to spread, more lives will be lost, and more human rights violations will take place.

The first week in July is the annual Global Week of Action to Control Arms. The week culminates with International Gun Destruction Day, at which guns are publicly destroyed across the world. In 2004, 5,137 firearms were publicly destroyed in Togo, and in the UK, where guns are tightly regulated, 300 gun replicas were crushed by a steamroller to publicise the issue.

The International Action Network on Small Arms (IANSA), together with Oxfam and Amnesty International, are campaigning for tougher arms control: www.controlarms.org

Brandon's Arms, an organisation committed to reducing deaths caused by firearms: www.brandonsarms.org

Brandon's battle to save lives

When he was seven years old, Brandon Maxfield was shot in the face and paralysed when staying with friends. Someone in the house had heard a noise outside and started to load a gun, which accidentally went off. The gun, manufactured by Bryco Arms, had a faulty design that required the safety catch to be turned off before ammunition could be loaded. Brandon sued the manufacturer and was awarded $24 million in damages.

However, the company declared itself bankrupt, and got permission from the Court to sell its assets, including its gun-making factory near Los Angeles, equipment and a stock of 75,000 unassembled guns. Just one bid was received – of $150,000 from the plant's manager. But the Court allowed 20 days for other bids to be made. Brandon, now aged 17, raised $505,000 and submitted a rival bid, determined to 'melt down all the guns to keep them off the street and to keep kids from getting hurt.' Unfortunately, the plant's manager topped this with a bid of $510,000, and Brandon's bid to save lives failed.

...for a safer world

Take action to control arms.

❧ **Sign the Million Faces petition.** This is the largest visual petition in the world. It will create a gallery of 1 million people who are prepared to take a public stand on gun control. You will be asked to submit a photograph of yourself plus personal details and choose a slogan. How about:

> Get tough on arms
> It's time for an arms trade treaty
> Make me safe from armed violence
> No more arms for atrocities
> Stop gun running
> Stop the terror trade.

BOYCOTT *the USA*

Country boycotts aim to hit where it will hurt most – by threatening a country's economic interests and thereby provoking change. The most successful country boycott was the Anti-Apartheid campaign against South Africa's white minority regime.

The USA is the most powerful nation on earth. Decisions taken in Washington D.C. have a global impact. But instead of using its superpower status to uplift and liberate humanity, the USA often abuses its political, economic and military might – which is to the detriment of the whole international community, including the American people. ⚽ The US government has invaded sovereign nations and torn up international trade and arms control agreements. Whilst lecturing everyone else about the evil of weapons of mass destruction, it has huge stockpiles of nuclear weapons that could annihilate the entire planet many times over. The US refuses to implement the Kyoto Treaty on global warming, and has rejected the right of the International Criminal Court to try war criminals and torturers.

American political and military power derives from its economic might. The USA depends on international trade to sustain its wealth. It has to sell goods and services abroad to maintain the affluence that funds its global political and military hegemony. ⚽ No one can force us to buy American. The people of the world – including US citizens – can use their collective spending power to change US policy and help shape a more peaceful and just world. ⚽ If people stopped buying US products, corporate profits would begin to slide. The US government would then come under immense pressure from the major corporations to moderate its policies.

The language that the US government best understands is money. To resist its bullying and domination, we need to hit US corporations where its hurts most – in the pocket. That means everyone, including Americans, boycotting US goods and services.

www.boycott-canada.com
www.boycottmadeinchina.org
www.boycottisraeligoods.org
For more information go to: www.ethicalconsumer.org

Some other country boycotts advocated by pressure groups:

Burma: for the annulment of election results and imprisonment of the elected leader.
Canada: for government-subsidised slaughter of 1 million seals over 3 years.
China: for the jailing of political and religious dissenters.
Israel: for refusing to withdraw from Palestinian territory seized in 1967.
Morocco: for the illegal occupation of Western Sahara and human rights abuses.
Turkey: for persecuting the Kurds and the eco-human disaster of the Ilisu dam project.

...don't buy American

Make this your Fourth of July promise: Don't buy American. Boycott large US companies such as American Airlines, American Express, AOL, AT&T, Citibank, Chevron/Texaco, Coca-Cola, ExxonMobil, FedEx, Ford, Gap, General Electric, Heinz, IBM, Kelloggs, KFC, Kodak, Kraft, Levis, McDonald's, Maxwell House, Microsoft, Nike, Pepsi, Revlon, Starbucks, Timberland, UPS and Wal-Mart (Asda).

bathing in # FRESHWATER

A group of hardy swimmers has won a battle to roll back the nanny state and bathe outdoors on winter mornings in the natural ponds on London's Hampstead Heath without lifeguards having to be present. In April 2005, Hampstead Heath Winter Swimming Club won a court case against the Corporation of London, which had claimed that it risked prosecution by the Health and Safety Executive if it allowed unsupervised dips.

Government over-regulation in the name of public health and safety, or a fear of prosecution for damages in the event of an accident, is making it harder for people to swim in lakes, ponds and rivers in many countries of the world. At the same time, governments are trying to encourage exercise.

The environmental impact of swimming in rivers and lakes is nil. But the use of swimming pools involves chemicals to disinfect the water and the energy for heating the water and the building, and for lighting.

People are fighting back and asserting their right to swim. The courts are upholding the idea that people should be able to do things at their own risk. Public authorities are being forced to keep open pools and ponds they have been seeking to close.

River and Lake Swimming Association: **www.river-swimming.co.uk**

The right to swim

In the UK, there is a right to swim in most tidal waters. Swimming is also allowed in many stretches of rivers that are not tidal, and in lakes where there is an established historic use by the public. You may also be allowed to swim where there are public navigation rights, but not in canals. Swimming is not allowed in most reservoirs. If access to a river or lake is privately owned, the landowner may object to you trespassing.

...skinnydip if you dare

Find a tempting river or lake, and take the plunge.

🌳 **Do it in a swimming costume**, or go skinnydipping if you dare.

🌳 **Do it at the height of summer**, or in the middle of winter.

🌳 **Go early or go late**, or any time in between.

Just do it. Assert your right to swim. You'll feel all the better for it.

CHEMICAL *soup*

Toxic chemicals can be found in virtually all creatures and in every environment. Manufacturers are making enormous quantities for agricultural use, for industrial use and for the products we buy and use in our lives. Most of these will be released into the environment – and once there they can travel great distances, persist for years, and become concentrated in living things that we may end up eating.

An estimated 1,000 new chemicals are created every year, in addition to the tens of thousands already in commercial use. Very few have been tested properly for their effect on wildlife and humans. There is growing evidence that some of these chemicals can alter sexual and neurological development, impair reproduction, cause cancers and undermine immune systems. ♣ If we can reduce the amount of chemicals that pass through our hands and bodies, this will be a small contribution to a safer world.

www.worldwildlife.org/toxics/you_do.cfm

WWF recipes to help make your home toxin-free:

All-purpose cleaner
3 tsp. liquid soap / 1/4 cup vinegar /
1/4 cup lemon juice / 1/4 cup Borax
(per gallon of water)

Window cleaner
1/4 cup vinegar
1 gallon warm water

Stain remover
Soak fabrics in
water mixed with
borax, lemon juice,
hydrogen peroxide
or white vinegar.

Oven cleaner
Baking soda, vinegar, salt, steel wool.

Clean grease with rag and vinegar. Sprinkle salt on spills. Let it sit for a few minutes, then scrape the spill and wash the area clean. For stubborn spots, use baking soda and steel wool.

Controlling cockroaches and ants
Combine powdered sugar
and borax in equal
parts and sprinkle
where they crawl.

...stop poisoning yourself

Reduce the chemicals in your life. WWF has created a list of actions you and your family can take to reduce your consumption and use of toxic chemicals at home and in your life. Do some or all of them:

Buy organic. This mainly includes cotton clothing, fruits and vegetables.

Thoroughly wash fruits and vegetables, and peel them whenever possible.

Stop using pesticides. Green up your garden using natural methods:
  Traps and biological controls such as parasites and natural predators.
  Disease- and pest-resistant plants.
  Plants that repel insects such as basil, chives, mint, marigolds, and
  chrysanthemums.
  Compost and mulch to improve soil health and to fertilise.

Use environmentally friendly cleaning products in your home:
  Don't buy or use chlorine bleach.
  Use simple and inexpensive cleansers such as soap, vinegar, lemon juice, and borax.
  Avoid air fresheners and other perfumed products: freshen your air by
  opening windows or using baking soda, cedar blocks or dried flowers.

slow CITIES

All cities now seem to look and feel much the same. This is partly as a result of globalisation. Everywhere you go you will now find a McDonald's and a Starbucks, and everyone is always in a hurry. 🌳 Inspired by the success of the Slow Food movement, 32 Italian towns and cities joined together in 1999 to create the Slow City movement to try to reverse this trend.

A Slow City is a place where people care about their town or city, enjoy living and working there, and value the things that make it special. Over 100 cities in 10 countries have now joined the movement. Ludlow in England was the first city in the English-speaking world to join. 🌳 The Slow City programme involves:

Enlarging parks and squares and making them greener.

Outlawing car alarms and other noise that disturbs the peace.

Eliminating ugly TV aerials, advertising hoardings and neon signs.

Promoting recycling, alternative energy and cleaner greener transport.

These are specific things that can be done to improve the quality of life in a city. Appreciation of the seasons, purchase of local produce and a slower and more reflective pace of life are some of the less tangible aims of the Slow Cities movement.

For a town to become a Slow City, the mayor has to make an application to the Cittàslow Committee in Italy, submitting a presentation about the town or city, giving reasons for wanting to apply, identifying goals that have already been met, setting out steps that will be being taken to meet the other goals, and giving details of who is involved in the project. 🌳 Towns and cities that subscribe to these ideals, and with a population under 50,000, can apply to join. Larger cities are considered to have become just too big to slow down.

Find out more about Slow Cities from: www.cittaslow.net and www.cittaslow.org.uk

Slow City principles

Encouraging diversity not standardisation.

Supporting and encouraging local culture and traditions.

Working for a more sustainable environment.

Supporting and encouraging local produce and products.

Encouraging healthy living especially through children and young people.

Working with the local community to build these values.

...where the living is easy

🌳 **Write a simple manifesto for slowing down** the town or city where you live – even if the population's bigger than 50,000.

🌳 **Try to get a debate going locally.** Write a letter to your local newspaper asking people to contact you if they are interested. Tell your local councillors about the movement you are starting. And if your town or city is small enough, float the idea of it joining the Slow City movement.

JULY 7

BARE *all*

PEACE – it's such a simple word, but it has many connotations in today's political climate. So, it takes a certain amount of courage to speak out against war these days. To speak out publicly, stripped of anonymity and clothing takes even more courage.

– Bare Witness

In November 2002, 45 women stripped off in Marin County, California, and formed the word PEACE with their naked bodies as a statement against the 'naked aggression' of US foreign policy.

This was the starting point for Baring Witness, a new style of campaigning. Baring Witness simply spells out a word or words using nude or clothed human bodies. This provides you with a great photo opportunity, and can bring press wide coverage for your cause. Getting access to the media will make the existence of the campaign known. It will also educate, inform, increase awareness and gather support. By baring witness you will achieve all of this.

Similar actions are now taking place all over the world – not just for peace but also as protests against GM crops, the World Trade Organization and other iniquities. In the UK, the first Bare Witness event took place in January 2003, when 30 people bared all for peace. They were sending a message to the UK government that invading Iraq was not the way to solve the problem. They could have stayed at home in the warmth and shaken their heads at the bad news streaming from their television set. But instead, they came out of their homes, and, in the middle of winter, they got out of their clothes in order to fight for peace.

In the UK, Bare Witness: www.barewitness.org
In the USA, Baring Witness: www.baringwitness.org

Bare Witness and Baring Witness are not affiliated to any political group. They support all efforts to bring about peace and inject a dose of common sense into the world. They are people who decided they had to do something, anything, to show that they cared, and that war is not the answer.

...for your beliefs

- **Do your own Bare Witness demo.** Get together a group of friends. Agree on an issue that you feel really passionately about. Think up a short slogan to spell out with your bodies. Then go for it – whatever the weather.

- **Download practical information** on using this stunt to get your message across from the Baring Witness website.

paint a MURAL

Does your local park need brightening up? Your office, or even your own garden? Why not paint a mural? You could paint an outdoor mural on a blank wall or a door, or an indoor one – anywhere there's a wall that's crying out 'Paint me!'

Murals can brighten up the environment. They can also assert the culture of a minority group, or promote a social or political message. ♠ People painted murals during the Great Depression in the 1930s as public art projects. Murals today are being painted on housing estates, in parks and in playgrounds. They can be painted indoors as well as outdoors. Murals can be painted by people from the community working together, or by a single artist as a piece of outdoor art.

If you're going to paint an indoor mural, why not do it with natural paints? Normal paints give off volatile organic compounds (VOCs), which can cause respiratory disease, and are stuffed with toxic chemicals and heavy metals. It is estimated that each household has several litres of leftover paint, and much of this will end up in the household rubbish, and then be dumped in landfill and leach out into the soil.

Natural paints are made with citrus-oil solvents rather than petrochemicals. They get their colours from minerals and clays. They may not be as bright, and mostly they are for indoor use. But they are eco-friendly. ♠ A green mural will show that you care about the environment in two different ways – artistically and chemically.

For information on eco-paints, go to: www.greenbuildingstore.co.uk
And go window shopping at: www.ecomall.com

Be inspired! To see some great examples of mural painting, visit these two archives of mural paintings in the USA:
Social and Public Art Resource Centre: www.sparcmurals.org
New Deal Mural Archive: newdeal.feri.org/library

...so long as it's green

♠ **Find a wall** that needs painting. It could be inside or outside.
♠ **Draw a design** for the mural you would like to paint. Do this with a group of friends, and discuss it with the local community where the mural will be painted. The theme could be something relevant to your neighbourhood and community. It could celebrate a person or event. Or it could simply be a public work of art.
♠ **Get permission,** if you need it.
♠ **Buy the paint.**
♠ **Draw an outline** of your design on to the wall.
♠ **Paint it!**
♠ **Admire your efforts.**
♠ **Have a party** to celebrate. Drink organic wine, of course.

BOMB *for peace*

Thailand has suffered decades of intermittent violence from Muslim separatists. In February 2004, the separatist movement in the nation's three southernmost provinces stepped up attacks on police, government buildings, and other symbols of the mainly Buddhist Thai state. The government responded with force and declared martial law in the region. Around 450 people were killed.

On 5 December 2004, the government of Thailand dropped an estimated 100 million origami birds as an attempt to promote peace, in a campaign devised by Prime Minister Thaksin Shinawatra. ❧ The crane is a widely recognised Thai symbol for peace, so people across the country folded paper cranes and wrote peace messages on them. ❧ The 'peace bombing' was scheduled to coincide with the 77th birthday of revered King Bhumibol Adulyadej. About 50 military planes and helicopters lifted off from three air bases and released the paper birds at low altitude. The airdrop took all day, but was completed by sunset after more than 150 flights.

As the birds fell to their targets in the provinces of Narathiwat, Yala and Pattani, schoolchildren rushed out to collect them and read the notes inside. Some students constructed giant nets stretched across schoolyards to capture birds. There was great interest in finding the bird that the prime minister himself had signed. Mr Thaksin promised that any student who found it would win a scholarship. ❧ Local officials responded with creative ideas for preventing a massive litter foul up. The Governor of Narathiwat offered to exchange ten paper birds for an egg and 30 collected birds for a kilogram of rice.

There were critics of this campaign, who said that it would not solve the complex problems causing the violence. However, it was a creative way of highlighting the need for a resolution of the conflict in the region.

Peace Pals has instructions for making a simple peace dove:
members.aol.com/pforpeace/ peacepals/project2.htm

For more information on how to create an origami bird and lots of links:
www.paperfolding.com/diagrams

Livio de Marchi, an Italian artist, has created a huge floating dove of peace:
www.liviodemarchi.com/ukmain3.htm

...with an origami bird

❧ **Create a flock of paper birds** with your own peace messages and display them around your workplace or school. Or hang them from trees in your neighbourhood.

❧ **Recruit as many friends as you can to help you with the project.** You can make your bird display more eye-catching by using an array of coloured paper.

10 JULY

ecological FOOTPRINTS

An ecological footprint is the area of productive land required to produce the food, energy and materials consumed by a person or a country, and to absorb the waste they produce, or cause to be produced. ♣ The organisation Redefining Progress has produced a table of footprints for each nation, measured in hectares of land per person.

10 largest footprints		10 smallest footprints	
USA	9.57	Pakistan	0.67
United Arab Emirates	8.97	Ethiopia	0.67
Canada	8.56	Tajikistan	0.65
Norway	8.17	Malawi	0.64
New Zealand	8.13	Burundi	0.63
Kuwait	8.01	Congo, Dem Rep	0.62
Sweden	7.95	Haiti	0.62
Australia	7.09	Nepal	0.57
Finland	7.00	Mozambique	0.56
France	5.74	Bangladesh	0.50

Selected others: UK 4.72, Russia 4.28, Germany 4.26, Japan 3.91, South Africa 3.52, China 1.36, Nigeria 1.10

A large footprint indicates a higher standard of living, but also a lifestyle that wastes resources. Differences between countries are also caused by factors such as the climate and the need to travel. Rich countries can mostly be found at the top of the list and poor countries at the bottom. ♣ The total footprint for all of humanity was 13.2 billion hectares. It continues to increase with the world's population and rising living standards, although growth is mitigated to some extent by technological advance.

Measure your ecological footprint by taking the Ecological Footprint Quiz at:
www.myfootprint.org
Redefining Progress: www.rprogress.org

Facts and figures on ecological footprint:
redefiningprogress.org/footprint/calculating.shtml

Big feet
Average footprint per person: 2.18 hectares
Average area of productive land available per person: 1.89 hectares
Global deficit per person: 0.29 hectares

The global footprint exceeds the Earth's capacity. This 'sustainability gap' must be addressed, as the human race cannot continue indefinitely to take more from nature than nature can provide.

...keep yours small

See what you can do to reduce your footprint:
♣ Walk and cycle whenever you can.
♣ Share car journeys and use public transport.
♣ Downsize your car and go electric or dual-fuel.
♣ Avoid air travel.
♣ Eat less meat and buy fresh food locally.
♣ Reduce, reuse and recycle as much as you can.
♣ Insulate your home and turn the thermostat down.

DOCTOR *yourself*

I am a district pastor in Ghana with churches in 26 towns and villages. I started using the book Where There is No Doctor *during my visits to these communities. With the help of the book, ailments such as headaches, diarrhoea, dysentery, skin diseases, convulsion, toothaches, constipation and dehydration have been treated at little or no cost at all.*

In the 1970s, a group of health activists in Mexico compiled a notebook of treatment information for some of the common medical problems they found in their village. This grew into a much bigger healthcare manual covering almost every common health problem villagers were facing, and giving advice on what to do about the problem in the absence of a doctor. ☺ The manual was aimed largely at village health workers. It was initially published in Spanish as *Dónde no hay Doctor*. Through the Hesperian Foundation this book has now been adapted and translated into 90 languages from Amharic to Urdu, and used all around the globe. ☺ The Hesperian Foundation has now developed a range of other health materials, all of which are published cheaply and distributed worldwide.

The distribution of low-cost health information helps people and communities deal with their urgent health problems and take preventive action. Providing good information that is appropriate to the health needs and living conditions of local communities is an extremely cost-effective way of improving health.

Hesperian Foundation: www.hesperian.org
Hesperian's Gratis Book Programme: www.hesperian.org/gratis.htm
Teaching Aids at Low Costs (TALC): www.talcuk.org

Gratis Books

The Hesperian Foundation has developed a Gratis Book Program to provide books free to those who can't afford them. Donate $15 to pay for one book plus shipment. Around 1,500 free books are distributed this way every year.

Where There is No Doctor helps people with their health problems, and to recognise problems which need to be referred to an experienced health worker. *Where Women Have No Doctor* helps women and girls to identify common medical problems and treatments. It covers sexual and mental health, diseases, pregnancy and childbirth, nutrition, disabilities and injuries. *Where There is No Dentist* helps people care for their teeth.

...books to save lives

☺ **Buy a copy** of *Where There Is No Doctor* either direct from Hesperian, or from TALC. Use it yourself as a self-help health manual.

☺ **Make a donation** to the Hesperian Gratis Book Fund.

☺ **Or, if you are travelling abroad** to a poor country, buy a copy of one of the books in the local language. Donate it to a village library or information centre. It may help save someone's life.

fight MALARIA

If you ever think you're too small to be effective, then you've never been in bed with a mosquito.

– Wendy Lasko

Malaria is one of the world's major killers, up there with HIV/AIDS and TB. Malaria causes over 1 million deaths a year – and it's on the increase. The majority of victims are children under five and pregnant women. Half the human race is at risk. The Roll Back Malaria Partnership, co-ordinated by the World Health Organization, aims to halve the impact of malaria by 2010 – but it's going to be a struggle.

Malaria is caused by a parasite, and transmitted to humans through bites by the Anopheles mosquito. Here are some worrying facts about the disease:

300–500 million people suffer from malaria every year, which is around 7% of the global population.

Africa has 90% of reported cases, and these account for around 10% of hospital admissions, 25% of doctor visits and 40% of public health spending.

Someone dies from malaria every 29 seconds.

There are four types of malaria, all of which produce a severe fever. But the most common can cause death and is becoming increasingly resistant to anti-malaria drugs.

Medicines for Malaria Venture has been set up to discover, develop and distribute new and affordable anti-malarial drugs for treatment and prevention. MMV is developing a new drug, ACT, based on a herbal Chinese remedy, which could be the biggest breakthrough for a generation.

Malaria Foundation International has information and lots of useful links: www.malaria.org

Medicines for Malaria Venture: www.mmv.org

Anti-mosquito software download: www.thaiware.com/main/topall.php

How to prevent the mosquito bites that may carry malaria:

Screen windows and doors.

Use mosquito nets on beds.

Use biological control – some fish in small ponds and water tanks reduce the larval mosquito population.

Stop mosquitoes breeding by closing off or removing stagnant water.

Have drug treatment, both to prevent malaria and for malaria patients.

Use insect repellents, including body lotions and mosquito mats and coils.

Treat interior walls and bed nets with insecticide.

...through your computer

Anti-mosquito software has been developed by a Thai computer programmer. It generates sound waves through the computer's speakers that repel the mosquitos, cockroaches and rats within a 2-metre radius. Fortunately the frequencies that annoy rats and cockroaches are undetectable by humans. There have been over 400,000 downloads to date, with an 85% approval rating.

☺ **Pass this idea on to friends** who live in tropical countries. Ask them to spread the message. This is one small step towards dealing with malaria.

JULY 13

THROW *a public party*

Parties are a great way for like-minded people to get together and have some fun. A street party can encourage everyone to get together and bring colour and laughter into their neighbourhood. But what about holding a party in an unexpected place? It will be a memorable occasion!

London has its own beach on the Thames – a small sandy stretch of the foreshore outside the Royal Festival Hall that was created for the Festival of Britain. It is exposed twice a day at low tide. ⌂ Technically, the beach is owned by the Port of London Authority, which inherited it from the City Corporation, which took it (along with most of London's foreshore) from George IV as payment for his gambling debts. But in reality it is belongs to all of us – an unownable public space.

Reclaim the Beach has been holding free public events on this beach, ranging from afternoons of family-friendly seaside fun to late-night raves that thousands have enjoyed. Everything is completely non-commercial; the people who put the events on are all volunteers, and the performers and musicians all give their time for free. The success of the events depends largely on the active participation of everyone who comes, and a policy of benign neglect by the authorities. ⌂ The whole thing started in 2000 when a group of friends brought a ghetto blaster, a picnic and a few bottles of wine onto the beach. By summer 2001 there were full-scale parties with sound systems, DJs, live bands, lighting, fireworks and bonfires. Family-friendly daytime events have featured sandcastle competitions, boat rides and Punch & Judy shows. ⌂ And when the tide rises, everyone goes home.

Reclaim the Beach: www.swarming.org.uk/recl/recl.htm
Space Hijackers: spacehijackers.org
Step-by-step guide to organising a street party: www.streetparty.net

And how about an underground party?

The group Space Hijackers campaign for public use of public spaces. In 1999 it 'hijacked' a London Underground Circle Line train and turned it into a moving disco. All the equipment was brought in suitcases and transformed on-site into a bar, a stereo deck, a nibbles counter and a disco light. Around 150 people attended the event, plus all the passengers who just happened to be on the train at the time – all of whom were given free vodka, tequila and sweets. After one and a half laps of the Circle Line, the party-goers dashed off to a pub to continue their partying.

...in an unexpected place

Organise a public party in an unexpected place, and have fun!

harness ENERGY

Solar electric power has become a realistic possibility, and not just for pocket calculators. Solar power can change lives in parts of the world that are beyond the reach of the conventional electricity network, and it doesn't produce any greenhouse gases or damage the environment.

Greenstar, an organisation working to deliver solar power to villages in the developing world, has designed a portable community centre that uses solar power to operate a water purifier, a classroom, a small clinic with a vaccine cooler and a digital studio with satellite or wireless internet connection. ❦ Greenstar then works with local people to develop a website that the villagers can use to conduct trade.

Greenstar plans to install 300 similar centres around the world. It uses 'virtual volunteers' to undertake specific assignments such as researching online sources of practical books on solar power, which will be used to create a Solar Bookstore, and finding out what work is being done on community health centres by other international organisations.

Greenstar: www.greenstar.org
The Barefoot College: www.barefootcollege.org
For more information on purchasing and installing a solar electric system in the UK, contact Solar Century: www.solarcentury.co.uk

Purchase solar energy devices for use in the developing world:
www.sustainablevillage.com

Solar Energy Alliance, a resource centre: www.solarenergyalliance.com

The Barefoot College in Tilonia (near Ajmer in northern India) has set up a 'barefoot solar engineers' programme. This trains unemployed young people, and women with low literacy skills, to install and maintain home solar-lighting systems in their villages. These solar engineers have electrified 300 Adult Education Centres in India, 521 night schools, and 1,475 houses in Ladakh, which is 3,350 metres high in the Himalayas. It has saved 12,000 litres of kerosene and diesel a year.

The college also runs training courses for participants from all over the world on the use of solar systems in sustainable development. All the electricity for their 7,500 m² training centre is supplied from a 40 kw solar unit. This project has received international acclaim and is well worth visiting – if you happen to be passing by...

...use solar power

❦ **Find out as much as you can about solar energy:** how much it costs; how much it will save; where to get it; and how to install it.
❦ **See if you can get a solar unit installed** at home or your workplace. Or why not run a campaign to get solar power installed in your school or college? Louise Ng is a 17-year-old from Golders Green in London who convinced her school that solar energy was both realistic and feasible. She raised enough funds to install a Solar Sun-Station that provides power for the school and feeds surplus electricity back into the National Grid.
❦ **Get started in solar energy by buying a solar LED torch** and a solar battery charger from Solar Energy Alliance.

JULY 15

SUDAN *take a stand*

After the holocaust in Nazi Germany, the world said that it would never be allowed to happen again. But it has happened, repeatedly and with no sign of ending. ❧ Over the past few years in Sudan, millions of people in Darfur have experienced a daily hell that we can hardly fathom.

The first thing we can do to help is conquer our ignorance about what is happening. A snapshot of the crisis in Sudan:

> **The Janjaweed Militia** are perpetrating atrocities against African farmers. They burn down entire villages, killing and raping everyone they can reach.
>
> **There is a severe water shortage** that leaves people lined up at pumps, waiting for up to ten hours to get enough water to survive.
>
> **Women are afraid** to leave their homes for fear of being raped by the pillaging militias.
>
> **With the onslaught** of torrential rains, malaria will ravage the population.
>
> **Over 1.2 million** people have been made homeless.

Southern Sudan news site: www.gurtong.org
Human Rights Watch reports: hrw.org/reports/2004/sudan0504
Darfur Peace and Development: www.darfurpeaceanddevelopment.org
Read personal accounts like Magboula's: www.cafod.org.uk

Who is Magboula?

When people ask you about your arm band, tell them about Magboula Khattar, a 24-year-old Sudanese woman. The Janjaweed Arab militia burned her village, murdered her parents and finally tracked her family down in the mountains. Magboula hid, but the Janjaweed caught her husband and his brothers, who were only four, six and eight years old, and killed them all. She escaped with her baby girl to a refugee camp in Chad. She is just one of the 1.2 million people who have been left homeless by the Janjaweed.

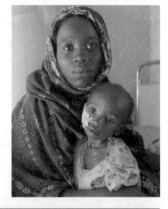

Remember that when Sudan is old news, there's bound to be somewhere else where atrocities we can barely imagine are taking place.

...on genocide

Make and wear an armband in support of the people in Sudan. This is what you need to do:

❧ **Get an old sheet** out of your cupboard and a thick marker pen. Cut the sheet into strips the width of your thumb and length of your forearm.

❧ **Write 'Ask me about Magboula'** on the centre of the strip.

❧ **Prepare a short information sheet** on Magboula and a brief overview of the situation in Sudan.

❧ **Wear the arm band** to work or school, or just around town. Bring extra arm bands with you. Give them out to people you meet during the day, and ask them to wear these to show their support.

And tomorrow, think about designing a t-shirt to reinforce your campaign.

16 JULY

Pets require a lot of care and attention, but they can be a fantastic addition to your life.

If you want a pet, there is no reason to go to a pet shop. Many puppies and kittens sold in pet shops come from pet breeders. Sometimes the animals are inbred and are not used to living in a home environment. ☘ Why not take care of an unwanted pet instead? Go and find a pet at your local animal shelter. Greyhounds, for example, make wonderful pets. Yet many are killed as soon as they are too old to race.

Find the pet that's just right for you. Understand the responsibilities of owning a pet (and the cost involved). And give your new pet a warm home and a lot of tender loving care.

If you don't want a pet you can still do something to help an animal. Go to the Animal Rescue website, and click on the icon. Your simple click will provide food for an animal in need. ☘ In 2004, over 4 million people clicked each month. This raised enough to fund 31.5 million bowls of food. Visitors who shopped at the on-site store funded an additional 3.1 million bowls of food. Like other 'click and donate' sites, your click costs you absolutely nothing. It simply triggers a donation by one of the site's sponsors.

The Animal Rescue Site: www.theanimalrescuesite.com
Cats & Dogs Online: www.catsdogsonline.com
Battersea Dogs and Cats Home: www.dogshome.org

An online matchmaking service

Cats & Dogs Online was created when Jacqueline Holstead had to find homes for her three cats – BB, a lovely, lively little black moggie; Rusty, a big cuddly teddy bear of a cat; Beatie, the talkative Tonkinese cat. The process of finding new homes was logistically and emotionally difficult. It became clear that adopting an animal is not an easy task, and finding the right new home for your pet is even more difficult.

Cats & Dogs Online brings animal-loving people together – people who wish to adopt a pet and people who find that they need to re-home their pet. The website helps provide new homes and happy endings.

...from an animal shelter

☘ **Next time you want a pet, get it from your local animal shelter or rescue centre.** You'll be making a poor animal very happy.

☘ **Make sure your pet is neutered,** otherwise you could end up with ten pets instead of the one you planned for. As a matter of course, many animal shelters will vaccinate, neuter and give a full battery of tests to your new pet in order to ensure that you take home a healthy animal. You won't get this five-star service if you buy a pet at the local store.

JULY 17

PLANT *diversity*

The total number of plant species in the world is estimated at around 300,000. Many are in danger of extinction, threatened by habitat transformation, alien invasive species, pollution and climate change. Their disappearance would lead to a loss of biodiversity. Maintaining plant diversity is a challenge the world needs to deal with – plant life may contain untapped secrets with the potential to meet present and future needs of humankind. 🌳 The terms 'native' and 'non-native' are used to distinguish between those species we believe would have been found growing in our country or region if no human beings had ever lived there; and those that have arrived or been developed with a helping hand from humans.

Planting native species in your garden is one simple way of safeguarding them – as well as providing a perfect habitat for native wildlife. 🌳 However, global warming is changing the climate so that native species in some areas no longer thrive. To protect native species for the future, we need to be aware of the bigger picture.

Royal Botanic Gardens, Kew: www.rbgkew.org.uk
The Natural History Museum can tell you which species are native to the UK: www.nhm.ac.uk/nature-online/life/index.html

Native species are considered preferable by conservationists because they are a product of the natural habitat and ecosystem. Species of plants, animals, fungi and other micro-organisms within any habitat are highly interdependent, and the introduction of a new species from outside can destabilise what exists naturally. For example, a non-native sycamore tree would take up a space that would otherwise have been occupied by a native oak. Compared with an oak, the sycamore supports only a limited variety of leaf-eating insects and small mammals. This, in turn, would affect the number and even the viability of other species, such as insectivorous birds or mammals. Although native species may not always support more biodiversity than an equivalent non-native, it is true in most cases, as native species have had much more time to develop stable links with each other.

...protect native species

- 🌳 **Find out what species are native to your area.** Find out where you can buy seeds – these won't cost much. There are native species of wild flower, pond plants, shrubs and trees to suit all tastes.
- 🌳 **Take an inventory of your garden** to see what native species you already have, and what non-native species are taking up space but not providing resources for wildlife.
- 🌳 **Designate areas of your garden for native species** (especially trees and hedgerow). Plant one native species each month. Over time you will turn your garden into something both you and the local wildlife can enjoy.

18 JULY

try out a WHEELCHAIR

The best way to understand the frustration that people with mobility problems face in their everyday lives is to experience it for yourself. You can do this easily by getting into a wheelchair for a day. The steps you did not notice become insurmountable barriers, the public transport you got around on is suddenly completely inaccessible to you, and there are no disabled toilets at the meeting you are attending.

Your day will become dominated by all the things you can't do, by all the opportunities that the rest of the population takes for granted being denied to you. But for those who need a wheelchair all the time, this is what their whole life consists of. ❌ Only when all of society comes to realise the importance of disability access as a basic human right – and at whatever the cost of provision – that things will begin to change.

Learn more about disability rights and disability issues from these websites:
British Council of Disabled People: www.bcodp.org.uk
RADAR, the disability network run by and for disabled people: www.radar.org.uk
Disability Rights Commission: www.drc.org.uk

There are lots of 'wheelchair for a day' projects to promote accessibility awareness. Here is one that took place in Vermont in the USA in 2002:

On the first day of the Wheelchair for a Day campaign, 16 biology students and four faculty members spent the day in 20 wheelchairs, which the students had obtained for the event. For the second and third days of the campaign, the wheelchairs were made available to staff and other faculty at five points on the campus. Those who were interested signed up to use the wheelchair at a specific time.

All participants received a free t-shirt designed by the students. This had the image of a person in a wheelchair at the foot of the hill leading up to the college Chapel. The slogan was 'Accessibility: It's an Uphill Battle'.

The week also included a panel discussion and a forum on the final day at which participants discussed their experiences as wheelchair users and decided what to do as a result.

...for greater understanding

❌ **Borrow a wheelchair for a day.** Get in it and go for a day out. Make a diary of your experience. Take a camera to photograph what you find most aggravating.

❌ **Join with disabled people** to campaign for better access throughout your neighbourhood or city.

JULY 19

GUERRILLA *girls*

Florynce Rae Kennedy, prominent civil rights activist and pro-choice campaigner, once famously said: 'If men could get pregnant, abortion would be a sacrament.' Maurice and Charles Saatchi, advertising gurus, sprang to public notice with a poster of a pregnant man, saying: 'If this could happen to you, you'd be more careful.'

The world looks different from male and female perspectives – not least when it comes to aggression and warfare. The architects of the Iraq war on both sides were all men. Would the situation have been different if the hormones coursing through their bodies had been oestrogen rather than testosterone?

Since 1985 the Guerrilla Girls have been reinventing feminism. Still going strong in the 21st century, they're a bunch of anonymous females who take the names of dead women artists as pseudonyms and appear in public wearing gorilla masks. ❌ Guerrilla Girls have produced over 100 posters, stickers, books, printed projects and public demonstrations to expose sexism and racism in politics, the art world, film and culture at large. They use humour to convey information, provoke discussion and show that feminists can be funny. They wear gorilla masks to focus on the issues rather than their personalities. ❌ Dubbing themselves 'the conscience of culture', they see themselves as feminist counterparts to the mostly male tradition of anonymous do-gooders like Robin Hood, Batman and the Lone Ranger.

Guerrilla Girls, fighting discrimination with facts, humour and fake fur since 1985:
www.guerillagirls.com
Life of Florynce Kennedy: en.wikipedia.org/wiki/Florynce_Kennedy

Guerrilla Girls on Feminism

We believe feminism is a fundamental way of looking at the world and recognising that half of us are female and all of us should be equal. It's a fact of history that for centuries women have not had the rights and privileges of men and it's time for that to end.

Despite the tremendous gains of women over the last hundred years, misogyny – the hatred or hostility towards women as a whole – is still rampant throughout our culture and in the larger world. We think that is the number one reason women need feminism.

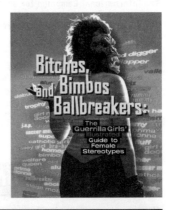

...re-inventing the F-word

Fight testosterone power and make politicians more peaceful. Got any leftover oestrogen pills? Send an 'Oestrogen Bomb' to Bush, Cheney and Rumsfeld, white men in power, with your own message suggesting a more feminine way of governing the USA and the world. Address: The White House, 1600 Pennsylvania Avenue, Washington DC 20500, USA.

20 JULY

campaign for **BHOPAL**

At five minutes past midnight on the night of 3 December 1984, the Union Carbide pesticide plant in Bhopal in central India exploded, releasing a toxic gas that caused 8,000 deaths within a few days, and more than 20,000 in the years since. An estimated 150,000 people have suffered serious health problems. 🌳 On the night of the disaster, six safety measures designed to prevent a leak were either malfunctioning, shut down or otherwise inadequate. The refrigeration unit was deliberately turned off, in order to save a measly $40 a day.

The site of the closed factory remains a toxic hotspot, with concentrations of carcinogenic chemicals and heavy metals. Chemicals continue to seep into the water supplies of an estimated 20,000 people who are living in surrounding communities. These people have no choice but to drink, wash and cook with this water every day.

The Indian government charged Union Carbide's CEO with negligent homicide, but Warren Anderson has not been extradited from the USA to stand trial in India. Dow Chemical purchased Union Carbide in 2001, but has refused to take responsibility for the Bhopal cleanup. 🌳 In 1999, 15 years on, Bhopal survivors filed a class action suit against Union Carbide in the US courts, asking that the company be held responsible for violations of international human rights law and for cleaning up the environmental contamination in Bhopal. This case will test the limits of a corporation's ability to use the laws of one nation to escape responsibility in another.

Read the stories and reports about Bhopal at the Greenpeace archive:
www.greenpeace.org/international/footer/search?q=bhopal
The Bhopal People's Health and Documentation Clinic: www.bhopal.org
The International Campaign for Justice in Bhopal: www.bhopal.net

Compare the compensation figures:

For the victims of 9/11: Congress authorised a $5,900 million compensation fund for the 2,963 deaths and about 4,400 injury claims arising from the disaster. The average death payment is just above $2 million, while the largest death payment to date has been $7.1 million.

For the victims of Bhopal: Five years after the disaster that claimed 8,000 deaths and an estimated 150,000 seriously injured people, Union Carbide agreed a compensation fund of $470 million. Victims each received less than $350 for injuries they are likely to suffer all their lives. The world's largest industrial accident cost Union Carbide just 48 cents a share.

...victims of Union Carbide

🌳 **Support the Bhopal People's Health and Documentation Clinic,** which is treating 1,000 victims each month and is documenting toxic deaths in the community. The clinic is funded entirely by donations. It was awarded the Margaret Mead Centennial Award in 2002 for its outstanding work.

🌳 **Join the International Campaign for Justice in Bhopal.** The campaign aims to bring justice to Bhopal survivors by keeping world attention focused on Dow Chemical's liability for the Union Carbide disaster.

JULY 21

SHOP *ethically*

Every time you go shopping, you have the power to make a difference to the world. Every pound you spend is a vote for the company that makes the product that you're buying. Buying ethical products sends support directly to companies working to improve our world, while at the same time depriving others that abuse it for profit. ⚽ Ethical consumerism means that when you go shopping, you take into account the issues that are important to you, and favour companies whose policies and activities you'd prefer to support.

Ethical shopping also means avoiding or boycotting companies whose policies and activities you disagree with. All too often, companies are involved in unethical practices, such as exploiting workers in the developing world, dumping toxic chemicals into the environment or producing products which involve the exploitation of animals. ⚽ Awareness of global poverty, animal welfare and green issues are at an all-time high. If we can carry this awareness into our shopping basket, we can all work together to help make the world a better place, and make sure that companies start treating it, and us, with more respect.

A small number of multinational companies own a large proportion of the country's favourite brands, but there are still plenty of alternatives out there, and a range of smaller companies who are as concerned with treating the world with more respect as making money. The Ethical Consumer Research Association researches the companies behind the brands so that you don't have to be a super detective to be an ethical consumer. This information is published in the bi-monthly *Ethical Consumer* magazine.

www.ethicalconsumer.org and on the www.ethiscore.org website.
Other ethical consumerism websites include: www.responsibleshopper.org

Ethical shopping list

Everyone has their own priorities when they go shopping, but consumers are beginning to take ethical issues into account as well as price and quality, and companies are responding accordingly. We all go shopping, and so ethical consumerism is an easy way of using your money to try and make a difference.

Fairly traded products
Local produce
Organic produce
Forest Stewardship Council (FSC) products
Fridge with energy efficiency A rating
Secondhand shirt from charity shop
Pay money into Co-operative Bank
Drop off recycling

...make your money talk

What else can I do?
- ⚽ **Write to companies** whose policies you disagree with, telling them why you are avoiding them.
- ⚽ **Join consumer campaigns** targeting companies whose activities you disagree with.

spot BUTTERFLIES

The job of air-raid wardens during the Second World War was to spot incoming aeroplanes and missiles, and raise the alarm in good time – thereby giving people time to make themselves safe. In much the same way, you can become a biodiversity warden, helping to watch out for impending environmental disasters so that something can be done about them.

More than 50% of the world's wildlife consists of insects, so what is happening to insect populations provides us with a good indicator of how well species are surviving, how many are endangered, and how many are becoming extinct in response to such factors as habitat loss and climate change. Because butterflies are distinctive, brightly coloured, easily spotted and have a short life-cycle, monitoring the butterfly population, and how it is changing, can provide us with an early-warning system.

Butterfly spotting is an excellent way of enjoying the outdoors and taking exercise, and you will also be contributing important scientific data about the state of the world's biodiversity. The Butterfly Monitoring Scheme consists of a network of volunteers who each select a small area and monitor the butterfly population in that area. Why not join them?

Butterfly Monitoring Scheme: www.ukbms.org
Butterfly Conservation: www.butterfly-conservation.org

The magnificent seven

Britain has seven species of blue butterfly:
    Common blue
    Adonis blue
    Chalkhill blue
    Holly blue
    Silver-studded blue
    Small blue
    Large blue
All are under threat to a greater or lesser degree.

...as an early-warning system

Contact the Butterfly Monitoring Scheme and become a monitor. This is what you will be asked to do:

🦋 Select a fixed-route walk 2–4 km long (45 mins – 2 hours) that takes in different habitats.

🦋 Record the butterfly population in a 5m-wide band along the route each week from the beginning of April until the end of September, between 10.45am and 3.45pm, in weather conditions suitable for butterfly activity.

🦋 Do this for a number of years.

🦋 Send your survey records to the Butterfly Monitoring Scheme, using the forms that they will provide you with.

JULY 23

BIG BROTHER

Government agencies and private companies are increasingly violating the privacy of people everywhere. Enormous amounts of personal data are being collected, stored and processed – often illegally – in the pursuit of more efficient marketing, greater social control, and more powerful mechanisms for monitoring of the citizen.

– Privacy International

Google uses a cookie that expires in 2038. This places a unique ID number on your hard disk. Any time you land on a Google page, you get a Google cookie if you don't already have one. If you have one, they read and record your unique ID number.

✦ About 75% of searches are done on Google. For all searches they record the cookie ID, your Internet IP address, the time and date, your search terms, and your browser configuration. Google retains this data indefinitely, and they won't say why they need this data or if they have ever been subpoenaed to disclose it.

In many countries, people are able to trace how you have voted. In the UK, for example, the number on your voting slip is recorded on the electoral roll used by the polling station to note down who has voted. It is then possible to find out the names and addresses of everyone who has voted for a particular party. A complete list of people voting for extremist parties could easily be compiled and handed over to the internal security services as a list of 'subversives'. The fear of being traced could deter people from expressing their true voting intentions.

Your mobile phone will show where you have made calls from, and soon satellite tracking systems for road pricing will record where your car has travelled. Your shop loyalty card and credit cards show what you have been purchasing. Video cameras are everywhere recording you walking in the street. You are being watched.

Privacy International: www.privacyinternational.org
Privacy.org, a news site established by Privacy International and the Electronic Privacy Information Centre: www.privacy.org

Privacy International runs its Big Brother Awards in Australia, Austria, Bulgaria, Denmark, Finland, France, Germany, Hungary, Japan, Netherlands, Spain, Switzerland, UK and USA.

Big Brother Awards are given to government agencies, private companies and individuals who have done something that significantly violates our privacy. The panels of judges worldwide consist of lawyers, academics, consultants, journalists, civil right activists and others.

...is watching you

Think about how your privacy is now increasingly being threatened.

✦ Is there is any person or any institution invading your privacy you would like to propose for an award?

✦ Tell Privacy International. Nominate someone for a Big Brother Award.

24 JULY

open source COLA

The ethos of the Open Source Software movement allows the free copying and modification of software whilst crediting the ownership of the original idea. This enables a piece of software to be continually improved through the input of others.

Opencola uses the same principles. It is a brand of cola for which the instructions for making it are freely available and modifiable. Anybody can make the drink, and anyone can modify and improve on the recipe. ⚽ It was originally designed as a publicity stunt to promote the Opencola software design company in Toronto and its services. But the drink took on a life of its own. It sold 150,000 cans, and the company became better known for the drink than the software it wanted to promote. The cola website is now run from Japan. ⚽ The success of Opencola partly stems from it being a quirky idea and partly from a widespread mistrust of big corporations. Opencola provides you with a great opportunity to create a no-logo, no-brand product, and use this to explain the benefits of 'open source' sharing and the issues of globalisation.

Opencola background and recipe: www.colawp.com/colas/400/cola467_recipe.html

Find out more about open source software and copyleft from the Wikipedia encyclopaedia: en.wikipedia.org/wiki/Open_source
en.wikipedia.org/wiki/Copyleft

Opencola recipe
7X (Top-Seekrut™) flavouring formula:

- 2 tsp 7X formula
- 3 1/2 tsp 75% phosphoric acid or citric acid
- 2.25 l water

- 2.25 kg plain granulated white table sugar
- 1/2 tsp caffeine (optional)
- 30 ml caramel colour

Mix the following oils together in a cup: 3.5 ml orange oil, 1 ml lemon oil, 1 ml nutmeg oil, 1.25 ml cassia oil, 0.25 ml coriander oil, 0.25 ml neroli oil, 2.75 ml lime oil, 0.25 ml lavender oil. Add 10 g gum arabic. Add 3 ml water and mix well in a blender. Keep in a sealed glass jar in the fridge or at room temperature.

Opencola syrup:
In a 4-litre container, take 5 ml of the 7X mixture and add the acid. Add the water and then the sugar. While mixing, add the caffeine (optional), and make sure it dissolves completely. Then add the caramel colour. Mix thoroughly.

To prepare the drink:
To finish, take one part syrup and add 5 parts carbonated water.

This recipe is licensed under the GNU General Public license. It is 'open source' cola, or, if you prefer, 'free' cola. You're free to use this recipe to make your own cola, or to modify it. If you distribute modified colas, you're expected to send an email to the recipe's author, Amanda Foubister at: amanda@opencola.com with your modifications.

...it's almost the real thing!

Make your own cola. Drink it at home, at parties, or at festivals and fairs where you can promote the idea of open source sharing.

GUIDE DOG *training*

Dogs can become canine superheroes. Guide Dogs are the eyes of the blind and Hearing Dogs are the ears of the deaf. ❌ These dogs are not born knowing hundreds of commands. They need to be trained. This is something you can help with. So why don't you help train a guide dog? ❌ The rewards will be enormous. The animal you help train will drastically improve the quality of life of a disabled person. You will be giving that person a constant companion, a best friend and the freedom to live their life in a more enabled way.

Guide dogs are generally from one of the following breeds:

Labrador Retriever

Golden Retriever

German Shepherd

Labrador/Golden Retriever cross

Guide dogs have to be trained to lead their partner in a straight line between two points and around any ground or overhead obstacles. The dogs can't read traffic signals, so are trained to stop at the kerb while their human partner listens for oncoming cars. But if the human partner begins walking and a car approaches, the dog is trained to stop. The dogs are trained to ignore all outside stimuli such as strange smells and sounds, other dogs and humans.

Guide Dogs for the Blind: www.guidedogs.org.uk
Hearing Dogs for Deaf People: www.hearing-dogs.co.uk

Puppy walking is an important part of developing a future guide dog. A volunteer puppy walker takes a puppy aged around six weeks into their home and nurtures it for the first year of its life – teaching it basic commands and getting it used to as many different environments as possible. This is done under the guidance of a Puppy Walking Supervisor.

...walk a puppy

Become a Puppy Walker. Help turn Fido into a 'Florence Nightingale'.

Puppy walkers have to meet certain criteria. To take on this role you need to:

❌ **Be at home** most of the day (puppies cannot be left for more than three hours).

❌ **Be over 18 years old.**

❌ **Live in a ground-floor dwelling** with a securely fenced garden or yard that has speedy access to a 'spending' area (where the pup can relieve itself).

❌ **Not have children under three.**

❌ **Have regular access to car travel.**

❌ **Be willing to take the puppy out** as part of your daily routine – to the supermarket, for example.

cast out # CASTE-ISM

Discrimination is often discussed on the basis of race, ethnic background, gender, age and sexuality. But discrimination on the basis of caste is a hugely important and worrying issue that is often ignored.

Caste-ism is most evident in Hinduism, which has four 'castes', based on occupation and ancestry. At the top are the priestly caste of the Brahmins; next the soldiers or Kshtriyas; then the merchants and farmers (the Vaishyas); finally those that serve them (the Shudras). ✖ Beyond these come the Dalits – who are completely outside the caste system ('out-castes' or 'untouchables'). Dalits are right at the bottom of the social hierarchy. In Hindu societies, many Dalit communities suffer extreme discrimination.

Dalits get the poorest shelter, often having to live in huts outside the perimeter of the village; they may be denied access to water for fear of their polluting it; they often have the worst, lowest-paid jobs, which also means that their nutrition and health is poor, and that their children have to work and are therefore denied an education. ✖ Hinduism even denies Dalits advancement in the next life. Dalits are condemned to return to the world over and over again as 'polluted' and 'outcast' people. A Dalit can never escape the oppression of the caste system. ✖ There are 160 million Dalits in India and 260 million in Asia as a whole.

National Campaign on Dalit Human Rights: www.dalits.org
International Dalit Support Network: www.idsn.org
A Dalit website with lots of links: www.ambedkar.org

Martin Macwan is a Dalit. He began life as a child farmhand. He then worked his way through school and went to college, graduating in psychology and then getting a law degree. In 1983, he started to work with tribal children and Pakistani refugees in Gujarat.

Macwan wanted to do more than just provide a social service. He started to work on Dalit rights and caste discrimination. In 1986, four of his friends were shot dead, 18

 more wounded and several villages set on fire in an attack by feudal landlords. The landlords resented what they saw as 'uppity Dalit activists' and wanted to 'teach them a lesson'. Macwan escaped death only because he had gone home sick earlier that day. Macwan held a dead friend's body and vowed: 'He died and I escaped. I swore with his corpse in my arms: your death will not be in vain.'

In 1989, Macwan started Navsarjan Trust in Ahmedabad to mobilise and empower the Dalits. Since then, Navsarjan ('New Creation') has grown into one of the most effective Dalit advocacy groups in India. In 1996, he launched the National Campaign on Dalit Human Rights, which is working for the abolition of 'untouchability'.

...it's as bad as racism

Support the Dalits in their campaign for human rights.

✖ Send Martin Macwan a letter of support: martin@icenet.net.

✖ And why not raise some money for the Dalit rights movement?

There are equivalents to caste discrimination in other societies and cultures. Any discrimination based on the accident of birth should be fought against.

JULY 27

GIVE TIME *to others*

A Time Bank enables everybody to give some of their time over to helping others, and at the same time receive other people's time for their own benefit. Time Credits are earned and then used to purchase what people need from other members of the Time Bank. ✋ This is a mechanism whereby everybody can help everybody else without anyone feeling that people are taking more than they are giving back. It is a mechanism for mutual aid within a community. ✋ Here are some of the things that can be converted into Time Credits, or which Time Credits can buy:

Do-It-yourself around the house, including painting and decorating.

Gardening and looking after houseplants.

Cooking and organising a brunch party.

A trip to the shops to do the shopping or collect a prescription.

Listening, mentoring and giving advice.

Dog-walking and babysitting.

Teaching new skills such as arts, crafts, music or sports.

Practising a new language by having conversation lessons.

Organising community events.

Professional assistance, including IT support and doing accounts.

Almost any sort of time or skill can be exchanged through a Time Bank – provided one member has that skill and another member needs it.

The basis for calculating the exchange value is that one hour of time contributed equals one Time Pound (or one Time Dollar). Everyone's time is worth the same. ✋ People should try to use up all the credits they earn. Or they can donate them to another individual or an organisation.

The Time Bank website explains how a Time Bank Works and gives you Ten Steps to creating your own Time Bank: www.timebanks.co.uk

Organisations can also participate in Time Banks. They can use the Time Bank to buy such things as help with:

Door-to-door leaflet delivery.
Getting repairs and decorating done.
Answering the telephone. Other assistance they require.

They can earn Time Credits through offering use of their resources, such as computers and photocopiers, or providing meeting space and training.

...and get help in return

✋ **Join a Time Bank.** See how much credit you can earn by helping others. Then start spending your credit by getting others to help you.

✋ **If there isn't a Time Bank in your community, start one.** Five or six people will be enough to get going. These could be friends, people from a local tenants' association, people you meet in the doctor's waiting room, or parents and teachers from your local school. Show people what they can achieve immediately by doing something together for the community.

identify GM MILK

There is an international debate raging about genetically modified foods. On the one side are the food manufacturers and the US government, who are pressing for free trade in GM products; on the other side are most consumers and the European Union, who want to restrict the trade. ☺ The real problem is that we don't know enough about the long-term impact of the release of genetically modified organisms into the environment, nor do we know whether eating GM products will have any adverse impact on our health.

Those opposed to GM crops have the following concerns:

Health: including toxicity and potential allergic reactions.

Environmental: including the possibility that GM crops will contaminate non-GM crops in nearby fields, increase pesticide pollution, damage the soil and reduce biodiversity.

Economic: particularly in the developing world, where farmers using seeds will become totally dependent on the GM seed suppliers. GM crops may hold a key to feeding the world's growing population – but their safety should be proved first.

The UK campaign to get GM out of food was led by Greenpeace and Friends of the Earth, and has been really successful. Because of public pressure, supermarkets and food manufacturers have removed GM ingredients from their products and no GM crops will be grown in the UK in the foreseeable future. ☺ However, one problem remains – animal feed. GM ingredients are still being used by animal-feed producers.

The Shoppers Guide to GM: www.greenpeace.org.uk/Products/GM/index.cfm
Greenpeace GM camapign: www.greenpeace.org.uk
Friends of the Earth's real food campaign:
www.foe.co.uk/campaigns/real_food/index.html

Greenpeace campaigns through direct action

Despite the ban on growing GM crops, there is no ban on the import of GM animal feed, much of which is fed to the nation's dairy cows. Many consumers are unaware of this,

but when made aware say that they would prefer it to stop. Marks & Spencer led the way, with a ban on milk produced by cows fed on GM feed. By late 2005 other supermarkets were considering following suit, but were clearly waiting to see whether customer power was going to force their hand.

Greenpeace is running a lively campaign, involving approaching shoppers outside supermarkets and offering to swop their GM milk for bottles of organic milk.

...pop the question

Copy the 'model' letter from the Greenpeace website (under Campaign/ GM/Get Active) and send it to the supermarket of your choice. Addresses are provided.

JULY 29

LOVE *your neighbourhood*

Your neighbourhood is special. Even if it's not perfect, you can learn to love it. Look around you and think about the things you really like. And do what you can to resist the way in which everything is becoming more and more uniform – the same shops, the same undistinguished new buildings, the same ways in which cars and parking are given precedence over people.

What's special could include parks and playgrounds, with people enjoying themselves, statues, architectural details such as a crazy chimney or interesting doorway, shop signs, road names, front gardens, trees and flowers…

Common Ground, with rules for local distinctiveness: www.commonground.org.uk

Some rules for local distinctiveness

Change things for the better – not just for the sake of it.

Let the character of the people and place win through. Kill corporate identity before it kills our high streets. Give local shops precedence.

Defend detail. Respond to the local and the vernacular. New buildings or developments need not be bland, boring or brash.

Enhance the natural features of the area – the rivers and brooks, the hills and valleys, the woods and heaths.

Get to know your ghosts. The hidden and unseen stories and legends of the area are as important as what is visible.

History is a continuing process, not just the past. Don't fossilise places. Celebrate time, place and the seasons with feasts and festivals.

Jettison your car whenever you can and use public transport. Places are for people and nature, not cars.

Know your place. Facts and surveys are not the same as knowledge and wisdom.

Buy things that are locally distinctive and locally made – such as food and souvenirs. Resist the things that can be found anywhere.

Names carry resonances and secrets. Respect local names and add new ones with care. It is not good enough to call a new estate 'Badger's Mead' when all the badgers have been destroyed.

Reveal the past. Decay is an important process. Don't tidy things up so much that the layers of history and reclamation by nature are obliterated. Let continuity show.

Use old buildings again. Find new functions for them.

…make your locality unique

🏠 **Take a camera** and photograph the 25 things that most please you about your neighbourhood.

🏠 **Prepare a virtual exhibition.**

🏠 **Contact your local paper** and offer to email your exhibition to anyone who is interested.

30 JULY

population PRESSURE

There were 6,607,480,457 human beings alive on the planet on 25 July 2007, at 15.52 GMT precisely, according to the US Census Bureau estimates. 🌐 The world's population has doubled since 1963 and increased by 75.6 million during 2005. By mid-2050, the population is estimated to rise to 9 billion. 🌐 Our planet has a limited supply of land, water and natural resources. Will it be able to support its increasing human population? What will be the environmental consequences? Will technology come to the rescue?

In the 1970s the world's two most populous nations took action to curb their growing populations. China instituted a one-child policy, and India introduced sterilisation camps and forced vasectomies. The side effects ranged from human misery to female infanticide. 🌐 It is now recognised that since poverty and gender inequality are key factors in population increase, the best way of slowing the rate of increase is by creating a social climate receptive to messages about family planning.

Providing a decent education for girls, so that they develop into women who have a much clearer idea of the options open to them, is an effective way of reducing the birth rate. Literate women are in a better position to act on information about how to limit their family and protect their children from disease. They are more likely to generate extra income to bring up a smaller family in greater prosperity.

World population information: www.census.gov/main/www/popclock.html
World Population/Overpopulation Awareness: www.overpopulation.org
United Nations Population Fund: www.unfpa.org

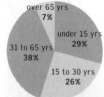

Population trends

Children under the age of 15 currently make up a large proportion of the world's population.

With birth rates falling, and people living longer, children will decline as a proportion of the population.

...help to relieve it

Whether you have a large family or a small family will not make much of a difference to the world's population. But you can make a difference by helping families and communities to get out of poverty. Your financial support will help meet basic community needs (such as health and sanitation), provide a better education, and help families find ways of increasing their income. You can:

🌐 **Sponsor a child,** where your support will help a family and the wider community. Organisations such as ActionAid and Plan International specialise in child sponsorship. It costs around 50 pence a day.

JULY 31

LEMONADE *for Alex* ☺

We have heard people say that Alex lost her battle with cancer. We believe that this could not be farther from the truth. Alex won her battle in so many ways ... by facing her cancer every day but still managing to smile; by never giving up hope; by living life to the fullest; and by leaving an incredible legacy of hope and inspiration for all of us.

– Jay and Liz Scott, Alex's parents

Alexandra Scott was an incredible eight-year-old. When she was only one year old she was diagnosed with neuroblastoma, an aggressive form of childhood cancer. At the age of four, she decided to set up a lemonade stand to raise money for her treatment. Her goal was to raise $1 million for paediatric cancer research, one glass of lemonade at a time. Now there are hundreds of lemonade stands all over the USA, raising money for Alex's paediatric cancer fund. Alex's fund has so far raised over $1.4 million.

Alex died on 1 August 2004. Her story is told in a book, *Alex and the Amazing Lemonade Stand*.

Childhood cancer facts:

One in every 600 children develops cancer before the age of 15.
Leukaemia and brain tumours account for more than half the cases.
The causes of most childhood cancers are unknown. At present, childhood cancer cannot be prevented.
Childhood cancer occurs randomly and spares no ethnic group, socio-economic class or geographic region.

Alex's Lemonade Stand: www.alexslemonade.com
Children's Cancer Web, information on childhood cancer:
www.cancerindex.org/ccw/guide2c.htm

How to make your own lemonade (sufficient for 50 glasses):

1 **Make a syrup.** Add ten cups of sugar to ten cups of water in a saucepan. Bring slowly to the boil, stirring until the sugar completely dissolves. Allow to cool. Refrigerate.
2 **Juice 50 lemons.** Make sure you remove the pips. Add the lemon juice to the syrup.
3 **Dilute to taste** with still or sparkling water. Add approximately three times the quantity of water to syrup.
4 **Decorate** with a half slice of lemon and a mint leaf.

...fight childhood cancer

Set up a lemonade stall in Alex's honour. Send the profits to Alex's Lemonade Fund at the Philadelphia Foundation: www.philafound.org/Alexslemonade.html or in the UK to CLIC-Sargent cancer care for children: www.clicsargent.org.uk

You will need:

☺ **A table,** lots of lemonade, a jug and plastic cups.
☺ **A sunny day** (hopefully).
☺ **A cheerful friend** to keep you company.
☺ **Posters and banners** that say what you are raising money for.
☺ **A cash box.**

1 AUGUST

buy a SHARE

Would you like to own Microsoft? When you buy a share in Microsoft, you become a co-owner of the company, along with all the other shareholders. You get these benefits:

    A share certificate, proclaiming your ownership.

    An annual report of the company's performance.

    Share dividends.

    The right to attend the company's Annual General Meeting and to vote on the resolutions put to the meeting. These include appointing Company Directors and agreeing their remuneration.

When you decide to sell your shares, you might even make a profit if the value of the shares has increased.

As a shareholder, you can vote against the appointment of a Director or against their proposed remuneration. Of course, your share of the company is tiny – so this will only have any impact if it is part of a wider campaign. 🚹 At the AGM, there will also be an opportunity to ask the Chair a question. You might ask about:

    Child labour: does the company use it?

    Waste disposal: does the company dispose of its waste safely?

    Global warming: is the company doing enough to address global warming?

Whatever your particular concern, you can ask the company for a response in front of a large audience with lots of journalists present.

Some companies find their shareholder meetings become a forum – sometimes a battleground – where social and environmental issues are raised: companies such as Nestlé (which markets formula milk in the developing world) and Exxon (which is not doing enough to counter global warming). All you need is one share in order to have the right to attend.

Information and ideas on shareholder activism:
www.coopamerica.org/socialinvesting/shareholderaction

Isabel Losada was campaigning with the Free Tibet Movement. They arranged for her to attend the AGM of BP to raise the issue of BP's investment in PetroChina, which was planning to build a pipeline through Tibet. Once she was in the meeting hall, Isabel changed into the costume of a Chinese soldier. Every time the Chair mentioned Tibet, she clapped and cheered. Every time her fellow Free Tibet protesters got to ask a question, she hurled abuse at them. And she congratulated the Chair on not letting terrorists disrupt the profits of the company. Humour is an excellent way to make a point. Read Isabel's book, *For Tibet with Love.*

...and have your say

Is there a company you would like to confront over an issue?

🚹 Buy one share in that company – through an online dealing service or a stockbroker.

🚹 Go along to the AGM. When the Chair asks for questions, stand up and have your say.

AUGUST 2

FOOD MILES

Food miles are a measure of the distance food has travelled from the field to your plate. Agricultural products and processed food now account for nearly 30% of goods travelling on our roads. They cause congestion and pollution, and add to the carbon emissions that are fuelling climate change.

A basket of fresh food bought in a supermarket in spring may contain:
- 🌳 brussel sprouts from Australia (10,562 miles)
- 🌳 sugar-snap peas from Guatemala (5,457 miles)
- 🌳 potatoes from Israel (2,187 miles)
- 🌳 chicken from Thailand (6,643 miles)
- 🌳 fish from the Indian Ocean (4,513)

Food miles are increasing, not only because food is coming from further afield, but because food processing involves ingredients being transported around the country, from factory to factory. Centralised supermarket distribution can also lead to food travelling many miles to be packaged at a central depot, and then being sent back to be sold near where it was produced. Next time you travel down a motorway, look out for the supermarket trucks criss-crossing the country.

Food matters: www.bbc.co.uk/food/food_matters/foodmiles.shtml
Life Cycles: www.lifecyclesproject.ca/initiatives/food_miles
National Sustainable Agriculture Information Service:
attra.ncat.org/farm_energy/food_miles.html

The story of a jar of yogurt

To produce a small glass jar of strawberry yogurt on sale in Stuttgart, researchers found:
- Strawberries transported from Poland to West Germany to be processed into jam and sent to Southern Germany.
- Yogurt cultures from North Germany; corn and wheat flour from the Netherlands; and sugar beet from East Germany.
- Labels and aluminium lids made over 300 km away. The glass jar and the milk were produced locally.
- To bring one lorry-load of yogurt pots to the South German distribution centre involved a distance travelled equivalent to 1,005 km, requiring some 400 litres of diesel.

The same story is repeated for almost everything you buy at the supermarket.

...reduce them

How to reduce your food miles:

🌳 **Walk to your local greengrocer or farmers market** and buy produce that is local, in season, and organic.

🌳 **Always ask where produce has come from.** Make a rule never to buy anything that has travelled further than 100 miles to get to you. You won't starve.

3 AUGUST

cleaning WATER

In February 2004 Coca-Cola launched Dasani in the UK. This bottled drinking water retailed for £1.69 (about $3.20). But its launch was followed by two fiascos. ☺ The first was when the press discovered that the water being used was actually common or garden London tap water, with impurities removed by a process called reverse osmosis. ☺ The second was when it was found that one of the minerals being added to improve the taste of the water exceeded safety levels. Following this double whammy, the product was withdrawn.

In the rich world, water is a 'lifestyle product'. We are willing to pay double the cost of a litre of petrol for a litre of water. ☺ In the developing world, lack of access to safe clean drinking water means disease and death. Clean water is a matter of life rather than lifestyle, and bottled water is bought at grossly inflated prices by those too poor to have a water source 'on tap'.

The technology that was used for Dasani has now been adapted for public use, making clean water a realistic possibility for everyone. Just digging wells is not sufficient if the ground water is contaminated with arsenic, fluorides or nitrates, as it so often is. ☺ The Bhabha Atomic Research Centre in Mumbai has installed small reverse-osmosis plants in a number of Indian villages. These plants are now commercially available, and can provide drinking water to communities of up to 1,000 people. The production cost of the water works out at about 0.03 cents per litre. Dasani was 1,000 times more expensive! This is technology solving the world's problems.

WaterAid: www.wateraid.org.uk

Water purifying units: As well as the small reverse-osmosis units developed in Mumbai, other mobile water-purifying units using waste heat, diesel or solar power are also available. A domestic water purifier based on an ultra-filtration membrane has been developed that produces 40 litres of safe drinking water a day. This could be used by any household with access to a well.

Schools & colleges...hotels...hospitals...can all use our water purification system to get water as pure as bottled water.

– Advertisement for a Pentair Water reverse-osmosis
system www.pentairwater.com

Their system costs $5,000, has a capacity of 500 litres per hour, and provides 1,500 glasses of clean water at a cost of just $1. Why can it not be used in villages, or in urban slums?

...techies to the rescue

☺ **Buy a bottle of mineral or filtered water, but once you've drunk it, promise never to do this again!** Put tap water into your empty water bottle, and nobody will know the difference. Refill as necessary.

☺ **When you go out to a restaurant, ask for 'local tap',** with ice and a slice of lemon.

☺ **Calculate how much you are saving from both these actions.** Donate this to WaterAid, which works to bring clean water to thirsty people around the world.

AUGUST 4

COMPOST *your waste*

Composting decomposes organic matter into a growing medium full of nutrients. It takes place when organic matter is kept warm and dry for some months. It can be speeded up by using worms – called 'vermicomposting'.

A third of all household refuse could be composted, as well as most garden waste: grass mowings, hedge trimmings and plants that have flowered (but not weeds). 🌳 Home-made compost makes an excellent soil conditioner and a rich source of plant food. The compost can be used in your garden and for your window boxes and pot plants. It cuts down on the need to buy peat-based products, thus saving the now nearly extinct peat bogs.

Detailed instructions on composting: www.mastercomposter.com

Can-o-Worms, an easy to use vermicomposter where the worms do all the work from: www.wigglywigglers.co.uk

Do compost:

Kitchen waste – fruit and vegetable peelings, tea bags, coffee grounds, crushed eggshells.
Garden waste – grass cuttings, hedge clippings, old flowers.
Crumpled or shredded card and paper – avoid heavily coloured paper.
Wood ash.
Human hair and animal fur.
Autumn leaves. Put large amounts in bin liners to rot down for mulch.
Old clothes – pure wool and other natural fabrics.
Sawdust, bedding and manure from vegetarian pets such as rabbits.

Don't compost:

Cooked food, meat and fish.
Droppings from meat-eating animals.
Magazines and heavily inked cardboard.
Nappies.
Coal ash and soot.
Diseased plants.
Roots of persistent weeds such as bindweed or couch grass.
Synthetic fabrics.
Glass, plastic and metal (to be recycled separately).

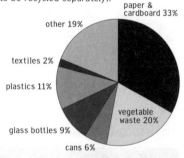

paper & cardboard 33%
other 19%
textiles 2%
plastics 11%
glass bottles 9%
cans 6%
vegetable waste 20%

A rough breakdown of UK household waste

...it's fun and easy

- 🌳 **Build a compost bin and recycle your waste.** If you have a garden or a yard, build a bin from old pallets or wood posts and wire-mesh netting, lined with old carpet or thick cardboard. Cover with a wooden lid or old carpet to keep the rain out and heat in.
- 🌳 **Buy a desktop wormery.** This is an educational toy, artwork and desktop paperweight all in one. The kit contains bedding, drainage chips, sand and 12 worms, which you assemble in a small glass-fronted case. Give it to your green friends or worst enemies – £40 from WigglyWigglers.

5 AUGUST

ambush MARKETING

Sport is big business all over the world, and relies on commercial sponsorship. The commercial interests of sponsors are now becoming much more important than the comfort and enjoyment of the people who come to watch sporting events (and often pay huge sums for their tickets).

The World Cup football tournament in Germany in 2006 attracted fans from around the world. A Dutch brewery produced short trousers in bright orange (the Dutch national colour), with the name of one of their beers, Bavaria, written prominently along one side. More than a quarter of a million fans purchased these trousers (which had extra large pockets to carry cans of drink), and more than 1,000 fans turned up to watch their side play the Ivory Coast wearing the trousers. But one of the sponsors of the World Cup was Budweiser, a rival beer. To protect the interests of their sponsors, the organisers made the Dutch fans pull down their trousers and watch their side in underpants. They weren't allowed even to bring the offending clothing into the stadium.

In England, the organisers of the 2004 Champions Trophy cricket tournament (sponsored by Pepsi) issued a list of what soft drinks fans could take into the ground. These included Pepsi, Tango, 7-up and Abbey Well water (all Pepsi brands); other brands were not allowed.

Coke ambush

In Evans, Georgia, in March 1998, the Greenbrier High School held a 'Coke in Education Day', focusing the whole day on Coca-Cola and its products. There was a talk by a senior manager on business economics, a recipe for a Coca-Cola cake was used in the home economics class, and there was a group photograph of students in Coca-Cola t-shirts.

Mike Cameron, a student at the school, did not want to be part of this marketing fest for Coca-Cola. He was wearing two t-shirts. Under the Coke shirt was another, promoting Pepsi. Immediately before the photograph was taken, Mike pulled off his Coke shirt to ambush the photo-shoot. He was suspended for his efforts.

Aside from the question as to whether schools should be plugging high-sugar carbonated drinks, there is also the important issue of freedom of speech that this incident highlights.

...undermine the power of sponsors

⚽ **At the next sponsored event you go to** – a concert sponsored by IBM, a gallery opening sponsored by Vodafone, or a tennis match sponsored by Stella Artois – make a point of dressing in competing logos and taking along rival products.

⚽ **Stand up for the freedom** of sports lovers to wear what they want and drink what they like (but be prepared to be thrown out).

AUGUST 6

CHICKEN *farming*

There are 30 million chickens in the UK. Despite the public concern about their living conditions, 85% still live in batteries and 70% are kept in huge sheds containing upwards of 20,000 birds. Most farms keep four or five birds in a cage no more than 50 cm x 50 cm. The minimum legal requirement for one bird is just under three quarters the size of an A4 sheet of paper. (This will be doubled by 2012 as a result of a EU directive.) ✋ The average hen lays eggs 338 per year. The chickens are kept for around 70 weeks before being slaughtered, mostly for pet food, although some enter the human food chain.

This is not just cruel to the birds, but dangerous for humans. Intensive chicken rearing makes diseases such as salmonella more likely. ✋ There are alternatives:

Better:
Barn hens, with 25 birds per m² on raised platforms Deep litter, part-solid cage and just seven birds per m².

Much better:
Freerange, with access to the outdoors, allowing 1,000 birds per hectare.

Best:
Your very own backyard chickens. The birds are not only decorative and entertaining, but provide delicious fresh eggs. This is your chance to change the world – one egg at a time!

Information about battery chickens: www.downthelane.net/battery.html
Compassion in World Farming: www.ciwf.org.uk
The Eglu is available from: www.omlet.co.uk

The Eglu is a chicken coop for the 21st century, featuring spacious open-plan living for two medium-sized chickens or three bantams. It is a stylish and practical addition to any garden. Designed to be comfortable for the chickens, and effortless for you, the Eglu makes keeping chickens rewarding and fun. It is fitted throughout with wooden roosting bars and an integrated nesting box with privacy screen to preserve your chicken's modesty when laying an egg. The chickens are kept warm in the winter and cool in the summer, thanks to modern twin-walled insulation. To make collecting your eggs easy, the Eglu has an eggport, which gives access to the nesting box. Available in three fantastic colours, you can make a statement in red, have fun with yellow or keep it subtle in green.

– from the Eglu sales blurb

Every Eglu comes complete with its own private secure area, enclosed with animal-proof wire netting to keep hungry foxes away from your chickens. You also get two chickens, well-suited to domestic gardens, friendly, organically reared to Soil Association standards, and at 'point of lay'. You can start getting eggs and turning them into omelettes right away.

...freerange in your garden

✋ **Become a backyard chicken farmer.** Buy an Eglu. The complete package costs around £350. Start saving right away and you'll never need to buy eggs ever again.

✋ **Adopt a chicken** and find out about trade injustice in Ghana. Click on each chicken and hear their stories on this hilarious Christian Aid website: www.mailorderchickens.org

7 AUGUST

decide to **GIVE UP**

Giving it up is good for your soul. Hindus go in for renunciation. Christians give it up for Lent (the 40-day period before Easter). Muslims have the holy month of Ramadan (a month when they fast from dawn to sunset). Jews have Yom Kippur (a fast which lasts about 25 hours).

But here's another take on the idea of giving up: There must be things you could give up that would make only a tiny difference to your life. But using the time or money you save, you could then make a big difference to the world. Here are some ideas for what to give up:

Give up drinking bottled water. Drink tap water instead. There's nothing wrong with it, and it's free (once you are connected to the mains). And it doesn't involve lorries thundering down the motorway to bring it to you, or empty bottles to dispose of.

Give up purchasing a cup of coffee on the way to the office each morning. Why? There are cheaper ways of getting your morning caffeine fix. Buy a thermos flask (one of those aluminium designer ones if you care about looking cool) plus a really nice cup and a teaspoon. Make your coffee at home and add milk and sugar as you wish. Use only the finest ingredients – the best coffee, freshly ground, fairtrade of course. Take this with you to work. Then enjoy.

Give up smoking. This is the single most sensible thing you can do for a healthier life. And it will make a huge difference to your finances.

Whatever you think you can give up, do! Then think of something creative to do with all the money you save.

H2G2 is a website inspired by The Hitchhiker's Guide to the Galaxy. It is a guide to 'life, the universe and everything'. It is an open-source guide, with visitors to the website contributing, adding to and amending content. You can contribute your ideas on how to give it up and how to get a life: www.bbc.co.uk/dna/h2g2

Here are some more ideas for things to give up:

Replace things with logos with things with no logo (read Naomi Klein's book *No Logo*).

Give up deodorant, and smell like yourself rather than a perfume factory (and save the world from volatile organic compounds).

Be alcohol-free at least one day a week.

...and get a life!

Answer these two questions:
1 What can I give up that I will barely even notice?
2 What will this then enable me to do?
Give it up. And do it!

AUGUST 8

FAIRTRADE *tea*

A community of forest dwellers in southern India has challenged the bastion of colonial rule and embarked on tea growing. The people are 'adivasis' – indigenous forest-dwellers. They live in forests about 5,000 feet up in the Nilgiri Hills. Over the years, the adivasis lost their rights over the forest lands, because of enclosure by powerful people who wanted to settle the land and fell the trees, and the Forest Department, who wanted people out of the forests for conservation reasons. ⚽ The Tribal Community Organisation (AMS) encouraged settled agriculture in order to make the adivasis economically independent and to protect tribal land rights. It came up with the idea of tea cultivation. This made sense because it was the predominant crop of the area, would generate a regular income, and because planting tea would provide evidence that the adivasis had tenure of the land. ⚽ Over the last ten years, more than 1,000 families have each planted tea on plots of up to one acre, and are now enjoying a steady income.

Tea growing provided the Tribal Community Organisation with a base for building a number of other enterprises:

A Tea Nursery to supply tea plants.

Co-operative tea marketing to negotiate a better price with the factories that cure the tea.

A 300-acre tea estate owned and operated by the community.

These initiatives led to the Just Change project, which promotes barter trading between communities of poor people in India, and markets the produce made by these communities to affluent consumers in India and overseas.

Just Change: www.justchangeindia.com
AMS, the tribal community organisation: www.adivasi.net
ActionAid's Chembakolli tea pack: schools@actionaaid.org.uk and www.chembakolli.com

Fairtrade tea

Unlike fairtrade coffee, which is produced by cooperatives of small farmers, fairtrade tea is produced mostly on large privately owned plantations in India, Sri Lanka and East Africa. To become fairtrade-certified, a tea estate has to provide its workers with fair wages and good working conditions, and ensure adequate housing and healthcare. Certified estates encourage sustainable farming, prohibit child labour, and the workers and managers together decide how the fairtrade premium will be used to benefit the workers – for housing, healthcare, education or income-generating projects. There are around 50 fairtrade-certified tea estates in India, employing more than 120,000 workers.

...sell it to your friends

Package and market tribal tea from the Nilgiris.

⚽ **Sealed bags** containing 25 tea bags can be purchased from Just Change for 90p. Design nice packaging and leaflets showing where the tea comes from.

⚽ **Sell as much as possible** to friends and colleagues. Make a good profit. Set up a thriving tea business.

⚽ **Organise a 'Mad Hatter's Tea Party'** as a fundraising event.

9 AUGUST

hug a TREE

Almost everybody understands the value of trees, whether they just add to the landscape or are essential to their lives and livelihoods. And people do some weird and wonderful things to protect them.

When a 400-year-old giant oak tree in Southern California was threatened by the widening of a highway for a new housing development, John Quigley came to its rescue. With the support of other tree-lovers, he ascended into the leafy heights of 'Old Glory', as the beautiful oak tree was named by local children, and stayed there for 71 days during the winter of 2002–03. Eventually he was removed by police, and in January 2004 the developers paid for the tree to be moved to a new home.

The Chipko Movement became world famous in the 1970s and 1980s. It showed the power of ordinary people to stand up to the rich and powerful. Local people on India's border with Tibet had used the forests in the foothills of the Himalayas in a sustainable way for many years. The forest had provided them with food, materials for shelter, medicines and fodder for their animals. Then the government restricted their access and sold licences to fell the trees to the highest bidder. When a sporting goods manufacturer arrived to fell the trees, local people, including many women, went out and hugged the trees to prevent them being chainsawed to destruction. This was the birth of Chipko Andolan (Hindi for 'Movement to Hug'). The movement leader, Chandi Prasad Bhatt, declared their aim: 'Let them know they will not fell a single tree without felling one of us first. When the men raise their axes, we will embrace the trees to protect them.' The loggers withdrew. Over the next few years, many forests were saved through what became the Chipko Movement.

> *Embrace the trees and*
> *Save them from being felled;*
> *The property of our hills,*
> *Save them from being looted.*   – Poem for Chipko

Read about the amazing efforts to save Oak 419: www.saveoldglory.com
For more information on the Chipko Movement:
www.unu.edu/unupress/unupbooks/80a03e/80A03E08.htm
The Ancient Tree Hunt: www.woodland-trust.org.uk/ancient-tree-hunt

The Ancient Tree Hunt: Unless you know exactly what you've got and where it is, you can't really protect it. That is the principle behind the survey organised in the UK by the Ancient Tree Forum, The Woodland Trust and the Tree Register of the British Isles. But they are relying on you to go out there and find the trees, measure them, and send in the details. It's a bit trickier than it sounds, so check out the website and find out how to do it properly.

...or hunt one if you prefer!

- Go out and hug a large and lovely tree in your local park or wood. Think about the heroism of the Chipko pioneers and about what you can do to preserve trees and woodlands.
- **If you are too embarrassed to hug a tree,** then go out and hunt one! And send the details to The Ancient Tree Hunt.

CIVILIAN *casualties*

We don't do body counts.

> – General Tommy Franks, US Central Command

War has distressing consequences for civilian populations. Even if civilians are not directly killed or maimed as a result of military action, they may suffer long-term injury or illness as a result of radiation, post-conflict contact with unexploded munitions, or pollution caused by the spillage of toxic materials. Populations become displaced and many people suffer deep psychological trauma. ❧ Documenting and assigning responsibility for the side-effects of war is a hard task, requiring long-term on-the-ground resources. But direct deaths and injuries from military strikes can be much more easily identified, both in place and in time, and responsibility can readily be attributed to the weapon that caused that death or injury. ❧ Despite this, the military forces operating in Iraq, predominantly from the USA and the UK, make no attempt to keep a tally of the civilian deaths caused by their actions.

The Iraq Body Count project has been created 'to record single-mindedly and on a virtually real-time basis one key and immutable index of the fruits of war – the death toll of innocents.' It aims to promote public understanding, engagement and support for the human dimension of the 2003 Iraq war by providing reliable, up-to-date documentation of civilian casualties.

For every American death there have been at least 19 Iraqi deaths:
  American servicemen killed in Iraq (end August 2007): 3,722
  Iraqi civilians reported killed by military intervention in Iraq calculated by Iraq Body Count, end August 2007: 70,749–77,272

Iraq Body Count: www.iraqbodycount.org
To find out about the cost of the Iraq war to the US ($185 billion as of July 2005) and what the money could have been spent on, go to: costofwar.com

How the Iraq body count is conducted

The information is gleaned by surveying the reports of news-gathering services around the world. An incident must be reported by at least two agencies, and by logging the following information the organisation aims to ensure that an incident is not counted more than once:

Date of incident
Time of incident
Location of incident
Target as stated by military sources
Weapon
Minimum civilian deaths
Maximum civilian deaths
Sources (at least two sources)

Start creating a dossier of facts and figures on an issue that particularly concerns you. Save press cuttings and read official reports. Use the internet to help you in this research. Very quickly, you may find yourself becoming an expert on the subject.

11 AUGUST

if you're **YOUNG**

These are ways in which young people can link together to change the world:

The Freechild Project was set up to advocate, inform, and celebrate social change led by young people around the world. Their website is a great resource list for youth action and many of the important issues being addressed by young people.

Free the Children is an international network of children helping children at a local, national and international level through representation, leadership and action. It was founded by Craig Kielburger in 1995, when he was just 12 years old. The primary goal is to free children from poverty and exploitation.

iEARN describes itself as the world's largest non-profit global network that connects young people and encourages them to collaborate in changing the world. It brings them together from over 20,000 schools and youth groups in more than 110 countries. There are more than 120 iEARN projects, each trying to answer the question 'How will this project improve the quality of life on the planet?'

Peace Child International, an international network promoting youth action. Peace Child focuses mainly on the issues of sustainable development and human rights. Every two years, it organises a World Youth Congress for up to 1,000 young people (Hawaii 1999, Morocco 2003, Scotland 2005, Bangalore 2007). It also runs a 'Be the Change' programme to encourage and support local youth-led initiatives for changing the world. You can get involved in 'Be the Change', attend a World Youth Congress or volunteer as an intern at their HQ near London, with full board and lodging provided.

TakingITGlobal is a global online community which inspires young people to make a difference. It provides a source of information on issues, opportunities to take action, and a bridge to get involved locally, nationally and globally. Membership is free of charge and allows you to interact with various aspects of the website to contribute ideas, experiences, and actions. There are profiles of 850 youth projects that TiG members are undertaking all over the world. TiG www.takingitglobal.org is closely linked to the Global Youth Action Network

Young People Change The World! runs international summer schools for young activists in the UK and southern Asia.

www.freechild.org
www.freethechildren.org
www.iearn.org
www.peacechild.org
www.youthlink.org
www.change-the-world.net

...join up with others

- **If you're a young person** (aged 16 to 25) check out all these websites. And become a member of TakingITglobal.
- **If you once were a young person,** you can still change the world!

SURFERS *against sewage*

Humans produce waste. They create a continuous supply of sewage that requires disposal. In many countries, sewage treatment and disposal methods are primitive: whatever goes down the toilet washes up on the beach or along the banks of rivers. People relieve themselves in a stream at the top of a hill village, and other people wash and brush their teeth in it at the bottom.

Toxic chemicals produced as by-products of industrial processes also require disposal. Most are discharged into rivers and run off into the sea. Products in everyday use at home contain a vast array of chemicals and organic compounds that are flushed, washed away after bathing or showering, or disposed of directly into the drains. There is no regulation of these discharges. ♣ Once in the eco-system, these contaminants can react with each other, making it hard to predict their impact on the environment. Many substances will remain in the environment indefinitely, either in the water itself or in the flesh and fat of organisms.

Surfers Against Sewage has been campaigning against sewage discharge and toxic dumping since 1990, when a wet-suited and gas-masked 'SAS hit squad' demonstration took place at the Royal Cornwall Show, with beach pollution fact sheets handed out to the public. ('SAS' is not just the acronym of Surfers Against Sewage, but it's also the name of the prestigious special forces regiment of the British army.) ♣ From this small beginning, SAS has become a national campaign, highlighting the problem of sewage disposal into the sea, providing information and monitoring compliance with legislation.

Join Surfers against Sewage: www.sas.org.uk

The recipe for Faecal Soup: Everything that goes into the drains – bleach, chemicals from domestic products, paint and solvents, oils and fats – and everything that is flushed down the loo will end up in the sewers. The result is a complex mixture of liquids and solids: a 'faecal soup'. The ingredients of this soup are:

Sewage-related debris
Bacteria and viruses from human intestines
Chemicals and heavy metals from household and beauty products
Nutrients (nitrates and phosphates)
Endocrine disrupting substances
Oils, fats and greases

You're making this soup every day. It's lucky you don't have to drink it. Make sure others don't have to swim in it!

...for cleaner waters

Here is a four-point action plan for safer beaches, rivers and lakes:

1 Don't chuck rubbish down the loo – the only thing going down your toilet should be human waste and toilet paper.
2 Enjoy your beach, but remember to bin your rubbish or take it home.
3 If you notice a pollution incident, report it immediately.
4 Buy organic. Once pesticides get into the water cycle, they can persist indefinitely.

13 AUGUST

build a FLY TRAP

A fly is any species of insect of the order Diptera, some of which can land on food and transmit bacteria to humans. Particularly the housefly (Musca domestica) is common amongst humans and has caused many diseases to spread in the past. Other flies, such as the horsefly (family Tabanidae), can inflict painful bites. The larva of a fly is commonly called a maggot.

— Wikipedia definition

Flies affect almost everybody. They may not be as much of a nuisance as mosquitoes, but they can be just as dangerous.

Trachoma is caused by *Chlamydia trachomatis*, a micro-organism that spreads through contact with eye discharge from an infected person. It is transmitted via towels, handkerchiefs and fingers, and also through eye-seeking flies, taking the infection from one person to another. ☺ After years of repeated infection, the inside of your eyelid may become scarred so severely that the eyelid turns inward and your eyelashes rub on your eyeball, scarring the cornea (the front of the eye). If untreated, this condition will lead to blindness.

It affects 84 million people, of whom 8 million have become visually impaired. It is responsible for more than 3% of the world's blindness, and is especially prevalent in many of the poorest rural areas in the world.

All about Trachoma, World Health Organization:
www.who.int/blindness/causes/trachoma/en
Teaching Aids at Low-Cost (TALC), fly trap instructions:
www.talcuk.org/free/html/flytrap/flytrap.htm

Build a fly trap

Slits or small holes are made for ventilation

Tube of plastic with only small hole at top

Bait bottle. Lower half with dark paint inside. 2 or 3 fly entry ports.

Go to the TALC website and and download instructions on how to build a fly trap. You will need:
  Two large clear plastic bottles, preferably identical, one with its screw top.
  One smaller plastic bottle, made of smooth plastic.
  A small quantity of black or dark paint.
  A sharp knife.
  A small piece of string.
  A pointed instrument.
  A candle.
The flies fly into the lower bottle, attracted by bait. They then make their way through a narrow tube into the upper bottle, where they are trapped. Various baits can be used. Chicken entrails are OK but tend to dry up. Flies seem to like the smell of 250 g of yeast in a litre of water with 6 g of ammonium carbonate added two days later. The Maasai of Kenya use a mixture of goat dung and cows' urine — you could try this!

...for a more comfortable life

We've all seen dying children filmed in refugee camps with flies crawling all over their faces. We've also been infuriated by flies buzzing around us. Here's a chance to address both of these problems.

☺ **Make a fly trap for your kitchen.**
☺ **Choose a country and circulate the instructions** for making a fly trap as widely as possible in that country.

AUGUST 14

GUNS *in the hands of babes*

They held a court and found her [a girl presumed to be a spy] guilty. They ordered me to lead her away and shoot her, and at first I hesitated; but then I did it. To [the guerrillas] it was a proof of my loyalty, but to me it didn't prove anything.

— Gloria, who joined the FARC in Colombia aged 11

I killed another child. I did this three times. I felt bad but I knew what would happen if I disobeyed. Now I see dead people and blood in my dreams and I know the spirits of the children are coming to haunt me.

— Bosco, who was abducted by the Lords Resistance Army from Gulu, Uganda at age 12

Over 300,000 children are involved in combat, taking part in all aspects of warfare. They are in the front line, carrying AK-47s and M16s. They go on suicide missions, act as spies, sex slaves, runners, messengers, lookouts, assassins, soldiers and human mine detectors. ♠ Child soldiers are used in more that 30 countries. They are a cheap and expendable commodity, so tend to receive little or no training before being thrust into the front line. They suffer higher fatality rates than their adult counterparts. ♠ Some are abducted, some volunteer. The main reason for volunteering is their personal experience of ill treatment by government armed forces.

The 'Straight-18' Plan: The international community is trying to ratify an International Ban on Use of Child Soldiers, setting 18 years as the minimum age for conscription, forced recruitment and participation in armed conflict.

Coalition to Stop the Use of Child Soldiers: www.child-soldiers.org

The World Revolution, information on child soldiers: www.worldrevolution.org/guide/childsoldiers

Human Rights Watch, stop the use of child soldiers: hrw.org/campaigns/crp/index.htm

Burma has the largest number of child soldiers in the world, according to Human Rights Watch. The national army forcibly recruits children as young as 11. More than 20% of active duty soldiers may be under 18. Armed opposition groups use children as well.

For a copy of HRW's report 'My Gun was as Tall as Me' go to: hrw.org/press/2002/10/burma-1016.htm

...stop child soldiers

Human Rights Watch provides a sample letter for you to email or fax to governments.

- ♠ **Let governments know that you care** about the use of child soldiers, and that they should sign up or ratify the Ban.
- ♠ **Encourage Cambodia, Colombia, Jordan, Nepal and the Philippines** to join the 35 countries that have already ratified the Ban.
- ♠ **Encourage Algeria, Eritrea, Fiji, Mozmabique, Thailand and Yemen** to sign up.

15 AUGUST

anonymous GENEROSITY

The best way to cheer yourself up is to try to cheer somebody else up.
— Mark Twain

God loves a cheerful giver.
— notice seen in Mother Theresa's office

Think about the idea of giving freely to someone, without being asked or being expected to give, without you knowing them or them knowing you.

For example: you are crossing a toll bridge, and you decide to pay not just your own fare, but also the fare of the car behind you. You leave a card, saying that this is an act of generosity from a complete stranger. Why don't they then do something that will make someone else happy... and pass the card on. They put a £5 note with the card next to an ATM machine, to be picked up by someone who needs the money. That person then buys an extra ticket at the cinema for the next customer, who buys a drink in a bar for a person selected at random... and so the process goes on. There will be lots of happy people who have taken pleasure in making lots of other people happy.

It is attitudes and not just acts that can make a difference. Making another person happy could be like a butterfly flapping its wings and causing a hurricane thousands of miles away. Your unattributable act of generosity could be the start of a wind of change.

Give It Forward Today: www.giveitforwardtoday.org

The eight degrees of charity

Charity is a part of every religion. Moses Maimonides was a Jewish sage who lived in the 12th century. He suggested that there were eight degrees of charity:

Bottom level: Giving to a poor person unwillingly. It is better not to give at all.

Seventh level: Giving to a poor person with a glad heart and a smile.

Sixth level: Giving to a poor person after being asked.

Fifth level: Giving to a poor person before being asked.

Fourth level: Not knowing who you are giving to, but allowing the recipients to know who their benefactor is.

Third level: Knowing who you are giving to, but not allowing the recipients to know who their benefactor is.

Second level: Giving to the poor, but not knowing who you are giving to, nor allowing the recipients to know who their benefactor is.

Top level: Investing in a poor person, so that a solution to his or her problem is found.

...a true act of charity

Perform two acts of generosity today.

Go to the Give It Forward Today (GIFT) website, created by 12-year-old Alex Southmayd. He gives lots of ideas, plus you can download GIFT Certificates for the recipients of your generosity.

 Download two GIFT Certificates with the message: 'You have been GIFTed. Your mission (if you accept it) is to GIFT two human beings with an act of kindness. Please pass this on...'.

AUGUST 16

PHOTOGRAPH *a day in a life*

Seeing the world through other people's eyes can be a big shock. Your neighbours may be living next door to you geographically, but your lives could be a million miles apart. Knowing more about their completely different life experiences could help you understand how they feel and even make you see things in a completely new light.

Misunderstanding can foster fear and hatred; unfamiliarity may become an obstacle to peace. The Photographing a Day in Our Life project aims to open your eyes to the perspectives and ideas of your neighbours, through the lens of a camera, and to develop mutual understanding.

Here is how the Photographing a Day in Our Life project works: People from adjoining communities who normally would not interact – or who interact minimally or with some reserve – are grouped into pairs. The two groups could be contrasted by age, gender, religion, race, conflict, sexuality, income and opportunity, domestic situations, disability... whatever. ✢ Each pair is provided with a digital camera. They are charged with the task of 'photographing a day in each other's life'. ✢ The photographer shadows the person they are paired with, and captures images of their daily routine – at work, at play, at home. Then the roles are reversed. The photographer becomes the photographed. ✢ At the end of the project, each pair has to make a short presentation in which they explain what caught their interest in particular, and why they chose to show certain photographs.

PhotoVoice: www.photovoice.org

PhotoVoice: capturing portraits of life at the edge.

PhotoVoice, set up by Anna Blackman and Tiffany Fairey, trains socially excluded groups in photojournalism to give them a voice and provide professional skills. PhotoVoice works with homeless people, refugees, street and working children, orphans, disabled groups and women living with HIV/AIDS in Afghanistan, Democratic Republic of Congo, Nepal, Vietnam and the UK.

So far, they have trained over 300 people. Their images offer extraordinary insights into how people live, captured by the very people whose lives are a daily struggle.

...how do others see you?

✢ **Organise a Photograph a Day in Your Life project** at your school, community centre or workplace. Or link your church with a mosque, or your temple with a synagogue.

✢ **Bring two groups of people together** who ordinarily would not interact, or who are divided by conflict. All you need are some digital cameras.

17 AUGUST

celebrate **CYCLING**

The Revolution will arrive on a bicycle.

– Salvador Allende, President of Chile, 1970–73

Critical Mass is many things to many people, but it is foremost a celebration rather than a protest. It is a bunch of cyclists riding around together, going from one point to another. It is not organised. It is a group of individuals who just happen to be doing the same thing at the same time. And because there's no organisation and nobody in charge, no permission needs to be obtained for organising an event in a public place and there is no organiser to hold responsible.

It started in September 1992 in San Francisco as a festive reclaiming of public space. It originally had a less catchy name: 'The Commute Clot'. The first ride attracted 60 cyclists, and the numbers have grown over the years. The idea has also spread to other cities. Independent Critical Masses have sprung up all over the world. Critical Mass has become a self-propelling global movement.

Critical Mass has a different flavour in every city. Some groups are big, some small. There are different approaches to respecting traffic laws (or lack thereof), interacting with motorists and relationships with the police. If you want to know more about Critical Mass, you need to find out what it's like locally.

Critical Mass groups in the UK: criticalmasslondon.org.uk/when&where
How to start a Critical Mass bike ride: www.criticalmassrides.info/howto.html
How to make a Critical Mass: www.critical-mass.org
How to Not Get Hit By Cars, 10 tips for safer cycling: bicyclesafe.com
A resource site for cycle commuters: www.BikeToWork.com

critical mass Liberate London by Bike
Central London Critical Mass ride together monthly
Meet last Friday of each month
6pm Waterloo outside NFT on the southbank
http://www.criticalmasslondon.org.uk

A Critical Mass happening

'What's this all about?' ask amused and bemused pedestrians on Market Street as hundreds of noisy, high-spirited bicyclists ride past, yelling and ringing their bells. There are a wide variety of answers: 'It's about banning cars.' 'It's about having fun in the street.' 'It's about a more social way of life.' 'It's about asserting our right to the road.' 'It's about solidarity.'

In riding round the city as part of a Critical Mass, many important questions come up. Why is there so little open space in our cities where people can relax and interact, free from the incessant buying and selling of ordinary life? Why are people compelled to organise their lives around having a car? What would an alternative future look like?

...create a critical mass

🌳 **Join a Critical Mass ride.** Have fun. Assert the power of the pedaller. Reclaim the streets for the most environmentally friendly (and often the quickest) form of urban transport.

🌳 **If there isn't a Critical Mass in your city...then start one!**

AUGUST 18

DEMOCRACY *support it*

If democracy is to mean anything, it should express the will of the people, and the ballot box is how the will of the people is manifested. There may not be an election this year or even next. But it is important that you prepare for next time. ♪ What issues concern you most? Are the political parties even addressing them, let alone adopting policies you think are sensible?

Now is the time to start getting a group of people together, discussing the issues with them, and planning how, together, you can make an impact when the next election comes. It is never too soon to start a campaign to encourage participation in the political process. Then, when the next election comes, you will be prepared. You will know the issues. You will also know how to get involved in the election campaign.

League of Pissed Off Voters: www.indyvoter.org

They Work For You: find out about your Member of Parliament, their voting record, how they stand on the issues. The website also profiles the political parties and their manifestos, and think tanks and what they are thinking:
www.theyworkforyou.com

EPolitix, online news and discussion of the issues, plus links to MPs' websites:
www.epolitix.com

The League of Pissed-Off Voters

This was formed to encourage the younger generation to learn the nitty-gritty of politics and invent fresh ways of playing the democracy game on their terms. The League's intention is to transform thousands of young adults who have never messed with politics before, into savvy political players.

The League is American, but their ideas can be used anywhere. They publish the following resources for participating in elections:

A 90-day plan of action.
How to host a Kickass strategy session.
A sample survey for contact collection.
The 'You get out the Vote' toolbox.
How-to-get-out-the-vote in 12 easy steps.

...encourage people to vote

Don't leave politics to stiffs in suits. Get out and get active. Do it in your way. Make democracy work... for you!

♪ **Organise a 'Politics 'n' Pizza Brunch'.** This could also be 'Politics 'n' Pancakes' or 'Politics 'n' Punk' – whatever works for you. Make the invitation simple: 'Brunch this wknd?' or 'My house Sat' will usually be more appealing than 'League of Pissed Off Voters blah blah blah'.

♪ **Get together in small groups,** and once everyone has had something to eat and drink, make a list of the issues you think are important to all of you and the policies you would like to see implemented. Once candidates have been selected, communicate with them and extract some promises from them.

19 AUGUST

circles of COMPASSION

A 'Circle of Compassion' is a gathering at which people sit in a circle on the floor. It is also a tool to help people communicate honestly and openly. The Circle allows participants to:

Listen without judging.

Understand one another, bridge differences and try to reach a consensus.

Devise and implement creative solutions to problems in a spirit of openess and collaboration.

Settle disputes in a spirit of reconciliation.

The World Conference on Women held in Bejing in 1995 was a milestone in the development of international collaboration between women and women's organisations. Circles of Compassion are being promoted by the Women's World Summit Foundation as a mechanism for discussing some of the critical areas of concern that were identified there. The Foundation's target is to achieve one million circles.

Women's World Summit Foundation. Their website has information on organising a Circle of Compassion: www.woman.ch

The 12 areas of concern

1 The persistent and increasing burden of poverty on women.
2 Unequal access to education.
3 Inequalities in health and in access to adequate healthcare.
4 Violence against women.
5 The effects of armed and other conflict on women.
6 Inequality in economic structures, policy-making and production processes.
7 Inequality in power and decision-making.
8 Insufficient mechanisms to promote the advancement of women.
9 Lack of awareness of and commitment to women's human rights.
10 Insufficient coverage in the media of women's contribution to society.
11 Insufficient recognition of women's contribution to managing natural resources and safeguarding the environment.
12 The girl-child.

...address women's inequality

Create your own Circle of Compassion. Take one of the 12 Beijing issues. Invite friends, colleagues and acquaintances to contribute to the discussion. Think of a positive action you can take together to address the issue.

How a Circle is run:

The start and end time for the session are agreed.

Start the session with a moment of silent reflection.

Each participant shares what is important for them now – a challenge or a joy.

Leadership of the Circle is shared by rotation.

Equality is the rule – each person is equal to everyone else.

Ground rules are agreed and stuck to – e.g. interventions should be in a spirit of observation, never of correction or 'setting things right'.

One person speaks at a time. They will hold a 'talking stick', and pass this on to the person speaking next.

Participants speak from their own experience and from the heart, keeping to the theme of the discussion.

COMPUTERS *donated*

More than 600 million perfectly good computers will be discarded by companies worldwide over the next five years. In the UK every year over 3 million computers are decommissioned and 1 million end up filling up landfill sites. Fewer than 20% of old computers are recycled. Effective disposal of old computers is becoming increasingly costly, with stricter environmental regulations and declining residual values.

A great many old PCs are in good working order and could continue to be used by someone else. In the developing world, 99% of schoolchildren graduate from high school never having seen or touched a computer in the classroom. There are commercial organisations that take old PCs for recycling. There are also specialist organisations, that refurbish PCs and then send them to charities, schools and low-income households in developing countries.

Prices are getting lower and specifications are rising year by year. So the old computers that are being discarded have higher and higher specifications. What you no longer need can be a wonderful opportunity for someone else.

In the UK, contact: www.computeraid.org
UK directory of computer recyclers from: www.icer.org.uk

Computer Aid International

This is a specialist non-profit-making organisation that renovates and ships computers to developing countries at a cost of around £65 per unit, depending on the quantity shipped. The computers are shipped without a Windows operating system, but Linux can be installed at no extra cost.

Computer Aid International is now shipping 25,000 computers a year, mainly to Africa. These can be used for non-commercial purposes such as:

Computers in schools;
Setting up an IT skills training project;
Creating a cyber café to generate;
income;
A computer loan scheme for university students;
For distribution to non-governmental organisations.

...to developing countries

Donate your old computer through a computer recycling scheme.

Or you can take an old laptop with you when you are travelling to countries in the developing world, and find an organisation or a school and just leave it with them. These will be especially useful in areas where the power supply is irregular.

Encourage your employer to donate all your company's computers when upgrading.

21 AUGUST

build a SKIP SCULPTURE

We live in a throw-away society:

7 million tonnes of paper are thrown away every year in the UK alone. It requires 80 million trees to make this paper.

8.5 billion cans, half for food, half for drinks, are produced each year in the UK – enough to reach to the moon and back and halfway there again.

Every year, an average European family with two children throws away 50 kilos of paper (six trees), 60 kilos of metal and 45 kilos of plastic. That last item may not sound a lot, but it's equivalent to 13,500 supermarket bags.

Here are three ways to deal with all this rubbish:

Reduce. Throw away less. Make sure you buy products with as little packaging as possible.

Reuse. Buy a proper bag for your shopping, instead of using plastic bags. Use both sides of a sheet of paper.

Recycle. 80% of domestic rubbish can be recycled, including paper, glass, metal and plastic.

See the WEEE Man at: www.weeeman.org

The WEEE man

WEEE stands for Waste Electrical and Electronic Equipment. To highlight the problem of electrical and electronic waste, the Royal Society of Arts commissioned Paul Bonomini to create the WEEE Man, a humanoid sculpture made out of all the electrical and electronic equipment that one person is expected to consume in a lifetime. It weighs 3.44 tonnes and stands 7 metres high.

To work out its weight, a simple calculation was made. The total electrical and electronic waste for the UK population (938,000 tonnes in 2003) was divided by the UK population (59,553,000), giving a figure of 15.75 kg per person per year.

Average life expectancy is 78.05 years. A 21-year-old in 2003 will live until 2060. Factoring in an e-waste growth rate of 4%, this person will produce 3.44 tonnes of WEEE in their lifetime. The same person born in 2003 would live until 2075 and produce 8.36 tonnes of WEEE. The WEEE Man would have to double its size.

...turn junk into art

🏵 **Make your own sculpture with a message.** Scavenge the local skips. Make a tour of your neighbourhood. See what people are throwing away. Retrieve bits and pieces that look interesting. Use these to build a sculpture in your front garden or a park.

🏵 **Get a picture of your 'skip sculpture' in your local newspaper.** Use the publicity to highlight the quantity of waste being generated. Produce a simple leaflet or poster telling people what to do about this.

AUGUST 22

POSTERS *to download*

Sometimes people are spurred into action by some event. The Sharpeville massacres in apartheid South Africa, the Vietnam war, and now the 2003 US-led invasion of Iraq as part of the 'war on terror'. All of these have led to an outpouring of protest.

Society may be divided on the issues, but it can produce great poster art!

There are a large number of websites where you can download, reproduce and distribute some great copyright-free posters. Here are some:

Peaceposters: print or email a poster at: www.peaceposters.org

Another Poster for Peace: www.anotherposterforpeace.com

Over My Dead Body, with Iraq posters plus a make-your-own educational toy on the G8: www.overmydeadbody.org

The Ronald Reagan Home for the Criminally Insane, also featuring a print-your-own $100 Hallibacon bank note: www.insanereagan.com/graphics.shtml

Insta-Protest – 'In a better world I would have never had to make them. The sooner these posters become unnecessary the better': 64.70.140.219/feb15/

...display your protest

Create your own art gallery of posters

- **Visit the websites listed above** and any others you can find.

- **Download those you consider most effective,** print them out (using A3 paper if you can), frame them and hang them up. Email them to your friends. Make and send your own postcards using these designs.

- **Add to your collection by designing and printing your own poster.** The Insta-Protest website features a 'design-your-own-poster' function.

23 AUGUST

Cigarette butts are a major litter problem in our cities. Almost one in three end up discarded on the streets. Globally, 4.3 trillion cigarette butts are 'littered' every year, and in many rich countries they account for around half of all street litter. 200 tonnes of butts are discarded each year in the UK. In the USA it's over 250 billion individual butts. In Australia, the smokers of New South Wales throw away enough butts to fill seven Olympic-sized swimming pools. Up to 350,000 butts end up in Port Phillip Bay, Victoria and the waterways every day.

Indoor smoking bans have led to a dramatic increase in 'butt litter'. What's good for our health can be bad for the environment:

> **It can take up to 12 years** for a cigarette butt to break down.
> **Cigarette butts can leach chemicals** such as cadmium, lead and arsenic into the water table and the marine environment.

BUTTsOUT is a global campaign on cigarette-butt littering, now active in five countries. It was developed by PlanetArk in Australia. Its goal is to see individual smokers taking financial and personal responsibility for the litter they create, and to develop sustainable solutions to the problem of cigarette butts.

The campaign seeks to engage smokers and non-smokers alike. Non-smokers can educate smokers to recognise that butts are litter, and suggest positive alternatives to stubbing them out in the street. But in the end it is only smokers who can stop the problem by changing their behaviour.

BUTTsOUT: www.buttsout.net

Personal portable ashtrays

BUTTsOUT produce a funky, re-usable, fire-resistant personal ashtray that can be used outdoors. 82% of smokers say they would use them because they are so easy to operate. They trap most smell and smoke, fit into a pocket or clip on to a belt, and are available in a range of colours.

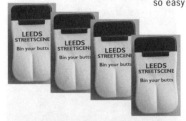

Leeds City Council distributed a customised version as part of a campaign to improve its streets. In Croydon, litter wardens have handed out free personal ashtrays to cigarette litterbugs, and tobacconists are being encouraged to stock them.

...keep your butt to yourself

 If you want to be nice: Buy your smoker friends a BUTTsOUT funky, re-usable, fire-resistant personal ashtray. Visit the BUTTsOUT website and select from a range of colours.

 If you are not prepared to be quite so nice: Buy an old tobacco tin (from a junk shop or car boot sale) and fill it with cigarette butts you have collected from the street. A pair of gloves and a face mask might be handy when you're doing this. Wrap up the box nicely and include a flyer from BUTTsOUT. Hey presto, a birthday present for a smoker.

A-B-C *make one*

We all tend to take our surroundings for granted. When you have lived or worked in a place for a long time you cease to 'see' it. You stop noticing the finer details of the architecture or the natural environment.

Your neighbourhood has evolved over the years. Understanding what makes it different from everywhere else – what makes it very special to you, what gives it a sense of place, what stories are attached to it, and what makes it the great place that it is – is important. It may be a street sign, a shop front, a carving on the brickwork, a tree or the fruit piled high on a market stall that makes you feel that your neighbourhood is special.

Why not celebrate your neighbourhood and raise everybody's awareness of their surroundings at the same time by producing an 'A-B-C': a graphic representation in 26 parts, based on the letters of the alphabet, of what makes your area special.

England in Particular, a Common Ground initiative:
www.england-in-particular.info/abc/ab-index.html

How to make an A-B-C

Decide the theme of your A-B-C. Will it cover everything, or just focus on one aspect of your neighbourhood in particular? Will it have a purpose? Is it for local interest? For tourists? As part of a local campaign? For citizenship education in schools?

Decide on the format. Your A-B-C could take many forms. Some are made entirely from photographs. Others include illustrations, linocuts, engravings or a mixture of all of these. Some have short captions. Others have longer descriptions.

Identify 26 places, objects or signs, each one linked to or depicting a particular letter of the alphabet. Take photographs of them. Using the pictures and captions, make these into a small booklet or a large poster.

You can use your A-B-C simply to show what delights you and what you care about – so that others will begin to see the neighbourhood in the same positive way as you do. You can use it as part of a campaign to save the area. You can even use it to show what's horrible, abandoned and in need of a bit of Tender Loving Care.

...of your neighbourhood

🏠 **Get together a small group of people.**

🏠 **Decide on the theme and the format** for your A-B-C.

🏠 **Choose an Art Director** to organise who does what and to create an overall design as well as preparing the artwork for the printer.

🏠 **Print and distribute it.** Decide on the selling price. Look out for possible outlets (such as bookshops, cafes, restaurants), and offer a good discount (40% at least) so that it's in their interest to help you sell it.

25 AUGUST

☺

give **BLOOD**

It must be a wonderful feeling to save someone's life. Although medical professionals, firefighters, coastguards, experience that satisfaction time and again, it seems beyond the reach of the rest of us. But you too can save a life simply by donating about an hour of your time – and a pint of your blood.

Few of us can predict when we might need a blood transfusion. And if we are lucky enough never to need one, then it is almost certain that our children, our parents, someone we know will need one sometime in the future. Giving blood couldn't be easier. It's quick, simple and safe. And all that most people feel is the satisfaction that they are helping to save lives.

Most people can give blood. If you're generally in good health, between the ages of 17 and 59 and weigh at least 50 kg (7 st 12 lb), you could start giving blood today. And when you do, find out how easy it is to save someone's life. ☺ If you are pregnant or have just had a baby, are taking antibiotics, have contracted or think you may have contracted HIV, had malaria, inject drugs, are a hepatitis carrier, then you will not be able to give blood. There are other criteria you have to pass as well, so contact the National Blood Service in advance, and they will send you a simple health-check form to fill in.

When you arrive to give blood someone will go through your health check form. If they consider that it is safe for you to be a donor, then a drop of blood will be taken from your finger and tested to make sure you're not anaemic. And if you're still OK, then just under a pint of your blood is taken – a procedure that takes about ten minutes.

National Blood Service: www.blood.co.uk

Helen's story

When Helen was born she was premature and weighed only 1.9 kg. When she was only a few weeks old she caught a chest infection and stopped breathing. She had to be put on a ventilator to keep her alive, and be pumped full of antibiotics to try and defeat the infection. It seemed as though she might lose the battle.

A blood test revealed that she was anaemic, and a blood transfusion was needed. Just a small amount of blood, donated on the spot by one of the hospital's support staff (who had been pre-screened), changed her from a pasty white to a healthy pink, and saved her life. She has never looked back.

...and save a life

If you're able to, give blood. Do this regularly.
Call up your local hospital or a national blood transfusion service for details of how to do it.

AUGUST 26

RAISING *water*

How can a children's roundabout provide people with water? In rural areas where water is scarce, fetching water will usually be done by women and girls. Water carriers will walk miles, often several times a day, in order to obtain their family's daily water requirements from local dams, springs, rivers, streams and farm reservoirs. 🌐 Boreholes, sunk into the ground, can provide better access to clean water. These are mainly operated by hand pumps. Although it is hard work pumping the water up by hand, petrol or electric pumps are too costly to install, run and maintain.

The 'Play-Pump' is a South African invention that uses the playful energies of children rotating a roundabout to raise water. It can provide up to 1,400 litres of water per hour, and is effective down to about 100 metres. Water is pumped into a 2,500 litre tank, 7 metres above the ground. A tap then provides access to the water. 🌐 Four billboards screen the tank. Two are used for health messages, but two have advertising, which provides money to pay for on-going maintenance. So far over 400 roundabouts have been installed in villages and primary schools.

Pump Aid, which provides simple but effective pumps in Zimbabwe and Mozambique, also introduces a sense of fun. The pumps it provides outside schools incorporate a 'bicycle system'. Most of the children have never had the chance to ride a bicycle so many come to school early to 'play' on the pump, thereby helping to fill the school water tanks. 🌐 The job of collecting water, once a tiresome chore, becomes fun, and children no longer have to leave their classrooms to walk miles carrying buckets of water on their heads from a distant muddy pool.

Roundabout Outdoor: www.roundabout.co.za
Pump Aid: www.pumpaid.org

The Play-Pump uses the energies expended by the children in making the roundabout go round and round to pump the water up from a borehole. Because the children are having fun, there is never a shortage of volunteers.

...in a roundabout way

Raise money to help African children play, attend school and keep healthy.

- 🌐 **A Play-Pump costs £5,000 to install,** and provides water for up to 2,500 people. Collect or raise just £100, and Roundabout Outdoor will send you a free hand-made wire frame replica of a Play-Pump as a thank you. This will make a nice collectable for your shelf; and will represent one-fiftieth of a continuous supply of clean water for a community.
- 🌐 **One of Pump Aid's 'Elephant Pumps' costs only £200.** They are made from local materials, use local labour, and are relatively simple to install and maintain. They can raise water from about 20 metres, at one litre of water every second.

27 AUGUST

Jill is a budding photographer who has put her portfolio online. Someday she might want to charge people for copying her photos. But now, when she is still trying to build her reputation, she wants people to copy her work as much as possible. Among her favourite photos are some dramatic black-and-white shots of famous skyscrapers.

Jack is making a digital movie about New York City using his new home computer. He wants to include a still photo of the Empire State Building, but he forgot to take one the last time he was in New York. He searches the internet for 'Empire State Building' and finds a collection of websites, some with photos. But he isn't sure if the photos are copyrighted or not. He uses a search engine that helps him look for files without copyright notices on them. But he knows that even things without copyright notices can be copyrighted. He worries that if he uses the photos he has found online and then posts his movie on the Internet, the people who took the photos will find the movie, get upset and sue him.

Creative Commons was set up to make it easier for Jack and Jill to find each other online, and then to develop the creative collaboration they both seek.

In 2002, Creative Commons released a set of copyright licences to enable people to dedicate their creative works to the public domain. Their range of licences covers such things as who can use the material for free, whether it can be adapted or has to remain in its original form, whether the licence allows the material to pass to another user under the same conditions (share alike), and the nature of the attribution to the original source. These licences can all be downloaded for free use. ✋ Creative Commons also wants to increase the amount of source material online, and to make access to that material cheaper and simpler. It provides a space for sharing your works and accessing the works of others.

Creative Commons licences: creativecommons.org/license
Creative Commons: creativecommons.org

...fostering collaboration

You've created something that you want to share with the world – a photo, a film, a theory, an equation, a slogan, or recipe, a poem, some music.

✋ **Put the best of what you've created online at Creative Commons.** This will get your work distributed, and you can borrow the works of others to use for your website, your newsletters and your pamphlets.

✋ **Help create a 'world bank' of common property** for the benefit of all, instead of tying your work up in copyright restrictions which make it difficult or expensive for others to use.

AUGUST 28

SEED *the world*

It's hard to understand how it feels to live right at the margin, if you have most or all of what you need. Having 'nothing' means having absolutely nothing for too many people in many countries. There are lots and lots of reasons why 36,000 people are dying of starvation every day, two-thirds of whom are children: war, drought, overpopulation, AIDS, absolute poverty. But seed shortage is one reason.

The only seeds available to many farmers in some of the poorest countries in the world, where food shortage is chronic, are for varieties of vegetables that do not produce their own seed. There is nothing accidental about this. The varieties, known as F1 hybrids, have been bred to be like it. Who on earth would do something so unnatural? Why, the companies selling the seed, of course. They claim that such varieties produce higher yields, but it locks the farmers into the need to purchase fresh seed each year, and if they can't afford it, they go hungry.

The mission of the Kokopelli Seed Foundation, which started in France and has now spread around the world, is to create a 'Community-Supported Seed Fund' to provide poor farmers in poor countries with the seeds they need for their gardens and small farms. Anybody can grow and collect seeds – including you. Gardeners and farmers from all over the world were doing this for thousands of years before the emergence of commercial seed growers – and more recently, the introduction of genetically modified seeds.

Kokopelli's website page devoted to seeds for the developing world:
www.kokopelli-seeds.com/third-world.html

How to become a Kokopelli seed grower

It's not as hard as you might think. Food plants provide plenty of seeds:
A pumpkin or melon contains hundreds of seeds.
A tomato contains around 70 seeds.
A lettuce going to seed may produce up to 10,000 seeds.

A 10 m x 10 m garden is big enough for 150 tomato plants, which would produce 6 kg of seeds. This would be enough to provide 40,000 packets, each containing 30 seeds.

The Kokopelli Seed Foundation will advise you on what seeds to grow and even provide you with starter seeds so that you can start up your 'seed factory'.

...to feed the world

- **Become a seed donor.** Grow plants, allow some to run to seed and donate the seeds to the Kokopelli Seed Foundation. Seeds produced by Kokopelli's seed-grower network are sent all over the world. If you haven't got a garden, then do it in gro-bags on your roof or balcony.

- **All seeds are welcome:** tomatoes, melons, lettuces, beets, carrots, grains, pulses, peppers. Every species will find a home somewhere.

- **For more details,** read Dominique Guillet's book, *The Seeds of Kokopelli.*

29 AUGUST

invest in YOUNG PEOPLE

Children living on the streets need to earn money just to survive. Many do this by begging or ragpicking. But it is difficult for them to keep the money they earn safe, and therefore impossible for them to use it to create a better future for themselves. ✋ In Delhi, a group of street children started their own bank, called Bal Vikas Bank (Children's Development Bank). It is a place to keep their money safe, it encourages them to save for their future rather than just live from day to day, and it makes loans to older children to help them set up a small business.

The bank gives them a chance to do something safer which will help them earn a better income, and get off the streets. For example, two boys started a mobile tea business. They strapped an urn to the back of a bicycle and sold tea to lines of taxi and rickshaw drivers who were waiting to refuel their vehicles with Compressed Natural Gas.

The amazing thing is that this bank is run entirely by the children. They make the rules, decide the loans, encourage saving and build the membership. The idea is spreading across India, and children's banks are also being started in Afghanistan, Bangladesh, Nepal, Pakistan and Sri Lanka. The children now want to spread the idea across the world.

The Bal Vikas bank programme: www.childrensdevelopmentbank.org
Centre for Innovation in Voluntary Action (CIVA): www.civa.org.uk
CIVA is the charity responsible for the 365 Ways project.

Taxi driving

A group of seven youths in Kisumu, Kenya, want to become taxi drivers. The 'taxis' are bicycles, which have been converted to include a pillion seat over the rear mudguard. This is an accepted form of transport in the town. As taxi drivers, the

boys should be able to earn a decent income.

The youths will be offered loans to purchase and modify a bicycle, and become a 'taxi driver'. They will repay the loans out of the money they earn, which will enable more youths to take loans to set up in business.

...support their enterprise

Organise a fundraising event to make a difference to the lives and futures of young people. Set yourself a target of £100. Send all the money you raise to support youth enterprise initiatives, without deducting anything for administration.

✋ Help street children in South Asia set up a children's bank.

✋ Help young people in Kenya become taxi drivers.

✋ Help other young people in other countries set up an enterprise of their own.

AUGUST 30

VEGAN *challenge*

I am a serious meat eater… but I accepted a challenge from a mate and went completely vegan for a week. It was eye-opening to have to think about everything I put in my mouth. I've gone back to eating meat, but going vegan made me think about my choices much more carefully.

– Will Poutney

A vegetarian is someone who abstains from eating any sort of meat or fish. A vegan doesn't consume or use any animal products at all. People become vegetarian or vegan for many different reasons. They may believe it is cruel to kill and eat animals, or that it is a drain on the environment to rear the meat and to dispose of the remains, or simply for health reasons.

Eating a well-balanced diet, free from animal products is good for your health. Here are some reasons why:

Fat: Vegan diets are cholesterol-free and low in fat.

Heart disease: The risk of developing heart disease among meat-eaters is 50% higher than for vegetarians.

Impotence: Meat-based diets can lead to impotence, as fat can clog up the arteries going to all your organs, not just to your heart!

Life-threatening illnesses: Cancer, stroke, diabetes, osteoporosis, obesity and other diseases have all been linked to meat and dairy consumption.

Unwanted chemicals: Livestock, poultry and cows are often pumped full of chemicals, hormones and drugs that are absorbed by your body when you eat these animals.

Toxins in fish: The flesh of fish can accumulate toxins up to 9 million times as concentrated as those in the waters they live in – and the seas are becoming more polluted.

A free Vegetarian Starter Kit: www.vegetarianstarterkit.com
30 reasons to go vegetarian: www.goveg.com/feat/chewonthis

Want some veggie beefcake or cheesecake? 'Lettuce ladies' and 'broccoli boys', dressed in strategically placed pieces of vegetable, raise eyebrows and open minds as they travel the USA, educating people about vegetarianism and serving up delicious veggie food. Apart from all the better-known health benefits of a vegetarian diet, this deliberately non-PC, humorous campaign places a heavy emphasis on the improvement a vegetarian diet brings to your libido.

Choose your favourite pin-up, join PETA (People for the Ethical Treatment of Animals) and get a signed photo as part of the membership package.

...try it for seven days

Are you man or woman enough to give up animal products? This will mean a change in your lifestyle and outlook. It's also a great way to see how meat affects the way your body feels.

☺ **Go vegan or vegetarian for a week** – or even a month.

☺ **After that, do what you want.** If nothing else, you will be able to say that you gave it a go.

31 AUGUST

waste is a BURNING ISSUE

The problem of waste is one of two halves: creating less waste, and then disposing of it in a safe and sustainable way. Most importantly, we must protect human health and the environment from toxic poisoning. ♣ Safe disposal of waste is as important in the developing world as in the industrialised world. Industrial countries export waste to developing countries for disposal where environmental laws are often softer or not enforced.

'We oppose incinerators, landfills, and other end of pipe interventions.' The Global Anti-Incinerator Alliance (GAIA) is an international alliance of individuals, non-governmental organisations, community initiatives, academics and others working to end the incineration of all forms of waste and to promote sustainable waste prevention.

GAIA works on municipal disposal, hazardous waste and medical waste. Each workgroup undertakes projects to prevent incineration and to promote alternatives. GAIA's first global campaign is to stop the World Bank funding waste incinerators.

> We recognise that our planet's finite resources, fragile biosphere and the health of people and other living beings are endangered by polluting and inefficient production practices and health threatening disposal methods.

> Our ultimate vision is a just, toxic free world without incineration. Our goal is the implementation of clean production, and the creation of a materials efficient economy where all products are reused, repaired or recycled back into the marketplace or nature.

Global Anti Incinerator Alliance: www.no-burn.org
Recycling fun facts: members.aol.com/ramola15/funfacts.html

How incineration works

The waste is unloaded from a truck into a bunker area, transferred into a hopper and fed into the furnace.

Combustion of the feedstock takes place in the furnace.

Heat recovery cools the exhaust gases; the recovered heat is re-used in the incinerator or used to generate electric power.

A gas cleaning system, typically consisting of a 'scrubber' to filter out pollutants, and an electrostatic precipitator or a fabric 'bag filter' removes fine particles and some polluting gases.

A fan draws exhaust gases through the system prior to discharge into the atmosphere via a chimney stack.

Solid waste and water residues are removed. Ash and clinker from the furnace fall into a quench tank. This sludge can be highly toxic.

...stop it going up in smoke

Join in the Global Day of Action.
Here are some actions they suggest:

♣ **Draw the public's attention** to local incinerators, waste facilities and landfills.

♣ **Picket government agencies** that support or promote 'burn' policies.

♣ **Join in the fax and email action** to demonstrate public opposition.

MUSLIMS *in the west*

Islamaphobia is currently a problem throughout the world. Since 9/11 (11 September 2001) and the start of the 'War on Terror', there has been a growth in Islamophobia (hatred of Muslims) in North America and Europe. This has increased following the 7/7 tube and bus bomb blasts in London (7 July 2005).

Young Muslims now feel vulnerable. They feel that people are thinking: 'If you look like a Muslim, you must be a terrorist.' They feel they might be picked up in a dawn raid, or be imprisoned indefinitely for nothing, without having any right to a hearing. They feel that the society they live in doesn't want them any more – that it wants them to hide their faith and become less visible. ✖ In France, the government passed a law which banned people from wearing religious symbols in state schools. So schoolgirls can't wear a 'Hijab', even if they feel strongly that they should be doing this as a matter of modesty.

Muslims from all over the world have come to our country and been offered citizenship. Their children have been born and educated here and English is their mother tongue. ✖ We will be better able to understand the terrorist threat and what to do about it, if we could better understand how young Muslims see the world.

muslimyouth.net: www.muslimyouth.net

Comments from young Muslims in the West:

❝ *How hard can it be to live as Muslim in the West?*

To accept that with every tick of the clock, things change. Fashion changes and just as long as none of it clashes with the Islamic rulings on clothing, then we can change with it. Because sometimes we have to.

Personally speaking, I like to mix-and-match. I love wearing Indian sequinned tops with English flare-bottom trousers. I like to get the best of both worlds.

❝ *It is clear that the events of 9/11 have had a major impact on the world on Muslims in particular. And so practising Islam freely in Britain has become a lot harder. This has caused many Muslims to value their religion a lot more and their citizenship a lot less.*

...deal with Islamophobia

Take a look at muslimyouth.net, produced by and for young Muslims. It is a good antidote to the way Muslim issues are being reported in the press.

✖ **Find out about Nasim Ali,** who set up Camden United, an anti-racist football project in Fitzrovia in central London, and who is now, aged 28, Deputy Mayor of Camden and adviser to the police and the Prince's Trust.

✖ **Hear about Hannah Al-Rashid,** who won a European gold medal for Pencat Silat, a Malaysian martial art.

✖ **Hear positive stories of these and other young Muslims** who are changing the world for the better.

✖ **Read it regularly.** Find out about the views of young Muslims on cultural identity, religious observance, the war on terror, and a whole lot more.

2 SEPTEMBER

free SOFTWARE

Free software is a matter of liberty, not price. To understand the concept, you should think of 'free' as in free speech, not as in free beer! When programmers can read, redistribute, and modify the source code for a piece of software, the software evolves. People improve it, people adapt it, people fix the bugs. ♛ This can happen at a speed that seems astonishing when compared to the slow pace of conventional software development. Just compare the evolution of the MS Windows operating system (owned by Microsoft) with Linux (which is free and open source).

Free software provides four kinds of freedom for software users:

The freedom to run the program, for any purpose (*Freedom Zero*).

The freedom to study how the program works, and adapt it (*Freedom One*).

The freedom to redistribute copies so you can help your neighbour (*Freedom Two*).

The freedom to improve the program, and release your improvements to the public, so that the whole community benefits (*Freedom Three*).

Access to the source code – 'Open Source' – is a precondition for Freedoms One and Three.

The Free and Open Source Software movement is built on the ideals of collaboration and sharing. It is an idea whose time has come. It is also enabling computer users in the developing world to access software without having to pay an arm and a leg for it or pirate it.

Software Freedom Day is held each September to promote the idea of Free and Open Source Software: www.softwarefreedomday.org

Free Software Foundation has developed free software, created a Copyleft licensing system, and publishes an online directory of free software: www.gnu.org

Open Source Initiative promotes the idea of open source development of software: www.opensource.org

A free software flood...

I'm from Skopje, Macedonia, and Microsoft organized a conference to promote the opening of a Microsoft office in my country. Over 600 IT people attended (managers mostly). This is a lot of people for Macedonia which has 2 million citizens (only 4% have access to the Internet).

Our organisation bought and recorded 1,000 CDs with free software (OpenCD/Knoppix) which we gave out. We called the operation 'Free Software Flood' because it was raining like hell that day and because all the participants where 'flooded' with free open software.

– Free/Libre Software Macedonia

...for a sharing society

MS Office has become the standard software package for office use. But try OpenOffice.org

♛ Download Open Office from: www.openoffice.org – read the licence conditions.

♛ Copy it on to as many CDs as possible.

♛ Distribute these to people could use them – free, of course.

CONKER *the world*

The horse chestnut tree was first introduced to Britain from the Balkans in the late 16th century. It is a popular ornamental tree in parks, gardens, town and village squares, churchyards and streets. The tree flowers abundantly from April to mid-May, and the 'candles' (which are white or red) seem to light it up.

The 'horse' connection is twofold. Horse chestnuts were fed to horses as a stimulant and to make their coat shine. And the leaf-scars on the twigs have the shape of a horseshoe, including nail holes. The fruits of the tree resemble chestnuts. They develop in prickly cases, which ripen in September and October. In the late 18th century, the fruits began to be used to play 'conkers' – before that, hazelnuts or cobnuts or snail shells were used.

There are about 470,000 horse chestnut trees in Britain. But the numbers will dwindle if local authorities have their way. Conkers and conker playing are now seen as dangerous in our risk-averse society, and conkers have been banned from school playgrounds. Local councils have been pollarding, chopping down or not replacing horse chestnut trees. This is because children may throw sticks to knock the conkers down near a busy road, or simply because the council is afraid that a conker will drop on somebody's head and they will be sued for damages.

Royal Forestry Society: www.rfs.org.uk
World Conker Champsionships: www.worldconkerchampionships.com

Building a reputation through conkers

Most towns and cities want to be seen as distinctive and special; some even want to achieve greatness. Ashton in Northamptonshire has done both through conkers. It all happened largely by accident. The village green in Ashton is surrounded by chestnut trees. In 1965, a group of friends at the local pub found themselves unable to go on a fishing expedition due to bad weather. Someone suggested they play conkers instead. A small prize was offered to the winner, and money was collected for a charity for the blind, as one of the group had a blind relative. This became the starting point for the World Conker Championships, which has become an annual international event, raising money for Talking Books. To date, around £310,000 has been raised.

...and make your mark

🏠 **Write to your local council** telling them not just to retain horse chestnut trees, but to plant more. They are beautiful trees in any neighbourhood.

🏠 **Go to Ashton** this autumn and participate in the World Conker Championships. Then think about what you could do to make your town or neighbourhood distinctive – just like the residents of Ashton have done.

🏠 **Read** *England in Particular*. Horse chestnuts and conker playing are just one of the aspects of English life featured in this encyclopaedia, available from: www.england-in-particular.info

4 SEPTEMBER

wearing # RIBBONS

Ribbons are used as symbols by different causes for promoting awareness. One of the best-known ribbon campaigns is the red ribbon used to promote HIV/AIDS awareness. Here are some of the other ribbon colours being used, and a weblink to get more information about the cause:

Gold: Childhood cancer (www.cancerindex.org/ccw/index.htm)
Grey: Asthma/allergies (www.asthma.org.uk);
Diabetes: (diabetes.diabetesjournals.org);
Mental illness (www.miepvideos.org);
Brain tumour (www.cancercenter.com/brain-tumors.htm)
Green: Clean environment (www.greenpeace.org);
Organ/tissue donation (www.organdonor.gov);
Missing children (www.missingkids.org); Leukaemia (www.leukemia.org/hm_lls)
Lace: Osteoporosis (www.nof.org)
Light blue: Prostate cancer (www.prostate-cancer.org.uk)
Orange: Hunger (www.hungerday.org); Lupus (www.lupus.org)
Peach: Uterine cancer (www.4woman.gov/faq/cuterine.htm)
Pink: Breast cancer (www.nationalbreastcancer.org)
Red: HIV/AIDS (www.unaids.org)
White: Alzheimer's disease (www.alz.org); Free speech (www.aclu.org)

For a list of lots more colours and causes, check out:
kiwijewels.com/awareness_colors_and_meanings.htm

How to make a ribbon
1 Cut a 7-cm length of narrow ribbon.
2 Lay the ribbon out horizontally on a table with the shorter edge on top.
3 Hold down the ribbon's midpoint with one finger. Move the left end of the ribbon so that it points downwards at a slight inwards angle.
4 Fold the right end in the same way, so the ribbon crosses itself about 1.5 cm below the fold.
5 Where the ribbon crosses itself, glue the top ribbon to the bottom ribbon. As an alternative, you can sew the ribbon at the crossover point using a thread of the same colour.
6 Pin a safety pin to the back at the crossover point; use this to attach the ribbon to your clothes.

...show you care

† Build awareness of different causes in your own school, office, or community by organising a 'Ribbon Week'.

† Make a different-coloured ribbon each day of the week, and encourage people to pin them on their dress, shirt or jacket lapel.

† Make a poster or leaflet for each 'cause of the day'. Hand these out with the ribbons.

SEPTEMBER 5

FOOTBALLS *fairly traded*

Football production has a reputation for using child labour. This was brought to public attention in the late 1990s. The response of most big companies involved in the trade was to ensure that they could provide a 'no child labour' guarantee. As a result production was concentrated in large factory units and many women lost what had been a good home-based earning opportunity.

The challenge for Fairtrade was to develop a way of producing footballs in the villages whilst ensuring children were not involved in the production process, and that workers receive a fair wage and were covered by health insurance. The $2 'fairtrade premium' provides for this and also supports a micro-credit fund for the families of stitchers to help widen their opportunities for generating income.

How a football is made: The inner structure of a football is made from layers of fabric, which are glued (with latex) on to the outer skin of stitched panels. A design can be screen printed onto the panels. A latex bladder is glued onto one of the panels. A professional ball has an air mattress which helps reduce the time a ball needs to regain its shape after being kicked.

Fair Deal Trading in the UK offers three footballs. The 'Premier' (£17.90) and the 'Pro' (£34.80) both conform to FIFA international match standards. A cheaper ball is being developed to retail at around £10. For more information, contact: www.fairdealtrading.co.uk

Alive and kicking

Although AIDS is one of the biggest killers in Africa, nine-year-old Alan Majisu has no idea what it is. Living in Karangware, a sprawling Nairobi slum, Alan loves football but misses out because his school lacks balls and equipment. Instead, he plays on the streets with a ball made from plastic bags.

Alive & Kicking was set up by Jim Cogan to revive local production of leather footballs in Africa. The leather panels are supplied by Bata and stitched by trained young Kenyans. The footballs carry an AIDS message, and are sold at a small mark-up to schools and community projects.

Contact: director@ aliveandkicking.org.uk

...buy three and have fun

Buy three footballs:

- **Use one** to play football with your family and friends.
- **Kick one** into a playground (as an unattributable act of generosity).
- **Donate one** to a youth football project in an African slum, where sport has a real role to play in engaging young people. Send it to National Youth Organisation (Bidii Foundation), PO Box 28838, 00200 Nairobi, Kenya.

6 SEPTEMBER

campaign for VOTES AT 16

Women worldwide have fought for the same voting rights as men.
Women were granted equal voting rights in 1928 in the UK and in 1920 in the USA.
In the UK, it was the suffragettes who led a campaign to get votes for women.
Emily Davison gave up her life for the cause; she stepped in front of the King's
horse in the 1913 Derby and was trampled to death.

Young people are now campaigning to get the voting age lowered to 16.
The arguments against this are the same as those used by earlier generations to
deny women and the working classes the vote, that they are too innocent of the
world and others know what's best for them. Those arguments are as wrong now
as they were then.

Download petition sheets from Votes at 16 Campaign: www.votesat16.org.uk

Ten reasons for young people to have the vote:

Young people suffer a double standard of having adult
responsibilities but not rights.

Young people pay taxes, live under the law – they
should have the vote.

Politicians will represent their interests if youth
can vote.

Young people have a unique perspective.

Sixteen is a better age to start voting; 16 year olds
are less mobile than 18 year olds.

Lowering the voting age will increase voter turnout.

If we let stupid adults vote, why not let smart
youth vote?

Young people will vote well.

There are no wrong votes.

Lowering the voting age will benefit the lives
of youth.

www.youthrights.org/vote10.html

...give young people a say

**If you live in the UK, sign this petition – and get all your friends to
sign too:**

*We, the undersigned, support the Votes at 16 Campaign. We believe that if 16
and 17 year olds are allowed to leave school, to have full-time jobs, to marry
and have children and to join the armed forces, then they should have the
right to vote in elections.*

*We believe that allowing 16 and 17 year olds to vote will strengthen our
democracy and lead to more interest in elections and higher turnouts. With
the introduction of citizenship education in schools we believe that young
people will reach the age of 16 with enough knowledge to cast a vote for
what they want and believe in.*

*We therefore call on the Government to legislate to lower the voting age to
16 for all UK public elections.*

SEPTEMBER 7

DONATE *your body*

Are you dying to go to medical school? But perhaps the exams are too hard and you can't manage the grades. Or you've set your hopes on a completely different and more fulfilling career. Here's an easy way for anybody to get into medical school without having to study to become a doctor.

Donate your body! Medical schools need it to help teach their students the principles of anatomy. You will be embalmed and frozen.

About 600 people a year in England donate their bodies, but the 6,000 students who get into medical school need around 1,000 bodies to dissect. The government's Chief Medical Adviser recently wrote to all doctors in England asking them to encourage their patients to leave their bodies to a hospital. So why not make this your choice?

Further information from HM Inspector of Anatomy, Room 611, Wellington House, 135–55 Waterloo Bridge Road, London SE1 8UG. Tel: 020 7972 4551

How to donate your body:

1. Contact a hospital or medical school to tell them you plan to donate your body to them.

2. Put your request in writing. Sign and date the letter, and get it witnessed. Tell your friends and family what you have done. If you do this, your family is legally obliged to hand over the body after your death.

3. You then need to die before the next step happens.

4. Immediately your death has been registered, your executors should hand over your body to your chosen hospital or medical school.

5. They will then assess whether they can use your body. Not all bodies are accepted (which is the ultimate humiliation). Your body needs to be intact and disease free.

6. Once your body has been accepted it will be embalmed and frozen. This needs to be done within three days of your death. Your body can then be used for up to three years.

7. About four medical students will work on your body, dissecting first an arm and a leg, then the head and the neck, and so on until they've finished with you.

8. Then your body can be returned to your family for a decent burial or cremation.

...teach doctors to do a better job

Decide to donate your body to a medical school. It will add an extra dimension of meaning to your life! You won't feel a thing. And don't be embarrassed. You won't be recognisable. The embalming will have turned you a colourless grey – something like a pumice stone.

the power of COMICS

Comics are a powerful medium. Words and pictures combine to tell a story or raise an issue. Comics can be serious or funny. They can stimulate, provoke and be used to urge people to action.

You don't have to be a professional artist to draw a comic strip. World Comics Finland and World Comics India have been running comic workshops with some of the world's poorest people to help them communicate effectively using comics; within their local community or to the wider world. 🖐 The idea is spreading, and World Comic projects have been active in India, Tanzania, Mozambique, Lebanon, and also in some European countries.

World Comics Finland: www.worldcomics.fi
World Comics India: www.worldcomicsindia.com

Tips for producing a good comic:

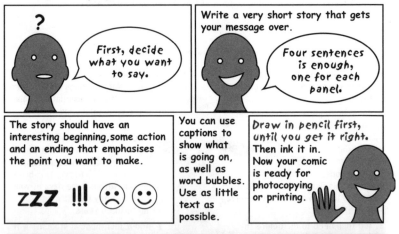

...tell stories in pictures

Take an issue you feel strongly about. Produce a wallposter comic about that issue.

🖐 **A wallposter comic is a good format to use.** Stick your poster up on a wall in a prominent place. A simple format is two sheets of A4 paper taped together. This provides space for a big headline and four panels, which should be enough to get your message across.

🖐 **The how-to section on the World Comics Finland website** gives some basic advice on how to set about producing a wallposter comic.

🖐 **Being able to draw well is not the most important thing.** You need a good story with interesting and engaging characters with which the readers can identify easily.

🖐 **Just try; and surprise yourself with the results!** When you have finished, pin your comic somewhere people can see and read it.

SEXUAL *harassment*

Sexual harassment is 'offensive behaviour of a sexual nature'. It includes, sexual innuendo, such as lewd comments about appearance or sex life; unwelcome physical contact, such as someone deliberately brushing up against you or trying to fondle you; an unpleasant work environment created by sexually explicit pictures being displayed, lewd emails being circulated or employees downloading internet porn.

These are two high-profile cases of 'Sexism in the City'. Both women won out-of-court settlements for alleged sexual harassment. In March 2001, Isabelle Terrillon, a 35-year-old trader working for Nomura Securities in London alleged that a company executive told her to wear short tight skirts, another asked her to strip and give him a massage, and male colleagues passed around pornographic emails that she found degrading. ❌ In July 2004, Elizabeth Weston, a 29-year-old lawyer working with US investment bankers Merrill Lynch, also in London, alleged that a senior employee had made lewd remarks, joked about her sex life and caused red wine to be spilt down her front.

Ron Davies, author and librarian at Exeter University, has been documenting leading financial scandals on his website, including allegations of sexist harassment at work made by female executives in the City of London.

Ron Davies's website: **www.ex.ac.uk/~RDavies/arian/scandals/behaviour.html**
I Spy Sexism at the Third Wave Foundation: **www.thirdwavefoundation.org**
Sexual harassment and what to do about it, from the Equal Opportunities Commission: **www.eoc.org.uk/EOCeng/dynpages/Sexual_Harassment.asp**

Stereotyping: The word 'stereotype' was originally a printing term, and meant a duplicate impression. This developed into a metaphor for an identical idea used in different situations. A 'cliché' has a similar meaning, and also comes from printing; it expressed the sound of molten metal being poured to form the type to be used for printing. Today a 'stereotype' is a simplified image of an individual or a group that is perceived to share certain characteristics. It is often used to portray negative qualities – of women, homosexual people, ethnic and racial groups, old people, young people...

The 'Don't Stereotype Me!' sticker from 'Bitches, Bimbos and Ballbreakers: The Guerrilla Girls Illustrated Guide to Female Stereotypes'. Download it from: www.guerrillagirls.com

...for a better workplace

Challenge sexual harassment!

❌ **When you encounter sexual harassment** or just sexist behaviour at the workplace, challenge the person concerned.

❌ **Download a postcard from the I Spy Sexism website.** Send it to the wrongdoer. Let them know that you are watching and that you will continue to watch, and that you will take firm action unless their behaviour changes.

blow the WHISTLE

Speaking out takes courage. If you witness wrongdoing at work or elsewhere, you must choose whether to remain silent, or bear witness and speak out. It is easier after the event to say that 'we should have spoken out'. But at the time, it can be a huge personal decision.

But whistle-blowing should be approached wisely. Is the wrongdoing substantial enough to warrant the risks of reprisal and the investment of time and resources to expose it? If you do decide to pursue the matter, then you should do so in a planned way, making a commitment to see it through, and not be put off by bureaucracy and stonewalling.

How to blow the whistle:

Before taking any irreversible steps, talk to your family and close friends.

Find out if there are other witnesses and if they are upset about the wrongdoing.

Consider first if you are able to make an effective complaint within the system.

If you do decide to blow the whistle, decide whether you want to 'go public' or do it anonymously.

Develop a plan of action, so you are in control of the process.

Keep a careful record of events as they unfold.

Identify and copy all necessary supporting documents before anyone has suspicions about you.

Get the support of potential allies, such as elected officials, journalists, activists and whistleblower networks.

Do it in your own time and with your own resources, not your employer's.

Invest funds to get a legal opinion from a competent lawyer.

Tell the truth; never over-egg your charges. You may find yourself and your own life investigated. Make sure you have nothing to hide.

Public Concern at Work: www.pcaw.co.uk
Government Accountability Project (USA): www.whistleblower.org
National Whistleblower Center (USA): www.whistleblowers.org
'The Whistleblower', an online newsletter: www.consumerwatchdog.org

Blowing the whistle on tobacco

Jeffrey Wigand was Vice President, Research and Development at Brown & Williamson, a Big Tobacco company. He blew the whistle on the tobacco industry in 1995, which had been minimizing the addiction and health issues of cigarette smoking, despite having evidence to the contrary. A huge settlement was awarded to victims of smoking, and this led to a complete change in the way tobacco was marketed. Dr Wigand has now set up Smoke-Free Kids to educate children on the harmful impact of tobacco.

Jeffrey Wigand inspired the Hollywood film *The Insider*: www.jeffreywigand.com
Make an evening of it. Also watch *Erin Brockovich*, starring Oscar-winning Julia Roberts as a whistleblower on toxic waste: www.erinbrockovich.com

...and expose wrongdoing

Speak out!

If you see wrong doing, have the courage and commitment to speak out.
Blow the whistle.

SEPTEMBER 11

TURN ON *and tune in*

BBC World broadcasts excellent programmes on international development, health, environment, human rights, gender and other global issues. Programmes can be informative and inspiring.

Here are some good sources of information on what's happening in the world. And what people are doing to change things:

New Internationalist reports on the issues of world poverty and inequality. It focuses attention on the unjust relationships between the powerful and powerless worldwide. It debates and campaigns for the radical changes necessary to meet the basic needs of all people. It brings to life the people, ideas and action in the fight for global justice: www.newint.org

Resurgence reports on environment and ecology, holistic science, creative living, spiritual well-being and sustainable agriculture, with articles written by theorists, visionaries, activists, scientists and artists: resurgence.gn.apc.org

Utne Reader reprints the best articles from over 2,000 alternative media sources. It contains 'Provocative writing from diverse perspectives ... Insightful analysis of art and media ... Down-to-earth news and resources you can use ... In-depth coverage of compelling people and issues that affect your life ... The best of the alternative media.' Some of the magazine is available on the web, some you need to subscribe to: www.utne.com

WorkingForChange, an online daily journal of progressive news and opinion published by Working Assets. Take action with ActForChange, which is part of the website: www.workingforchange.com

Third World Network, a research and information service based in Malaysia providing a Southern perspective on global issues. It publishes a daily SUNS bulletin as well as the fortnightly Third World Economics and the monthly Third World Resurgence. It also distributes books published in the Third World: www.twnside.org.sg

Sign up to receive e-newsletters from BBC World to alert you to forthcoming programmes: **www.bbcworld.com**

Radio Ga Ga

It's not just TV, websites and newspapers that report on world events. Radio is also a great way to find out about current affairs. Listen to programmes on OneWorld Radio: radio.oneworld.net. Or seek out pirate radio stations for a unique take on the world.

...the latest on BBC World

Tune in to find out about what's happening in the world.

🔊 **Listen to BBC World documentaries on your computer.** Go to: www.bbc.co.uk and click on 'Listen to shows you've missed' and then 'World Service'. If you don't have Realplay, then you will be given instructions on loading a free version.

🔊 **See the latest news in words and pictures at 10x10.** This website displays the top 100 words and pictures in the world every hour based on what's happening in the news. www.tenbyten.org

12 SEPTEMBER

clean up **A BEACH**

Our exploitation of the deep seas and oceans is 'rapidly passing the point of no return', according to a United Nations report of June 2006. There are, on average, around 46,000 pieces of plastic litter for every square mile of ocean worldwide. This leads to the death of over 1 million seabirds and over 100,000 marine mammals every year, due to entanglement or ingestion. Greenpeace recently discovered that there is a vortex of floating pieces of plastic in the southern Pacific the size of Texas.

Plastic can take 1,000 years or more to degrade in seawater, and even then continues to pollute our environment with thousands of microscopic fibres. Samples of sand taken from a Northumbrian beach were found to have over 10,000 fibres per litre of sand.

The International Coastal Cleanup takes place in mid-September each year. Over a weekend, 300,000 volunteers in 90 countries – from Argentina to Vietnam – help clean up over 11,000 miles of shoreline. It is also about preventing pollution. Volunteers record the different types of marine debris, leading to a better understanding of the causes, This enables organisations such as Ocean Conservancy to educate the public, business and government officials about the problem. Understanding the problem is the key to finding long-lasting solutions.

International Coastal Cleanup: www.coastalcleanup.org
Marine Conservation Society: www.mcsuk.org
Adopt a beach 'Litter as Art': www.adoptabeach.org.uk
Fran Crowe: www.flyintheface.com
The Ocean Conservancy: www.oceanconservancy.org

Fran's 46,000 challenge

Fran Crowe has resolved to 'save' one square mile of ocean by collecting 46,000 pieces of litter while walking on the beaches near her home in East Anglia. She posts reports and photographs of her walks on her website, and has found packaging from crisp packets that are over 30 years old!

She has sold some of the smaller items as 'souvenirs' to raise money for marine charities. She has also makes art installations out of some of the rubbish and uses some of her finds in workshops with schools. Eventually, she will try and recycle as much as possible.

She and other artists around the UK are using beach rubbish to draw attention to this huge environmental problem.

...and turn it into art

🏆 **Participate in a Coastal Cleanup event this weekend.**

🏆 **Join Fran Crowe in her endeavours.** Take some carrier bags with you when you go for a beach walk and fill them with flotsam and jetsam. You never know what you might find.

SEPTEMBER 13

POLLUTANT *persistence*

Persistent Organic Pollutants, or POPs, are among the most dangerous chemicals ever created. They include many pesticides, industrial chemicals and chemical by-products. ☘ POPs have become an urgent global environmental health problem. POPs break down very slowly in soil, air, water and living organisms. They persist in the environment for a long time. They get into the food chain, and then into the tissues of living creatures, including humans. POPs damage reproduction, the body's development and immune system, and create nerve disorders, cancers and hormone disruption.

Every living organism on earth now carries measurable levels of POPs in its tissues. POPs have spread throughout the environment to threaten human health, and damage land and water ecosystems all over the world. ☘ POPs travel long distances in air and water currents. They do not disperse in high-altitude, low-temperature regions of the globe. Peoples and ecosystems of the Arctic and Antarctic are at high risk. In 2001, a treaty banning the use of POPs was signed by 91 countries. It comes into effect when 50 countries have ratified it.

It's VOCs as well as POPs. Beauty comes at a price. Fragrances are chemicals which vaporise easily – that's why we can smell them. They are added to products to give them a scent or to mask other ingredients. ☘ The volatile organic chemicals (VOCs) emitted by fragrance and cleaning products contribute to poor indoor air quality, and are associated with headaches, allergic reactions and other side effects.

From fleas to weeds, factsheets for pesticide-free solutions:
www.pesticide.org/factsheets.html

Pesticide Advisor, alternatives at home, in the garden and on humans and pets:
www.panna.org/resources/advisor.dv.html

Pesticide Action Network: www.pan-international.org
Fragranced Products Information Network: www.fpinva.org
Health Care without Harm: www.noharm.org

Chemicals in agriculture are not always essential to high productivity.

2,000 Bangladeshi farmers were trained to grow rice without insecticides and with reduced amounts of nitrogen fertilizer. The yield was not affected and the farmers saved money.

This scheme is being replicated across the country. Around 12 million farmers could benefit from higher incomes and improved living standards, whilst creating environmental benefits for everyone.

– www.irri.org

...threatens life on earth

☘ **Understand what POPs are and the danger.** Know what you are buying and using.

☘ **Then take steps to reduce (better still eliminate) your use of POPs.**

☘ **Don't use toxic insecticides,** for example. Careful sanitation, door and window screens kept in good repair, fly swatters, flypapers and fly traps will all help reduce the fly population.

14 SEPTEMBER

promote # BREAST MILK

A mother has a right to independent information and freedom from pressure from companies. If she chooses to bottle feed she should be aware of the risks and costs.
– International Baby Food Action Network

Breastfeeding is the best start in life: it is free, safe and protects against infection. Breastfeeding reduces the risk of illness in all countries. Breastfed babies need no other food or drink for about the first six months of life. They also have reduced risk of diabetes, pneumonia, ear infections, and some cancers. It is extremely rare for a woman to be physically unable to breastfeed.

In the developing world, formula milk is expensive. It is often mixed with unclean water, which can cause diarrhoea; and it may be over-diluted to make it last longer, so leading to malnutrition. Where water is unsafe, UNICEF says that babies are 25 times more likely to die if they are bottle fed, and that reversing the decline in breastfeeding could save the lives of 1.5 million infants every year.

Nestlé says that it is socially responsible in distributing and promoting formula milk. They state that: 'Breastfeeding is best for babies. Chemist Henri Nestlé stated this in his Treatise on Nutrition soon after founding our company in 1867, and it is still true today. We are committed to ensuring that the best interests of mothers and babies are served by our employees around the world.' ⚽ Nestlé is the world's largest baby food company. It sells formula milk in both the developed and the developing world.

Baby Milk Action, the UK campaign against Nestlé:
www.babymilkaction.org/pages/campaign.html

International Baby Food Action Network: www.ibfan.org
For Nestlé's point of view: www.babymilk.nestle.com
Express Yourself Mums: www.expressyourselfmums.co.uk

Campaigners say that Nestlé:

Provides information to mothers which promotes artificial feeding and discourages breastfeeding.
Donates free samples and supplies to health facilities to encourage artificial feeding.
Gives inducements to health workers for promoting its products.
Does not provide clear enough warnings on labels of the benefits of breastfeeding and dangers of artificial feeding.

...save infant lives

Make up your own mind about who's right and who's wrong. If you think that Nestlé needs to do more, join the Boycott and bring pressure to bear:

⚽ **Stop buying Nescafé coffee and other Nestlé products.** Tell your friends and workmates to do the same.

⚽ **Write to tell Nestlé that you support the Boycott.**

⚽ **Collect petition signatures** to present to Nestlé at its AGM.

⚽ **Encourage support** from community groups, unions, churches and other organisations.

⚽ **Hold a day of action** in your community and get publicity for it.

SEPTEMBER 15

GREENSCORE *yourself*

We can all live a greener, more environmentally sustainable life. But this will mean changing what we buy and how we live.

Some things will require a bit of effort. For example, reducing the number of car journeys we make or not buying cheap air tickets to get away on weekend breaks.

Some will require money: loft insulation, draught excluders, double glazing. Some will be a bit less comfortable until we get used to things: turning down the heating and switching off the lights and TV remote. Some will be a bit more expensive, such as buying organic food and drink. But on the other hand, we will save money in the long run on things such as long-life electric bulbs.

GreenScore and Eco-Teams are projects of Global Action Plan:
www.globalactionplan.org.uk

To set up an Eco-Team, email: ecoteams@globalactionplan.org.uk
To take the GreenScore test, register at: www.greenscore.org.uk

To buy green, use the following websites: www.thegreendirectory.co.uk
www.greenchoices.org or www.gooshing.co.uk

Green tips for everyday from Greenpeace Canada:
www.greenpeace.ca/e/resource/green/everyday.php

Flintham Crusaders

Seven young people from the village of Flintham, aged between 12 and 17, formed a youth Eco-Team. They cajoled their parents into cutting down household waste, composting and saving energy and water. Their efforts saved their families an average of £19.28 per week and reduced the amount of waste going to the landfill by half.

Tom, the youngest member of the team, was fired up by his experience. After completing the programme, he decided to expand his hobby of keeping ducks and chickens to provide eggs to sell to villagers. He produces over 200 eggs a week, which he delivers by rollerblade to 'increase the danger level'!

...reduce your impact

To help you become greener, take the GreenScore test to see how green you are.

🌳 **The questionnaire covers around 80 practical things** you can do to become more energy efficient, reduce the impact of your travel, save water, shop sensibly, and reduce, re-use and recycle your rubbish. How did you score?

🌳 **Now try to improve on it!** Get together with half a dozen or so of your neighbours and set up an Eco-Team. Then over the next four months together try to reduce your environmental impact from energy and water use, household waste, transport and shopping.

🌳 **From time to time, take another GreenScore test** to measure your improvements. If every member of the Eco-Team improves their score, this will help create a cleaner, more sustainable future for everyone.

speak up # SPEAK OUT

Speak up for what you believe in. If you have something important to say, if you disagree with what someone else is saying, or if you agree and want to add some points, then it is important for you to have your say.

Here are some opportunities for you to get your voice heard:

At conferences and public meetings you attend. Don't just sit there thinking about what you might say. Stand up and say something. Mention who you are (and the organisation you represent). Then say what you need to say clearly and succinctly. And bring along lots of literature to hand out afterwards.

Call into a phone-in programme with your point of view. They will ask you what you would like to speak about before they let you on air. So make sure that it's something sensible.

Send your views by phone or email to viewers' and listeners' feedback programmes on TV and radio.

Write a letter to the editor of your local newspaper.

Write to your Member of Parliament or Congressperson. They often refer to their postbag, but in actual fact get very little correspondence except through orchestrated campaigns.

Your view may not be heard or be published this time. But no matter, try again. And keep trying. See yourself as an expert with something important to say on an important issue. And one day, perhaps, people will be trailing after you to get your point of view.

SpeakersBank provides training to non-profits, local communities and young people to encourage people to Speak Up and Speak Out about the issues they care about. See their publication for young people: Untie Your Tongue, and Get Life Licked! www.speakersbank.co.uk

Tips for public speaking
Breathing: give yourself enough air to get the words out
Eye contact: you're communicating with them personally
Straighten up: speak tall
Talk with your hands: gestures reinforce what you're saying
Volume: don't eat your words
Emphatic pauses: to make a point
Slow down: make each syllable count
Tonal variation: for emphasis and impact
...or **B-E-S-T V-E-S-T** for short. Give it your best shot!

...get your voice heard

👪 **Make a list of ten things** you could do to get your voice heard. Then try to do them all.

👪 **Make a diary of what you have done,** with the dates and details of each approach. If you get no response, then telephone to ask why.
It pays to be assertive.

👪 **Get something published or broadcast** at least once during the month, if you can.

SEPTEMBER 17

STORY *telling*

The imagination is a place all by itself. A separate country. You've heard of the French Nation and the British Nation. Well, this is the Imagi Nation. It's a wonderful place.

— George Seaton

Storytelling is as old as humanity. 30,000 years ago, hairy, grunting cave dwellers threw down their tools to sit by the fire and share tales about the day's hunt. A millennium ago, entire fiefdoms and kingdoms gathered together to hear their storytellers perform.

Through stories, we are introduced to the rise and fall of empires, the world's great and passionate loves. We taste what it would be like to live in another time in the past or in the future or in another body. Entire cultures and histories have been passed down through the ages through oral tradition. Public libraries, schools, playgroups, day-care centres, women's refuges, after-school clubs and youth centres would all jump at the chance to have you come in and do some storytelling.

Information about storytelling, conferences, tips and networks: www.storynet.org
Stories and information about storytelling: www.storyteller.net
Spooky stories from the American South: www.themoonlitroad.com
Folktales and legends from all over the UK: www.mysteriousbritain.co.uk
Stories for all ages from all over the world: www.dancingponyproductions.com

It was a dark and stormy night…

…the rain fell in torrents, except at occasional intervals, when it was checked by a violent gust of wind which swept up the streets (for it is in London that our scene lies), rattling along the housetops, and fiercely agitating the scanty flame of the lamps that struggled against the darkness…

— from *Paul Clifford* by
Edward George Bulwer Lytton (1830)

'It was a dark and stormy night…' is the most quoted opening sentence of a story. The annual Bulwer Lytton Fiction Contest awards a prize for the worst opening sentence of an imaginary novel. Why not have a go? You might even win! www.bulwer-lytton.com

…become the local oracle

Call your local library, and arrange a time when you can come in and enthral a group of kids with a nail-biting adventure or a heart-wrenching romance. Show them a wider world. Tell them stories about people who will inspire them to great things.

Through your storytelling, you will become a feature of your local community. You will feed people's imagination and you will brighten up their lives. And why not persuade your local Talk Radio to give you a weekly slot.

18 SEPTEMBER

declare INDEPENDENCE

In 1977, the 120 residents of Freston Road (in London) were threatened with eviction to make way for a giant factory estate. They held a referendum on declaring independence from the UK: 95% were in favour. They applied for membership of the United Nations. Everyone could be a Minister. The Education Minister was a two-year-old, and the Foreign Minister was a dwarf, who wore a t-shirt saying 'Small is Beautiful'. There was no Prime Minister.

There was media attention from around the world. The *Daily Mail* printed a leader column and a report 'from our Foreign Correspondent in Frestonia'. Coachloads of tourists were shown the borders and received passport stamps. Frestonia applied to join the International Postal Union, and printed its own postage stamps. Frestonia was eventually rebuilt to a community design with several million pounds of foreign aid from the UK.

Frestonia: www.globalideasbank.org: search on Frestonia
Transition Towns: www.transitiontowns.org

Print your own money

One idea for strengthening the local economy and becoming more self-reliant is to create your own local currency. This is just what has happened in Totnes as part of the Transition Town Initiative. Three hundred Totnes bank notes were printed and handed out, to be used in 18 participating local businesses for a limited period. By mutual consent they were deemed to be worth £1 each.

As Rob Hopkins, the originator said:

This is just a small experiment designed to get people thinking and talking about money. Totnes used to issue its own money and one side of the Totnes Pound is a facsimile of an old Totnes banknote. One day in the not-too-distant future Totnes might have its own local currency again.

...and build a state

Design a currency for your own community. Who will feature on the banknote? Will it be some prominent local person from the past? Or an important person of today? Or the local Big Issue seller? The wording on your banknote should clearly state that it is only a virtual currency, so that you are not breaking banking regulations. Give your banknote limited validity. After the cut-off date, it will become just a piece of paper.

Persuade local shops and services to accept it as a valid currency for transactions. Issue just a few banknotes to start with. Number each with a unique reference number. Ask holders to tick a box each time the banknote changes hands — to keep track of how well it is being used as a local currency.

Then see how things go. If it takes off, you will either have created a natty fundraising idea or a truly viable new currency

SEPTEMBER 19

TRAVEL *to other countries*

Do you have any idea how many countries there are? Boundaries shift when wars, treaties or totalitarians muddy things up, but there are currently around 190 countries in the world.

How many have you seen? Not many, very likely. So get moving! There's an entire world to explore, with cultures and styles of living that are very different from your own. Seeing the world may inspire you. It could even change your life.

Some ideas to inspire you:

Witnessing war and peace: Why not find out about countries that have experienced war and conflict? Don't just rely on what you see on TV. Check it out at firsthand. But check the security situation first. You can travel independently, but you could also join a peace tour.

From Fiji to Cyprus and back again: The School for International Training allows you to engage with regional experts, work with local organisations and understand local and regional issues.

Palestine: The Palestine Summer Encounter, organised by the Holy Land Trust, aims to create a dialogue between overseas visitors and Palestinians. In two months, you learn Arabic, volunteer with a Palestinian non-profit organisation and visit important sites in the region.

Colombia, Cuba, Mexico, Nicaragua: In a Witness for Peace delegation you will gain an insight into issues of peace, economic justice and sustainable development, and the chance to meet those fighting for a better world.

Bosnia: Builders for Peace is a summer programme that includes hands-on restoration of historic sites damaged during the war that followed the break-up of Yugoslavia, plus teaching conversational English at a free summer school for high-school students.

Builders for Peace: thomas.butler3@comcast.net
Witness for Peace: www.witnessforpeace.org
School for International Training: www.sit.edu/studyabroad/index.html

Get the money together to pay for your trip.

Put a big jar on a table just inside your front door. Stick a label on the jar that reads 'BRAZIL' in big letters, or whatever country you'd like to go to. Every time you enter or leave your apartment, 'BRAZIL' will be staring you in the face, reminding you of your plans.

Ask everyone who comes to your home (and that includes you) to put their change in the jar. It doesn't matter whether it's a pound or a penny. It all adds up. As soon as you have enough money, pack your passport and go and see the world.

...to broaden your mind

Be a net-jetter!

During your trip, write a travelogue and take photographs recording your daily experiences and encounters. Email this to everyone you know, or put it on a website or a blog you have created for your trip.

campaign for PEACE

All over the world people campaign for peace. In 2001 the United Nations General Assembly declared 21 September as the International Day of Peace (Resolution 55/282).

> *... a day of global ceasefire and non violence devoted to commemorating and strengthening the ideals of peace both within and among all nations and peoples... the observance and celebration of which makes in strengthening the ideals of peace and alleviating tensions and causes of conflict ... an invitation to all nations and people to honour a cessation of hostilities for the duration of the Day ... and an invitation to all Member States, organisations and individuals to commemorate in an appropriate manner this International Day of Peace.*

The government of the USA spends 25 times as much on the military as it does on overseas aid; the UK spends over eight times as much; France six times as much; Germany and Japan five times as much.

International Day of Peace website: www.un.org/events/peaceday

Marching for peace and justice

In 1930, Gandhi, with 78 followers, led a Salt March to protest the injustices of the British Empire. This became a turning point in India's struggle for independence. They walked 241 miles in 24 days from the Gandhi ashram in Ahmedabad to the seaside village of Dandi, where they proceeded to make salt from sea water (which was illegal at that time, as the British rulers imposed a hefty tax on salt).

The Salt March was re-enacted in March and April 2005 in order to reawaken the people of the world to stand up for peace and non-violence. Find out more from: www.saltmarch.org.in

...seven simple actions

Here are seven things you can do for World Peace Day:

🕊 **Organise your own event** to celebrate World Peace Day. A fast, or a disco with peace movement music: 'All we are saying is give PEACE a chance'.

🕊 **Give £5 and get nine of your friends to do the same.** Then together use the £50 to support a peace initiative.

🕊 **What's your big idea for world peace?** If a world leader could do something, what should they do? Write a letter to them with your idea, and send a copy to your local newspaper.

🕊 **Be inspired by Gandhi:** 'Be the change you wish to see in the world.' If there is one small thing you could do for world peace, what would it be? Go and do this today.

🕊 **Measure happiness in smiles per hour.** Today on World Peace Day, smile at people, people you meet, people in the street.

🕊 **Choose an issue or a region of conflict,** and then find out as much as you can about what is happening. Try to hear both sides. Keep up to date with breaking news.

🕊 **Find a pen pal 'from the other side'** and share your thoughts and ideas.

PEDESTRIAN *rights*

We're all pedestrians and many of us also drive cars. As drivers we demand congestion-free roads and the right to drive as we wish; but when we are not in our cars, we hate the traffic noise, the polluted air, the dangerous driving, our streets jam-packed with traffic and parked cars, traffic signs everywhere. And when traffic is banned, we suddenly realise how much nicer our streets could be.

The car culture is not going to suddenly disappear. But we can fight to make it less dominant in our lives and landscapes.

Carbusters is an organisation which campaigns against traffic. They stage events and protests to cut down the use of cars. Carbusters organises pedestrian-crossing actions to contest the fact that cars always get the right of way, even when they are outnumbered by pedestrians. Protesters dress in solid black or white outfits, march into the middle of the road and lie down, creating a human zebra crossing.

The World Carfree Network is a clearing house for information from around the world. Their annual World Carfree Day in September has over 1,500 cities in 40 countries participating: www.worldcarfree.net

Carbusters provides tools for taking on car culture: www.carbusters.org
Carfree.com, a website linked to the book Car Free Cities: carfree.com

Carbusters Campaigns

Get hold of an old car, park it in the centre of town and invite people to destroy it. Whilst they are doing this, tell them about the destructiveness of the car.

Offer a free roadside counselling service for all car addicts. Give them the opportunity to undertake the 'Eight-step Programme to a Car-free Life' on the Carbusters website.

Hand out fake parking tickets, designed to look like the real thing, 'fining' drivers for hogging public space or contributing to climate change.

Sticker a car parked on the pavement or in a pedestrian zone with footprint-shaped stickers and leave a note saying:
> *Warning, You have parked illegally in a pedestrian area. Next time your car will be walked over.*

...people before cars

🏆 **Pay a parking meter** for parking time and use it as a venue for a party.

🏆 **Make it a huge party,** using a whole row of parking meters in the busiest area of town at the busiest time of day.

🏆 **Have lots of banners and placards** so that everyone knows exactly what you are doing.

have a healthy **HEART**

World Heart Day takes place at the end of September. It is held in more than 90 countries around the world and receives a great deal of positive publicity. The aim is to increase awareness of heart disease and encourage people to adopt healthier lifestyles. The World Heart Day slogan is 'A Heart for Life'.

Heart disease has become the Number One killer. This is not just in Europe and North America, but across the developing world, especially amongst the middle classes in urban areas. Cardiovascular disease accounts for one in three deaths each year, adding up to 17 million people. ☺ Changes in diet, involving the consumption of more pre-prepared and fast foods, which contain too much fat, sugar and salt, is one of the reasons for the growth. Smoking and lack of exercise are also important factors.

The main risk factors for heart disease include: high cholesterol, which furs up the arteries, high blood pressure, smoking, lack of exercise, unhealthy diet, being overweight or obese, drinking too much alcohol, stress, and genetic factors.

World Heart Federation: www.worldheart.org
World Heart Day: www.worldheartday.com

Some ideas for incorporating exercise into your daily routine:

Get off the bus or train a few stops earlier and walk the rest of the way.

Go for a walk during the workday break or at lunchtime.

Take the stairs instead of the lift.

Go and speak to someone instead of phoning or emailing them.

Stand while on the phone.

Schedule exercise time into your diary.

Why not do salsa or go line dancing, or get together with a group of your friends to jog, play football, swim together on a regular basis?

...be fit for life

First start with yourself. Try not to die young. Small changes to your lifestyle can bring big rewards.

☺ **Check the shape you're in** by going to: www.worldheartday.com/heartforlife/Obesity.asp

☺ **If you smoke, stop.** It is also important to have a smoke-free environment at work and at home, so make others around you aware of the dangers of passive smoking.

☺ **A balanced diet and regular exercise are both important.** Even 30 minutes of moderate exercise every day will help.

FOOD *for thought*

Whilst the human population grows, there is a crisis at sea. Nature's limits have been breached by too many fishing vessels catching too many fish, often in extremely wasteful and destructive ways.  Over-fishing what is considered a 'free resource' is leading to a catastrophic decline in fish stocks. What was once found in abundance has or will soon become endangered species.

If nothing is done, the oceans will turn into fish deserts. The human communities around the world that depend on fishing will be forced to find alternative livelihoods. There will also be disastrous consequences for marine life.

In his book The End of the Line, Charles Clover suggests these actions: The fishing industry fish less, especially the giant trawlers that scoop up everything. Consumers eat less fish, or eat fish that have been less wastefully caught. And we should all know more about how fish are caught and reject fish caught unsustainably.

For information on the Marine Conservation Society and on what not to eat: **www.mcsuk.org**

Don't eat:

Atlantic cod	Skates and rays
Atlantic salmon	Snapper
Chilean seabass	Sturgeon
Dogfish	Swordfish
European hake	Tuna
European seabass	Tropical prawns
Grouper	
Haddock	
Ling	
Marlin	
Monkfish	
North Atlantic halibut	
Orange roughy	
Shark	

Do eat and enjoy:

Bream	Mackerel
Brill	Megrim
Brown crab	Mussels
Catfish	Oysters
Clams	Pollack
Cockles	Poulting
Coley	Red mullet
Dab	Scallops
Dover sole	Turbot
Flounder	Witch
Gurnard	
Herring	
Langoustine	
Lemon sole	
Lobster	

at the right fish

Favour fish caught by the least wasteful fishing methods.

- **The Marine Conservation Society lists 20 fish not to eat,** giving reasons and suggesting possible alternatives, as well as 25 fish that you can eat with a clear conscience (see above). Follow these recommendations and you will know that you are not contributing (at least for the moment) to the destruction of a particular fish stock.

- **Campaign for the government to give fishermen tradeable rights to fish,** accompanied by new responsibilities for marine conservation. And to create nature reserves in the oceans, where fishing is banned.

- **Think before you eat.** Eat fish with a clear conscience and make sure that you don't eat any of the fish from the 'Don't eat' list.

- **Read** *Cod* by Mark Kurlansky, for the story of how a once abundant fish has come to be nearly extinct.

24 SEPTEMBER

make someone SMILE

Tell people how important they have been to you.

I decided that I was going to find one person a year and write them a letter and tell them how they had changed my life. I wrote to my 3rd grade teacher and said what I remembered most from what she had taught me. Then I forgot all about it. But I was visiting my parents on vacation and we went shopping, I heard my name being called. My teacher ran up to me to say that when she and her husband read my letter it made them both cry and that it was such a nice thing to write.

Give other people a chance to do good. A priest in Indianapolis preached about kindness. Then she held up 50 envelopes. An anonymous donor had filled each with a $50 bill. Anyone could take one, no strings attached. All the donor asked was that the money be used for good. 'We can make this world a better place,' the preacher told her congregation. Those who picked up the envelopes spent weeks pondering how best to spend the money and make a difference. The donor had trusted them to use the money wisely. They took that trust and passed it on.

Be unexpectedly kind.

One time when I was at a bookstore, I noticed that the shop assistant was the only person working. She was trying hard to be really pleasant even though she was overwhelmed with waiting customers. I crossed the road and bought a potted plant, walked back to the bookstore, handed the plant to the shop assistant and said, 'I hope your day gets better.' She smiled and said, 'It just did. Thank you so much.'

You can visit the makesomeonesday.org website and write about what you have done as an inspiration for others: www.makesomeonesday.org

Some other ways to make someone's day:

Praise people and mean it: 'I saw what you did, and it was really great!', 'You're really important to me', 'You're looking great'...

Smile at people as you pass them in the street, when you are sitting opposite them in a subway or when you're stuck in a traffic jam.

Lend a hand when someone needs it. Help an old person across the street, or someone with a pushchair trying to navigate some steps, or someone with heavy shopping. Do this without them having to ask.

And there are lots and lots of other ways to make someone's day!

...make people feel good

👫 Today, do something that will make someone's day.

👫 And if you've enjoyed doing it, then do it again tomorrow... and the next day... and every day!

SEPTEMBER 25

SCHOOL LUNCH *rethink*

Children are not eating well enough. And many children today have little understanding of how food is produced, how it gets to our plates and the connection between our health and well-being and what we eat. A school lunch should be seen as being more than just a meal.

Thinking outside the lunch box: Rethinking School Lunch is a programme developed by the Centre for Ecoliteracy in the USA to show that school lunches are more than just providing a plateful of food. ☺ Students visit local farms to understand the local farm economy and to see local cottage-scale food production. They can compare this with the global market for foods colonised by international brands. ☺ Students can work with kitchen staff to plan healthy meals. They also develop the messages that will persuade their peers to eat more healthily.

The most important meal of the day. Children concentrate less well if they arrive hungry at school in the morning or if they've just had a bar of chocolate or a packet of crisps. A quarter of UK children are turning up at school each morning without having had a proper breakfast. Magic Breakfast, the brainchild of Carmel McConnell delivers nutritious bagel breakfasts to children in London schools.

Rethinking School Lunch: www.ecoliteracy.org
Feed Me Better: www.feedmebetter.com
Magic Breakfast: www.magicbreakfast.com
Parents Jury: www.parentsjury.org

Feed Me Better

Jamie Oliver, nicknamed 'The Naked Chef', is a young celebrity chef with his own TV cookery series and string of best-selling books. In 2004, he started a campaign to improve school dinners by showing that something could be done. Working in an area of South London in a TV series broadcast on Channel 4, Jamie developed new menus, worked with school catering staff to prepare more nutritious food within the budget, and persuaded the children to abandon junk food and start eating better. Side effects were: better concentration, better behaviour and better health. When the series ended, Jamie had persuaded the UK government to invest in feeding children better.

...more than just a meal

☺ **Download the 'Road Map' to a re-thought school lunch** from: www.ecoliteracy.org/rethinking/rsl-guide.html and send a copy to the Headteacher of your local school.

☺ **Join a Parents Jury.** The Jury, coordinated by the Food Commission, works to improve the quality of children's food and drinks. It comprises 1,700 parents with children aged between 2 and 16. If you live in the UK, feel strongly about child nutrition and have a child in this age range, apply to join. If you live outside the UK, set up your own Parents Jury. The original working title for the Jury was 12 Angry Parents.

fun lovin' CRIMINALS

Arthur Koestler, well-known author of *Darkness at Noon*, had a good idea: to stimulate prisoners to make constructive use of their time inside by creating something. Their painting, craft, writing or music could be exhibited, and prizes given. This would help the prisoners' self-development and provide an outlet for their creative talents. Both would help prevent re-offending. 🏠 The Koestler Awards Scheme was introduced into UK Prisons in 1961.

Changing Tunes creates music in prisons. Richard Pendlebury was a rock musician. Whilst volunteering at Horfield Prison, he realised that there was a fantastic pool of musical talent amongst the prisoners. He put together a band of prisoners and began a music class. He then established an organisation, Changing Tunes, to take his ideas forward.

Changing Tunes operates in six prisons. Each has equipment (mainly drums, guitars and keyboards). The prisoners choose the type of music they wish to learn or play; rock, pop, jazz, classical, or gospel. A musician organises the session. There will often be a target, such as putting on a performance or producing a CD. Changing Tunes invites ex-prisoners to perform in its concerts. None of the prisoners with whom Changing Tunes has worked closely has so far re-offended.

Prison Radio: www.prisonradio.org.uk

Radio Wanno 999 is the first project of Prison Radio, devised by James Greenstreet, Director of Radio for Development. This has four components:

A learning centre: prisoners study for a qualification in media production.

A broadcasting unit: prisoners run a talk-based radio station for the whole prison community.

A CD production unit: producing and distributing material of benefit to prisoners – including advice to new inmates.

A prison outreach project: helping prisoners after their release.

Radio Wanno's output is as varied as the people who produce it. A poignant piece on what it's like to be a father in prison might sit alongside a comedy drama about cockroaches, and a dynamic vox pop package in which prisoners talk about the latest exploits of a Premiership football team.

...listen to what they say

Go to: www.prisonradio.org.uk and listen to these audio clips:

🏠 An inmate at Wandsworth reading his own poem.

🏠 An atmospheric piece telling the story of former Wandsworth inmate Derek Bentley, the last man in Britain to be hanged.

🏠 Is it possible to be happy in prison? A feature originally broadcast on Radio Wanno.

🏠 An audio diary made by Mark Williams charting the lead-up to his release.

SEPTEMBER 27

AIR *pollution*

Every time we breathe in, dangerous air pollutants enter our bodies. These can cause short-term effects, such as eye and throat irritation. More alarming, however, are the long-term effects such as cancer, and damage to the body's immune, neurological, reproductive and respiratory systems.

Air pollution is not just a city problem. Many air pollutants are dispersed hundreds of miles away from their source, and so can affect distant ecosystems. Some pollutants remain toxic in the environment for a very long time and will continue to affect ponds, streams, fields and forests for many, many years. Most air pollution is the result of energy consumption: the burning of fossil fuels to produce electricity or to power transport.

Pollutants in the air include:
Sulphur Dioxide and Nitrogen Oxides, produced from the burning of fuel, and which cause acid rain.
Carbon Monoxide, which is toxic, produced in vehicle emissions.
Particulate matter, such as smoke and vehicle exhausts. Legislation for cleaner air and substantial decreases in the amount of coal being burned have reduced this problem in America and Europe.
Lead, which is produced from a chemical added to petrol to make engines run more smoothly (lead tetra-ethyl); lead-free petrol has become the norm.
Other chemicals and increasing amounts of additives in petrol mean that many other pollutants are being released into the atmosphere.

US Department of Homeland Security's Ready America website has simple instructions for making your own face mask:
www.ready.gov/america/getakit/cleanair.html

Be an armchair activist. Click and donate to clean air projects at:
www.iwantcleanair.com

How one man brought clean air to Delhi

In 1986, environmental lawyer M C Mehta asked India's Supreme Court to protect fundamental constitutional rights by directing government ministries and departments to implement the 1981 Air Act in Delhi. In 1986 in response, the Court pressed Delhi's administration to explain what it was doing to reduce air pollution. In 2002, all public service vehicles (buses, taxis and auto-rickshaws) had to convert to Compressed Natural Gas. The impact on air quality was marked and immediate. www.cseindia.org

...every breath you take

Wear a face mask whenever you go out into the street.

- **This will protect you from pollution.** It will also make a public statement that the air is not clean enough for people to breathe safely. This will get others thinking.

- **Most cycle shops sell face masks** because cyclists are at more risk from vehicle pollution. They are in the street, with exhaust fumes all around them, at red traffic lights stationary vehicles pump exhaust fumes into their faces, and physical exertion means that their air intake is increased.

responsible **BUSINESS**

All big corporations have a Corporate Social Responsibility policy. This sets out how they wish to relate to their external stakeholders: the communities where they operate, the customers they serve and wider society.

These are statements made by some leading oil companies:

BP: 'We support the fundamental rights of people around the world: we run our business in accordance with the principles set out in the Universal Declaration of Human Rights.'

ChevronTexaco: 'Our approach to corporate responsibility is to conduct business in a socially responsible and ethical manner; support universal human rights; protect the environment; benefit the communities where we work; learn from and respect cultures in which we work.'

ConocoPhillips: '[Our] longstanding commitment to the communities in which [we] operate reflects our belief that no individual or corporation can be a good citizen without becoming involved; by exercising imagination, donating time and skills and providing financial support.'

ExxonMobil: 'We condemn human rights violations in any form. We seek to be responsible corporate citizens, and recognize that we have both the opportunity and responsibility to improve the quality of life wherever we do business.'

Shell: 'Contributing to sustainable development is not only the right thing to do, but it makes good business sense. It helps us to maintain our licence to operate, manage risk better, lower costs through improving energy efficiency, and enables us to grow.'

Download the Hands on Corporate Research Guide from CorpWatch:
www.corpwatch.org

Corporate Social Responsibility Newswire for information and contacts:
www.csrwire.com

What makes a company socially responsible? Should it:
Support community organisations in the local communities and the countries where it operates by donating cash and encouraging employee volunteering?
Pay fair wages and provide good working conditions to all its employees?

Trade fairly with its suppliers?
Make products according to accepted standards of safety and durability?
Have an environmental policy which is based on the principles of sustainability?
Deal with the pollution it produces?
Provide leadership on social and environmental issues?

...judge corporate policy

🌐 **Find a company that interests you.** Go to its website, and examine its Corporate Social Responsibility policy. Read its annual report to see how it pursues this side of its business. Find out from other sources some of the issues and controversies around the company and its operations.

🌐 **Make up your own mind** as to whether the company seems to be pursuing its role as a 'good corporate citizen' in a satisfactory way. What can you do to make it more socially responsible?

SEPTEMBER 29

DIARRHOEA *prevention*

Most people will be affected by diarrhoea at some time in their life. But for many, especially babies and children, it can be deadly. ☺ Diarrhoea leads to dehydration, the main cause of death. Children are more likely than adults to die, because they become dehydrated more quickly. ☺ A drug that will stop the diarrhoea safely within a few hours does not exist. Yet the deaths of more than a million children a year could be prevented by a method that is cheap, safe and so simple it can be learned and used by anybody.

The treatment is Oral Rehydration Therapy, which is effective in most situations. Oral reydration does not stop diarrhoea, but it does prevent the body from drying up by replacing the water and salts that help it retain water. This gives the body time and strength to do battle with whatever is causing the diarrhoea. ☺ ORT consists of salt and glucose. It is extremely cheap, costing as little as 5p per sachet (or you can make your own from these commonly available household ingredients). It *does* need to be added to clean water, however, which can prove problematic in areas where none is available. ☺ No other single medical discovery of the 20th century has the potential to prevent so many deaths at so little cost. It currently saves the lives of around 1 million children a year.

The Rehydration Project: www.rehydrate.org
Find out how many people have had diarrhoea so far today and how many people have died. Go to: www.rehydrate.org/diarrhoea/index.html

It is in the developing world that the impact of diarrhoea is most severe:

1.8 million people die every year from a diarrhoea-related disease (which includes cholera).
90% are children under five.
88% of diarrhoea-related disease is caused by an unsafe water supply, inadequate sanitation and poor hygiene.
Washing one's hands (better personal hygiene) and an improved drinking-water supply would do a great deal to improve the situation.

...with a little sugar and salt

Teach yourself how to rehydrate a child suffering from diarrhoea:

☺ **Wash your hands** with soap and water.
☺ **Prepare a solution in a clean pot** by mixing one teaspoon of salt and eight teaspoons of sugar with one litre of clean drinking water (boil and then cool the water). Stir until the contents dissolve.
☺ **Wash your hands and the child's hands** with soap and water before giving
the solution to the child.
☺ **Give the child as much of the solution as it needs;** in small amounts.
☺ **Give the child alternately other fluids,** such as milk and juice.
☺ **Continue to give solids** if child is older than four months.
☺ **If the child still needs rehydration after 24 hours,** make up a fresh solution.
☺ **If the child vomits,** wait ten minutes and give them more solution. Usually the vomiting will stop by itself.
☺ **If the diarrhoea increases or the vomiting persists,** then take the child to a health clinic.

30 SEPTEMBER

be a **PHILANTHROPIST**

Money is sitting in your bank account right now, waiting for you to spend it. It may be collecting interest but only very slowly. It is contributing to the profits of the bank and doing nothing for you. You could be spending it to change the world.

If you could do one thing to make a positive impact on the world, what would it be? Think miniscule, think mammoth, think traditional and think outrageous. If you have a vision, your money could help make that vision come true.

You could leave your money to charity in your will. But why wait? You could do something by yourself. Or you could join with others.

The Funding Network: **www.thefundingnetwork.org.uk**

The Funding Network is a group of people who meet regularly to give their money away. There are 100 or so active members of the Network, and most give at least £1,000 a year.

Members of the Network also suggest projects to support. This could be a disco run by and for people with learning disabilities, or an international Roma group lobbying for human rights, or a project that is making the Sahara green. Funding days are held every three or four months, when members get together. Half a dozen selected projects are each given ten minutes to present their case and answer questions. Most come away with at least £5,000 given by those present.

The Funding Network is a chance for like minded people to get together, enjoy themselves, hear about some really interesting ways of changing the world and give away their money.

...give away your money

You could join The Funding Network, or you could set up your own network of like-minded philanthropists.

Think of one thing that will make a real difference. It could address a problem, an issue or a cause which you care about passionately. This is a chance to put your money where your mouth is.

Set up your funding network. Find nine friends who would like to join you in giving money away. Agree how much you each will give. It could be a lot or a little. It could be the same amount for everyone, or everyone could give a percentage of their income. You decide. Then look around for really interesting projects to support. Remember that your money will make much more of a difference by supporting a small initiative or giving direct to a project, than by making a donation to a large charity.

OCTOBER 1

CONSERVATION *holidays*

I spent two weeks in Romania on an eco tourism project in the delightful village of Salasu de Sus in the foothills of the Retezat Mountains. We came from England, Wales, New Zealand and even Malaysia to work with a group of local volunteers for a fortnight – and to gain a fascinating insight into a very different way of life. Our first challenge was the construction of a children's playground out of a few large logs.

– BTCV volunteer

The British Trust for Conservation Volunteers organises conservation holidays. These offer a creative alternative to sitting on a beach. Holidays last one to six weeks. Turtle monitoring in Thailand, Greece or Grenada, endangered primate surveys in India, footpath construction in Iceland, wetland management in Hungary; these are just a few of the things you can do.

You will meet people you wouldn't normally meet. You'll work alongside local people, helping them to protect their environment. You'll do some physical work and get your hands dirty. But in return, the stress and routine of normal everyday life will be washed away and replaced by beautiful scenery, a sense of achievement and new friends. And in the evenings there will be free time to relax, explore the locality and socialise even more.

BTCV conservation holidays: www.btcv.org

Biosphere Expeditions: www.biosphere-expeditions.org

Calculate your carbon emissions at Climate Care:
www.co2.org/calculator/index.cfm

Survey elephants in Sri Lanka

This is just one of the conservation holidays organised by Biosphere Expeditions. You will survey the forests, jungles, grass plains and water holes around and within the Wasgamuwa National Park for elephants and help to build a database of individual movements and associations. You will interview local villagers outside the Park about elephant crop raiding, and assess and record any damage done. You will also spend some time in tree-hut hides, attempting to observe and record elephant herds at water holes. All this in an effort to help resolve the conflict between humans and elephants and to gather data to promote the establishment of the first national park in Sri Lanka that crosses climatic zones.

...go somewhere nice

🌳 **Go on a conservation holiday.** You will be asked to pay. But it will be a cheap holiday doing something really worthwhile. If you want to go to Albania, Australia, Bulgaria, Canada, Ecuador or around 20 other countries, or just stay in the UK, a BTCV conservation holiday may be just what you need.

🌳 **Calculate the carbon impact of your air travel in getting there,** and plant some trees to compensate.

stay in an EARTHSHIP

Earthships are solar-powered homes or work spaces. They're built from something that's causing a massive waste problem: used tyres. They work with the planet's natural systems, using the sun's energy and rain to provide heat, power and water. The use of earth-filled car tyres also provides excellent insulation.

Earthship living is autonomous living: very cheap and very cheerful. Living in an earthship means that you do not need to make use of power stations emitting greenhouse gases, or rely on mains water or waste services. 🌳 Tyres filled with compacted earth are strong, and require a low level of building skills. It creates a use for a waste material which is a real and growing environmental problem. At least 240 million tyres are scrapped each year in the USA and 150 million in the European Union.

The UK generates 40 million used tyres each year, many of which end up in landfill sites. From time to time tyre fires have started in rubbish tips, releasing noxious fumes into the atmosphere. But 20,000 new earthships could be built each year out of our growing used-tyre mountain. 🌳 Building and living in an earthship makes a significant contribution to reducing greenhouse emissions. Cement manufacture causes 10% of greenhouse gas emissions worldwide. And in the developed world, other building materials create a further 10% of emissions. Energy used in the home for heating, lighting, cooking, cooling contributes 30% of total emissions.

Earthship Biotecture: www.earthship.com
Low Carbon Network: www.lowcarbon.co.uk

Make use of used tyres

John Dobozy, an Australian inventor, has developed a process to extract the greatest amount of value from a used tyre, turning it into a number of useable and saleable products, leaving practically no waste, and with the potential to generate around $3 of income per tyre. Find out more from:
www.abc.net.au/catalyst/stories/s1185584.htm

...for sustainability

Find out about earthships.

🌳 **Have a holiday in an earthship.** Earthships were pioneered by Earthship Biotecture, which is based in Taos, New Mexico, USA. They have earthships available for holiday lettings at around $50 per person per night for a party of four. Experience recycled zero-emissions living.

🌳 **Buy the t-shirt.** If you're really committed, they will sell you 'how to' books, plans or even a fully built Earthship.

🌳 **Visit an earthship** being built near Brighton by Low Carbon Network. This is an educational resource. They also run two- and four-day courses in earthship building skills.

WALK *to school*

When I was about 10 years old, I used to walk to school, but was supposed to catch the bus home in the afternoon. My mother never knew that I used to spend the bus fare at the sweet shop. The walking journey home was always more pleasurable knowing that I'd got four fruit salad chews and a couple of sherbet flying saucers for the price of a bus fare.

The school run accounts for a sizeable chunk of morning rush hour traffic. It causes congestion, pollution and danger outside most schools. If more children were to walk to school, then communities would experience the environmental and health benefits associated with having fewer vehicles on the road.

Children can walk to school on their own if they're old enough. Or they can be accompanied by their parents. Or you can organise a 'walking crocodile', where parents and children meet up at some agreed point, and then walk to school together.

There are also crocodiles in the jungle. In Gudalur, in the South India Nilgiri hills, children from tribal settlements in the forests walk together with a community worker two or three kilometres to school each day along forest trails. As a result, more children (and especially more girls) go to school.

International Walk to School Week: www.iwalktoschool.org
The UK Walk to School campaign: www.walktoschool.org.uk
Living Streets has information on how to do it: www.livingstreets.org.uk

10 reasons to use shoe rubber not tyre rubber:
- **Pushchairs** are easier to park than cars.
- **You save** money.
- **You cut down** on pollution.
- **You see more** of your neighbourhood.
- **You meet** and make friends on the way.
- **You can chat** with your children about this and that.
- **You can put** road-safety theory into practice.
- **You're making life easier** for those who need to use the road.
- **It can be fun.**
- **It keeps** you and your children fit.

...for healthy kids

Take part in walk to school week.

Three million children, parents, and community leaders from 29 countries around the world do something for International Walk to School Week.

Make sure all your friends and family know about it and participate. Go with them. Dress in fancy dress. Make a large placard with a catchy slogan. Play a big trombone... You'll be highlighting a major source of pollution and congestion.

International Walk to School Week is the first week of October **4 OCTOBER**

African school LINK UPS

School link ups are a great way for teachers and pupils to see a different world perspective. A link with an African school (or indeed a school in any other part of the world) can teach children about the wider world and help them develop into active global citizens. It provides an opportunity for staff and pupils to make lasting friendships. And it also makes the curriculum more interesting and immediate.

Link Community Development pioneers school linking between the UK and Africa. It supports over 300 links between schools in the UK and schools in Ghana, South Africa and Uganda. A key aim is to improve the African school, so that more children have a better education. Headteachers are provided with training and given help to produce a school development plan.

The school raises some money from its local community. It is then given a grant to spend on one of the priorities in the development plan. The link provides an opportunity for pupil and teacher exchanges, and for shared educational projects. The UK link school also helps with fundraising and support in kind. If every school in Africa had a link, it would transform education for millions of young Africans.

Link Community Development: www.lcd.org.uk

North-South School Linking, an EU resource: www.schoollinking.net

Windows on the World: a free, easy to use British Council resource for schools and colleges seeking international links: www.wotw.org.uk

Upper Culunca is a remote rural secondary school in South Africa. The infrastructure of the area is poor: no electricity, no water supply, dirt roads impassable at certain times of the year. Unemployment is around 70%, and people leave to get jobs in the cities. Upper Culunca has three classrooms, as many toilets and a staff room.

Ken Stimpson School near Peterborough has a diverse mix of pupils, and decided to take part in the link-up project. At Ken Stimpson, students did a sponsored run to raise money. Another group, stunned by how little their African peers had to live on, started recycling; and a World Citizenship conference for young people was held. Over £1,000 has been raised in the UK to buy water butts to save rainwater and build two new classrooms. And a school farm project is being developed with support from the Rotary Club.

...children share their lives

Get your local school linked up.

🦊 Find out as much as you can about school linking.

🦊 Choose a country and find a school that is interested.

🦊 Arrange to give a talk in your local school to the students as well as to the teachers.

BILLBOARD *liberation*

A can of spray paint, a blithe spirit, and a balmy night are all you really need.

– The Billboard Liberation Front

When was the last time you read a billboard with a positive message? Corporate giants have enough cash to bombard you with any message they want. Everywhere you look there are billboards (advertising hoardings), sending out complex coded messages, trying to make you feel somehow lacking if you don't buy this or that product. No one spends £20,000 to put up a billboard that just says 'Perform an act of kindness today'.

It's time to fight back and turn billboards into a tool for good. As most of us don't have £20,000 spare cash to put up our own advertising, groups like the Billboard Liberation Front 'adjust' someone else's message. But you must understand that liberating a billboard is completely illegal, you will get arrested if you are caught.

The opening to the Billboard Liberation Front's manifesto reads:

In the beginning was the Ad. The Ad was brought to the consumer by the Advertiser. Desire, self worth, self image, ambition, hope; all find their genesis in the Ad. Through the Ad and the intent of the Advertiser we form our ideas and learn the myths that make us into what we are as a people. It is now clear that the Ad holds the most esteemed position in our cosmology.

Billboard Liberation Front: www.billboardliberation.com
Adbusters, a global movement fighting consumerism: www.adbusters.org

From the Billboard Liberation Front website Obligatory Disclaimer

This website is intended for entertainment purposes only. No one involved in the production and hosting of this website encourages any action which would violate state, federal, local or international statutes and treaties. We may be stupid, but we're not dumb.

...for positive messages

Dream about liberating a billboard! Think about what you would write. Billboard Liberation Front offer these tips:

- **Consider just altering it** by adding a symbol, a word, or a thought bubble.
- **Plan escape routes.** Check the site out day and night for activity. How will you reach the billboard safely? Do you need a ladder?
- **Go up on the billboard prior to your 'alteration';** make sure you feel safe.
- **Have a ground team to assist you** and to alert you to danger.

humanity in HARMONY

Daniel Pearl was an American journalist working for the Wall Street Gazette. In January 2002 he was in Pakistan, investigating the links between fundamentalism and terrorism. He was captured and beheaded. The video of his beheading was circulated by his murderers and shocked the world. His widow, Mariane, told her story in her book, *A Mighty Heart*.

Mariane has now set up the Daniel Pearl Foundation in memory of her late husband. In the spirit of Danny's love of music and commitment to dialogue, she has created Daniel Pearl Music Days which are held during the first ten days of October each year (10 October was Danny's birthday).

Concerts for peace are organised around the world. The number of events has been doubling each year. Tens of thousands have already joined this global community, celebrating the ideals for which Daniel Pearl stood: cross-cultural understanding, mutual respect and tolerance. Small bands of amateur musicians to international music stars, drum ensembles to big symphony orchestras have all participated. Over 400 concerts were held in 39 countries in 2004.

Daniel Pearl Foundation: www.danielpearl.org

For participation guidelines in Daniel Pearl Music Day, please go to: www.music-days.org

Just Vision: www.justvision.org/profile

Just Vision website presents the stories of Israeli and Palestinian civilians who are working for peace. By the end of 2005, there were 180 such stories. This is a fraction of the courageous Israelis and Palestinians whose peace-related efforts receive too little media attention. There are four main criteria for being included. People must be engaged in work that involves people on both sides of the Green Line; they must be living permanently in Israel or Palestine; they are pursuing non-violent approaches to peace building; and they are civilians, not elected officials.

Just Visionaries include people like Inas Radwan, from Jenin, who organises summer camps in the USA for young Israelis, Palestinians and Americans. And Gershon Baskin, from Jerusalem, founder of IPCRI, an Israeli–Palestinian think tank.

...play music for peace

Stand up to hatred and intolerance in the world; play music for peace!

🕊 **Promote the spirit of peace.** Have some fun. Give fun to others. Organise your own gig for Daniel Pearl Music Day, or persuade your favourite venue to dedicate a performance.

🕊 **Participation is open to anyone** who wishes to promote tolerance, understanding and global harmony. You are not expected to raise funds.

TV *helps*

Get a 'dot tv' internet address, and you will be supporting a threatened nation. All internet and web addresses end in a 'suffix': .com .org .biz . gov .coop .net .info, which show the nature of the organisation that is registering (a commercial company, a civil society organisation, a business, a government body, a cooperative, etc.). 🌴 Or .uk .fr .pk .in, which show where the internet address is registered (UK, France, Pakistan, India, etc.). Each country has a different suffix, apart from the USA, which was the heartland for the developing WorldWideWeb.

Tuvalu, which is a group of islands in the South pacific, has .tv as its suffix. This is a real asset for the country, as the two letters 'TV' are recognised all over the world as having media glamour. But Tuvalu is so small that it does not even have its own TV station. When you get a .tv web or email address, you will also be contributing to the economy of one of the smallest and strangest countries on the planet, as the .tv suffix has been leased to the VeriSign corporation under a profit-share agreement with the government of Tuvalu.

So get a .tv internet address, and help the Tuvaluan economy. But also think about global warming and what you could do to bring the plight of the Tuvaluans to the attention of a gas-guzzling complacent world.

Sign up for .tv at: www.tv
Find out more about Tuvalu by going to: www.tuvaluislands.com

Tuvalu

There are 11,500 Tuvaluans living on nine islands and atolls in the South Pacific with a total area of 26 sq kms. The place is remote and really small. The islands are no more than 5 metres above sea level. Global warming and the melting of the polar icecaps, means that the sea is rising. The islands are in danger of disappearing; they get flooded not from waves, but through water bubbling up from the ground, and the flooding is becoming more frequent. Tuvalu is likely to disappear off the face of the earth; it is likely to be either the first or the second victim of global warming.

...support a threatened nation

Get a .tv internet address. It's simple... and it's cool.

If your email or website address is yourname.tv or yourorganisation.tv, this will look different and it will get you noticed.

To register, go to: www.tv and it'll cost you US$50 for one year or as little as US$300 for ten years.

write A LETTER

> *Dear Forest Service staff,*
>
> *I am deeply concerned about the Forest Service's plans to remove Yellowstone's grizzly bears from the endangered species list. As the Forest Service revises the plan, I strongly urge you to select Alternative 4, which would protect important wildlands, restore degraded habitat and maintain habitat within and between grizzly bear ecosystems. Please choose Alternative 4 and do everything possible to ensure Yellowstone's grizzlies remain adequately protected.*
>
> *Yours faithfully...*

If you feel strongly about something bad that is being planned or already taking place, you need to make your views known to those who are causing the problem or who can help with a solution.

Letter writing is one way of doing this. It's not the only way. Demos, marches, stunts, publicity campaigns and lobbying are other things you might do. But sending a letter will let you get your views across and make it clear that you care. One letter may not make much of a difference. But lots of letters show that lots of people care.

Protecting Grizzly Bears may not be your passion. Perhaps what you really care about is protecting areas of outstanding beauty, ancient monuments, heritage sites, other wildlife, campaigning against superstores and shopping malls, SUVs...

These two letter-writing websites are small ones run by committed individuals:
Global response with 5,500 members from 92 countries: www.globalresponse.org
Earth Action Network campaigning in the US: www.earthactionnetwork.org

ActionNetwork with over 750,000 activists taking action on mainly US issues: www.actionnetwork.org

Earth Action Network was started by Dr Mha Atma Singh Khalsa, a Los Angeles chiropractor. He wanted to do something to help the planet, and read in an activist guidebook that a single letter received by a government or company was considered to represent the views of 100 to 1,000 people. As a result, he began writing letters to influential people, based on information he got from environmental newsletters and reports. A friend pointed out to him that there were many others who felt as strongly as he did and who would love to have a chance to do the same, and Earth Action Network was born.

...make your views known

Rapid-response letter writing has developed with the internet. All the big campaigning organisations encourage it, whether the issue is human rights, conflict or the environment.

⚐ **If you are concerned about an issue,** then join a Rapid Response Network of your choice. Sign up and start writing.

⚐ **Write your own letters** in your own words.

BULLY *awareness*

Question: What do Ms Dynamite, Tom Cruise and David Beckham have in common?

Answer: All of them were bullied at school.

Bullying can happen at school, at the workplace and within families. It's particularly horrid when the bullying is homophobic or racist. If you are being bullied, tell someone. This can be quite hard; so it may be easier to write a note explaining how you feel. ◄ Bullying won't stop unless you do something. Keep a diary of what's happening; record the incidents and also your feelings, so that you have a record if you need this. If you know someone who is being bullied, then it's important to do something to stop it. Anti-bullying websites give information on what to look out for.

The Wikipedia encyclopaedia gives these as some examples of bullying:
Spreading (negative) gossip and rumours.
Constant criticism for unspecified allegations.
Taking the victim's possessions or exerting control of their work.
Making the victim do what they do not want to do with a threat of violence or disciplinary action if they refuse.
Actually following through with a threat to ensure the victim will comply with all future orders.

Bullying Online: www.bullying.co.uk
Kidscape: www.kidscape.org.uk
Two Canadian anti-bullying websites: www.bullying.org and www.cyberbullying.ca

Stamp out cyberbullying

Cyberbullying is sending or posting harmful or cruel text or images using the internet or other digital communication devices. Cyber-bullies:
Send cruel, vicious, and sometimes threatening messages.
Create websites that ridicule others.
Break into email accounts and send vicious or embarrassing material.
Engage someone in instant messaging, trick the person into revealing sensitive personal information, and then forward it to others.
Take embarrassing pictures of people using a digital phone camera and then send these pictures to others.
The Center for Safe and Responsible Internet Use provides advice and guidance on online cruelty: responsiblenetizen.org
The Center's cyberbullying website is at: cyberbully.org

...they ruin people's lives

Do an anti-bullying survey.

◄ **Download some suggested questions from Bullying Online,** and include an open-ended question for respondents to tell you about how the bullying is affecting or has affected their life.

◄ **Survey school students, or adults,** asking them about their experience of being bullied at school. Make the response anonymous. You may well be surprised at the extent of bullying and the impact it has had on people's lives.

the gift of SIGHT

There are an estimated 45 million people in the world who are blind. The majority of these are poor people in the developing world. This year nearly 2 million people will lose their sight. If no action is taken, there will be 75 million blind people by 2020. ☺ More than two-thirds of blindness is treatable and preventable; 30 million people could see, if we could address the problem.

Restoration of sight is one of the most cost-effective interventions in health care. It costs surprisingly little to make a blind person see, and it brings enormous benefits to those who are enabled to see again.

'2020 Vision' means perfect sight. 'VISION 2020: The Right to Sight' aims to eliminate needless blindness by the year 2020. This initiative has been jointly launched by the World Health Organization and the International Agency for the Prevention of Blindness, working with more than 20 international NGOs involved in eye care and the prevention and management of blindness.

20/20 Vision: www.v2020.org
SightSavers International: www.sightsavers.org.uk
Project Orbis: www.orbis.org

Main causes of blindness

Corneal blindness: caused by malnutrition.
Cataract: a clouding of the lens; 100 million people could benefit from a simple operation.
Glaucoma: caused by increased pressure in the eye through malfunction of the drainage system.
Trachoma: an eye infection caused by poor hygiene and environmental factors, which is transmitted by flies. Trachoma can lead to blindness. Children can be treated with antibiotics, adults with a simple operation.
River blindness: endemic in sub-Saharan Africa and parts of South America, can be treated with drugs.
Childhood blindness: usually caused by Vitamin A deficiency. There are 1.5 million blind children worldwide.
Retinal detachment: due to ageing or accidents.
Refractive error and low vision: usually corrected by providing spectacles.

...give it to someone in need

It costs so little to help someone see again. There are lots of organisations that run eye camps, which involve setting up a 'production line' for treatment and operations. They all want your money to help them do more work. Project Orbis (a US agency) and SightSavers (an international agency) both are actively looking for support. For example:

£3 protects 25 villagers from river blindness
£5 buys a lens needed to replace a cataract
£10 treats 8 people suffering from trachoma
£17 restores sight to a cataract sufferer

Or you can buy the Gift of Sight from www.goodgifts.org

A little generosity can transform someone's life.

LIBRARY *building*

Books document the ideas of a culture and a generation. For example, Jews settled in Calcutta (now known as Kolkata) at the end of the 18th century, and developed a vibrant community with its own culture, cooking and lifestyle which was significantly different from Jews in other parts of the world.

Today only a handful of Jews remain in Kolkata, and they are very elderly. Tomorrow their presence will be forgotten, their synagogues abandoned, their graveyards fallen into disrepair. All that will remain will be the memoirs, the genealogies and the cookery books published by this community. And if these are lost, so will all memory of the Jews of Calcutta.

Collecting and preserving books is a way of preserving a heritage. Whether it is the Jews of Calcutta, the antics of the hippies of the 1960s or the early history of the Beatles.

National Yiddish Book Center: www.yiddishbookcenter.org

How one man saved 1.5 million books and an entire culture from extinction

In 1980, Aaron Lansky was a 23-year-old graduate student. He was alarmed by the fact that all over North America thousands of Yiddish books that had survived Hitler and Stalin were now being thrown away. The older generation was passing on, and their children and grandchildren were unable to read Yiddish. The books seemed to be of no value to anybody.

Yet this was an entire literature from a vibrant Jewish civilisation from central Europe that existed until the Pogroms and the Holocaust led to mass emigration and genocide. If this literature was destroyed, so would be our knowledge of the civilisation that created it.

Lansky realised something had to be done before it was too late. So he took a two-year leave of absence from graduate school, rented an unheated factory loft, and issued a public appeal for unwanted and discarded Yiddish books. Lansky has now recovered 1.5 million books and established the National Yiddish Book Center, which translates books and supplies Yiddish books to libraries around the world. His efforts have been hailed as the 'the greatest cultural rescue effort in Jewish history'. Read Lanksy's story in his book, *Outwitting History*.

...for future generations

Think of some small part of today's civilisation that particularly fascinates you.

- **Start photographing it,** keeping cuttings of newspaper articles about it, and buying all the books you can find on the subject.
- **Begin to build up a library.** Some time in the future this could become a valuable archive, preserving for future generations knowledge of this special interest of yours.

from ipod to E-WASTE

Digital equipment causes toxic waste. Lurking underneath Apple's beautifully designed digital music players and computers are poisonous chemicals like lead, mercury and cadmium that can cause birth defects and disabilities. Every computer manufacturer, every mobile telecoms provider, every digital download system is developing ever-newer products, and this is making the older models obsolete. These are then discarded. It is becoming a major issue.

About 40% of the heavy metals in landfills comes from electronic equipment discards. If this seeps out, the impact could be horrendous. Just 1/70th of a teaspoon of mercury is sufficient to contaminate a 7-hectare lake, making the fish unfit to eat. Silicon Valley Toxics Coalition estimates that up to 600 million desktop and laptop computers in the USA alone will soon be obsolete. All these obsolete computers would create a pile 1.6 km high covering 2 hectares. This would be the same as a 22-storey pile covering the entire 1,275 km^2 of Los Angeles. E-waste is growing almost three times faster than municipal waste.

Less than 10% of discarded computers are currently recycled. Most of the rest are either stored in basements, garages, offices and cupboards or, in ignorance of the hazards of doing this, tossed out with the rubbish.

The Computer Take Back campaign: www.computertakeback.com
Silicon Valley Toxics Coalition, calling to account the global electronics industry: www.svtc.org

Send a letter to Steve Jobs, CEO of Apple Computer.

On the principle that the 'Polluter Should Pay', computer companies should be reducing the amount of toxic materials and taking back their products for recycling. Steve Jobs has already agreed to take back iPods. This letter could encourage him to do more. Send this letter from the Computer Take Back website:

Recycling iPods at Apple stores is a great thing; but why not go all the way and accept all obsolete Apple products at your retail outlets?

If you can do it with iPods, you can do it with all your products! Old computers like the Apple II, IIe, and the Mac Classic contain toxics like lead, mercury, and cadmium, and end up in landfills or incinerators, polluting our land, air and water.

By offering free recycling for all Apple products, including to those who don't happen to live near an Apple store, you can be the real innovator and green leader I thought you would be.

...minimise toxic waste

🌳 **Continue to use your computer if it is still usable.** You almost certainly don't need the extra specifications that suppliers are offering.

🌳 **Donate your old computer** to a charity at home or abroad if you want to trade up.

🌳 **Find out how to dispose of your computer safely,** if you can't find anyone to donate it to (or if it's just too old or broken down).

GRAND *challenges*

Most medical research is directed toward diseases of the rich. If similar efforts could be made towards the poor, this could save millions of lives. In 2003, the Bill & Melinda Gates Foundation challenged researchers to come up with solutions for some of the world's major health problems.

Fourteen 'Grand Challenges' were selected from more than 1,000 suggestions to address these goals:

> **Create childhood vaccines** that don't need refrigeration, needles or multiple doses.
>
> **Use the immune system** to guide the development of new vaccines for malaria, TB and HIV.
>
> **Find ways** of preventing insects from transmitting diseases such as malaria.
>
> **Grow** more nutritious staple crops to combat malnutrition.
>
> **Discover** ways to prevent drug resistance.
>
> **Develop methods** of treating latent and chronic infections such as TB.
>
> **More accurately diagnose** and track disease in poor countries, where sophisticated laboratories or reliable record keeping systems are not available.

In 2005, the Foundation gave $436 million for 43 projects.

Grand Challenges: www.grandchallengesgh.org
Bill & Melinda Gates Foundation: www.gatesfoundation.org

Crops play a part in malnutrition:

Many people's diet consists largely of a single 'staple food', but in many cases this does not meet their nutritional requirements.

Cassava: This starchy root crop is a staple for more than 250 million Africans; it provides less than 30% of the protein needed for a healthy diet, and can be toxic if not prepared properly.

Rice: Rice is the primary source of food for more than half the world's population, but it is deficient in many essential micronutrients.

Sorghum: More than 300 million people in arid regions of Africa rely on sorghum, but it is low on essential nutrients and difficult to digest.

...for health solutions

Define your challenge. It may be to solve a problem, or to come up with good ideas.

- **Get some money together.** See what you can afford to contribute; badger your friends; write to rich people, big companies, the newspapers, telling them about your dream of solving a major social problem and ask them to contribute something. Set yourself a challenging target, and see if you can better it!

- **Set up a judging panel** (of illustrious people) to decide the winner.

- **Issue your own grand challenge.** Use websites, blogs and newsgroups to spread the word. If the challenge is interesting and there's a cash prize, then lots of people might reply.

14 OCTOBER

world-changing WOMEN

Did you know that women:

Produce 60%–80% of basic foodstuffs in Sub-Saharan Africa and the Caribbean.

Undertake over 50% of the labour involved in intensive rice cultivation in Asia.

Perform 30% of the agricultural work in industrialised countries.

Head 60% of households in some regions of Africa.

Meet 90% of household water and fuel needs in Africa.

Process 100% of basic household foodstuffs in Africa.

Contribute an estimated $15-trillion-worth of unpaid work in the home and the community.

But…

Women have not achieved equality with men in any country.

866 million women live below the poverty line; two-thirds of all poor people.

20 million women are refugees; 75% of the world total.

660 women are illiterate; two-thirds of illiterate adults.

86 million girls are not in school; two-thirds of all absentees.

Women earn about three-quarters of the pay of men for the same work, outside the agricultural sector.

Only 24 women were elected heads of state or government in the 20th century.

Only 7 of the 185 highest-ranking diplomats to the UN are women.

Women's Creativity in Rural Life: **www.woman.ch**

Women who make a difference:

Amina Bio Yau Bio Nigan from Gomparu, Benin created her own micro-enterprise: transforming local fruits, vegetables, spices and roots into syrups, jams and cosmetics, and selling quality products at an affordable price.

She uses traditional methods and organic ingredients.

'Bio Nigan' products are now well known and even sold in neighbouring countries (Burkina Faso, Niger and Togo).

Betty Makoni from Harare, Zimbabwe teaches English. Most of her girl students have been victims of sexual abuse so she created a club where they can exchange accounts of their experiences and encourage each other to sue the guilty. The club concept has spread over the whole country, with 166 (involving more than 3,000 girls) being formed. Betty grouped them into the 'Girl Child Network'.

In 2001, Betty built a 'safe village' in Rusape as an information dissemination centre and a refuge for abused girls.

...a force for development

⊗ **Take part in Women's Rural Development Day.** Reflect on and learn from the extraordinary contributions that women are making.

⊗ **Read about the winners of the Prize** for Women's Creativity in Rural Life, and what they have achieved. Select some favourite stories. Tell other people about their achievements.

FEED *the world*

The good news: progress is being made on the war on hunger. The number of hungry people in the world dropped from 959 million in 1970 to 791 million in 1997.

The bad news: between 1995 and 2005, the number of hungry people has increased by almost 4 million each year. In 2002, there were 852 million underfed people worldwide (one in seven of the world's population): 815 million in developing countries; 28 million in transition countries; and 9 million in industrialised countries.

Hunger is the main risk to health worldwide. Its impact is greater than AIDS, malaria and tuberculosis combined. ● The hunger hot spots in the world are: Haiti, West Sudan (Darfur), Afghanistan, North Korea, Colombia, Democratic Republic of Congo, Bangladesh, Nicaragua. ● The main reason for hunger is poverty; war and natural disaster account for just 8% of the problem. ● Causes of hunger include overpopulation and land degradation; population movements (refugees); shortage of water and drought; floods and tropical storms; locust infestation; severe heat or cold; natural disasters, such as earthquakes; man-made emergencies, such as the consequences of conflict.

The World Food Programme is the food aid arm of the United Nations. It provides food aid to save lives of refugees in emergencies, improve the nutrition of vulnerable people including children in school, and help build infrastructure through food for work programmes.

Food Force: www.food-force.com
FightHunger: www.fighthunger.org
Facts about hunger: www.bread.org/hungerbasics/international.html

What is hunger?

Hunger: a signal that the body is running short of food.

Undernourishment: food intake does not provide enough calories to meet the body's minimum needs. This results in chronic hunger.

Malnutrition: food intake is insufficient to support natural bodily functions such as growth, pregnancy, lactation, and resistance to and recovery from disease.

Wasting: substantial weight loss usually associated with starvation or disease.

Stunting: shortness for age, which indicates chronic malnutrition.

Underweight: a low weight compared with a well-nourished, healthy person of the same age.

...and fight global hunger

● **Download the World Food Programme's video game,** 'Food Force'. Play and enjoy it. Distribute copies. You will learn about the problems of hunger and the difficulties of delivering food aid. There are six missions to complete.

● **Go to the FightHunger site.** Click and trigger a 19-cent donation, which is the cost of feeding one child for one day.

0.7% is the AID TARGET

When people tell you that aid and debt relief don't work, you say that what doesn't work is doing nothing.

– Gordon Brown, as UK Chancellor

In 1970, rich nations promised 0.7% of their gross national income for development. The intention was to raise the level to 1%. By 2003, only six of 19 OECD countries had managed to achieve more than half the 0.7% target. ● The USA was giving just 0.15%, the UK 0.34%. But Sweden, Netherlands, Luxembourg, Denmark and Norway were all exceeding 0.7%. ● In 2005, a pledge was made by the European Union that member states would achieve 0.56% by 2010, and reach the 0.7% target by 2015. This is too little and too late.

The Millennium Goals were agreed by the international community in 2000 to address poverty, hunger, universal primary education, health care, access to clean water and proper sanitation; all problems that the people of the rich world do not have to face, but which are part of the daily struggle for most of the people living in the poor world.

An immediate annual injection of at least $50 billion per year is required. This figure would ensure progress towards the Millennium Development Goals. For the goals to be met, $94 billion a year is needed.

Global Call to Action Against Poverty: www.whiteband.org
Organisation for Economic Cooperation and Development (OECD): www.oecd.org

Living on less than $1 a day

Whilst you drink a cappuccino at Starbucks, consider that one sixth of the world's population are having to live on just a dollar a day.

Meanwhile, every cow in the European Union (one of which will have made the frothy milk for your coffee) receives a subsidy of more than $2 per day (which is more than the income of half the world's population).

...make sure you're giving it

Put your money where your mouth is. Build on the goodwill shown by the Make Poverty History campaign and Live8 in July 2005, when 2 billion people worldwide tuned into, or attended, concerts aimed at raising awareness of global poverty.

● **Shame your government** into moving towards the 0.7% commitment much more quickly by setting up your own 0.7% Campaign.

● **Pledge to give 0.7% of your own annual income** as development aid. Ask your friends to do the same, and use the Pledge Bank to challenge others to join with you: www.pledgebank.com

● **Send your cheque** to the International Development Minister in your country saying that you are giving your government 0.7% of your annual income as a voluntary contribution to help them address world poverty, and challenging them to do the same.

OCTOBER 17 *International Day for the Eradication of Poverty*   302

WATER *monitoring*

Millennium Development Goal 7 pledges to ensure environmental sustainability. One of its targets by 2015 is to halve the proportion of people who lack access to clean water and proper sanitation. Water monitoring, to provide data on the state of the world's water resources, is essential if progress towards achieving this goal is to be measured. ♣ A water monitoring kit costs $13.00 plus shipping. This includes everything you need to test the four key indicators, plus a step-by-step guide to using the kit. Each kit includes one set of hardware (collection jar, pH test-tube, dissolved oxygen vial, thermometer), and enough pH and dissolved oxygen tablets to perform 50 tests. ♣ The kit is suitable for all ages and experience levels. A large group will require more than one kit.

World Water Monitoring Day is held annually, and was created with the following aims:

To promote the importance of water monitoring.

To connect people with efforts to protect and preserve their local watersheds, and get them involved in doing this.

To develop information about the health of each watershed as this changes over time.

On 18 October, people all over the world go out and test four key indicators of water quality:

Temperature

Acidity (pH)

Dissolved oxygen

Turbidity (how clear the water is, the amount of suspended particles).

They assess the health of their local rivers, lakes, estuaries and other waterbodies. Everyone is invited to participate.

Water on the Web, all you need to know: www.waterontheweb.org
World Water Monitoring Day: www.worldwatermonitoringday.org
Young Water Action Team: www.ywat.org

The Young Water Action Team

YWAT is a global network of young water professionals, activists and students, aged 18 to 30. Their mission is to increase awareness, participation and commitment of young people to water-related issues. There are members in more than 40 countries. If you are in the right age range, interested in helping tackle the world's challenges regarding water, sanitation and hygiene, and would like to be part of an international network, join YWAT.

...increasing awareness

Participate in this global water monitoring initiative. Not just this year, but next year too.

♣ **Order a water-monitoring kit.**

♣ **Go out and measure the water quality** of all the lakes, rivers, streams and estuaries near you.

go on a PILGRIMAGE

We went into the depth of the bush in Highgate Cemetery. When the highest tombstone came into view, we saw the familiar statue: an amiable old man, wise scholar, fearless fighter and giant who predicted and created a new world. On the tombstone was inscribed: 'Proletarians of the World, Unite!'

– Xue Baosheng

Karl Marx, founder of communism and author of *Das Kapital*, is buried in Highgate Cemetery in North London. Pilgrims from all over the world come to visit his grave.

The idea of pilgrimage is found within almost every religion. The 'In the Steps of the Magi' tour organised by the Holy Land Trust aims to develop a better understanding between people from different regions and to give first-hand opportunities to explore the culture and people of the Middle East. 🏃 The journey begins near Jerash in Jordan, and ends in Bethlehem. Pilgrims visit Petra, Jericho, St. George's Desert Monastery, Jerusalem, Hebron, Nazareth, Ramallah and Bethlehem. Travel is by a variety of methods, including car, camel and a lot of walking – which gives the opportunity to observe and interact with local people and communities.

Make a virtual pilgrimage without leaving your house. Choose to visit one of these 'heroes':
Nelson Mandela on Robben Island: www.freedom.co.za
Gandhi's virtual ashram: www.nuvs.com/ashram
Karl Marx in Highgate: www.redrocks.net/travel/london/image23.html

Shantum Seth is an advisor to the United Nations Development Programme on volunteering and livelihoods. He is also actively involved in Ahimsa Trust which is working on peace and development. Shantum is a Buddhist. He explains:

In the footsteps of the Buddha provides an opportunity to explore areas that few tourists visit and to understand some of the structures and subtleties of Indian life. We go for country walks and visit villages that have changed little since the Buddha's time 2,500 years ago. We visit schools, stop at mango groves for picnics take a boat ride along the Ganges and even shop for silk! We go at a slower pace than tourists usually do, which allows us to be mindful, have discussions and time for ourselves. At each of the sacred sites I tell stories of the Buddha's life and teachings.
travel.vsnl.com/footstepsofbuddha/shantum.htm

...develop your understanding

What sort of pilgrimage would you like to make?

Would you like to go to:

🏃 **Woodstock,** the venue of the concert that defined a counterculture?

🏃 **Rochdale,** to see where the co-operative movement started?

🏃 **Selma,** Alabama to see where Martin Luther King once stood?

🏃 **Hiroshima** to see the epicentre of the first atomic bomb?

The choice is yours.

OCTOBER 19

ROOM *to read*

World change starts with educated children

– John Wood, Room to Read

School is unaffordable in many parts of the world. Many poor people survive on less than a dollar a day. Even if there is a school nearby, some children may be two hours' walk away, and there may not be a teacher in attendance. Or the child may be required to look after the family or work in the fields. The cost of books, school uniforms and sometimes school fees can also make school beyond the reach of many families. ◆ As a result, over 100 million school-age children in the developing world are not enrolled in primary school.

The situation is worst for girls. The girl child is last in the pecking order when it comes to allocating family resources. She may be required to look after the younger children in the family, do the housework and fetch water; and in some societies will get married whilst still very young.

More than two-thirds of women in some countries never attain literacy. Room to Read is creating educational opportunities in Asia by building schools and libraries. Room to Read gets villages to raise part of the overall expenditure (through donated land, labour, materials and cash). This community involvement has enabled Room to Read to grow so quickly. In its first four years, Room to Read:

Helped over 510,000 children.
Built 110 schools and 1,475 libraries.
Published 33 children's books in local languages.
Donated 300,000 new books.
Established 48 computer and language labs.
Funded 975 long-term scholarships.

Room to Read: www.roomtoread.org

The story of two eight-year olds

Eight-year-old Karpali in Tennessee organised a read-a-thon, which raised over $6,000 for Room to Read to build a school in Nepal.

Eight-year-old Renu lives in Phutung Village in Nepal. She wants to become a doctor – a big ambition for a daughter of subsistence farmers. When her parents could no longer afford school fees, Room to Read provided a scholarship. Now Renu's goal of becoming a doctor is back on track.

...an opportunity to learn

Help Room to Read provide communities with schools and literacy.

◆ **Go to the website.** See a slide show about their work.

◆ **Adopt a project.** Raise money to help a community build a school or library. It's an achievable target. And you'll be proud of having done something really worthwhile.

◆ **Become a virtual volunteer,** anything from website development to speaking at local schools.

20 OCTOBER

buy ethical DIAMONDS

A diamond may be 'forever', but thousands of miners, many of them children, work in unpleasant, unsafe conditions, risking injury and death, to produce this symbol of love and fidelity.

Mining can affect local ecosystems, harm wildlife and deprive communities of their natural resources. The dust from mines can cause respiratory diseases in both the diamond workers and those living nearby. The diamonds could be funding armed conflicts, as was the case in Sierra Leone. And there is concern about a possible link with money laundering and the financing of drugs and terrorism.

Can diamonds ever be ethically produced? A number of organisations are attempting to guarantee to customers that the stones offered for sale in their shops and online are 'conflict-free diamonds' – in other words, the income it generated was not used to fund war, and it was mined and produced under ethical conditions.

Conflict-Free Diamond Council: www.conflictfreediamonds.org
Diamonds for Africa Fund: www.diamondsforafricafund.org

Diamonds for Africa Fund

Corey Frayer bought a diamond engagement ring for his fiancée, and was appalled to discover the poverty and suffering behind the diamond. So he decided to donate it to make a positive contribution to Africa, and he created the Diamonds for Africa Fund in partnership with Brilliant Earth and the Indigenous Land Rights Fund.

The Fund set itself some goals: to raise $300,000 for the San Bushmen in Botswana, to improve health and education in villages in the Congo (DRC), and to help children in Sierra Leone affected by conflict diamonds.

To support the Fund, you can make a donation, or you can buy your diamonds from Brilliant Earth, which will donate 5% of its profits to local communities affected by the diamond trade.

...sparkle with a clear conscience

Make sure you buy ethically:

- **Only buy conflict-free and responsibly mined diamonds**, where the gemstone can be traced from the mine through to the point of sale.
- **Purchase your diamond in a recycled or responsibly mined** metal setting.
- **Buy a second-hand or antique ring**, where no diamond has to be newly mined. Go to an antique shop, or buy at auction, or find it on eBay.

GO MAD *in October*

Make A Difference Day started in the USA in 1992 with a simple idea: 'Put your own cares on hold for one day to do something for someone else or for your local community'. It is the USA's largest single day of volunteering, with 3 million people doing their bit. It has been copied successfully in the UK, and other countries are now beginning to do it. Soon it will become a worldwide event.

Make a Difference Day is always the fourth Saturday in October. But if you can't make that day, just do something that week or that weekend. For example, following a drug-related murder, the young people on a Sheffield housing estate wanted to restore trust in the community, and prove that they were not all 'vandals', 'thieves' and 'druggies'. The young volunteers created an inter-generational book, profiling children's and grandparents' experiences as a way of bringing young and older people together.

Charity organisations also make a special effort to make a difference. Disabled members from Surrey-based charity, Reach Out Youth and Disabilities, undertook a surprise renovation for a fellow volunteer and her disabled daughter, while they were away on holiday. They joined forces with New Malden police to renovate the interior of Pat Begley's house. They laid a new carpet, carried out repairs, and spring-cleaned the house. The team also worked hard to revamp the exterior of the house; paving and landscaping the garden, laying a new lawn and installing a water feature.

In the UK: www.csv.org.uk/Campaigns
In the USA: www.usaweekend.com/diffday

Cinnamon Trust

Cinnamon Trust held a 'Fun Dog Show' for Make a Difference Day 2003. The awareness-raising event was attended by around 200 people from the local community and 71 dogs. There were six categories in the show, including 'waggiest tail', 'prettiest bitch' and 'most appealing eyes'.

Organiser Pat Sanderson said:
The event was great fun. The dogs got a lot of attention and the phone hasn't stopped ringing since, with people wanting to find out more about our organisation. We've already recruited half a dozen new volunteers!

...on Make A Difference Day

Register as an official participant for Make A Difference Day. Or you can just do something independently.

Do something big or small, with lots of people, by yourself or with a friend; such as picking up the litter in your street, planting a few flowers around the base of a tree or helping old people across a busy road.

Make A Difference Day is the fourth Saturday in October **22 OCTOBER**

sleep ROUGH

There is no single reason why children run away from home. It may be because of sexual or physical abuse, violence, bullying, depression, loneliness, feelings of failure or low self-worth. A breakdown in communication with parents could be a deciding factor. ● According to ChildLine, the free helpline for children in distress: 'Many of the children and young people who call us about running away or being homeless have argued with their families; most desperately want to re-establish good communication, and get on again with their parents and siblings.' Others may have been released from child-care institutions with nobody they can turn to.

In the UK more than 100 children and young people run away from home every day. That is 35,000 each year, according to estimates from The Children's Society. Most go on the streets because there is nowhere else to go. Street life then lures them into crime, drugs and prostitution.

Most of us will never have to experience homelessness. If we could understand better what homelessness is like, then we might be able to deal with the problem more effectively. ● MuslimYouth.Net devised a homelessness experience project for young people to directly experience homelessness (under controlled conditions) and to report on it.

The MuslimYouth.Net online magazine for young Muslims: www.muslimyouth.net
National Coalition for the Homeless: www.nationalhomeless.org
Homeless Link: www.homeless.org.uk

Experiencing two days of street life

In March 2005 a group of six young people took part in the 2 DAYZ OF STREET LIFE project. Each participant was given £3 spending money, which had to last them two days (the duration of the event). There were strict rules. The following were not allowed:

Additional funds or credit/debit cards.

Mobile phones or other electronic equipment.

A change of clothes or personal hygiene products (such as toothbrush or soap).

Sleeping bags, blankets and other bedding materials .

They could only make contact with family and friends through a payphone (paid out of their spending money), and all food had to be purchased from their allocated spending money.

The group was asked to keep in contact with a Project Manager during the two days. Participants were photographed and videoed discreetly. They had to submit a detailed diary, which was published on the MuslimYouth.Net website.

...end homelessness

Organise your own homeless experience.

● Sleep out with limited funds for as long as you dare.

● Get a friend to photograph you.

● Write up a record of your experience.

You must think about your personal safety before you embark on this.

OCTOBER 23

SCORE *a Millennium Goal*

The world community came together in 2000 to agree a plan to solve world poverty. They would work together to achieve eight goals by the year 2015. They set themselves 18 targets, so that they could measure their success.

The Eight Millennium Goals are:

1 **Extreme poverty and hunger must be halved.** Halve the number of people living on less than $1 a day, and the number who suffer from hunger from the 1990 level.
2 **Universal primary education must be achieved.** All boys and girls must have proper schooling at primary level.
3 **Promote gender equality and empower women.** Eliminate gender disparities at all levels of education by 2015.
4 **Child mortality must be reduced by two-thirds.** Reduce the under-five mortality rate by two-thirds from the 1990 level.
5 **Maternal mortality ratio must be reduced by three-quarters.** Reduce the maternal mortality rate by three-quarters (from the 1990 level).
6 **The spread of HIV/AIDS and malaria must be halted.** Halt and begin to reverse the incidence of HIV/AIDS, malaria and other major diseases.
7 **Environmental sustainability must be ensured.** Reverse the loss of environmental resources. Halve the proportion of people who lack access to clean water and proper sanitation. Improve the lives of at least 100 million slum dwellers.
8 **A global partnership for development must be developed.** Rich and poor countries must work together. All rich countries should increase their development aid to 0.7% as a minimum. There must be equitable rules of trade. Heavily indebted poor countries should be helped.

Millennium Development Goals: www.developmentgoals.org
The Millennium Campaign: www.millenniumcampaign.org
TakingITGlobal's youth MDG website: www.takingitglobal.org/themes/mdg
Global Call to Action Against Poverty: www.whiteband.org

Only with your voice... The Millennium Campaign
The Millennium Campaign has been set up to ensure the eight goals are met. As part of the programme a number of celebrities have dedicated their support for the cause. Actors like Angelina Jolie and Richard Gere, and singers like Shakira, have publicly joined the 'Only with Your Voice' campaign and spoken out on these issues.

...solve world poverty

🌐 **Score a goal for the future of the world.**
Organise a 'Penalty Shoot Out'. Invite your friends along. Get them to pay a small entry fee for each kick. Give it to solve world poverty. Hand out explanatory literature.

🌐 **How to play:**
Players shoot at eight hoops hung from the crossbar with string, one for each Millennium Goal.
When the ball goes through a hoop, play stops for a discussion of the relevant Goal.

United Nations Day **24 OCTOBER**

war on the ARMS TRADE

I watched a Hawk attack a village in the mountains. It used its machine guns and dropped incendiary bombs ... They have a terrible sound when they are coming in to bomb, like a voice wailing ... They fly in low ... and attack civilians, because the people hiding in the mountains are civilians. Four of my cousins were killed in Hawk attacks near Los Palos. — Jose Gusmao, refugee from East Timor

Since the 1970s Indonesia has waged a brutal war in East Timor, involving bombings, arbitrary arrests, torture, kidnapping, sexual abuse and extra-judicial killings. ✹ Since 1994, over half of Indonesia's weapons have come from the UK. These have included the Hawk jets described by Jose Gusmao, and British Scorpion tanks used in attacks on peaceful demonstrators in 1998, which killed students and protestors. ✹ These are just a couple of examples of the worldwide impact of the arms trade: fuelling wars, snuffing out lives, and consuming vast sums of money.

Money spent on arms is money *not* being spent on development by poor countries. In 2004, wealthy countries sold arms worth US$22 billion to developing countries. ✹ Half of this amount would enable developing countries in Africa, Asia, the Middle East, and Latin America to put every child in primary school. ✹ The deadly trade continues because of massive government support to the arms industry, providing large financial subsidies, promoting arms sales abroad and watering down export controls.

The Campaign Against Arms Trade suggests three ways of reducing the arms trade:

Genuine export controls, putting human rights, development and an end to conflict before arms company profits.

Ending government subsidies to the arms industry.

Converting arms production to civilian industries.

Campaign Against Arms Trade: www.caat.org.uk
Find out about your Member of Parliament at: www.theyworkforyou.com

The major exporters of arms are all wealthy countries.
In 2004 the value of the arms being exported was:

USA	$18.6 billion
Russia	$4.6 billion
France	$4.4 billion
UK	$1.9 billion

...to make peace in the world

✹ **Stopping the supply of arms in conflict zones** and to dubious regimes should be a part of the ethical dimension to any country's foreign policy. Write to your MP asking that she or he presses the Government to end arms export subsidies.

✹ **The next time newspapers report a massive arms deal,** write to the editor of your newspaper pointing out the potential suffering to the inhabitants of the recipient country.

✹ **Get involved in campaigning** for an end to the deadly trade in weapons – join a local CAAT group in your area.

WORDS *for the future*

New words and phrases are added to our vocabulary every day. As society evolves, as new technologies are developed, as new ideas become current, so new words and phrases are created and existing words and phrases come to acquire new meanings. For example:

Spam, once a brand of canned meat, is now used to describe junk email.

Bootylicious, an amalgamation of beautiful or rather 'bootiful' and delicious.

Nuke and **Mutual Assured Destruction (MAD),** part of Cold War speak.

Text messaging and **ringtone** are part of our mobile phone society.

The 'Future Dictionary of America' lists words compiled in 2004. Intended to be read as though it was produced 30 years in the future, and to reflect the social and political issues of our times, the Dictionary comes with The Future Soundtrack of America, a musical expression of current policies. Nearly 200 contributors, mostly famous writers, have invented words. For example:

Wolfowish: Hoping for that which is highly unlikely. Believing that the residents of Sadr City would greet the approaching Humvees with rose petals and chocolates was, in hindsight, probably indulging in a bit of wolfowishing.

Errorgance: A feeling of smug superiority over those who do not share one's own erroneous or misguided convictions.

Wiktionary: en.wiktionary.org
McSweeney, the publishers of Future Dictionary: www.mcsweeneys.net

Theofandtoainthatiswas….

WordCount is an interactive presentation of the 86,800 most frequently used English words, ranked and scaled in order of commonness and displayed side by side as one very long sentence. www.wordcount.org

TREEMENDOUS

...add one to the Wiktionary

🌱 **Invent a new word or phrase for a new idea or a recent innovation.** That's the easy bit. Now try to get it in the Wiktionary. Wiktionary is a free online dictionary of words in every language with definitions of words, and information on their origins and pronunciation. It is a companion to the Wikipedia free encyclopdaedia.

🌱 **To get into the Wiktionary,** a word needs to satisfy at least one of the following criteria:

The word is in widespread use.

The word has been used in a well-known work.

Common usage of the word has been confirmed in a reputable work.

The word has been used in at least three independently recorded instances over a period of at least one year in publicly available written texts or in audio-visual productions.

🌱 **Once your new word qualifies,** write the Wiktionary entry for it.

26 OCTOBER

change your 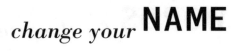 **NAME**

You might want to change your first names or family name for any number of reasons. This could be because you:

Are getting married or are making a commitment to live with a partner.
Are getting divorced.
Want to reclaim an old family name which has gone out of use.
Are fed up with the silly name your parents gave you.
Want to be noticed.

These are some of the more usual reasons. You might also want to change your name to bring attention to a cause or an issue – but you need to feel really strongly about the issue to do this.

Names can be changed in two ways. You can pick a new name and consistently use it. This is called 'common usage', and is used for stage names and aliases. But you will still have to use your original name to sign official documents.  Or you can get a Court Order changing your name. In the UK this is called Deed Poll.

Type 'change your name' into Google, and you'll find a lot of online name-change services which will do the necessary.

The soyouwanna website will tell you more:
www.soyouwanna.com/site/syws/changename/changename.html

Deed Poll Limitations

You can not change your name with 'fraudulent intent,' for example to trying to avoid bankruptcy or impersonate someone else.
Your new name should not be blasphemous, offensive or vulgar.
You should use only letters, hyphens and apostrophes.
Use of your new name should not result in a breach of a trademark (if you are a singer, giving yourself the name of Mick Jagger to promote your music would not be allowed).

Lesley Presley

...to promote a cause

Is there a cause you feel absolutely passionate about?
Do you want to draw attention to this cause by giving yourself a new name?
Do you want to be seen as being intimately identified with that cause?
Are you prepared to give up your existing name (although you can always use the same process to change your name back to what it was originally)?
Do you have the courage to have a really unusual name which people will notice, comment on and even have a good laugh about?

If the answer to all these four questions is 'Yes', then start making plans for your new name.
What's it going to be? You can be sensible or outrageous. For example:
Edward Goldsmith, an environmentalist, could become Edward Going Green.
Emily Pankhurst could have become Emily Votesforwomen.
John Potter, a cycle activist, could become Free Wheeler.
Hans Blix, a UN arms inspector, could become Guantánamo Sucks.

PICK UP *a piece of litter*

It is easy to get cross with people who litter the street, but this will not do anything to stop them doing it. You can also blame the local council for not having enough streetcleaners to clear up the mess. But there is another approach – to pick up the litter yourself. This is what the Litter Movement advocates.

The Litter Movement was started by Tuula-Maria Ahonen in Finland. There are now members on all the continents of the world, and from Argentina and Australia in the south to Lapland in the north. There is no joining fee and you don't have to fill in any forms to become a member. All you have to do is to make a commitment to pick up at least one piece of litter each day and put it in a rubbish bin, and to invite at least one other person to join the movement.

The less litter there is on the ground, the less people will litter. The Litter Movement has made many people who used to drop litter question and change their ways. It's a simple idea. It's a first step to a cleaner world.

The Litter Movement: koti.welho.com/jpeltora/littermovement.htm
Rob the Rubbish: www.robtherubbish.com

Rob the Rubbish

Robin Kevan is a 61-year-old retired social worker who lives in the tiny Welsh town of Llanwrtyd Wells (which happens to be the smallest town in Britain). Almost every day, Rob goes out first thing to pick up litter. Armed with the simplest of equipment – gloves, a pick-up stick, yellow jacket and black bin bags – he does the biz.

Not content with this, he also decided to clean up the countryside around his home, picking up the litter left on the surrounding Cambrian Mountains and the Brecon Beacons. His litter-picking activity got publicity in the national press. Word began to spread. He became known as 'Rob the Rubbish', and is now known throughout the world for what he does.

He regularly cleans up other mountains and beautiful places, amongst which are not only the UK's highest mountains, Ben Nevis, Snowdon and Scafell Pike, but also the Everest Base Camp trail in Nepal – which must count as 'the peak' of his mission to make the world a cleaner place.

...today and every day

- Pick up one piece of litter today and bin it.
- Commit to doing this as a daily action.
- Join the Litter Movement.
- If you come across someone who is littering, don't tell them off. Don't be aggressive; just ask them nicely if they would like to join.

28 OCTOBER

living on LESS

The average person requires 2,500 calories a day to survive. In the developed world, and also for the rich in the developing world, people are consuming 40% more than this norm. ⚽ Obesity is fast becoming a problem of epidemic proportions, whilst 600 million people in the developing world, mainly the rural poor, are seriously malnourished.

Plenty and waste are taken for granted in the rich world, whilst hunger and need exist in the poor world. The inequalities are growing wider. Could you live on less? ⚽ Doing this will make you more sensitive to what many of your fellow human beings are experiencing, simply as a result of where they happened to have been born.

Human Development Reports: hdr.undp.org/statistics/data
Living on Less, reflections of a blogger: livingonless.journalspace.com

Percentage of people living on less than a $1 a day in 2004

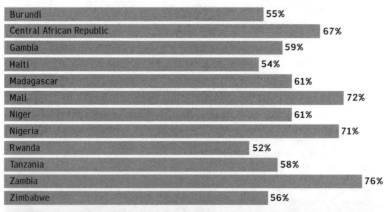

Country	Percentage
Burundi	55%
Central African Republic	67%
Gambia	59%
Haiti	54%
Madagascar	61%
Mali	72%
Niger	61%
Nigeria	71%
Rwanda	52%
Tanzania	58%
Zambia	76%
Zimbabwe	56%

...could you do it?

Live on less: Try some of these exercises in marginal living:

⚽ **Go without having your rubbish collected for a month.** Go through the bin to analyse what you have been throwing away.

⚽ **Confine your water consumption to 10 litres a day,** equivalent to one flush of the toilet.

⚽ **Live without electricity** for a day or a week.

⚽ **Do without motorised transport.** Walk or cycle if you need to travel.

⚽ **Spend as little as you can for three months.** Make a diary of everything you spend, with your comments on each spending decision.

⚽ **Buy only basic food,** no convenience foods, and with as little packaging as possible.

⚽ **Entertain yourself for a week;** no TV, no radio, no CDs, no video games.

Examine the things you did to make do. What were the things you most missed? How much reduction in consumption could you bear without feeling excessively inconvenienced? What can you do about global inequality?

OCTOBER 29

AIDS *living with it*

Shawn Decker has a story to tell about living with HIV/AIDS:

I'm a positoid. In the early 1980s I was infected with HIV through the use of tainted blood products. At the age of 11, after being diagnosed HIV positive, I was expelled from the 6th Grade because local school officials thought I was a danger to other students. That was in 1987, a time when certain communities believed that HIV/AIDS was something that could not happen to them.

Eventually I was readmitted to high school, and graduated as 'Homecoming King'. In part, I think this gesture was my classmates' way of showing that they not only liked me, but they supported me as well. Even though I wasn't speaking openly about HIV at the time, they respected me for being 'goofy, wisecracking, HIV positive Shawn'. ☺ Later, when I came out of my AIDS closet, I used that humour as my main tool in educating others about life with HIV. Nearly 20 years later, I'm healthy, happy and in love.

One way that I try to raise awareness about HIV/AIDS issues is through public speaking. My partner, Gwenn, shares my passion for HIV education, and we travel the US through CAMPUSPEAK, talking to college students about our relationship – I'm HIV positive and she is not. ☺ Much of the conversation has to do with our sex life, and by 'opening our bedroom door', so to speak, we give people a chance to learn that those living with HIV are normal beings with normal emotions.

My advice to young people is to be open and honest about the topic of sex. Know that you cannot tell that someone is HIV positive by looking at them, and in many instances people who are HIV positive themselves do not even know; so how could they tell you?

Shawn's websites:
www.positoid.com
www.mypetvirus.com

Love, Shawn Decker and Gwenn Barringer

Aboyagirlavirus.com is an engaging, honest look at two people in love. Shawn has HIV and Gwenn doesn't. They answer all the questions you can think of, and then some.

Gwenn has her own site, and she makes one excellent point; if she can stay HIV negative, then anyone should be able to.

...keep informed, keep safe

☺ **Go to Shawn's website** to see what it's like to live with HIV/AIDS.

☺ **Wear a red ribbon** to show your support for people with AIDS.

☺ **Never put yourself at risk of contracting HIV.**

30 OCTOBER

spread some HAPPINESS

Most of us are not as happy as we might be. We tend to obsess about the things that make us miserable: doing jobs we don't enjoy, travelling nose-to-bumper or crushed inside a bus to get to work, the strains of family life, never quite having enough money to afford what we want.

Despite growing affluence, happiness levels are remaining fairly constant. Once people have enough income for their basic necessities, then money does not make much of a difference. And the people who spend more time pursuing money are often less happy.

Slough, a town near London, started a programme called 'Making Slough Happy'. The aim was to raise the level of happiness. They encouraged singing and dancing, communal art projects visits to lottery winners to see if money made a difference – even a trip to a graveyard.

Reminding yourself that life is short can really boost your appreciation that it's wonderful just to be alive!

They developed a 10-point manifesto, which you are recommended to follow for at least two months, after which you may well find you feel a whole lot happier.

How To Be Happy, available from BBC Books: www.bbcshop.com

Happiness Manifesto
1. **Exercise** for half an hour, three times a week.
2. **Count your blessings** – at the end of each day reflect on at least five things you're grateful for.
3. **Pass an hour in uninterrupted conversation** with your partner or closest friend each week.
4. **Plant something** – a window box or pot plant – then keep it alive.
5. **Cut your TV viewing by half** – more if you can.
6. **Smile or say hello to a stranger** – at least once each day.
7. **Make contact with a friend or relation** you have not seen for a while, and arrange to meet up.
8. **Have a good laugh** – at least once a day.
9. **Give yourself a daily treat.**
10. **Do an extra good turn** for someone each day.

...follow the manifesto

Before you change the world, you need to change *your* world.

🏠 So, print out the Happiness Manifesto, and put it somewhere prominent in your home. Pledge to do all 10 things for two months. Then see how you feel.

🏠 Spread a little happiness. Print out the manifesto and circulate it to your 10 best friends, or the first 10 people you meet.

🏠 Think about how to make your town happier.

OCTOBER 31

AFGHANISTAN *women*

We work hard for women's rights in Afghanistan. We need the solidarity and support of all people around the world.

– RAWA

The perception of Afghanistan as a country where women are most oppressed was reinforced under the rule of the Taliban (which ended in 2001), when women were only allowed out in public dressed in a burka, and many suffered substantial abuse to their human rights.

RAWA, the Revolutionary Association of the Women of Afghanistan, was founded in 1977 by Meena, then aged 21, for Afghan women to fight for human rights and social justice. Meena was assassinated ten years later in Pakistan by Afghan KGB agents, in connivance with fundamentalist warlord Gulbuddin Hekmatyar.

RAWA runs education, health and income-generation projects alongside its political campaigning. RAWA needs all the support it can get. Since the overthrow of the Soviet-backed regime in 1992, the focus of RAWA's struggle has been against fundamentalism and its ultra-male chauvinistic and anti-woman outlook.

RAWA: www.rawa.org
And these organisations work closely with RAWA:
In France, FemAid: www.femaid.org
RAWA Supporters UK: rawasupporters.co.uk
In the USA, Afghan Women's Mission: afghanwomensmission.org

What FemAid supporters worldwide are doing:

USA: A large number of kites were donated and distributed to two RAWA orphanages. Kite flying had been banned by the Taliban. A jazz musician gave a concert for his 40th birthday and sent the proceeds.

UK: A charity football match was organised, and supporters of both teams raised money. Stella McCartney sold signed and numbered t-shirts for a RAWA orphanage.

France: Schools in the Bordeaux area collected school supplies to send to Afghan refugees in Pakistan.

Canada: Funds were raised for medical aid for a Quetta hospital (in Pakistan near the Afghan border) and for training midwives.

FemAid UK: Sadie Brinham filled 150 shoe boxes for Afghan orphans with necessities such as school supplies and toothbrushes, plus New Year's presents. Sadie then set up a UK branch of FemAid: sadiebrinham@yahoo.co.uk.

...act in solidarity

- **Read** *Meena, Heroine of Afghanistan* by Melody Ermachild Chavis.
- **Buy some music** to support RAWA. There is a choice of two CDs:
  Azadi, a benefit compilation for RAWA. 100% of proceeds goes to RAWA:
  www.museumfire.com/azadi.htm
  Dropping Food on their Heads is not Enough; 50% of proceeds goes to RAWA:
  www.gcrecords.com/benefit.html

1 NOVEMBER

surprise **SHOEBOX**

Christmas is still weeks away. But you may already be finding the commercialisation distasteful, and you will almost certainly be wracking your brains as to what to buy your family and friends. Why not give yourself a treat, and enjoy putting together a box full of small items for someone you can be sure will appreciate them? ♣ There are several schemes that distribute donated gifts, packaged in shoeboxes, to people in countries where children are living in such poverty that a toothbrush, a packet of crayons, or a skipping rope will be a treasured gift.

But why wait until Christmas? This really simple idea was found on the www.honduras.com website:

> *When you pack your luggage, please include a shoebox full of school supplies such as pens, pencils, chalk, paper, crayons, etc. Also take an extra $20 along. When you arrive in Honduras, keep an eye out for a small, poor school. Walk up to it, and give your box to a teacher or to the director. Then as you continue your vacation, keep an eye out for an obviously poor person (preferably a woman). Walk up to her and give her the $20. The reason for giving to a woman is because it is usually a woman who has to feed and clothe the children; so your money will more than likely go where it is desperately needed.*
>
> *You will be surprised at how good this will make you feel. And believe me, you will have done a great service to Honduras, even though it may seem to be a very small amount. Have a great trip! Have a great vacation! And have a great life! Thanks.*
>
> *– Gringo Jak*

Samaritan's Purse is a Christian organisation that runs a shoebox scheme in North America, Northern Europe and Australia: www.samaritanspurse.org

The Rotary Club distributes shoeboxes year round: www.rotary1280.org/shoebox

How to pack a box

If it's a gift box, indicate whether it's for a boy or a girl and their approximate age.

About 14 items fill a box. For a school, pens and pencils, marker pens, solar-powered pocket calculator, geometry instruments, scissors are all useful. Toy suggestions include doll, ball, toy car, cards, marbles, skipping rope, yo yo, dominoes.

Other popular items are toothbrush, toothpaste, soap, comb, sunglasses, caps, socks, t-shirts, hair clips, watches, small books.

Don't include used items, knives, battery-powered or electrical equipment, perishable items, medicines, breakable items, flammable or caustic materials or religious items.

Tie your box with string so that it can be opened easily in case of enquiries at customs. Take it with you when you travel abroad. Or deliver it to a charity running a gift-box scheme.

...a gift that really helps

Remember to keep the shoebox next time you buy a pair of shoes.

♣ **Wrap the box** with some bright wrapping paper. Wrap the lid separately.

♣ **Collect things** to fill up your shoebox: assorted supplies for a school, or gifts for a child in an orphanage.

♣ **Get a group of friends** to join you in filling a shoebox.

NOVEMBER 2

NON-VIOLENT *movies*

Every day, we are bombarded with images of violence and death. Video games, music lyrics, television shows, commercials, radio, and movies entertain us; but they also spew out images of aggression, violence and killing. ❧ *Rambo, The Terminator, James Bond, Spiderman, Indiana Jones* are all about men who win out by blowing up buildings, shooting opponents, pushing the enemy off a cliff.

Some movies you could watch:

Gandhi (1982): This film swept the 1983 Oscars, winning eight awards, including Best Picture, Best Actor (Ben Kingsley), Best Screenplay, and Best Director for Richard Attenborough. It is the awe-inspiring story of how a diminutive lawyer stood up to the British Empire and became an international symbol of non-violence and understanding.

Martin Luther King Jr: The Man and the Dream (2004): This is a film about one of the most loved, respected, and influential leaders in American history. In this look at the life and work of Martin Luther King. Writer and director Tom Friedman explores how Dr King's ideas evolved in the face of the rapidly changing climate of the Civil Rights Movement.

Free at Last: Civil Rights Heroes (2004): Witness the amazing, courageous stories of Emmett Till, Medgar Evers, The Birmingham Four, Viola Liuzzo and more. The story of the Civil Rights struggle played out in the small acts of peaceful defiance by individuals.

www.movies.go.com

Or for a different thought-provoking movie marathon:

Amandla! A Revolution in Four Part Harmony (2003): The struggle to eradicate apartheid in South Africa and the vital role music played in this challenge.

Apocalypse Now (1974): Possibly Francis Ford Coppola's greatest work, based on Joseph Conrad's *Heart of Darkness*.

Hotel Rwanda (2004): Amid the genocidal butchering, one ordinary man musters the courage to shelter more than 1,000 people in the hotel he manages.

The Killing Fields (1984): All hell is breaking loose in Cambodia, Khmer Rouge's genocide has begun. The true story of *New York Times* journalist Sydney Shanberg, who stayed on after the American evacuation.

Schindler's List (1993): Steven Spielberg's Holocaust epic shows factory owner Oskar Schindler exploiting cheap Jewish labour. In the midst of WWII, he became an unlikely humanitarian, losing his fortune whilst saving 1,100 Jews from Auschwitz.

...for a peaceful night in

Challenge the culture of violence.

❧ **Invite your friends** to join you in a Non-Violent Movie Marathon.

❧ Get some popcorn, fluff up the couch, and enjoy several movies that do not contain explosives, car chases, guns, bombs or kick punches.

❧ **Explain to your guests** the idea of your movie marathon, which is to think about the impact of violent images on society.

❧ **Challenge your guests** to come up with ideas for addressing this issue.

theatre of PROTEST

A simple play reading can become a theatrical act of protest. In Aristophanes' ancient Greek play *Lysistrata*, a group of women organise a sex strike to try to stop the endless warfare that their menfolk are pursuing. On 3 March 2003, the Lysistrata Project organised 1,029 readings of Aristophanes' play in 59 countries around the world to protest against the war in Iraq. A secret reading in northern Iraq was organised by members of the International Press Corps, who had to keep quiet about it or risk losing their jobs. A reading in Patras, Greece, was held by Greeks and Kurdish refugees in an abandoned factory serving as a Kurdish refugee camp. There were secret readings in China. The readings raised $125,000 for peace and humanitarian aid in the Middle East and elsewhere.

How they did it: The organisers wrote a letter that said: 'Are you frustrated by the build up to war? Do you feel like there isn't anything you can do? Well, here's something you CAN do....' They emailed this to everyone they knew. And they forwarded it to everyone *they* knew. The next day the organisers started hearing back from people all over the world. Within two weeks, they had been interviewed on national radio, readings were scheduled in over 70 cities, a documentary team started filming, and a couple organised an internet auction to raise money.

The Lysistrata Project: www.lysistrataproject.com

Kathryn Blume is one of the founders of the Lysistrata project: www.kathrynblume.com/LysProj.htm

'Put the Act back into Action', a Friends of the Earth how to guide to using street theatre: community.foe.co.uk/resource/how_tos

Ten steps for a successful local play reading:

1 Clarify your aims: Why are you doing it? What do you want to achieve? Be realistic, but also be ambitious.

2 Get a location: in a living room, at a community centre, on the steps of city hall, anywhere!

3 Pick a time.

4 Pick a charity to benefit.

5 Get the script: online, from a library or a bookshop.

6 Cast the roles: friends, celebrities, whoever's willing.

7 Get help! Send an email asking for volunteers. Give everyone who offers something to do.

8 Make the project visible: Get as much publicity as you can.

9 Put up a website.

10 Be green: Show that you also care about the environment. Use recycled paper for programmes and fliers.

...be an accidental activist

Stage a public reading of a political play.

- **Try a play by Richard Norton Taylor**. The words are entirely those spoken by participants at an important public enquiry. *The Colour of Justice*: racism and the police response; *Bloody Sunday*: civil rights in Northern Ireland; *Justifying War*: the legitimacy of the invasion of Iraq.
- **Or read**: *The Accidental Death of an Anarchist* by Dario Fo; *Execution of Justice* by Emily Mann; *Fires in the Mirror* by Anna Deveare Smith; *The Syringa Tree* by Pamela Gien; *Jody's Body* by Aviva Jane Carlin.

LANDMINE *adoption*

Each year, 26,000 people are killed or mutilated by landmines. 8,000 of these are children. The lives of 71 people each day are being damaged or destroyed. ❧ They didn't lay the mines; but they suffer the consequences. And their lives are at risk with every step they take.

There are between 60 to 100 million landmines in the ground worldwide. It costs between $3 and $30 to purchase an anti-personnel landmine. It can cost as much as $1,000 to remove it. Landmines destroy livestock and prevent the cultivation of arable land. They are an ever-present menace to those who live in affected areas.

Rebuilding war-torn communities and economies is difficult in any circumstances. But in many communities, recovery, reconciliation and long-term development are all but impossible because of landmines. ❧ The 'Ottawa Convention on the Prohibition of the Use, Stockpiling, Production and Transfer of Anti Personnel Mines, and on their Destruction', has now been signed by 136 nations. But not by China, Russia and the USA, three of the world's most powerful nations.

Adopt a Minefield: www.landmines.org.uk
Canadian Landmine Foundation: www.canadianlandmine.com
International Campaign to Ban Landmines: www.icbl.org

The Night of 1,000 Dinners

This is co-ordinated by Adopt A Minefield and it takes place on or around the first Thursday of November each year, although people can hold dinners whenever it is convenient for them.

Thousands of people around the world host dinners in their homes, at work or in community venues to raise funds to clear landmines and help landmine survivors.

Dinners have been hosted on the sand dunes of the Sahara, in bedsits in Balham, in embassies in all sorts of weird and wonderful places.

...help mine casualties

Host an Adopt A Minefield dinner. This is a chance for you to make a difference while cooking and eating a meal with your favourite people.

❧ **Find out this year's date** from the Adopt A Minefield website, put it in your diary, invite your friends and download some of the recipes that have been donated for the occasion.

❧ **Raise lots of money.** It costs about £1 to clear a square metre of minefield, and about £50 to help an amputee child walk again.

Adopt A Minefield passes 100% of the funds received from the general public to projects clearing landmines and helping landmine survivors. Adopt A Minefield tells every donor where their money is allocated and, when the project has been completed, what impact their money has made.

plant a **PEACE POLE**

Peace is a daily, a weekly, a monthly process, gradually changing opinions, slowly eroding old barriers, quietly building new structures.

— John F Kennedy

Peace Poles are a memorial to peace. Wherever a peace pole has been planted, it is an indication that that specific place on Earth has been designated a place of peace. ❧ A peace pole ceremony can serve as a memorial to a tragedy that has taken place. The major of New York City, Michael Bloomberg, planted a 9/11 Memorial Peace Pole. ❧ A peace pole can also be a symbol of a community making a commitment to achieving peace. It can serve as the symbol of a new beginning between two previously warring factions.

Over 200,000 peace poles have been planted in over 180 countries on Earth. There are peace poles in:

The Pyramids of El Giza, Egypt
The Magnetic North Pole in Canada
Sarajevo
The Allenby Bridge between Israel and Jordan
Baghdad
Robben Island, South Africa
New York
Gorky Park, Russia
Confucius burial site, Taiwan

The Peace Pole Project, a project of the World Peace and Prayer Society:
www.worldpeace.org/peacepoles.html

Peace Pole Makers (USA): www.peacepoles.com

Peace poles are usually 2.5 metres tall. They can be made out of a sustainable material; for example, in North America they are often constructed out of Western Red Cedar cut from renewable forests. They can also be constructed of metal or plastic.

They are planted in the ground or placed on stands if they are indoors. Desktop models, 50 cm high, are also available.

Every 'official' peace pole has the words 'May Peace Prevail On Earth' written on one side; and often that phrase is written on the other sides in different languages.

...reserve a space for peace

Plant a peace pole in your community.

❧ **Pick a spot** such as a public space or park; or even someone's backyard. The more people who pass by and see it, the better. You can make your peace pole. But make sure it is solid and durable in sun and rain.

❧ **Or if you prefer, buy a ready-made peace pole.** The Peace Pole Project publishes a list of suppliers in countries all over the world. Outdoor poles cost between £200 and £750. A miniature version for a flower pot costs £7.

❧ **Organise a dedication ceremony.**

MOBILE PHONE *recycling*

You know how it is, you're now with the latest model. And your old mobile phone, the one you used to love and take everywhere with you, is left at home, unwanted and abandoned. It doesn't have to be like this. Your old mobile can have a new life, full of meaning and purpose... but with someone else...

– Oxfam, Bring Bring

Millions of mobiles are obsolete, broken or otherwise unused. And more are discarded every year. Most are put into the household waste. They end up in landfill sites, where the toxic material contained in the battery and LCD display leak out. Your old phone really does need to be disposed of safely. The best thing to do is recycle it.

The developing world is taking a technological leap into the mobile phone age. A really interesting Village Phone scheme is run in Bangladesh by Grameen Telecom, in partnership with the Grameen Bank. ♣ Rural women are given mobile handsets, which they pay for with a small Grameen Bank loan, and they are taught to use them. They then sell phone services to villagers, and this provides affordable telephone access to the village and contact with the outside world. It also provides the women with a livelihood.

Fonebak is a scheme endorsed by the mobile phone industry whereby you can return your old phone to a collection point or put it in an envelope and FREEPOST it to them: www.fonebak.com

Oxfam does something similar through its 'Bring Bring' Scheme. Take it into any Oxfam shop: www.oxfam.org.uk/what_you_can_do/recycle/phones.htm

Three small charities have set up: www.cartridges4charity.co.uk
The Campaign to Recycle Unwanted Mobile Phones supports Child Advocacy International: www.childadvocacyinternational.co.uk/fundraising/recycle.htm

Grameen Telecom: www.grameenphone.com

Turn your old mobile into a sunflower

Researchers at Warwick University have developed a mobile-phone case that you can plant and transform into the flower of your choice.

The case is made from an easily biodegradable plastic. When it is placed in a compost heap, a seed, embedded behind a small window in the case, germinates. The prototypes have used dwarf sunflower seeds. Watch a film about this:

...new owners, new uses

When you get a new mobile phone, make sure that your old one is recycled.

♣ **If it is in good enough condition to be reused,** it can be tested, refurbished, re-branded and sent to a developing country for re-use.

♣ **If it is not,** metals can be extracted for re-use from handsets, batteries and chargers. The handsets are incinerated to generate heat. The plastics from chargers are recycled into such things as traffic cones and buckets.

world KINDNESS

No act of kindness however small is ever wasted.

– Aesop

Glen Bornais from Ottawa, Canada writes:

Despite my preoccupation with the big problems of the day (perhaps because I've studied political economy at a critically spirited institution) and despite my natural tendency towards the dramatic, I've recently come under the power of one truly simple idea: we could improve our lives, our communities, our families, our friendships, our world simply by engaging in a random and unsolicited act of kindness every day.

This approach to life will not likely resolve or reverse the unequal distribution of wealth, nor the damage we do to our planet, nor third world debt, nor suffering and hunger of the deepest kind, but acts of kindness as unsolicited compliments, smiles, simple charity, community trash pick up can help us regain faith in each and every person, and sometimes even in ourselves.

The World Kindness Movement was set up in 1997 to promote kindness. There are now branches in a dozen countries. Their work is 'in acknowledgement of the fundamental importance of simple human kindness as a basic condition of a satisfying and meaningful life.' ⚕ The second week in November has been designated 'World Kindness Week' and one day in that week is 'World Kindness Day'.

Inspiring quotations on kindness: www.kindness.com.au/quotations.htm

Calendars and bookmarks with ideas for acts of kindness from Random Acts of Kindness Foundation: www.actsofkindness.org/inspiration/graphics.asp

Or send an e-card: www.actsofkindness.org/inspiration/ecards.asp

Join the Coinspiracy....

The Coinspiracy is an initiative of the KindActs Network Association of British Columbia in Canada to engage young people in creating positive global change.

The campaign uses a kindness coin called a 'UNI', which is short for the universal nature of kindness. To participate, the 'Coinholder' commits three kind acts: one for him or herself, one for the environment and one for someone else. The coin is passed on to the recipient of the kind act who in turn commits the three kind acts and passes it on.

The first Coinspiracy campaign was piloted in 2002. Over 100,000 humanitarian acts were performed, and an estimated $30,000 was raised in donations. Clothing, books, medical supplies and food were donated to orphanages, families in need and inner-city schools.

On World Kindness Day in 2003, 77 schools and youth groups in Australia, Bermuda, Canada, India, Italy, Nepal, New Zealand, Nigeria, Scotland, Singapore, South Africa and the USA, participated in the Coinspiracy.

...make people happy

⚕ **Perform an act of kindness** right now to the person you next see. Think of this as a start for leading a kinder life.

⚕ **Join the Coinspiracy campaign** and experience for yourself the multiplier effect of kindness and its endless possibilities. To participate contact: www.investinakinderworld.com

BUY ONE *give one free*

Ever heard of a BOGOF? Supermarkets, pharmacies, even bookshops, use the 'Buy One, Get One Free' strategy to shift slow-moving stock, or to get one over a rival retailer. Everyone likes getting something for nothing, so these promotions are extremely popular, even though we often don't actually want the extra item.

Why not donate the item you've been given? It will make you feel good, and won't cost you a penny. This is what Los Angeles resident Blake Mykoskie wants you to do with his comfortable Argentine shoes. And something similar happens when you buy a Harrods Crisis Pud. For each Christmas pudding sold, Harrods donates enough for Crisis to provide a homeless person with a Christmas dinner.

Crisis Pud: www.crisispud.com
TOMS: www.tomsshoes.com

Blake Mysoskie tells the story of TOMS

I went to Argentina for three weeks to play polo, and a lot of the farmers and polo players wore shoes called 'alpagata',with a rope sole and cardboard interior. They are the most comfortable shoes I have ever worn. A lot of the children in Argentina don't have shoes, and get cuts and scrapes. When these get infected, it turns into a big health issue.

I turned to my friend and I said I'm going to start a shoe company – and every pair we sell, we're going to give a pair to a child in South America. We used a flip-flop-type sole, and a leather insole so your feet would stay dry if you wore them all day long. And we designed about 15 different styles. We called them TOMS – shoes for Tomorrow.

I came back to the USA and started giving them away to my friends and different celebrities, and in three months we sold 5,000 pairs, had been in half a dozen publications, and it just really exploded. We called them TOMS – shoes for Tomorrow.

It's really important to us that we go to Argentina ourselves to distribute the shoes in the villages. Our shoes represent hope. Our gift shows the children that someone cares.

...the BOGOF way to give

- 👫 TOMS shoes cost $38 a pair. Buy one... and give one free. Buy two or more pairs and they are shipped free worldwide.
- 👫 Buy a Crisis Pud and provide someone with a Christmas dinner.
- 👫 Next time you pick up a BOGOF item, share your good fortune with a neighbour, or, if it's non-perishable, save it as a raffle/tombola prize.

9 NOVEMBER

prevent GENOCIDE

After WWII the international community pledged never again would genocide occur. Yet it has. And it is occurring again and again. Genocide is defined as the systematic and planned extermination of an entire national, racial, political, or ethnic group. It has eight stages:

1 **Classification.** Dividing people into 'us' and 'them'.

2 **Symbolisation.** Giving names or symbols to the group.

3 **Dehumanisation.** One group denies the humanity of the other group. People are equated with animals, vermin, insects or diseases.

4 **Organisation.** Genocide is always organized, usually by the state, though sometimes informally, or by terrorist groups. Special militias are armed and trained. Plans are made for mass killing.

5 **Polarisation.** Extremists drive the groups apart. Laws are passed denying rights or forbidding social interaction.

6 **Preparation.** Victims are identified and separated. Death lists are drawn up. People are often segregated into ghettoes, forced into concentration camps, or confined to a famine-struck region and starved.

7 **Extermination.** The killing begins, and quickly escalates.

8 **Denial.** This follows the genocide. The perpetrators dig up the mass graves, burn the bodies, try to cover up the evidence and intimidate the witnesses. They deny that they committed any crimes, and often blame what happened on the victims.

Genocide Watch: www.genocidewatch.org
The Genocide Watch pledge: www.genocidewatch.org/Pledge.htm

Country	Websites for more information
The Nazi Holocaust	www.nizkor.org
Armenians in Turkey	www.armenian-genocide.org
Rwanda	www.hrw.org/reports/1999/rwanda/
China	www.gendercide.org/case_infanticide.html
Sudan	www.genocidewatch.org
Cambodia	www.yale.edu/cgp
Burundi	www.endgenocide.org/genocide/hutu.htm
Former Soviet Union	www.endgenocide.org/genocide/soviet.html
Iraq	www.gendercide.org/case_anfal.html
Indonesia	www.endgenocide.org/genocide/indonesia.html
Ba'hai in Iran	www.endgenocide.org/genocide/bahai.html

...pledge 'never again'

Sign Genocide Watch's pledge:

✤ **I pledge** to do my part to end genocide: the intentional destruction, in whole or in part, of a national, ethnical, racial, or religious group.

✤ **I commit myself** never to be a passive bystander to genocide anywhere.

✤ **I will assist** the victims of genocide and will help them escape from their killers. I will support the victims with humanitarian relief.

✤ **I will not stop my protests** against a genocide until that genocide is stopped.

PEACE *for a moment*

After catastrophic events – either natural or human-induced – there is now a well-established tradition of people gathering together, or just pausing in their daily routine, and spending some moments in silent contemplation.

11 November is Armistice Day or Remembrance Day. At the eleventh hour on the eleventh day of the eleventh month, two minutes' silence is observed to remember all those who died in WWI, and in subsequent wars. As well as the red poppies, distributed by the British Legion, there are white poppies, distributed by The Peace Pledge Union to symbolise the belief that there are better ways to resolve conflicts than killing strangers.

On 6 August 1945, the first atomic bomb ever used in warfare was dropped on Hiroshima; and on 9 August, the second was dropped on Nagasaki. On 9 August 2005, Pax Christi Ireland observed One Minute for Peace at 10.02 GMT.

Global Minute for Peace Day takes place on 22 December, the Winter Solstice – traditionally a time for rejoicing, as the days start getting longer, bringing a new hope into people's lives. On the first Global Day, the voice of President Kennedy speaking at the United Nations was broadcast, saying: 'Together we can save our planet'. GMPD is an initiative of John McConnell, who also promotes International Earth Day on the Spring Equinox.

Just a Minute of Peace (JAMOP) is a Canadian initiative, linked to an international concert for peace. People are urged to spend a minute in silence on 7 July 2007 at 23.59 GMT.

See what conflict took place in the world during the 20th century by exploring the Conflict Map: <u>nobelprize.org/peace/educational/conflictmap</u>

Peace Pledge Union: <u>www.ppu.org.uk</u>
Just a Minute of Peace: <u>www.jamop.com</u>

Total deaths in 20th century from war and oppression:

Genocide and tyranny:	83 million
Military deaths in war:	42 million
Civilian deaths in war:	19 million
Man-made famine:	44 million

– Matthew White's *Historical Atlas of the 20th Century:*
users.erols.com/mwhite28/20centry.htm

...time to commit

- **Sign up to JAMOP** and make a symbolic gesture to advocate peaceful solutions to international conflict, to advance human rights and to promote responsible economic and social development in the world. And join together with others on 07/07/07.

- **One minute of silence provides a time for reflection,** and for you to think about what part you can play to end war. Take a minute now to think about this, and commit yourself to taking one simple action for peace.
  Sit down; stand up; write a letter; lobby your elected representative; do something.

11 NOVEMBER

compile a **DIRECTORY**

Right under your nose, there's a whole heap of things going on. Most of which you probably don't even know about. There may be:

A sailing club that meets to sail model boats on a nearby lake.

A kite-flying group showing off their latest creations.

People learning salsa, yoga, karate, tai chi, or flower arranging.

Poker or bridge clubs.

Reading circles, amateur dramatic societies and groups that play music.

One o'clock clubs for young mothers to meet and share their experiences.

Tea dances for senior citizens.

The local soccer or baseball team that's about to make it big in the Local League.

Self-help groups such as Alcoholics Anonymous, WeightWatchers.

Local chapters of Greenpeace or Amnesty planning a campaign to change the world.

Church groups, school groups, youth groups

... and much more.

Groups are a good indicator of how well the community is functioning. The more the better. If people knew about what was happening when and where, or if organisers had a place to advertise what they were doing, then many more people might join in. It would become easier to find what to do, and easier to attract people for something you want to organise.

The Nicholas Albery Foundation: **www.alberyfoundation.org/**

> **Nicholas Albery**, a UK social inventor, promoted the idea of community notice boards, where people could post information on events that they were organising.
>
> You could do this electronically, by creating a website for your neighbourhood. You could do it in print by persuading your local newspaper to provide you with a listings column each week, or on air through your local radio station.
>
> Or you could get an outdoor space on a busy street for people to put up their posters (as well as in public libraries, which are expected to provide this facility). Some local councils now provide community notice boards.

...of community activities

Create a Neighbourhood Yellow Pages for your local community or town.

🏠 **Make a list** of all the activities and services taking place in your neighbourhood. Provide enough information on each for people to know if it is something they might be interested in.

🏠 **Provide contact details** for people to find out more.

🏠 **Publish your list**. Set up a website, which will cost little or nothing.

🏠 **Produce a printed directory,** and try to recoup your money from sales of a hard copy or from advertising.

NOVEMBER 12

FOOD *not bombs*

It is a scandal that there is hunger in the midst of plenty. Hungry people include: single-parent families, low-waged employees, the unemployed, the elderly and those unable to work through illness or disability. 🏠 Before you eat the meal in front of you, your food has gone through a chain of farmers, distributors, manufacturers, wholesalers and retailers. At every point in the chain, perfectly good food is discarded. The USA wastes 20 million tonnes of food a year (about 80 kg per person). Just one tenth of this would end hunger in America.

Food Not Bombs started in 1980 with two ideas: bombs, militarism and war are a bad thing, and no person should go hungry in today's world. Food Not Bombs provides free vegetarian food to hungry people. 🏠 They recover food that would otherwise be thrown out, fresh produce near the end of its shelf life, and turn this into hot vegetarian meals, served in city parks to anyone who wants it. Food Not Bombs also campaigns against war and poverty throughout the world.

Food Not Bombs groups have been started in nearly 50 countries. Join or start a group in your city: www.foodnotbombs.net

Food for Life: The International Society for Krishna Consciousness runs free vegetarian food programmes in around 16 countries: www.ffl.org

Many homeless projects organise soup runs, going out in the evenings to provide free meals to people on the streets. Contact Homeless Link for details of local projects: www.homeless.org.uk

Crisis organises Christmas shelters for homeless people, providing temporary accommodation over the festive season, plus food, entertainment and health services. The biggest of these in 2004 was at the Millennium Dome, and was attended by 1,500 people: www.crisis.org.uk

These projects require volunteers to collect, cook and distribute the food. If you've got the time, why not give it a go?

...feed the hungry

🏠 **Collect food for** distribution to the hungry. You'll need a vehicle and a small group of committed volunteers.

🏠 **Approach supermarkets,** grocers and greengrocers, markets, restaurants, and ask them to donate food to you on a regular basis. Take literature to explain what you are doing.

🏠 **Deliver the food** you collect to night shelters, day centres and soup kitchens. Find out what they need and arrange a regular delivery schedule.

🏠 **Prepare meals** to serve on the street. This is hard work, but also fun. Pick central locations, as this will make the problem of homelessness more visible.

🏠 **You've just started a Food Not Bombs group.** The *Food Not Bombs Handbook* on their website will tell all you need to know.

13 NOVEMBER

become an ENTREPRENEUR

Social entrepreneurs do for society's problems what entrepreneurs do for business: they provide practical solutions by combining innovation, resourcefulness and opportunity. They innovate by finding a new product or service to meet a need, or by developing a new approach to an existing problem. They get started immediately, confident that they will find a way of succeeding.

The Ashoka Foundation supports social entrepreneurs around the world by providing them with three-year bursaries to develop and implement their ideas. ✋ Veronica Khosa was a nurse in South Africa. Around her she could see sick people getting sicker, elderly people unable to get to a doctor, and hospitals with empty beds that would not admit patients with HIV. So Veronica started Tateni Home Care Nursing Services, pioneering the concept of 'home care' in her country. Starting with practically nothing, her team took to the streets providing care to people in their homes. ✋ A few years later, the government adopted her ideas, and home-care schemes are now spreading beyond South Africa. Social entrepreneurs are unstoppable people with great ideas; they are people who get things done.

If you are based in the UK and have a good idea for changing your community, or the world, apply for a grant from UnLtd. Grants range from £250 to £20,000.

These organisations support social entrepreneurs. Visit their websites to see the sorts of people and projects they are supporting:
Ashoka Foundation: www.ashoka.org and www.changemakers.net
Skoll Foundation: www.skollfoundation.org
Schwab Foundation: www.schwabfound.org
Social Capitalist Awards: www.fastcompany.com/social

Apply for a grant to UnLtd: www.unltd.org.uk

Join these networks to meet other change makers:
Pioneers of Change: www.pioneersofchange.net
International Young Professionals Foundation: www.iypf.org

Ashoka success story

Rodrigo Baggio wanted to help poor people make use of information technology to improve their communities and their own lives. In 1995, he set up a technology school in a Rio de Janeiro slum. This worked so well that his organisation, Committee for Democracy in Information Technology, has since established more than 900 schools in Latin America, and in South Africa and Japan.

The students learn how to use computers and discuss issues facing their communities. They then devise a project that involves the use of computers – such as publishing a community newspaper or launching a small business or organising a civic group – which they then work to make happen. Over ten years, more than 600,000 people graduated from CDI schools.

...lead social change

Get on with it! If you see a problem, and if you have an idea for how it could be dealt with, get on and do something. Don't make excuses for doing nothing; don't wait for someone else to do something. Do it yourself... and do it now!

NOVEMBER 14

IN-YOUR-FACE *politics*

The Biotic Baking Brigade is a movement that actually moves: a network of political pranksters who literally practise in-your-face politics. They target is assorted greedheads, hitting them right in the smacker...with pies! But it is worthy work. The BBB's pies are the Boston Tea Party of our modern day, sending a serious message softly to the corporate oligarchy.
— Jim Hightower

It's an assault on public officials. It's an assault on government. It should not be condoned.
— Michael Yaki, San Francisco Supervisor

Humour is an important weapon in the armoury of an activist. What do Bill Gates, Milton Freidman, Sylvester Stallone, Canadian Premier Jean Chretien, Swedish King Carl Gustaf, Ronald McDonald, Timothy Leary, Eldridge Cleaver, World Trade Organization Director Renato Ruggiero and Andy Warhol have in common? They've all been 'pied' by the Biotic Baking Brigade and its sympathisers around the world. The Brigade consists of activists involved in ecology, social justice, animal rights and feminism, with a sense of humour and an 'in your face' courage.

Slapstick and politics can mix. The fine art of landing a freshly baked cream cake in the face of a reactionary, pompous but otherwise deserving person has a long and venerable tradition. As a way of highlighting a particular cause, gaining often spectacular media attention, or merely bringing a lofty demeanour down a crust or two, there is nothing quite as good as a pie.

Biotic Baking Brigade: www.bioticbakingbrigade.org

Watch The Pie's the Limit, a delicious documentary featuring a cornucopia of political pie throwings in San Francisco and beyond; plus behind the scenes interviews with real underground pie tossers. Watch with delight as half a dozen demagogues are served up their just deserts! View it or download it at: www.whisperedmedia.org/piepage.html

Pie Any Means Necessary: buy the book

This anthology cooks up an intoxicating melange of history, analysis, tactics and recipes for this most edible of the political direct action techniques. Tips from experienced pie-ers on the best way to slip into a shareholders meeting unobserved, ammunition in hand, blend deliciously with tried and tested recipes for delectable vegan pastries (perfect for launching, or dining upon). Generously sprinkled with some of the punchiest, wittiest communiques explaining just why those responsible for environmental destruction might be in line for their just desserts.

...how to pie for publicity

Step 1: Get hold of a copy of *Pie Any Means Necessary: The Biotic Baking Brigade Cookbook*. Find it in bookstores, cafes, bunkers, caves, and police station lockups everywhere. Or order it straight from the publisher, AK Press: www.akpress.org

Step 2: Choose a recipe from this or another cookbook, and bake your pie. Sloppy is good!

Step 3: Choose your target, and go for it.

15 NOVEMBER

people *MIXING*

You are probably missing out. There are interesting people everywhere, but most of us tend to stick with the groups of people we're used to. Most of us remember the way 'cliques' or 'gangs' formed at school, and most adults still experience them to a degree. Every group has its own territory and its own rules. Almost everyone remains locked into their small group.

The reality is that people can't really be slotted into 'types'. One of the human race's most spectacular attributes is its phenomenal diversity. You might share the political opinions of your bank manager, or a favourite food with your boss at work. You really don't know until you ask. There may be lots of really interesting people out there whom you never get to talk to.

Some people are more dedicated to mixing up their social groups. On Tuesday 16 November 2004, more than 4 million students at nearly 8,000 schools across the USA participated in the third annual Mix It Up At Lunch Day. They stepped out of their comfort zones to meet someone new.

So try mixing it up. Organise a day where everyone gets to meet new people. It's a great way to break down social, economic, racial, gender, ability, disability and even age barriers. You could allocate tables according to birth month, or the first letter of last names. Break down the barriers, and you might find people have more to talk about than they realise.

Tolerance.org: www.tolerance.org/teens/lunch.jsp

Where else you can mix it up?

In bars and restaurants, make a point of sitting next to strangers and chatting to them.

At parties, go and talk to all the interesting looking people you don't know.

Using a telephone directory, invite everyone in town with the surname 'Rice' or 'Bush' or whatever to meet for a drink one evening after work.

Mix It Up encourages people to cross lines and meet new faces. You want to make a difference, so start by meeting someone new.

...meet someone new

Organise a Mix It Up event:

A Mix It Up at Lunch Day.

A Mix It Up at Work for employees at your office, college or wherever you can.

Tolerance.org has instructions on how to set up a Mix It Up Lunch. It includes e-cards to send to everyone and posters to download.

CO-OPERATION *is the key*

Anyone can make a difference and feed hungry people. Eric Samuel gave up a full-time job as a banker to fight food poverty and health inequality as a volunteer in the London Borough of Newham, one of the poorest parts of the city. ✋ He started off by going to the wholesale market once a week early in the morning, and getting fresh fruit and vegetables. He then sold these at a low 10% mark up. Eric has now created a whole network of food projects in the area through the Newham Food Access Partnership.

Eric's food programmes have spread. His food access schemes include food co-ops (with 14,000 customers), breakfast clubs (serving 40,000 meals a year), free fruit for primary school children, fruit tuck shops, lunch clubs and fruit delivery schemes. ✋ Whilst Eric has been encouraging food access, he has also been developing a sustainable social enterprise, which aims to alleviate food poverty, create local jobs and enable the community to play an active role in improving its health.

All this started with one man in a borrowed van getting up early to go to market!

Newham Food Access Partnership: www.nfap.org.uk

Model rules for cooperatives for the UK are available on the Cooperatives UK website: www.cooperatives-uk.coop

Co-operatives are businesses based on collective ownership. Instead of having an MD, or a partnership of directors, the executive decisions are handled by a team.

Co-operatives can be an extremely difficult business model to start up, but once up and running often prove a superior decision-making body than other companies. A co-operative aims to trade fairly with their customers. Profit is rarely a primary aim.

You could set up an informal co-operative buying group for you and your friends or neighbours. You'll get fresher fruit and vegetables a whole lot cheaper, because you will be buying from the market at wholesale prices.

...to decent living

✋ **Get a group of people together** who would like to join the co-op and make a list of the things that everybody seems to want.

✋ **Go and buy from the wholesale market** (or you could buy direct from a local farmer). Everyone gets what they ordered, and everyone contributes their share of the cost.

✋ **Next month another person from the group will go and do the buying.** Everyone will take their turn doing this. Everyone has to do something for the group. Everyone will benefit.

To start with, just buy a few boxes of the things that are in season. As the scheme develops, you can decide to expand the range of the things you buy. Shopping will never be the same again!

17 NOVEMBER

be a responsible **PET OWNER**

There are lots of problems with pet ownership: fouled pavements and gardens, the unnecessary consumption of resources, the expense of caring properly for it, and the health and safety issues around irresponsible ownership.

The RSPCA, Britain's biggest organisation promoting animal welfare and campaigning for animal rights, encourages people to think before getting a pet, and has a cyberpet game to help young people to explore the issues of pet ownership. They say:

> *There are a lot of important things to think about when deciding whether or not to get a pet. Will you be able to afford food and vet's bills? Do you have time to play with it? To help you think about these things, and of course for a bit of fun, why not adopt an RSPCA Cyberpet. Play with it, feed it and watch it grow. If you treat it well, it will grow up to be strong, healthy and happy, but if you don't look after your Cyberpet, the RSPCA will come and take it away from you!*

Find out more at: rspcapet.onlinemagic.com/intro.html

Check out the following for links to the wonderful world of cyberpets: www.virtualpet.com/vp/links/links.htm

The Virtual Pet Project: web.mit.edu/sturkle/www/vpet.html

The Virtual Pet Project

Researchers at the Massachusetts Institute of Technology are collecting stories from virtual pet owners around the world. If you have any kind of robotic, digital or virtual creature or toy, tell them about your experience with it. These are some of the things they are interested in:

1. What kinds of things do you and your creature do together?
2. Do you feel that you have a special relationship with it?
3. What do you like (and not like) about it?
4. What is it like to be a caretaker for a virtual creature?
5. How do friends, family members, and live pets react to your creature and to you spending time with it?
6. Is your creature smart? Does it have feelings? Does it think? How do you know?

Access their website, and email them your answers.

...and do it virtually

Be a responsible pet owner:

- Get an electronic toy such as a Tamagotchi, which gives you your own pet to feed, walk and look after.
- Adopt a virtual pet online.
- Join a virtual pet community, such as ShowDog, where you become the breeder, owner, handler, trainer, and groomer of your dog. You get to manage and budget the rations of food your dog receives, how you breed your dog, which shows you enter, and more: www.showdog.com

NOVEMBER 18

STOP *child pornography*

The internet can be a dangerous place for children. A research group at the University of Cork collected more than 50,000 child pornography pictures via the internet over a two-year period. There are about 2,000 children involved in these pictures. On average, two children, not previously seen, are added each week. Perhaps up to 70%–80% of these pictures are as much as 30 years old. For the children forced to participate, this violation continues as long as the pictures circulate. It is like a rape that never ends.

Complaints about child pornography are on the increase. Between 1997 and 1998 Save the Children Sweden received three tip offs. The following year this rose to more than 700. New sources of internet child pornography include Russia, Romania, the Baltic states and the Czech Republic. Live webcasting of sexual acts involving children is now being reported. All indications are that internet usage will increase, and that the problem of child pornography will grow with it.

Paedophile organisations and networks are becoming more daring and cunning in using the internet. Not only do they use it to display images of children but also to make contact with children through chat rooms. Police appear to lack the resources to deal adequately with the problem – despite the distribution of pornography in any form being illegal virtually everywhere.

Radda Barnen's Child Pornography Hotline: www.rb.se/hotline/ehome.htm

In Sweden 53 paedophiles created a net community whereby members could post photographs and film clips in categorised archives. There was also a message site and a chat room, where members could discuss pictures and fantasies and exchange images. The members used only nicknames and anonymous email addresses.

A technical oversight by the group allowed an intruder to listen into members' exchanges. This person tipped off the Child Pornography Hotline, and the police were able to investigate, gather evidence and take action.

The pictures and film clips on view in the room were hardcore child rapes involving children as young as 4 years old and even a three-month old baby.

The paedophiles included an unemployed 27-year-old, a university faculty head and a female farm worker.

...police the net

Support the campaign. Save the Children Sweden ('Radda Barnen' in Swedish) is campaigning to end the use of the internet as a marketplace for child pornography.

- **Join them in their fight against child pornography on the internet.** They need our help.
- **Report any instances of child pornography** on the internet you come across.

rights for CHILDREN

2.2 billion of the world's population are young people under 18. Almost all of these are protected by the Convention on the Rights of the Child, apart from the 80 million children who live in Somalia and the USA, neither of which has signed up to the Convention.

The Convention was launched on 20 November 1989 with these basic ideas:

Every child has the right to have his or her basic needs fulfilled.

Every child has the right to protection from abuse and exploitation.

Every child has the right to express his or her opinion and be respected.

Some important children's rights:

The right to have a name and be registered as a citizen in your home country. *Of 132 million born each year, 53 million children are never registered. There is no written proof that they exist.*

The right to a home, food, clothing, education, health care and security. *Around 600 million children live on less than $1 a day, 900 million on less than $2. Three-quarters of the world's children are very poor.*

The right to be protected from economic exploitation and against work that damages health or prevents the child from going to school. Children under 12 years may not work at all. *Over 100 million children under 12 do work: 90% of these are involved in harmful work; 9 million are enslaved; 1.2 million are sold each year as merchandise.*

The right to go to school. Elementary school should be free of charge to all. *Over 113 million children never begin school, 60% of these being girls. Around 150 million children leave school before the fifth grade.*

The World Children's Prize: www.childrensworld.org
Information on the Convention on the Rights of the Child: www.unicef.org/crc

The World Children's Prize for the Rights of the Child (WCPRC)

The WCPRC invites all schools and children to be part of the world's largest annual forum and educational programme about the rights of the child, democracy and global friendship.

The WCPRC has one unusual feature. Only children can vote to choose the laureates. In 2005, 2.3 million votes were cast from 7,821 schools and young people's groups in 73 countries.

Past laureates have included:

Maggy Barankitse (Burundi), for child welfare work.
Barefoot College and Children's Parliament (Rajasthan, India), where the Prime Minister is just 12 years old.
James Aguer Alic (Sudan), for fighting to free slave children.
Nelson Mandela (South Africa) and **Graça Machel** (Mozambique).

Hear their inspiring stories on the WCPRC website.

...defend them

Enlist your local school or young people's group as a Global Friend of WCPRC. They will then receive the prize magazine (which, as well as the prize web, is published in nine languages) and can vote from January to April for who has done the most for children's rights.

TV-FREE *zone*

Bhutan is a Buddhist sanctuary, a refuge from the world and its ills. In the 1930s all that was known of Bhutan in the Western world was what could be gleaned from James Hilton's novel, *Lost Horizon*. He called Bhutan 'Shangri la'. ♀ The King of Bhutan decided that, as a spiritual society, happiness was the most important thing, and in 1998, defined Bhutan's key aim as 'Gross National Happiness'.

Bhutan was the last country in the world to introduce TV. It arrived in 2002, with 46 cable channels. This has thrown Bhutan headlong into the global culture of the 21st century. Everyone underestimated the impact that TV would have on local life and culture. One third of Bhutan's girls now want to look more American (whiter skin, blonde hair). A similar proportion of girls also aspire to a new approach to relationships (boyfriends not husbands, and sex before marriage).

An editorial in a Bhutanese newspaper warns: 'We are seeing for the first time broken families, school dropouts and other negative youth crimes. We are beginning to see crime associated with drug users all over the world, shoplifting, burglary and violence.' Swapping Gross National Happiness for the joys of *Big Brother*, *Baywatch* and *I'm a Celebrity, get me out of here*, may not be such a good thing after all.

The TV-Turnoff Network encourages children and adults to watch less television in order to create healthier lives and communities: www.tvturnoff.org

White Dot, international campaign against TV. Read their survival guide 'Get a Life' for what to do after you've turned your TV off: www.whitedot.org

TV-B-Gone: www.tvbgone.com

Technology to the rescue

TV-B-Gone is a universal remote control device that hangs on your key chain. It enables you to 'turn off virtually any television' at home or in a public place from a distance of about 14 metres. Point, press, keep pointing for just over a minute. It's that easy. Launched in October 2004, the TV-B-Gone device was sold out in just two days, and the suppliers have been battling to keep up with demand ever since.

It must have been a useful tool in late April 2005, when TV Turn-Off Week was celebrated in countries as far apart as the USA and Australia, the UK and Brazil.

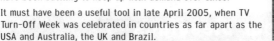

...turn off the box

Spend less time watching TV. US children spend more time each year in front of the television (1,023 hours) than in school (900 hours a year). A BBC survey in 2004 showed four-year-olds in the UK spending four hours a day in front of TV. Adults are also 'glued to the box'.

♀ **Turn off your TV**. Reduce your viewing by 50% for starters. Later, consider reducing the number of TVs in your home to just one.

♀ **Think about what you could do with all this extra free time...** talk, exercise, change the world?

say THANK YOU

Giving thanks is traditionally associated with autumn. Throughout history and all over the world, people have celebrated the harvest each autumn with some sort of thanksgiving ceremony.  Demeter, the ancient Greek goddess of grain, was thanked at the festival of Thesmosphoria. On the first day of autumn, married women built leafy shelters. The second day was a fast day, and the third was a feast with offerings to Demeter. ✝ The Romans had Cerelia on 4 October, when the fruits of the harvest were offered up to Ceres. Cerelia was celebrated with music, parades, games and a feast.

The Chinese harvest festival is Chung Ch'ui, held at full moon in the 8th month. This is the moon's birthday, celebrated with special 'moon cakes', stamped with a picture of a rabbit (the Chinese see a rabbit, not a man, in the moon). ✝ The harvest festival of the Jews is called Sukkoth, the feast of tabernacles. They build small huts out of branches and foliage, which are decorated with the fruits of the harvest. ✝ The Festival of Thanksgiving in the USA commemorated the first year in the New World of the founding Pilgrims, and a harvest that was plentiful. This is a day of family get togethers and turkey dinners.

View the Wellcome Medical Photographic Library: **www.wellcome.ac.uk**
Find out about Tim Berners-Lee: **www.w3.org/People/Berners-Lee**

Healthcare achievements in the 20th century to be thankful for:

Antibiotics, vaccines and anaesthetics, which have transformed medicine.

Insulin which saves the lives of diabetics.

Anti-retroviral drugs, which mean that you don't need to die of AIDS.

The understanding of malaria, which means that it can be treated.

The Human Genome project, with its potential to eliminate hereditary disease.

...count your blessings

Thanksgiving is a great day to say 'Thank You'. In every area of human endeavour, you will find things that have made life so much better. Today's the day to reflect on all that's good in the world.

✝ **Say thank you to all your funders and supporters.** To be good at fundraising, you need to build good relationships with those who give you their money or time. This means thanking them nicely. Keep in touch, tell them what you have been able to achieve with their help, share your successes. Today, tell them how much you value their support.

✝ **And say a special thank you to Tim Berners-Lee.** Tim devised the World Wide Web, one of the great ideas of the 20th century, which has profoundly changed all our lives.

NOVEMBER 22 *Thanksgiving Day is the fourth Thursday of November*

STICK 'em up

A bath and a washing machine both use 80 litres of water, a power shower uses 70, a dishwasher 35, flushing a toilet 9. A garden hose will use 450 litres an hour. This water is delivered to your door. It's high-quality stuff too, clean enough to drink. It's usually available on demand. And although you may be charged for the amount you use, it's almost free. This is amazing when you consider that people in other parts of the world may need to walk several kilometres each day to get a few gallons from the local water source.

Turning off the tap should be a reflex action. But people often forget to do it. They leave the water running when they are brushing their teeth, when they are staring at themselves in the mirror, when they are combing their hair... or even after they have left the bathroom. This is a waste of a precious commodity – especially in long hot summers or in areas where demand is threatening to exceed supply. The same is true for turning off the lights when you leave a room. It's so basic, but your laziness or forgetfulness will translate into higher electricity bills, more pollution and more greenhouse gases contributing to global warming.

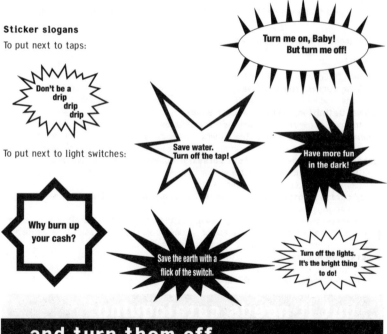

Sticker slogans

To put next to taps:

Don't be a drip drip drip

Turn me on, Baby! But turn me off!

Save water. Turn off the tap!

Have more fun in the dark!

To put next to light switches:

Why burn up your cash?

Save the earth with a flick of the switch.

Turn off the lights. It's the bright thing to do!

...and turn them off

- **Make some stickers.** Buy a pack of large blank labels. Cut them into interesting shapes. Think up some provocative slogans and use marker pens (non-water-soluble will be best for obvious reasons) to write and illustrate your slogans.
- **Put them next to taps and light switches** as a reminder to everyone (including yourself).
- **Put your stickers up at home, at work and in public places.**

23 NOVEMBER

information is POWER

The Open Directory describes itself as 'The Republic of the Web'. The project is the largest, most comprehensive human-edited directory of the internet. It is constructed and maintained by a global community of volunteer editors.

The World Wide Web continues to grow at staggering rates. In fact, growth is such that automated search engines are increasingly unable to turn up useful results to search queries. So, instead of fighting the explosive growth of the internet, the Open Directory provides a means for the internet to organise itself. ♪ Volunteer editors each organise a small section, culling out the bad and the useless, and keeping only the best content.

So far the Open Directory has catalogued over 4 million websites: 590,000 categories in 76 languages, using 66,849 editors. Just as the *Oxford English Dictionary* became the definitive book on words through the efforts of volunteers, the Open Directory aims to become the definitive catalogue of the Web. ♪ The Open Directory has been founded in the spirit of the open source movement. It is free. There is no cost for submitting a site to the directory, and use of the directory's data is free, subject to terms of the Copyleft licence.

Open Directory Project: dmoz.org

Damn it!
The Open Directory has eight entries in English for 'Curses':
Breaking curses from our lives; biblical curses, how they affect the lives of Christians, and how to be free of them: www.bible.com/answers/acurses.html
Curses: Definition, history, modern usage:
www.themystica.com/mystica/articles/c/curses.html
Generational curses, sins of the fathers; curses carrying down a family line, with descriptions of various types of curses: hometown.aol.com/godswaitn/genealgy/index.htm
Global psychics, the truth about curses; fraudulent scenarios by unethical practitioners claiming to remove curses for cash:
www.globalpsychics.com/lp/Tips/curses.htm
Gypsy curses incorporated; free random curses or individually tailored curses for a fee: members.tripod.com/~Curses_Inc
Irish curses; traditional Irish curses: www.ncf.carleton.ca/~bj333/HomePage.curses.html
An tinneall Mallachtai, the curse engine; choose from English phrases to generate a curse in Irish: hermes.lincolnu.edu/~focal/scripts/mallacht.htm
Understanding curses; the effect of curses in a biblical context:
hermes.lincolnu.edu/~focal/scripts/mallacht.htm
dmoz.org/Society/Folklore/Magic/Curses/

...but it needs cataloguing

♪ **Join the Open Directory Project.** Apply to become an editor using the form on the website. Editors select, evaluate, describe and organise the websites to be included in the Directory. Indicate a category that corresponds with your interests.
♪ **All you need is an interest in the subject area**, plus a computer, a genuine interest in building a global directory that is objective in its outlook and free from commercial interests.

DEFEND *yourself*

There are all sorts of situations where we may be in physical danger of attack. Whether it is being mugged, sexually assaulted or simply a random act of violence, and whether we are in Houston or Harare, Moscow or Manila.

Girls are particularly vulnerable to assault. In the USA:

Women and girls represent 86% of all victims of sexual violence.

Children aged 6–17 years old account for 53% of all victims of sexual assaults.

A young woman is at greatest risk of sexual assault at age 14.

40% of all young people have witnessed violence.

These startling facts should shock us all into finding ways to create safer lives for ourselves, our families and our communities. We need to understand the threats and the best course of action in a violent situation. We need to think about acquiring basic self-defence skills, which will help to conquer fear and boost our confidence.

Girls' Leap, a community programme in the USA to help girls understand and deal with violence: www.girlsleap.org

AWARE: arming women against rape and endangerment: www.aware.org

Question 1: You are walking to your car in a deserted parking area after working late one evening, and you hear someone behind you quickly approaching. You realise that they can reach you before you can get to your car. What would you do?

a Don't look back, walk faster, try to get into your car before they reach you.
b Put your hand on whatever defensive tool you are carrying, turn your head so you can see who is approaching.
c Stop and turn around, pull out a weapon if you are carrying one.

Question 2: You are on a long drive and stop at a fast-food restaurant late at night. When you return to your car in the deserted parking lot, you encounter a man with a knife in his hand who orders you to go with him. What would you do?

a Scream.
b Cooperate with him and look for an opportunity to escape.
c Try to talk him out of it.
d Refuse to go with him and resist in the strongest way possible.
e Pretend to faint.

Find the answers at:
www.aware.org/quizzes/quizindex.shtml

...learn martial arts

⊗ **Answer the questions above.** Think carefully about what's the best course of action. One day you might find yourself in a similar situation.

⊗ **Download and photocopy the four 'Fighting Back' posters** on self-defence for women and girls published by *the F word*, an online magazine on feminist issues: www.thefword.org.uk/static/fightingback/page1

International Day for the Elimination of Violence against Women **25 NOVEMBER**

stop SPENDING

Around 20% of the world consumes over 80% of the world's natural resources. This is in part because we buy so much stuff we don't need. World Buy Nothing Day is when 'you can turn the economy off and talk about it'.
Buy Nothing Day gives you a breather to think about whether you need to buy the things you feel you need. It will focus your mind on the environmental and ethical consequences of consumption: who you buy from and whether they are socially responsible businesses.

Buy Nothing Day is held near the end of November each year. There is only one rule: don't spend a single penny all day for the whole day. It all started with No Shop Day in 1994, organised by Ted Dave, a Canadian advertising executive, as a collective protest against the unrelenting calls to over consume.

These are some of the things that people do to support Buy Nothing Day:
Ask friends to bring stuff to swap.
Create a shopping-free zone, hanging out with friends in a public space.
Interview shoppers on video about what they are purchasing and why.
Get people to pledge to shop responsibly for a month.

World Buy Nothing Day: www.ecoplan.org/ibnd/ib_index.htm
Buy Nothing Day UK has a toolkit for organising a Buy Nothing Day, including posters, ideas on how to celebrate the day, and ways to get people involved: www.buynothingday.co.uk
101 things to do instead of shopping: www.buynothingday.co.uk/101.html
Buy Nothing Christmas: www.buynothingchristmas.org
Adbusters: www.adbusters.org/metas/eco/bnd

And some more things to do instead of buying:
Turn your mobile off and chill out.
Go to the top of a tall building and look at the view.
Paint your fridge or washing machine a bright colour.
Collect wild food: windfall apples, blackberries, mushrooms.
Have a bath in candlelight.
Learn to count up to ten in ten languages.
Grow your own beansprouts.
Go out in the evening and look for bats.
Take up jogging.
Take your toaster apart and try to mend it.

...buy nothing for a day

Buy nothing on Buy Nothing Day. Throw a Buy Nothing Day Party. Spend the whole of the day with friends instead of spending hard-earned cash.

SCHOOLING *for all*

Education is a fundamental right. But this right is being violated for over 24 million children in Africa and 125 million children worldwide. Gender equity in education by 2005 and universal primary education by 2015 were among the Millennium Development Goals for ending world poverty. But on current trends, these targets will be missed.

More pressure is needed to make governments provide education. This must be available and affordable to all, and also allow girls an equal chance. The Global Campaign for Education is an international attempt to put pressure on governments. ◀ In April 2005, The Global Campaign ran an international week of action on the theme 'Education to End World Poverty'.

Part of this was the 'Send my Friend to School' action. This involved people making a life-size cut-out of a school-age child. Politicians were then invited to visit a school, a non-formal education centre or adult-literacy programme, and to accept all the cut-out friends as a pledge of their commitment to education for all. National rallies were held with people and their cut-out friends.

Universal education
Global Campaign: www.campaignforeducation.org
UNICEF, campaigning for girl's education: www.unicef.org

Mentoring in the UK
Mentoring and Befriending Foundation: www.mandbf.org.uk
SOVA: www.sova.org.uk

Supporting streetchildren
Consortium for Street Children, a network for projects all over the world: www.streetchildren.org.uk

Maria is a friendly, confident 13-year-old Bolivian. Until recently she was selling newspapers on the streets and in the bars of La Pas. Her family forced her to go to work at the age of eight. This was dangerous work, which involved walking through the streets while it was still dark to collect the newspapers.

Educators from a girls' hostel met Carla and invited her to come and live with them, where she is one of the youngest of the 25 girls. She now attends school. Her dream is to go on to university and become a teacher.

...give a child an education

Make a pledge to get one child back to school.

◀ **This could be someone in your own country.** Talk to them about the importance of education. Be a big brother or sister to them, mentoring them through a difficult period when guidance and wisdom might help.

◀ **Or find an organisation that's doing good work abroad and support it.** Start with street children, who have no parents and must fend for themselves. A non-formal education class or a street school can provide basic literacy and numeracy.

27 NOVEMBER

freedom of EXPRESSION

Writers have a critical role to play in countries where freedom of expression is denied. They can write about what's happening, and get their writings smuggled out and published in the free world. But if they remain true to their convictions and write the truth, they lay themselves open to imprisonment.
Alexander Solzhenitsyn, Nobel prize-winning author of *One Day in the Life of Ivan Denisovich* and *The Gulag Archipelago*, was the first to bring to the world's attention the scale and barbarism of the Gulag system in the Soviet Union. He had been imprisoned and exiled in his country for many years, and was eventually allowed to seek refuge in the USA.

Václav Havel, a prominent Czech playwright, spoke out against Soviet oppression. The publication of his plays was banned, and he spent five years in prison because he had co-founded Charter 77 and was a member of the Committee for the Defence of the Unjustly Prosecuted. In 1989 he was elected his country's first post-Communist President.

Writers need to speak out. It is important to show solidarity with those who do, and who are imprisoned for doing this. PEN is an international campaign against the persecution and imprisonment of writers anywhere in the world. PEN has 130 branches in over 100 countries.

English PEN, which founded the worldwide movement: www.englishpen.org
International PEN: www.internationalpen.org.uk

Raul Rivero Castañeda, poet and journalist, founded the independent news agency Cuba Press in 1995. Together with nine others he called on Castro to free prisoners of conscience and reform the socialist regime. In April 2003 he was charged with 'Crimes against the State' and given a 20-year sentence, following a one-day trial for which he was given insufficient time to put together a proper defence. He was released in November 2004, after being transferred from prison to a military hospital.

Naushad Waheed, cyber-dissident and a prominent artist in the Maldives, has been an outspoken critic of his government for many years. His most recent arrest took place in 2001. He was then held in detention for about five months before being transferred to house arrest. In October 2002, he was tried without access to a lawyer or the opportunity to defend himself, and was sentenced to 15 years imprisonment. In an account smuggled out of jail, Waheed describes the horrific scenes of torture inflicted on himself and others.

...support writer's rights

Join the campaign.

English PEN organises a Writers in Prison campaign. Each month one writer is featured. Find out as much as you can about that writer by searching on the web. Go to: www.amazon.com, and see if any of that writer's books are available. If so, order copies. Read as an act of solidarity.

Join PEN's Rapid Response Network to campaign against the oppression of writers.

NOVEMBER 28

PALESTINIAN *olive oil*

Olive oil is the backbone of the Palestinian agricultural economy.
Since the 2000 Intifada, farmers have encountered enormous difficulties in
picking their olives. Some cannot reach their fields without a special permit, as
they are cut off by the so-called 'separation wall' (the barrier the Israelis are
building between Israel and Palestine). In other villages, the olive groves are near
to Jewish settlements, and access is hazardous or impossible.

The Israeli Occupation is devastating the lives of many Palestinians,
who depend on olives for a living. Ironically, the olive branch is a symbol of peace
in a region where olive picking is wracked by conflict. As part of the 'Olive
Picking Coalition', 255 peace activists from the Gush Shalom peace movement (in
Hebrew, this means 'The Peace Bloc') took part in the olive picking at Yassouf and
Jama'een villages in Palestine. The villagers feared harassment by the settlers of
neighbouring Tapuakh and that dogs would be set on them.

Gush Shalom staged a peaceful protest. Together, the families who own
the groves and the peace activists shook the trees and climbed to the highest
branches, whilst talking in a mixture of Hebrew, Arabic and English. The olives
were collected on nylon sheets, put into sacks and taken away by tractor.

Gush Shalom: www.gush-shalom.org/english/index.html

Holy Land Olive Oil sells Palestinian extra-virgin olive oil in the US and Canada:
www.palestineoliveoil.org

Olive oil produced by Jews, Arabs, Druze and Bedouin working together:
www.peaceoil.org

Gush Shalom want to see:

An end to the Israeli occupation.

An acceptance of the right of the Palestinian people to establish an
independent state in all of the territory occupied by Israel since 1967 (with possible
minor exchanges of territories agreed between the parties).

Jerusalem as the capital of both states, united
physically for municipal governance.

**A recognition of the right of Palestinian
refugees to return,** allowing each refugee
to choose freely between compensation and
repatriation, with a fixed annual quota for
those able to return to Israel.

The security of both peoples, ensured by
mutual agreement and guarantees.

An overall peace between Israel and all Arab countries, and
the creation of a regional union.

...buy it in solidarity

Buy Olive Oil from Palestine. Zaytoun sells pesticide-free fairtrade extra
virgin olive oil and high-quality soap made from olive oil in the UK as an act
of solidarity with Palestinian farmers: zaytoun.org

Go olive picking in Palestine next October with Zaytoun.

support **LOCAL ARTISANS**

Robib in rural Cambodia is six small villages, with a total population of 4,000. The annual average income per person is around $40. The villagers harvest rice once a year, and this barely feeds their families. There is no surplus to sell. In bad years or when there is a flood, there is not even enough food to go around.
🖐 Robib has a health centre but there is a shortage of medicine. Seriously ill patients have no access to expert medical care, so little chance of survival. Like most of rural Cambodia, Robib's population is vulnerable to malaria, TB and some tropical diseases. AIDS, which is growing uncontrollably in the larger urban centers, has not yet hit Robib because of its isolation.

Bernard Krisher, a 69-year-old former journalist, has brought IT to Robib. A satellite link was provided free by the Thai company Shin Satellite. The dish provides a continuous 64,000-bits per second connection to a small group of computers in the village, which are run for part of each day using solar power.
🖐 In addition to providing computer education and internet access to the school (attended by 400 students), the project has brought telemedicine to the village, using doctors in Boston.

Krisher is showing how the internet can really help a single village. His American Assistance for Cambodia programme has also constructed 200 rural schools, using matching funds from the World Bank. 🖐 Villagers have been trained in traditional weaving skills, which vanished during the Pol Pot years. Silk scarves and table runners are now produced. The hotel in Tokyo where Krisher lives processes credit-card purchases made from the village website.

Robib Village Website: www.villageleap.com
American Assistance for Cambodia: www.cambodiaschools.com
Handmade products from North Africa at the World Bank-supported Virtual Souk: www.tedjohnson.us/resume/peoplink/vsouk
Arts and crafts from Africa from the Ghana-based: www.eShopAfrica.com
Arts and crafts from Novica, which is run in association with National Geographic: www.novica.com

The Virtual Souk

The Virtual Souk creates an online trading environment for local crafts. It offers handmade products by artisans of Morocco, Tunisia, Lebanon and Egypt who would not traditionally have access to the international market.

...via the web

Next time you want to give someone a present:
🖐 Buy a silk scarf from Robib.
🖐 Or buy a product from one of the other websites we've listed that links producers with consumers.

AIDS *is preventable*

AIDS is a global challenge. It is having a huge impact on the world's most vulnerable and poorest people. The HIV virus infects 13,500 people every day, swelling the total number infected with HIV to 37.2 million adults and 2.2 million children at the end of 2004. ◉ 95% of these people live in the developing world. ◉ 3.1 million people died of AIDS in 2004, which means that, on average, somebody died every 10 seconds. 25 million people have died since AIDS was first diagnosed in 1981, 6 million of whom were children. More than 15 million children have been orphaned by AIDS.

There is hope for the future. The political will exists. The resources are there. Medicines that inhibit new infections now allow many to survive with the disease – and they are becoming more affordable through pressure on the drug companies and the wider availability of generic drugs. ◉ The UN has set up UNAIDS to encourage global action, and the Global Fund to mobilise funds. The Apathy is Lethal campaign promotes awareness and encourages action. You can:

Educate yourself to better understand the disease, and what you can do to minimise the risk to yourself.

Educate others as to what actions they can take on a personal level.

Volunteer with an AIDS organisation – providing anything from office help to buddying. Raise funds for the global effort.

Apathy is Lethal: www.unfoundation.org/campaigns/apathy/forum/info.html
United Nations Programme on HIV/AIDS: www.unaids.org
AVERT has a useful website: www.avert.org
Terrence Higgins Trust, the UK's first AIDS charity: www.tht.org.uk

Major challenges

Women account for 57% of the people living with HIV in Sub-Saharan Africa, largely as a result of gender inequality, sexual violence and ignorance.

Young people (aged 15 to 24) account for nearly half of all new HIV infection worldwide.

Prevention programmes currently reach only 1 in 5 people at risk of infection.

Only 1 in 10 pregnant women in poorer countries is offered services for preventing mother-to-child HIV transmission.

Anti-retroviral treatment is available for only 7% of the people who need it in developing countries: a total of 400,000 people at the end of 2003.

...apathy is lethal

◉ Erase the tax on condoms The high price of condoms acts as a disincentive to consistent use, particularly for at-risk groups and young people. Condoms in the UK are almost twice as expensive as in the USA, and dearer than elsewhere in Europe. They can be obtained free of charge on the NHS, but clinics ration them and they are hard to ask for. Ask your MP to write to the Secretary of State for Health, requesting he/she remove VAT from condoms.

◉ Play the Tony Blair drugs test game at:
www.actionaid.org.uk/1394/hiv_aids.html
and Supershagland at: www.kikass.tv

　　　　　　　　　　　　World AIDS Day **1 DECEMBER**

have another CHOCOLATE

When people eat chocolate, they are eating my flesh.

— Drissa, a child slave in Côte d'Ivoire

Child slaves may have made your chocolate. According to the television programme, *Slavery*, made for the BBC by Kate Blewett and Brian Woods of True Vision, thousands of children in Central and West Africa are being stolen from their parents, shipped to Côte d'Ivoire and sold as slaves to cocoa farmers. These children earn no money for their work, and are barely fed. They are beaten if they try to escape, and most will never see their families again. Nearly 50% of the world's cocoa supply is grown in Côte d'Ivoire.

Steven Millman saw the television programme and was so appalled he had to act:

> *Suddenly I could taste every bit of chocolate I'd ever eaten in my life, a taste so sour at the thought that child slaves had produced it that I thought I would vomit. Since then I've done some research to see where chocolate might safely be purchased, and I decided to make that information available to the world.*

> *This information takes two forms. First, I've written over 200 letters to many of the world's great chocolate manufacturers to find out who is making sure that their chocolate has no slavery involved and I am posting their responses. Second, I have compiled a links page with relevant information about news sources and organisations.*

Anti-slavery cocoa campaign:
www.antislavery.org/homepage/campaign/cocoaaction.htm
True Vision website: www.truevisiontv.com/

How to avoid slave chocolate

This is the letter that Steven sent to over 200 chocolate manufacturers:

> *Hi! – There has been a ton of information in the news over the last few months about the child slavery used in the harvesting of cocoa in the Ivory Coast. I love your chocolates, but I can't bear the thought of eating chocolate made by child slaves. Do you guys do anything to ensure that no child slavery is used in the production of your cocoa?*

> *Thanks, Steven*

All replies and the companies that didn't reply are posted on Steven's website.

...but be sure it's slave-free

Go to Steven's website: www.radicalthought.org

- **Click on the Companies Page** to find out whose chocolate is made with child slavery. Don't eat it. One easy way of identifying slave-free chocolate is to buy chocolate made organically. There are no organic farms in the areas where slavery is used. Any chocolate bearing a 'Fairtrade' or 'Max Havelaar' logo will also be free of slavery.

- **If you are inspired by what Steven did,** then do something similar about an issue close to your heart.

DISABILITY *access*

It is part of a modern, humane society that people with physical disabilities should have proper access to the offices they might work in, the public buildings they might need to visit, the events they might wish to attend, and the streets and public transport they might wish to use. ✖ The Graphic Artists Guild Foundation in New York designed 12 symbols that can be used to promote and publicise accessibility of spaces and activities for people with a range of disabilities. These include:

 An event or location accessible to people who are blind or have low vision.

 Availability of a text telephone.

Large Print Large print books, pamphlets, guides and programmes for the visually impaired.

 Accessible to people with limited mobility, including wheelchair users: step-free access, disabled toilets and low public phones.

 Availability of telephones for the hard of hearing.

OC Open Captioning, where captions are available all the time.

AD))) Audio-description at performances for people who are blind or have low vision.

Amplified listening systems, such as loop systems to amplify sound via hearing aids.

Braille Availability of printed material in Braille.

Symbols can be downloaded from: www.gag.org/resources/das.php

...it's a basic right

✖ **Download these symbols** and print them on to sticker paper.

✖ **Design a second version** with a diagonal red bar superimposed on the symbol contained within a red circle to indicate that these facilities are **NOT** available, but should be made available in order to provide disability access.

✖ **Use your stickers to praise good practice** and publicise a lack of proper access.

stand up for YOUR RIGHTS

Now, I say to you today my friends, even though we face the difficulties of today and tomorrow, I still have a dream. ... I have a dream that one day this nation will rise up and live out the true meaning of its creed: 'We hold these truths to be self-evident, that all men are created equal'.

– Martin Luther King
from his speech at Civil Rights March on Washington, 28 August 1963

Is there an issue you feel really strongly about? Is there an injustice that is so outrageous that you boil with rage and feel that you have to do something about it? Take your inspiration from Rosa Parks (see below). This previously very ordinary woman did something that was both very simple and very extraordinary. Her single action changed the course of her own life and was a trigger for the Civil Rights Movement in the USA. So, stand up for your beliefs by starting a campaign or undertaking some sort of non-violent direct action.

Until her death at the age of 92 in 2005, Rosa Parks was continuing the work she and her husband, Raymond, undertook throughout their lives with youth in the community, through the Rosa and Raymond Parks Institute for Self Development. Pay tribute to a brave and great lady by visiting her website: www.rosaparks.org

Rosa Parks, civil rights pioneer

Rosa Parks worked as a seamstress in Montgomery, Alabama, at a time when the southern states of the USA operated a kind of apartheid. She was arrested on 1 December 1955 for refusing to give up her seat on a segregated bus to a white male passenger, as demanded by the bus driver. She was tried and convicted of violating a local ordinance. Her act sparked a city-wide boycott of the bus system by blacks.

The Montgomery Bus Boycott started on 5 December 1955 and lasted 381 days. Rosa Parks' courage catapulted her into world history, and she is now affectionately referred to as the 'Mother of the modern-day Civil Rights Movement'.

The boycott also brought a young Baptist minister, Dr Martin Luther King Jr, to world prominence.

...sitting down ain't easy

Do something!

What? Is there an issue or an injustice that you feel really strongly about? Then do something that addresses that issue or injustice.

When? Today. Now's the time to get started.

Who? You of course!

How? You decide. But taking that first step is the most important thing.

Hear the voice of Dr Martin Luther King Jr at the King Centre:
www.thekingcenter.org

DECEMBER 4

PLEDGE *to change the world*

Changing the world all on your own might seem an impossible task. And indeed it would be. But it's OK, because there are others out there just like you: they feel the need to act, but don't want to do it alone. And the way to make contact with them is through the Pledge Bank. 👫 The idea is simple. You enter a pledge online, promising to do something but only if a certain number of other people do the same. When enough people have signed up, everyone undertakes their pledge. This is a really good way of multiplying the impact of your actions to change the world.

Tips for successful pledges:

Keep your ambitions modest. Why ask for 50 people when five would be enough? Every extra person makes your pledge harder to meet.

Think about how your pledge reads. Will an outsider understand it? Read it to someone else. If they don't understand it, you'll need to rewrite it.

Make your pledge imaginative, worthwhile, fun, and reasonably easy to complete.

Don't imagine that your pledge will sell itself. Tell the world. Email your friends, print leaflets and stick them through your neighbours' doors. Get some publicity in the local newspaper.

Pledge Bank: **www.pledgebank.com**

Some examples of successful pledges:

Jeff edited 100 pages for Project Gutenberg: www.pgdp.net once 50 other people had agreed to do the same.

Andy installed low-energy long-life bulbs throughout his house once 20 other people had agreed to do the same.

Matthew bought only Fairtrade tea, coffee and chocolate bars during July 2005 once 20 other people had agreed.

Ellie did all her shopping locally and not in a supermarket chain in July 2005 along with 20 other people.

Tom wrote to his MP asking for Wireless Internet Access to be provided at the British Library, and 200 other people pledged to write to their MPs with the same request.

Find out why these things are the secret of a successful pledge

Other pledge requests include displaying posters on 'How TB kills 1,500 Africans a day' in your car, planting 10 trees to offset your carbon dioxide emissions, giving 1% of your gross annual salary to charity, refusing to register for an ID card but pledging £10 to a legal defence fund, switching to green electricity and cleaning up a river bank in South Wales.

...but only if others do too

Pledge to do something to change the world. Put your pledge on PledgeBank. Persuade family, friends, colleagues and complete strangers to sign up. Achieve your target by the cut-off date.

I will... *(enter your pledge)*, but only if ... *(enter number)* of other people will do the same. The other people must sign up before *(enter date by which the pledging has to be completed)*.

dress a **TREE**

We need to care for and protect our trees, take them into our lives and look after them. They are the lungs of our planet, breathing oxygen into the air. Without them, we would die. ♣ Tree Dressing Day encourages the celebration of trees in the city or in the country, in the street or on the village green, in your garden or in a park.

Trees have been honoured and decorated throughout the ages, and still are in many parts of the world. And not just at Christmas time...

Examples of tree dressing at: www.england-in-particular.info

What they did then...

Xerxes, the famed ruler of Persia, on discovering a plane tree that he considered beautiful, is reputed to have honoured it by dressing it with jewels.

The prophet Mohammed, on his night journey along the Axis Mundi with the Archangel Gabriel as a guide, encountered a tree glowing with emeralds, rubies and sapphires, perhaps the miraculous Tuba Tree which stood at the heart of paradise.

Alexander, explorer and conqueror of ancient times, found a talking tree with the heads of animals and people growing in its branches, which rebuked him for his ambition and forewarned him of his death far from home.

At Satterthwaite in the North of England, an old oak tree by the village fountain was reported in 1889 to be dressed every year with coloured rags and also with crockery.

...and what they are doing now

In Mexico during December, *pinatas* (bags full of sweets) are suspended from the trees as a treat for children to celebrate the bounty of the trees and the riches they provide.

In Provence, South of France, on May Day may trees (hawthorn) are decked with flowers and ribbons.

In some parts of Russia on Maundy Thursday, the people of a village select a young birch tree from the wood and dress it in women's clothing or with ribbons and beads.

At Chir-Ghat in India, local women, as an act of devotion, tie pieces of their clothing to the branches of the ancient tree that reputedly witnessed the appearance of the god Krishna to the cow-girls.

On the North American prairies, the Lakota, Ongala and Dakota Sioux put rags in trees as part of an ancient ritual connected with spiritual purification. Red is an offering to the sun, blue to the sky and green to the earth.

...make it feel appreciated

Go dress a tree. Use anything you feel like: lights, big hanging numbers cut out of card, cloth, huge rosettes, objects you've collected for recycling.

You can use the decorations to put across a specific message, or just make your tree look so beautiful that people notice and appreciate it.

LIGHT UP *your message*

Do you want to change the world while you sleep? You can be curled up in your warm bed, dreaming of desert islands and exotic fruit cocktails complete with miniature umbrellas – and still be sending out a message to passers by. 🏠 We all have our own ideas about how to improve the state of the world. Why not write up a message in lights and hang it up outside your house or apartment?

Be as political, as fun, as serious, or as silly as you want. You are only limited by your ideas, your spelling, the space you have available, and how many lights you can afford. Change your message whenever you feel like it... or when you think up an even better slogan. 🏠 This is a great way of spreading a message in an innovative way. Don't be surprised when people all over your neighborhood pick up on your idea. Here are some ideas for messages to light up the world:

P-E-A-C-E	if you're anti-war, or just as a seasonal message
V-O-T-E	at election time
W-A-L-K--T-O--W-O-R-K	to reduce greenhouse gas emissions
S-M-I-L-E	because tomorrow will be a nice day
S-A-V-E--W-A-T-E-R	in a drought
S-M-O-K-I-N-G--K-I-L-L-S	a dear friend has just died of lung cancer
F-A-I-R--T-R-A-D-E	to support fairtrade, of course
U-S-E--A--C-O-N-D-O-M	do your bit to combat HIV/AIDS

There are lots of 'novelty lights' on sale. Try matching your lights to your message: yellow ducks for a watery theme, red chilli peppers for a particularly spicy slogan and pink elephants to give people a laugh. 'Rope lights' are especially easy to 'write' with and come in a range of colours.

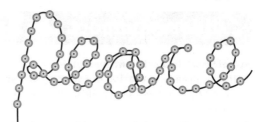

...while you sleep

🏠 **Get one or several strings of lights.**

🏠 **Spell out a message for night-time drivers and midnight amblers to see.**

🏠 **Hang it up in your front garden**, a window or a balcony facing the street.

　　　　　7 DECEMBER

get STREET SMART

It's the season of goodwill. Christmas is coming very soon. You've gone out to a restaurant to have a meal with some good friends. Do you feel a warm glow of satisfaction? 🏠 If you do, then this would be a really good time for someone to persuade you to give to the homeless — to help people who are living a very different life from your own, who wouldn't be able to afford the meal you've just eaten, and who certainly wouldn't even be allowed into the restaurant.

This was the starting point for StreetSmart, a simple fundraising scheme whereby participating restaurants add £1 to the bill for each table as a voluntary donation. The restaurant passes on the money raised to StreetSmart, which then distributes it to local charities for the homeless. 🏠 London diners help the London homeless, and Newcastle diners help out in the Northeast. The costs of running StreetSmart are sponsored by Bloomberg and all the money raised goes directly to the people who need it.

The donation is voluntary. The scheme is publicised through a small card placed on each table. Diners have a chance to say they don't want to pay the donation. But almost everyone is happy to do so, and most don't even notice.

StreetSmart: **www.streetsmart.org.uk**

StreetSmart started in London in 1998. It has now spread across the UK to 13 cities. In its first seven years, it raised and distributed over £1.8 million to 149 projects.

The projects all aim to get people off the streets, and back onto their feet again. Some of the money goes to basics such as a bed, a shower, or a pair of shoes. But money also goes to rehabilitation — helping homeless people through crucial stages in their progress from vagrant to valued community member.

...diners support the homeless

StreetSmart is a brilliant fundraising idea.

🏠 **If it's already operating in your city and you're eating out,** pay your £1 and think of the good it is doing. Discuss the scheme with your fellow diners.

🏠 **If you notice that the restaurant hasn't signed up,** then talk to the restaurant manager. Ask them to agree there and then to sign up to StreetSmart.

🏠 **If there is no StreetSmart scheme in your city,** contact StreetSmart and ask if you can tell local restaurants about it and get something started.

🏠 **And if you live in another country,** this could be a great opportunity for you to start your own version of StreetSmart. Find out as much as possible about how the scheme works, and then get going on setting up your own scheme.

DECEMBER 8

PRESERVE *material culture*

To understand the present it is important to know about the past. We can do this through documents and what is written in books (personal memoirs as well as great histories), but also through the buildings, landscape and historic artefacts that survive.

How will future generations view the present period if nothing remains? How will they get a balanced view of our age if the great events of our time are remembered, but the experience of ordinary people living ordinary lives is forgotten? ♛ Each of us has a responsibility to value the objects of our contemporary culture, to help ensure their preservation, and to use them to tell our story. ♛ One way of doing this is by making a time capsule. Around 10,000 people around the world have already done so.

International Time Capsule Society (Oglethorpe University, Georgia, USA): www.oglethorpe.edu (then type name of society into website search engine)

Smithsonian Centre for Materials Research and Education tells you how to make your own time capsule with a contact list of suppliers: www.si.edu/scmre/takingcare/timecaps.htm

The British Library advises on time capsules: www.bl.uk/services/npo/faqtime.html

Ideas for what to put in a time capsule: www.appliedhistory.com/suggest.html

The rescue game

Gather a group of friends and ask everybody to imagine that they have been given a ten-minute warning that their house is in imminent danger of being flooded.

Invite everyone to make a list of the ten things they would rescue, and a brief explanation of why they would save it, and what it means to them.

Compare lists. Look for similarities; look for differences; and examine each other's choices, rationales, and histories. The aim is to give you all a better understand of the meaning of the objects in your world and how they define you.

...make a time capsule

Make a time capsule.

♛ **It needs to be airtight and watertight.** Or you can buy one made in lead (around £250) or plastic (around £50).

♛ **Include in it some of the things** that you think best represent life on earth as it is now – photographs, recordings, CDs and DVDs, articles from newspapers and magazines, predictions about the future, clothing, equipment, objects, seeds, identity documents, whatever.

♛ **Produce a guidebook for your collection.** Try to explain to someone who might be opening it in 100 or 500 years' time what the objects are, how they work, their significance and why you selected them.

♛ **Bury it,** but not too deep, in the hope that someone sometime in the distant future will unearth it and discover the secrets of the early 21st century.

9 DECEMBER

stand up and BE COUNTED

Human rights provide a foundation for building a just and peaceful world. Every human being on the planet has the right to dignity, respect, and freedom – whatever their race, colour, sex, sexual orientation, language, religion, political or other opinion, national or social origin, wealth or other status. ♩ On 10 December 1948, the General Assembly of the United Nations adopted and proclaimed the Universal Declaration of Human Rights. This has been translated into over 300 languages and dialects – from Abkhaz to Zulu. It is the holder of the Guinness World Record for the document that has been most translated. ♩ Unfortunately, unlike the US Constitution or the European Convention on Human Rights, the Declaration has no legal force.

The Declaration contains 30 articles. Amongst these are:

Article 1: all human beings are born free and equal in dignity and rights...
Article 3: everyone has the right to life, liberty and security of person.
Article 4: ...slavery and the slave trade shall be prohibited in all their forms.
Article 5: no one shall be subjected to torture or to cruel, inhuman or degrading treatment or punishment.
Article 18: everyone has the right to freedom of thought, conscience and religion...
Article 19: everyone has the right to freedom of opinion and expression...
Article 20: everyone has the right to freedom of peaceful assembly and association...

World Human Rights Day is a time to reflect on how lucky we are to have our rights enshrined in a UN Declaration, and to pledge to do something for the many people across the world who are denied these rights.

Information on the UN and human rights: www.un.org/rights
Read the Declaration in almost any language: www.unhchr.ch/udhr

Ngawang Gyaltsen is a senior monk from Drepung monastery near Lhasa. He was imprisoned for a year in 1987, rearrested in 1989 and sentenced to 17 years in prison, plus 5 years' deprivation of political rights. He had been singled out as the leader of a group of monks accused of producing literature critical of the Chinese government and 'passing information to the enemy'. The group's first publication was a Tibetan translation of the Universal Declaration of Human Rights.

...celebrate your human rights

♩ **Put human rights on a t-shirt.** Get together with a group of friends and each choose a basic right from the Declaration. Get a local t-shirt screening shop to design colorful shirts with your chosen slogans. Assemble in a public space, stand in a line and proudly advertise your selection of human rights to promote World Human Rights Day.

♩ **Make a series of Tibetan prayer flags,** each one focusing on a different human right. Visit the website of an Amnesty International group in Pasadena, whose idea this is: www.its.caltech.edu/~aigp22/flags/home.shtml

SHARE *your books*

bookcrossing n. the practice of leaving a book in a public place to be picked up and read by others, who then do likewise.

added to the *Concise Oxford English Dictionary* in August 2004

You probably have lots of books on your shelves, gathering dust. Why not share them with others? Select one that you really like. Nobody is reading it at the moment. Register it on the Bookcrossing website, and start its journey into the unknown.

BookCrossing is a book-lovers' community. It's a global book club that crosses time and space. It's a reading group that knows no geographical boundaries. It has 300,000 members, sharing 1.5 million books, all over the world. And it's completely free. ♥ A BookCrossing member leaves a book around for someone else to pick up and read; and registers this book on the BookCrossing website. The person who finds the book reads it and then passes it on to another reader. The book continues from one reader to another, until it gets lost or someone breaks the chain by not passing it on. ♥ Each reader can comment on the book, putting their comments on the BookCrossing website. The person who originally supplied the book can keep track of its journey.

BookCrossing: www.bookcrossing.com

The Three Rs of BookCrossing

R1: Read a good book... a book that you would recommend to others.

R2: Register the book with BookCrossing. First you log in your details. This takes a couple of minutes. You will be given a BookCrossing identification number and the URL of the BookCrossing website. Label your book with these references, and put in a note asking the reader to pass it on after they've finished reading it. You can buy printed labels from the BookCrossing website.

R3: Release the book for someone else to read. There are three ways of doing this. You can give it to a friend. You can leave it somewhere for someone to pick up – on a park bench, in a coffee shop, etc. Or you can release it 'into the wild', which means that people have to search for it. The BookCrossing website enables you to say you have left it or give clues to help people find it.

Then wait and see what happens.

...help create a public library

♥ **Sign up** as a member of BookCrossing.
♥ **If you happen to find** a BookCrossing book left by someone else, read it, enjoy it and pass it on.
♥ **Encourage all your friends to join.** The more BookCrossing grows, the better it will get!

buy a GOOD GIFT

There are all sorts of occasions when you may need to buy a present: someone's birthday, Christmas, Mother's Day, Valentine's Day, to celebrate a wedding, as an in memoriam gift for someone who has just died, because you've been promoted, or just because you feel like giving someone something...

How often do you find that you can't think what to give? How often have you given (or been given) something that the recipient doesn't need and doesn't like, which is then quietly hidden away and forgotten, or taken to a charity shop, or given to someone else as a present (which they won't like either)?

So here's a really great alternative: buy a good gift. Choose a gift from the Good Gifts Catalogue and your Good Gift is actually delivered by a charity to a person or a family or a community in need. What you are paying for enables something very specific to happen. 👫 The recipient gets a card with details of the project and a badge to tell them that they are 'Gifted'. They can take pleasure in their gift, which is doing something positive; and they do not need to worry about how to get rid of yet another unwanted and unneeded present. You feel good, and your gift will make a difference to someone's life.

The Good Gifts Catalogue: www.goodgifts.org

A selection of Good Gift ideas:

Life Cycle: give a bike for a midwife in places like Cambodia and Ethiopia. This will enable her to get around more quickly when she's needed. £35

Gift of sight: fund an operation to remove cataracts or repair the damage of trachoma and help someone to see again. £27

Adopt a vegetable, and save it from extinction. £12

Pedal power in Kigali: give a young Rwandan a bicycle with a pillion seat, and he'll earn an income by giving people rides around the city. £55

A nomadic camel for a nomadic family, to provide transport, milk and good company as it wanders between Ethiopia and Somalia. £125

Ducks for peace: cows, goats, bees are all given to families to generate more income. The latest good idea is ducks. Four plus starter feed. £15

There are gifts for all occasions, and for all sorts of people. You can even give your worst enemy a brain cell — for medical research! The gifts are fun to give and fun to receive.

...make three people happy!

👫 **Buy a Good Gift** for someone's Christmas present.

👫 **Once you've done it once,** do it again for someone else. Giving will never be the same with a Good Gift.

👫 **If you're getting married,** put Good Gifts on your Wedding List. Everything you're given is sure to be wanted.

HUNGER *banquet*

Our planet produces enough food to feed every woman, man, and child – and with some left over. The problem is that the food does not reach everybody who needs it. And we're not talking here only about those who go hungry as a result of drought or conflict, but about people who are just too poor to buy enough food to keep them alive and healthy. ☻ Children are particularly at risk. Malnutrition stunts their physical and mental development and makes them more prone to disease.

Millennium Development Goal no. 1 is to halve the number of people suffering poverty and hunger by 2015. But if hunger is not really about an overall shortage of food, but about its unequal distribution, we should be able to do much better than that. We should be able to abolish malnutrition altogether.

Oxfam America's Hunger Banquet website gives you a chance to learn about hunger from the point of view of those who experience it every day:
www.hungerbanquet.org
www.oxfamamerica.org

Gloria Narua is surviving on the edge; and it wouldn't take much for her life to fall apart. She lives in Mozambique, where she grows crops on a small plot of land called a mashamba. It's not much, but most years she can produce enough maize, groundnuts, eggplant, carrots, and kale to feed three children. She even owns a few chickens.

Unfortunately, she doesn't earn enough to send her children to school. Her oldest, Eduardo, is nine years old and desperate to learn how to read and write. She'd do anything to educate him, but simply can't afford it. Besides, this year, she'll need his help in the field. It's October – time to bring in the maize. Last year, her husband gathered the harvest with her, but he died in the spring. People say it could have been AIDS, but she can't be sure.

She misses her husband – now more than ever. For, as she looks forward to the harvest, she's worried. The rains were not good this year. This could make for a tough year to come...

...experience life's lottery

Organise a Hunger Banquet. Each person attending is randomly assigned a role.
- ☻ **15% of the people are in the high-income group;** they sit at a table and enjoy a three-course meal.
- ☻ **25% of the people are in the middle-income group;** they sit on chairs and eat rice and beans (delicious and nutritious).
- ☻ **The remaining 60% are the world's poor;** they sit on the floor, and get only rice and water. They will be suffering the fate of the billions of poor people throughout the world who are undernourished and go to bed hungry each night.

You can use a hunger banquet to raise money to fight global poverty. But make sure the rich pay more!

13 DECEMBER

go on a # SEX STRIKE

Sometimes there is nothing for it but to show you mean business. If you want to bring about change, or at least persuade your partner to see your point of view, you may just have to hit them where it hurts.

Sex strike in Sudan: Samira Ahmed, a university professor, launched a sex strike in 2002 to try to end 19 years of civil war. She called it 'alHair', Arabic for 'women sexually abandoning their men'. The action (or rather the inaction) began with 20 women from the Lou and Jekany tribes, who were most involved in the fighting.

Stripping off against strip mining: Birsel Lemke campaigned against a proposal to develop highly poisonous cyanide-based gold mining in sites across Turkey. Inhabitants of one village near the site of a proposed mine ran naked, bearing signs with the slogan, 'Before Eurogold strips us, we'll strip'. The women refused to have sex with their husbands until the men had expelled the gold mining company.

Sex strikes have been used around the world:

> **In Colombia:** to protest against the violent drug wars.
> **In Poland:** to fight for legal abortion
> **In Amsterdam:** by sex workers to protest against harassment.

Birsel Lemke's Right Livelihood Award: www.rightlivelihood.org/recip/lemke.htm

The Global Women's Strike held on 8 March each year to highlight how much of the world's work is done by women, and how much difference it makes when their contribution is withdrawn: www.globalwomenstrike.net

No Water, No Sex

In 2001, a group of women in the village of Sirt in Turkey banned their husbands from their bedrooms in an effort to get a mains water supply to their village. The 27-year old water system had broken down, and the women were having to collect water from a fountain and carry it home over long distances.

The strategy had an immediate effect. The men petitioned the authorities to repair the water system, and offered their labour free. The local authority provided pipes to bring a nearby water source to the village. The women continued their protest until water actually started gushing out of the taps. Islam requires people to bathe after sex, so there was a connection between the method of protest and what was being fought for.

...to get things done

If there's an issue you care passionately about, write to the partners of those who are causing the problem urging them to go on a sex strike. Get as much publicity as you can for your campaign.

If there is something your own partner is doing that is causing harm to others or to the planet, why not start your own sex strike to persuade him or her to desist.

DECEMBER 14

DRIVE *to Africa*

Are you ready for a challenge? Have you got three weeks to spare, a sense of adventure and lots of courage? Do you want to raise loads of money for local African charities? Do you want to export vehicles to Mali or Gambia?

The Challenge is to drive the route from Plymouth, UK to Bamako in Mali or to Banjul in Gambia, on a limited budget with the principal aim of raising money for local charities. The first challenge was held in 2003, from Plymouth to Dakar in Senegal. Since then, interest has grown enormously. In 2007, nearly 300 teams participated.

The rules are as follows:

> **Cost:** competing cars must cost less than £100. Maximum budget for the vehicle rally preparation: £15
>
> **Assistance:** Once the rally is underway, there will be no formal assistance from the organisers. Your team is on its own. You are likely to be travelling in small groups of five or six cars, and other people will try to help you out.
>
> **Auction:** All the vehicles that make the full distance must be handed over to be auctioned in aid of local Gambian charities.
>
> **All vehicles must be left-hand drive:** This rule is necessary because Gambia is a left-hand-drive country. RHD vehicles are not really welcome there.

Plymouth–Banjul Challenge: **www.plymouth-dakar.co.uk**

Maxine's story

I'm 15 days into the Plymouth–Banjul challenge. The queue on the Western Sahara side of the Mauritanian border is five hours long. Two guys from Cornwall drape their washing from their van to dry. I chat to a young couple from Sheffield who've travelled and slept in their 2CV for six weeks. Our passports and car documents are being painstakingly processed. There is no café, no toilet. People disappear periodically behind a dilapidated wall, watching carefully where they tread.

Suddenly my name is called and I retrieve my papers. There is nothing to keep me here, no one to wait for. I pull out of the queue and head for the border post. The guard checks the stamps and waves me through. 'Where do I go?' I ask. Ahead there are no road markings – no road even, just sand. 'Straight on for four kilometres,' he says. Mines are scattered across this no-man's land. If I follow other tyre tracks, I'll be fine, I tell myself.

...on the Plymouth–Banjul challenge

Buy a car and drive just over 4,000 miles. Have a lot of fun and help raise over £100,000.

15 DECEMBER

🏠 *support the* CLOWN DOCTORS

The clown doctors have become shooting stars in my life. I can count on them when I need some cheering up. Thank you for your smiles, your jokes, your fun. No words could ever describe what you have done for me!

– Brooke

Humour relaxes people, reduces pain and stress, makes people laugh and feel good and generally promotes a positive outlook. All in all it's a good medicine. And it doesn't have the side effects of some more potent drugs. 🏠 This is where clown doctors come in. Imagine being in hospital, away from the comfort of your home, and feeling sad, anxious, frightened, lonely or in pain. Clown doctors treat children in hospital with a dose of fun and laughter. 🏠 The clown doctors programme was developed by the Humour Foundation in Australia, where 40 clown doctors entertain around 60,000 patients a year. A similar scheme was set up by the Theodora Foundation all over Europe. In the UK, the Theodora Children's Trust recruits and trains special clowns to work in selected hospitals in England and Wales.

Theodora Children's Trust: www.theodora.org.uk
Humour Foundation, Australia: www.humourfoundation.com.au

Clown doctors receive considerable training in the very special skills needed to divert children's attention during painful procedures, help calm them in emergency, or

just brighten up their day. They learn how to develop their mastery of magic, storytelling, acting, mime, balloon sculpture, and juggling, and adapt these skills to each child's needs in widely differing situations. When working on the wards, they have to behave with sensitivity, only approaching children when it is clear that they will be welcome, judging how best to involve the children and their carers, and bring them some relief from the distress and pain they may be feeling. As one grateful parent remembers:

It was an extremely stressful time, but as if by magic the clown doctors would always arrive on the ward at the right time and brighten everyone's day. The children would perk up, parents would have their minds taken off the awful and often harrowing situations they were finding themselves in, and even the staff would smile!

...bring happiness to a hospital

🏠 **If you think you have what it takes to become a Clown Doctor,** make enquiries with the Theodora Children's Trust. Or you could make a donation.

🏠 **If you know a child who is ill** and could do with some cheering up, download the Clown Doctors Activity Book from: www.humourfoundation.com.au

🏠 **Bring a little happiness** into an old people's home or a day centre for homeless people, and organise a Christmas entertainment for them.

DECEMBER 16

STREET CHILDREN *speak out*

Children are living on the streets for many reasons. They have run away from physical or sexual abuse at home. Their families are too poor to feed an extra mouth. They are physically disabled and unwanted. They are attracted by the idea of 'the bright lights'. In the developing world, they are 'street children'. In the rich world, they are 'runaways'. The causes may be slightly different, but the result is the same: vulnerable children living on the street, having to fend for themselves just to survive.

Once on the streets, they need to earn money just to eat. Some beg. Some sell – anything from sweets to magazines. Some do shoe-shining. Many are ragpickers – recycling cloth, plastic, glass, metals, often in dangerous conditions. And some work is traditionally done by gangs of street children, such as erecting wedding tents in India. It is hard to comprehend what life for children on the streets must be like. When we encounter street children, we see them as a nuisance. But they are human beings who are being denied access to some fundamental human rights we take for granted.

Consortium for Street Children: www.streetchildren.org.uk

Street children have their own ideas about the world and its problems:

With unity amongst ourselves, we can do anything! – Mannar

We should work to protect all children and uphold their rights. We should see that the police who make the lives of street children so miserable are punished. – Suresh

Education is the most important thing to bring about change. With education comes respect. And with respect we can build our lives. – Papu

Employment is the big issue. Every young adult should have the opportunity to earn a living. – Anuj

After a brainstorm on how to change the world, a group of children in Delhi aged from 9 to 17 came up with the idea of organising a National Street Children's Day, when they would do things for other people for free, which would challenge the stereotype that streetchildren are parasites who are up to no good.

...listen to what they say

- **Remember:** George Bernard Shaw's wise words: 'The worst sin towards our fellow creatures is not to hate them, but to be indifferent to them; that is the essence of inhumanity.'

- **Understand:** Read Trash by Gita Wolf, a storybook which shows the life of a group of ragpickers in South India, compiled from a workshop when the children told the stories of their lives.

- **See:** Contact the Consortium for Street Children to find out about street children's organisations in countries you plan to visit. When you get there, visit a night shelter and meet some of the children. Take some of your old toys (such as Lego) or school materials to leave with them.

- **Do:** Next time you are accosted by street children, buy them an ice cream!

17 DECEMBER

make friends with **AFRICA**

The state of Africa is a scar on the conscience of the world. But if the world as a community focused on it, we could heal it. And if we don't, it will become deeper and angrier.

– Tony Blair, British Prime Minister, 2001

People are the real wealth of nations. The United Nations Development Programme (UNDP) defines 'human development' as much more than the rise or fall of national incomes. It is about creating an environment in which people can develop their full potential and lead productive, creative lives in accordance with their needs, interests and choices. Economic growth is only one means, although an important one, of enlarging those choices.

The Human Development Index is a 'league table' compiled by the UNDP. It tries to reflect the wider view of human development by taking into account the following factors: life expectancy, adult literacy rate, education enrolment, gross domestic product per capita. The bottom 20 nations in 2004 were all in Africa:

Rwanda	0.450	Zambia	0.407	Central African Rep.	0.353
Nigeria	0.448	Malawi	0.400	Guinea-Bissau	0.349
Guinea	0.445	Dem. Rep. Congo	0.391	Burkina Faso	0.342
Angola	0.439	Mozambique	0.390	Mali	0.338
Tanzania	0.430	Burundi	0.384	Sierra Leone	0.335
Benin	0.428	Ethiopia	0.371	Niger	0.311
Côte d'Ivoire	0.421	Chad	0.368		

Substantial numbers of Africans now live and work in Europe and North America. Some are passionate about 'doing something' for Africa and have started their own organisations to raise money and support development programmes.

The African Foundation for Development (AFFORD) is a network of African diaspora initiatives in the UK: www.afford-uk.org

News from all over Africa can be gleaned from: www.allafrica.com

UNDP human development website: hdr.undp.org.

Stand up for Elsie

Elsie Nemlin, who is from the Ivory Coast, founded Stand Up For Africa in 2003 with three main objectives:
To raise funds for the disadvantaged in Africa and facilitate their self-sufficiency.
To provide volunteers from the African Diaspora to share skills for African development.
To lobby for justice and fairness.
SUFA's first programme addresses the child slave trade in West Africa:
www.standupforafrica.org.uk

...help it to a better future

Volunteer to help one of the small 'diaspora development initiatives' in whatever way you can. You will be working with a group of highly motivated people and make some exciting new friends.

EAT *in darkness*

See what it's like in the dark. Here, we're on an equal footing with other people. And for once we can hold a hand out to others.

– a visually impaired waiter in a pitch-black restaurant

The idea of eating in total darkness may seem strange if you are sighted, but of course is perfectly normal to an unsighted person. In 1999, a blind clergyman, Jorge Spielmann, had the idea of opening a restaurant in Zurich staffed by blind waiters. It is called *Die Blinde Kuh* (The Blind Cow), and the waiters wear bells on their feet, so you can hear them approaching. Diners are met at the entrance and led in procession to their tables. The toilets are lit, but diners have to be guided there by a waiter. ❌ The venture has a serious purpose – to give blind people work, and at the same time to teach sighted people what it is like to live in a blind world. ❌ Before opening his restaurant Spielmann sometimes used to blindfold guests at his home to encourage them to pay more attention to the food and the conversations going on around them. 'I just want people to experience the world on our terms.'

Dans Le Noir? (In the Dark?), which has branches in Paris and London, is run on much the same lines. The venture was established by the Paul Guinot Association, which helps France's blind and visually handicapped. 'We hope the restaurant will serve as a bridge between people who can see and people who can't.' ❌ The idea is certainly of interest to experimental psychologists, who are keen to find out how lack of vision affects our experience of taste. And, if an account of a one-night experiment along these lines in New York is anything to go by, the darkness can make for a very intimate dining experience.

Die Blinde Kuh: www.blindekuh.ch
Dans le Noir?: www.danslenoir.com
Unsicht Bar: www.unsicht-bar-berlin.de

Adapting a building to make it totally blacked out
is an expensive and time-consuming process. It also runs into difficulties when it comes to health and safety regulations. The *Unsicht Bar* ('Invisible Bar') in Berlin gets round the problem by requiring diners to wear masks over their eyes. The restaurant was started by an organisation of blind and visually impaired people, and most of the staff are blind.

...a blinding experience

- ❌ **Is a blind restaurant a good idea?** Could the idea catch on? Might blind restaurants spring up in other cities? What do you think?
- ❌ **If you go to any of the cities** featured above, make a point of going to dine at a Blind Restaurant, and find out for yourself.
- ❌ **Back home,** contact an organisation for blind and visually impaired people active in your town or city, and suggest that you work together to organise a blind evening (with masks) at a local restaurant.

19 DECEMBER

become an ENCYCLOPAEDIST

Thanks to the internet, you can play a part in creating the world's most ambitious information project. Wikipedia is an internet encyclopaedia ('wiki' means 'quick' in Hawaiian), which is being created entirely by volunteers, who contribute new articles and update and revise existing ones. Contributions have to comply with Wikipedia's 'neutral point of view' policy, so that there is no bias in what is published. ⚘ Articles can be edited by anyone (except by banned users and there are a few protected pages). The entries in the encyclopaedia develop, as amendments and additions are made, and flaws are quickly repaired. Everything is copyright free.

Wikipedia is the world's largest and fastest-growing encyclopaedia. It was started in 2001 and in its first year over 20,000 entries were created. By September 2004, over 1 million articles had been completed (350,000 of which are in English). ⚘ There are articles under active development in over 100 languages. Nearly 2,500 new articles are added to Wikipedia each day, along with ten times that number of updates to existing articles. Wikipedia is one of the ten most popular internet reference sites.

There are a number of related projects supported by the Wikimedia Foundation, including: Wiktionary (a dictionary and thesaurus), Wikiquote (a compendium of famous quotations), Wikibooks (a collection of manuals and textbooks and Wikisource (a repository of public domain documents). All of these projects are being developed using similar principles to Wikipedia. ⚘ The Wikimedia Foundation is funded by appeals on its websites, which have raised $150,000 for this work. Compare this with the cost of creating a new edition of the Encyclopaedia Britannica.

en.wikipedia.org
www.wikimediafoundation.org

Translators wanted
In France, between 1751 and 1772, a remarkable book was published that attempted to put all human knowledge between two covers. This was the *Encyclopédie*. Compiled largely under the direction of Denis Diderot, it comprised 28 volumes, 71,818 articles and 2,885 illustrations. A second, edition, in 66 volumes, was published from 1782 to 1832.
You can help translate the *Encyclopédie* into English: www.hti.umich.edu/d/did/call.html

...contribute to Wikipedia

⚘ **Write an article** for Wikipedia on some obscure subject that you are an expert on. Start by finding out whether the subject already has an entry and what related subjects have entries.

⚘ **Open your article** with a concise paragraph, defining the topic and mentioning the most important points. The reader should be able to get a good overview by only reading this first paragraph. Then write the rest of the article. Guidance for contributors is published on the Wikipedia website.

⚘ **Or, take a subject that you are really interested in** and know something about, find the article in Wikipedia, and then edit it, adding all the bits that are missing.

DECEMBER 20

BRIGHTEN *up your community*

It's the middle of winter. The days are short. Around 500,000 people in the UK suffer from Seasonal Affective Disorder (also known as SAD), which is the most common winter depression. It is caused by a biochemical imbalance in the hypothalamus (the gland responsible for regulating body temperature and food intake) caused by the shortening of daylight hours and the lack of sunlight in winter. The symptoms include a general lassitude and depression.

Many of us find the winter months bring us down, even if we are not as badly affected as sufferers of SAD. Our surroundings never look as good under grey skies as they do in the summer sunshine. But maybe this is the time to take a fresh look at the community we live in – when it is at its worst. 🏠 What can be done to improve it? Remove the graffiti? Paint a mural? Hang up banners in the streets? Encourage window boxes? Plant trees? Tidy up the road signs, pedestrian barriers and other street furniture? Banish the motor car? Build sitting-out areas? Encourage live music? Provide more sunlight? Whatever it is, if you want it done by the end of the summer, you had better get started now.

Information on SAD can be found on: www.sada.org.uk

Resources for redesigning your community:
The Community Planning Website: www.communityplanning.net
Christopher Alexander's famed Pattern Language: www.patternlanguage.com

From SAD to happy

On one side of a valley is the Austrian village of Rattenberg, with a population of 455. This sits in the shadow of a high mountain, which deprives the village of sunlight for four months of each year. On the other side of the valley is Kramsach, which basks in the winter sun.

An array of computer-guided solar reflectors known as 'Heliostats', each 6.5 m² and computer programmed to adjust their direction according to the sun's position, bounces the sun's rays from above Kramsach to a rocky outcrop close

Rattenberg, where a second bank of mirrors directs the light to the village.

There is not enough reflected sunlight to bright... the whole village. But selected streets, building facades and public spaces are lit up, and the villagers now feel much less sad during the long winter.

...with a ray of sunshine

Spend an afternoon walking around your neighbourhood. Make a note of all the things you don't like and all the things you would like to have but which are not there. Then categorise your suggested improvements:

🏠 **Things that can be done easily** and with very little or no money.

🏠 **Two or three things** that are really important and which would bring maximum community gain.

🏠 **Everything else.** Talk to your neighbours and try to get a consensus for your community improvement plan. Talk to your councillor to see what your local council could do. Talk to your neighbourhood association to see how they might help. Try to get at least one thing on your list done within the next three months.

don't buy COCAINE

For once the politicians and the police are actually right – cocaine is bad news. But not just for the reasons you might be thinking. You've probably heard all about how coke rots your nose, causes heart attacks, is highly addictive and fuels cartels and corruption.

But there's another reason not to buy cocaine that people don't talk about. It is that cocaine isn't 'fairtrade'. Far from it. Although many farmers initially turn to growing drugs because low commodity prices mean that they can't make a decent living from more traditional crops, less than 1% of the profits from cocaine go back to the producer.

Every time you purchase a gramme of cocaine the people who cultivate coca leaves are being completely ripped off. They are breaking their backs and employing child labour just so you can get high for a few hours. It must be a bit of a downer knowing that kids have had to work themselves to the bone just so that you could indulge yourself.

The Drug Policy Alliance website explores the drug war, and is a good source of information on every drug under the sun: www.lindesmith.org

Educate yourself on what people have been eating, inhaling and injecting for centuries. HuumeBoikotti is a Finnish website with lots of interesting information on the drugs trade: www.huumeboikotti.org/en

Fairtrade products and where to get them: www.fairtrade.org.uk

Drug facts to share with your friends:

Opium was being cultivated from 6,000 BC.

In the 19th century, the opium business was one of the most profitable businesses of the British Empire.

When Coca-Cola was first produced, the 'health tonic' contained small amounts of cocaine in the recipe.

According to rough estimates, there is more money in circulation annually in the drugs trade than in the oil refinement industry, and almost as much as in arms trafficking.

Did you know that in the UK:

3 million people use illicit drugs (5% of the population).

Of 280,000 people using Class A drugs, only 20% are receiving treatment or are in jail.

The annual cost of crime by cocaine and heroin users is £16 billion.

Drug users commit 36 million crimes each year – 56% of total crime.

...it's not fairtrade!

Support fairtrade.

☺ **Stop using cocaine.** If you haven't yet started, more power to you!

☺ **Tell your friends to stop.** Spread the word.

☺ **Eat fairtrade chocolate,** unzip a fairtrade banana, have a fairtrade cup of tea instead. It's better for you... and better for the world.

DECEMBER 22

COMPUTING *power*

Two heads (or in this case tens of thousands) are better than one. Some problems are so complicated that it is difficult to find enough computer power to solve them. To get over this, a mechanism has been developed for harnessing together the unused computing capacity of PCs all over the world so that they can work together.

One very complicated problem is predicting climate change. The climateprediction.net project has over 95,000 computers in 150 countries. They work together to investigate how sensitive the different climate change models are to small changes in the underlying assumptions that have been used to create them, and also to changes in climatic conditions.

www.climateprediction.net

Climateprediction.net

This is the world's largest climate modelling experiment. It will provide decision makers with a much better scientific basis for creating policies to address global warming.

Each simulation divides the globe into thousands of sectors, and estimates the future temperature, based on certain assumptions such as cloud coverage, the rate of heat movement and rainfall rates.

The first results of climateprediction.net suggest that average temperatures could rise by as much as 11°C by the middle of the 21st century unless deep cuts are made to greenhouse gas emissions. This is double the warming predicted by the Intergovernmental Panel on Climate Change.

...help predict the future

Link your computer to the 95,000 others around the world that are already working on the climateprediction.net project.

To run a simulation will take between 10 and 22 days, depending on your computer power. If you switch your computer off and then back on again, the simulation will continue from where it was left off until it has been completed.

What to do

- **Decide to join in.** It's not a huge decision to make. You are not using your computer up to its full capacity. If you want to use your employers' computer, get their permission.

- **Check whether your computer meets the minimum requirements.** It it's less than 5 years old, it probably will. The operating system can be Windows, Mac or Linux.

- **Go to climateprediction.net,** which should answer any questions you might have.

- **Register** and accept the license agreement.

- **Run the programme;** and the results will be sent back automatically to: climateprediction.net.

forecast your FUTURE

Christmas Eve is make-or-break time for children fortunate enough to be expecting gifts. Has anyone paid attention to their wish-list? Will Santa Claus bring them that much-desired gift? Over 750,000 children a year in the UK alone write a 'letter to Santa' in the run-up to Christmas. His address and special postcode is Reindeerland, SAN TA1. 👫 What happens to these letters? The Royal Mail replies to all such letters, and the process is covered on a webcam at: www.royalmail.com/santamail.

What is on your wish-list? Maybe you don't care too much what you receive by way of a Christmas gift, but would dearly love to see a more caring society, a more peaceful world, or a healthier environment. Well, these certainly aren't going to be brought by Santa Claus – or by any single individual. They are problems that you are going to have to help sort out yourself.

Letters to Santa is a website that was inspired by New York's Operation Santa Claus. You can download Christmas carols (words and sheet music), classic Christmas stories, safety tips, and even track Santa's progress on Christmas Eve: www.operationlettertosanta.com

Operation Santa Claus

At the New York Post Office in the 1920s, postal clerks started opening some of the letters to Santa and, touched by some of the requests, dug into their own pockets to pay for presents. This has now become Operation Santa Claus, and the idea has been copied by other post offices in the USA.

The idea is simple. Postal staff volunteer to sort through the mail (around 200,000 letters to Santa are received each year) and select those that appear to be from needy inner-city children. Members of the public come to the Post Office, read through some of the mail and take away letters they would like to reply to with a gift.

...write a letter to yourself

Write a letter to yourself, which you will open and read in 10 or 25 years' time.

👫 **Write about the issue** that you want to do something about. What impact do you think you will be able to make? How would you like things to be in the future? And what do you think things will actually be like then?

👫 **You could add some personal thoughts** – your current state of mind, how you spend your time, if you are in love with anyone, how you see your life evolving, your ambitions for the future...

👫 **Hide the letter,** or, if you think you will lose it or be too tempted to open it before the time is up, give it to someone else to keep for you.

It will be fascinating to read your letter in the future. You will be able to compare how things are now, with the world as it will be then. And your current aspirations and emotional state with those of the person you will have become.

BAND AID

25 November 1984: There was widespread famine in Ethiopia. Images were being shown on TV of people literally starving to death. Bob Geldof, a rock singer with Boomtown Rats, felt he had to do something. So, with Midge Ure, he wrote a Christmas song, called up his famous singer friends to help record the song, and produced 'Do they know it's Christmas?'. It was the first single ever to sell over 3 million copies in the UK. All the proceeds were given to the Band Aid Trust for African famine relief.

28 January 1985: Inspired by what Geldof had done, 45 musicians got together in New York to record 'We are the World', written by Michael Jackson and Lionel Richie. The group called itself USA for Africa – United Support of Artists. This was also a Number One hit.

13 July 1985: Geldof organised Live Aid: a rock concert held simultaneously on both sides of the Atlantic (in London at Wembley Stadium and in Philadelphia at the JFK Stadium), and broadcast around the world. (Geldof estimated that nearly 85% of world's TVs were tuned into it.) The concert raised nearly $100 million.

Geldof raised millions for Africa. But he also invented two big fundraising ideas: the pop single recorded and produced entirely free, and the mega-concert broadcast globally. He alerted a whole generation of young people to the idea that the world needed fixing. And he went on to help set up the Commission for Africa and organise ten Live8 concerts on 2 July 2005 to get the G8 rich nations committed to eliminating poverty in Africa.

Live Aid: www.liveaiddvd.net
The 20th anniversary version of 'Do they know it's Christmas': www.bandaid20.com
Live8: www.live8live.com
The unofficial Live Aid site: www.live-aid.info
All about Band Aid at: en.wikipedia.org/wiki/Band_Aid
All about USA for Africa: en.wikipedia.org/wiki/USA_for_Africa

Band Aid Charitable Trust

New recordings of 'Do they know it's Christmas' were made in 1989 and 2004. The Band Aid Charitable Trust continues to receive income from sales and royalties, which it donates as aid for Africa.

In 2003, it supported food security, fresh water, eyecare and healthcare projects in west and east Africa. The 2004 recording helped victims of famine in Darfur, Sudan.

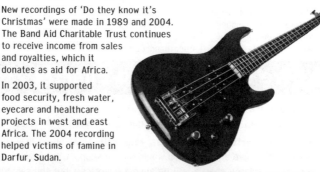

...do they know it's Christmas?

Buy the various Band Aid, Live Aid and USA for Africa CDs.

make a WILL

Almost everyone has some assets, and everyone is going to die sometime. Your life expectancy might be high, but the unexpected can happen – today, tomorrow, whenever.

It is important to make a will, because it allows you to:

Choose how to dispose of your assets. If you die without a will, there are rules that dictate how your assets are distributed. This may not be in the way you would wish.

Inherit from an unmarried partner. Unmarried couples (same sex or not) cannot inherit from each other without a will.

Make arrangements for your children. Couples with children under 18 may want to consider arrangements for their children if either or both die.

Minimise tax payments. It may be possible to save inheritance tax.

It is your most recent will that determines what happens. So if your circumstances change, for example if you separate from your partner or you hit the jackpot in the lottery, then you should make a new will.

Why not include a charitable bequest in your will? This could be a simple charitable gift, or you might establish a fund for a specific purpose, which will continue to operate for many years (for example, a bursary fund to provide books, uniforms and school fees to a child in the developing world). Or you might fund the planting of a grove of trees as a memorial.

Take the Make-a-Will quiz at: <u>moneycentral.msn.com/retire/home.asp</u>

Living Wills

A Living Will sets out how you would like to be treated as you near death, when you are no longer able to make decisions for yourself. It covers such things as the degree of medical intervention, pain management, feeding that should be administered, and where you would like to die. This can take the burden of decision away from your family.

A Living Will is an expression of wishes, rather than a legally enforceable instruction. Buy The Natural Death Handbook, or download an older version from: www.globalideasbank.org/natdeath/ndh0.html

...give something to charity

Go and write your will today. Type 'make a will' into Google, and you will find many do-it-yourself guides and online will-writing services.

Include a charitable bequest in your will. Think about how much you would like to give and what you would like to support. Remember that a small bequest to a large charity will be almost unnoticed, but the same money could support really interesting work by a smaller organisation.

Remember that the charity will get nothing until you die, and that the gift will cost you absolutely nothing and may save tax when you die. So be generous!

DECEMBER 26

STUFF *do we need it?*

Michael Landy, a British artist, catalogued and destroyed all 7,226 of his possessions in a 2001 art installation called *Break Down*, held in a vacant C&A clothes store on Oxford Street in central London. ⚽ Landy stood on a platform overseeing a production line staffed by ten assistants. Every single one of his possessions was first catalogued and then destroyed – his passport, his keys and his credit cards, right down to a last dirty sock. The objects were shredded or ground up, and then put into plastic trays and sacks for disposal.

The things Landy valued most he had left until last. One of the last objects to be destroyed was his father's sheepskin coat. Over 45,000 people came to see what was happening, and the final day attracted a crowd of 8,000.

> *When I finished I felt an incredible sense of freedom, the possibility that I could do anything. But that freedom is eroded by the everyday concerns of life. Life was much simpler when I was up on my platform.*

The event got a huge amount of publicity. Sermons were preached on the morality of consumerism. Landy was attacked for wanton destruction. Some saw it as an attack on capitalism. And others saw it as an act of madness and offered counselling. Landy described the event as an 'examination of consumerism'. ⚽ Since then, he has been drawing street flowers. These are flowers that live in the cracks in paving stones in the street. They don't need many nutrients. They can survive in harsh conditions.

Find out more about Michael Landy at:
www.tate.org.uk/magazine/issue3/michaellandy.htm

We live in a consumerist society. We are urged to purchase much more than we need. And when fashion changes, we just buy something else – whether or not the thing we have is still functioning. Maybe, like Michael Landy, you could experience a sense of freedom by ridding yourself of possessions – maybe not all of them, just those you no longer need.

...or are we better without?

- ⚽ **Make a catalogue of everything you own.** Think about each item on your list: about how and why you came to acquire it, whether you still use it (or indeed ever used it), whether you still need it (or think you need it), and whether you really do want to keep it.

- ⚽ **Set aside everything that you don't need or want.** Then either take these to a charity shop or sell them on eBay. Or, if they are completely worn out or of no use to anybody, then throw them away (in a recycling bin, of course).

- ⚽ **Keep your list. In five years' time,** repeat the exercise and see if you have continued your consumerist ways, buying more than you need.

27 DECEMBER

auction it on EBAY

If you no longer need it, someone else might really want it. And they may be prepared to pay good money for it. So why not auction it on eBay? You will find a new user, liberate some space in your home and raise money to help you change the world – all in one go!

eBay was created in 1995 by Pierre Omidyar as an online marketplace for buying and selling. He wanted to create an efficient internet trading space for individuals and small businesses.  eBay pioneered an auction format with a simple, easy-to-understand mechanism that lets buyers and sellers decide the true value of items, build relationships with others, and become part of the eBay community. Pierre and co-founder Jeff Skoll are now major philanthropists.

eBay now has 114 million registered users, trading in more than 50,000 different categories in 29 different countries. At any time there will be more than 25 million items for sale. 3.5 million new items are added each day. People have auctioned everything from genuine Glastonbury mud (sold for a staggering £490) to a 40lb buffalo head (complete with detachable horns). If you are not already hooked on eBay, there are simple instructions on the website on how to buy and sell. You can also buy a guidebook to help you through the process.

eBay charity page: pages.ebay.co.uk/charity/information.html

Download a factsheet on buying and selling on ebay:
www.harriman-house.com/ebay/factsheet.htm
based on The eBay Book by David Belbin.

Information about the charitable foundations funded by Omidyar: www.omidyar.org
and Skoll: www.skollfoundation.org

The Great Chicago Fire Sale

This was the first charitable eBay auction, organised by a municipality to raise money for the arts. Items donated for the sale included a 1960s Playboy bunny costume, a dinner party prepared by Art Smith, personal chef to Oprah Winfrey, the opportunity to dye the Chicago River Green, and much more: www.greatchicagofiresale.com

...create hope from junk

Go through your possessions, identify all the things you no longer need and which you think someone else might want to buy from you. Then start selling. See how much you can raise!

In the UK, eBay has a Charity Page, where non-profit making organisations can publicise their auctions. Selling fees still have to be paid, but this provides some free additional publicity.

Approach celebrities, and see if they will give you things to sell. They may sign something, provide some bit of memorabilia or get you tickets to an upcoming film premiere. Dave Rowntree, drummer with Blur, offered to auction two hours of his time for a drumming lesson and a glass of champagne.

DECEMBER 28

THINGS *to do*

In this world, nothing is certain but death and taxes.

– Benjamin Franklin

The rest of your life is up to you. But, remember that you have only a limited amount of time before you go.

So start making a list of all the things you want to do before you die. Then start doing them. Right away. You never know how much longer you have left...

A list of 100 simple things to do: brass612.tripod.com/cgi-bin/things.html

Grow a Brain is a website all about things to do before you die, with lots of links: growabrain.typepad.com/growabrain/things_to_do_before_you_die/

Some things you simply must do:

Scour the night sky for comets, with the chance of following Halley or Donati and having a comet named after you.

Extract your own DNA. Spit gargled salt water into diluted washing-up liquid and slowly dribble ice-cold gin down the side of the glass. The spindly white clumps that form in the mixture are, basically, you.

Measure the speed of light by melting chocolate in a microwave oven. You measure the distance between globs. Various calculations produce the answer. You can still eat the chocolate afterwards.

Write your name in atoms at IBM's Almaden research laboratory, San Jose, California. While you're saving up to go there, simply go and see an atom by visiting a university lab with equipment to trap and cool atoms. Barium is best.

Help nail a murderer. Register ahead with Tennessee's body farm and donate your corpse. It will be left out in the open to decompose before a trainee forensic scientist gets to work on it. An estimated 100 murderers have been convicted as a result of this training.

Become a diamond. LifeGem of Chicago, Illinois, will take a few grains of your cremated remains, subject them to high pressure and temperature. You emerge from the process 18 weeks later as a sparkling one-carat diamond.

From *100 Things to Do Before You Die*, ideas from scientists put together by Valerie Jamieson and Liz Else, Profile Books.

...before you die

Think about all the good you might to do before you die.

♀ **Make a list of things you would like to do** to address some of the world's big problems. Your list can be as long or as short as you like. The problems are those you believe important. The actions are what you want to do to address them.

♀ **Put the list somewhere where you can see it.** Make sure you do at least one thing on the list each month – and try to do everything before you die.

29 DECEMBER

go to the next WSF

The World Social Forum is a huge annual event, attended by people from NGOs, community groups and civil society movements from all over the world who are 'opposed to neo-liberalism and world domination by capital'. ⚽ The WSF is an open meeting place for reflection and creative thinking, for democratic debate of ideas and issues, for free exchange of experiences, and for networking and linking up with other people and groups in order to plan effective action for a better world.

The first WSF was held in January 1998 to coincide with the annual World Economic Forum in Davos, when 192 organisations from 54 countries launched a 'Declaration against the Globalisers of Misery'. The next year, in 1999, a Davos Forum aimed to show that the economic issues addressed by the World Economic Forum only served a small group of interests, and that other mechanisms were needed for addressing issues of social justice and world development. This led to the first World Social Forum held in Porto Alegre, Brazil in January 2001. Some 20,000 participants came together around the slogan 'Another World is Possible'.

The number of people attending has continued to grow. Over 55,000 people from 131 countries came to the second WSF in 2002, and 100,000 attended in 2003. ⚽ In 2004, the WSF was held in India, attracting around 250,000 participants. There are also regional and thematic WSFs, which explore specific issues and issues of regional significance.

World Social Forum: www.forumsocialmundial.org.br/index.php

And these are the regional forums linked to the World Social Forum:
European Social Forum: www.fse-esf.org
Americas Social Forum: www.forosocialamericas.org
Pan Amazonian Social Forum: www.fspanamazonico.com.br
Mediterranean Social Forum: www.fsmed.info
...and watch out for the next Asia Social Forum

What it's like at the forum
The programme includes lectures, presentations, workshops, film and video, cultural events, marches and demonstrations, the issuing of declarations and much else. If you go, you will learn about the world and its problems, what people's movements are doing to address these, new ideas for development, and new skills for making change. You will meet old friends and make new friends – and you should come away believing that another world *is* possible.

...another world is possible

⚽ **Change your plans for January.** Take a trip to the next World Social Forum. It will open your eyes to what people are doing to create a better world. It could inspire you. And you should have a great time.

NEW YEAR'S EVE

Never doubt that a small group of thoughtful committed citizens can change the world. Indeed it is the only thing that ever has!

– Margaret Mead, anthropologist

New Year's Eve is a time to look back and to reflect on all that has happened in the past year. What have you been able to achieve in your efforts to change the world? What has been your most successful action? What was most fun? What had most impact? What have you learned? What new friends have you made? How have you changed?

But it is also a time to look forward – to make a commitment to continue your efforts next year and into the future.

Through your actions, you can do your bit to change the world. You can also inspire others to action. Congratulations on what you have done so far. Keep up the good work. And best wishes for an enjoyable and successful New Year of making a difference!

Bethesda Arts Centre: www.bethesdafoundation.org

Nieu Bethesda is a poverty-stricken township in semi-arid desert of South Africa attached to the town of Bethesda. It has become a popular tourist attraction because

of 'The Owl House', a tiny museum devoted to the work of the eccentric sculptor Helen Martins, who lived and worked there. The township also has underground pools from which the local people draw water with windmills.

The New Year of 2005 was welcomed in by a choir and a procession of lantern bearers, who walked through the streets and alleyways of Nieu Bethesda. Before the event, workshops were held to involve as many local people as possible in lantern making. Long withies (willow sticks) were bound together to form a three-dimensional framework, which was covered with tissue paper and decorated with patterns. Some of the lanterns were geometric and others were in the shape of wild animals and birds.

When night fell, candles were placed inside the lanterns and the procession started off. The local police and volunteers were there to ensure safety. It was a great night, which will be long remembered.

...light up the future

⋔ Say goodbye to the old year and welcome in the new with an outdoor celebration, even if it's only in your street or garden. Use some kind of illumination – home-made lanterns, torches, tea-lights – anything you can lay your hands on at short notice to symbolise your hopes for a bright future.

⋔ And next year, think about involving your whole community in a lantern parade.

Turn your ideas into actions: 24 tips for social inventors

Here is some advice for making a success of your project:

Idea generation

1 Define the problem as clearly as you can; then think how you can solve it. Brainstorm to overcome worthy-but-dull ideas.

2 Look for synergy, for win-win-win situations that solve lots of problems all at the same time.

3 Gather other people's ideas; and find a way of rewarding them for their contribution.

4 Be prepared to be flexible. Lots of ideas develop in ways you can't foresee at the outset.

5 Be patient. Take a long view. Some ideas might take ten years or more for the results to develop.

6 Use humour. This can tilt the scales when confronting bureaucracy, and can be much more effective than simply trying to 'persuade' people.

Structural

7 Involve your friends – together people can move mountains.

8 When you start out, think about linking with a NGO that is able to receive grants on your behalf.

9 Delegate as much as possible to other people (for particular initiatives, to run a committee, etc). But make sure everyone who promises to help actually delivers.

10 Invite celebrities, business leaders, politicians and other important people to become patrons and to attend events.

11 Celebrate successes as you go.

Financial

12 Make a budget for your project. Keep your overheads low and try to get as much as possible for free.

13 Ask friends and colleagues to support you by giving you regular (small) donations.

14 Find the funds you need. Persevere. There will be someone out there who is interested in supporting what you are doing.

15 Think about charging for things that you might otherwise provide for free.

16 Keep your accounts simple; and keep them up-to-date.

Outreach and publicity

17 Create a great website, and use it to disseminate information. Make it interesting and interactive.

18 Polish up your DTP (desktop publishing) and design skills, and make your leaflets and posters look really nice. But remember that simple = effective.

19 Get access to a good photocopier that does double-sided leaflets reliably. Some offices may help you by providing this facility as an 'in kind' donation.

20 Get to know journalists, especially those who are most likely to be interested. Try to get publicity at every opportunity.

21 Maintain an email press list. Send out regular press releases telling people what you're doing.

Keeping going

22 Keep a diary charting how your project is progressing.

23 Ask for advice when you need it. There are lots of people with the experience and skills you need.

24 Keep up the momentum. Don't give up. Deal with the problems that come up from time to time.

Adapted from advice given by Nicholas Albery, social inventor, to students at the School for Social Entrepreneurs, London. To help you plan your project, download 'How to be a Community Champion' from www.millenniumcampaign.org

Index

Go to
www.365act.com
to submit your own ideas
for changing the world
and to sign up to receive
a regular newsletter

Thank you for changing the world

ALSO FROM MYRIAD EDITIONS

"The threat of global warming may make you weep,
but Kate Evans' brilliant cartoons offer hope and inspiration.
And they're funny too." **Independent**

"A dialogue between a sceptical businessman, an idealistic youth and a
scientist, with cameos from Gandhi, George Bush and a Geldof lookalike...
if you think this all sounds a bit weird, you would be totally right
– but then the best cartoons often are." **Guardian**

"Scientifically rigorous, politically and economically literate and astute,
and deeply engaging at a human level." **Ecologist**

"More comprehensive than most weighty scientific tomes,
and a good deal funnier." **Mark Lynas**

"Very comical and extremely accurate."
Tyndall Centre for Climate Research

"Brilliant: funny and shocking and apt and beautifully drawn."
George Monbiot

"Essential reading." **Big Issue**

£6.99 pbk
ISBN: 978-0-9549309-3-6
Available from Amazon and all good bookshops

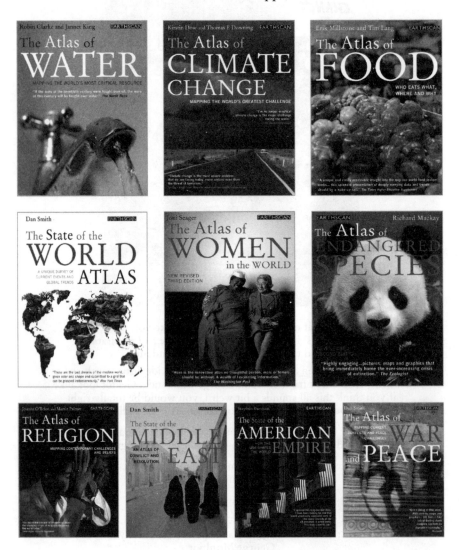